SHOCK EXCHANGE

How Inner-City Kids From Brooklyn Predicted the Great Recession and the Pain Ahead

FOREWORD

In 2006 I started a youth mentorship program called the New York Shock Exchange (Shock Exchange) as a vehicle to share my passion for investing and basketball with my 11-year-old son and other boys his age. I figured that using basketball as a "carrot" would be a cool way for kids to learn about the stock market and the economy. Besides, just coaching basketball would not have been much fun for me. Somehow I had to make it educational as well. And after having played basketball in college and spending over a decade involved in corporate finance and mergers & acquisitions, I was just the person to teach it to them. And just as I had suspected, with their ability to spot trends before adults, inner-city kids from Brooklyn knew more about investing than I, Peter Lynch, Bill Miller, and any hedge fund manager or Wall Street analyst on the planet. We not only helped them perform due diligence on their stock picks, but documented how macroeconomic forces were affecting their picks and the market in general. In the process, we noticed how key drivers of the economy – housing starts and auto sales – were dismal. Along with rising oil prices caused by wars in Iraq and Afghanistan, the U.S. economy was in the midst of stagflation not seen since the early 1990s and the Nixon administration of the '70s. Since the "Great Recession" that the Shock Exchange foretold, financial literacy has been championed by the Wall Street community.

The Shock Exchange's observations on the Great Recession – and the steps needed to address it – have been repeated by politicians, economists, Wall Street analysts, and even the president. However, they conveniently forgot to cite the source of their information. But it's not over. The next recession will be more painful than the last. I will take you on a journey of how we came to know this, the progenitors of the financial crisis, and the pain ahead.

FARMVILLE, VIRGINIA – HISTORY

I was born in Farmville, Virginia in 1967 on what my Aunt Anna describes as one of the coldest February days ever in the state of Virginia. My great grandmother, Ola Layne Allen, and Mr. Allen had to rush my mother to the hospital in Mr. Allen's 1962 Dodge pickup truck . . . you know, the old one with the stick shift on the steering wheel. Legend has it that since it was so cold, everybody knew it was going to be a boy. It would only be surpassed by the frigid February day I would get married there 28 years later. Farmville, located within Prince Edward County, is about 60 miles southwest of Richmond, the state's capital. For Civil War buffs, many of the stops of Lee's final retreat and the operations of General Grant's successful campaigns against the confederacy occurred in Prince Edward. Lee eventually surrendered in neighboring Appomattox County. Blanche K. Bruce, the first black man elected to the U.S. Senate (1875 – 1881), grew up about five minutes from my house. Prince Edward is not known for much else than being your typical, small, college town. Both Longwood University and Hampden-Sydney College ("H-SC" or "the College") are located there.

Longwood was founded in 1839 as Farmville Female Seminary Association, the third oldest public university in the state behind the College of William & Mary and the University of Virginia. Built on a reputation as a teachers college, it became a university in 2002 and has grown to over 4,000 students. Its two most famous sports alumni are Jerome Kersey (Portland Trailblazers) and Michael Tucker (Kansas City Royals, Atlanta Braves). Kersey enrolled there as a 6'3", 175-pound 18-year-old and left a 6'7", 225-pound grown man. His battles with Charles Oakley of Division II powerhouse, Virginia Union, are still a part of Farmville lore. Oftentimes the two had to be separated during heated exchanges. Whenever Longwood played a home game during Kersey's tenure, the entire town literally shut down. My friends and I would recap the exploits of Kersey and other Longwood greats like Joe Remar and Ron Orr. We would recant how if Oakley had tried to step to Kersey, we would have rushed the court and jumped him . . . yeah right. Ron Orr used to attend some of our high school games; during my sophomore year he even asked me to come down to Longwood to play pick-up with him and the rest of the guys, but I never took him up on it. I was a bit flattered but I really did not think Ron Orr seriously wanted to play with little ol' me. In hindsight I think I actually went to play with them once. Kersey had just graduated and was working out to prepare for camp with Portland. Dude grabbed a rebound on the far end of the court and took the ball coast-to-coast for a dunk, running over anybody who got in his way. I had never seen anybody that big move that fast before. After my self-preservation skills kicked in, I acted like I had to go to the men's room and hauled my behind home.

Founded in 1775, Hampden-Sydney is the 10th oldest college in the country, and along with Morehouse and Wabash, one of three traditional all men's institutions. It was founded by former Princeton graduates who wanted to build a liberal arts institution in Central Virginia. Patrick Henry and James Madison were members of the College's first group of trustees. I grew up less than a mile from the

1

College and my brother Mark and I attended the Log Cabin School there, a pre-school taught by Ms. Frances Scott who also sang on the choir at Mercy Seat Baptist Church where we attended. Every year the college boys would have an Easter egg hunt for the kids at our Sunday school, something we looked forward to. Hampden-Sydney was somewhat of a Division III football powerhouse back then. We were not allowed to ride our bikes in the street during home games because the College boys would get a little out of control. We would sit on my grandfather's porch and watch them fly up and down the road after the games. That would be our entertainment for the weekend. Farmville pretty much caters to the college students given that they drive so much of the town's economy. Having Longwood and Hampden-Sydney in the county was something we took for granted because they were always there. In today's upside-down economy, college towns are generally the only ones still thriving. The anchors that they provide may come at a cost, just as Longwood's growth, both outward and upward, has caused some angst amongst the townspeople. Whether Hampden-Sydney will add to that angst remains to be seen.

Farmville was made famous amongst African Americans by W.E.B. Du Bois in 1898 when he wrote *The Negroes of Farmville: A Social Study*. Du Bois' aim was to study the economic condition of the American Negro. Under the direction of the U.S. Commissioner of Labor, *The Farmville Negro* was the first of a series of small, well-defined studies of Negroes in the U.S. and predates Du Bois' more famous study, *The Philadelphia Negro* which was published in 1899. It is no wonder that Du Bois' focus was on Farmville, because Prince Edward County was a happening place for blacks at that time. In 1790 the county's population was 8,100 and about half was black. By 1890, the population had grown to almost 15,000 and approximately 68% was black.

Population of Prince Edward County

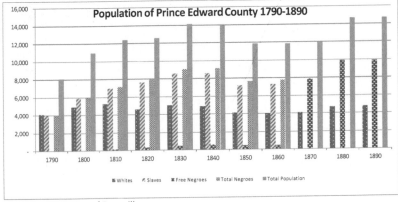

Source: The Negroes of Farmville

There was a community of blacks in Prince Edward who had been "free" decades prior to 1865, when Lincoln officially freed the slaves. Prince Edward was near the economic center of Virginia's biggest industry – tobacco. In Du Bois' words, it was the "black belt" of the state, the region where the majority of its inhabitants were of Negro blood. Trading and merchandising took place in the town of Farmville, located in the northern-most section of the county. According to Du Bois, Farmville was the trading center for six counties; tobacco and an assortment of agricultural products were marketed there. On Saturday, the regular market day, the town swelled to twice its normal size due to the influx of people – mostly Negroes – who came into town to trade and do business.[1]

Farmville was in a constant state of change – unusual for towns of its size. It attracted a steady influx of immigrants while many of its boys and girls were attracted to the city life of Richmond, Baltimore and New York. The town gained a reputation for taking kids from the farm to train elsewhere for industrial life. Du Bois surmised that the emigration of blacks to northern cities quelled Negro population growth. The main occupation was working in tobacco factories, of course. Other popular occupations were laborers, domestics, mechanics, carpenters and brick makers. Of note is that the entire brickmaking business was controlled by a black man who had bought his and his family's freedom, purchased his master's estate and later hired his master to work for him.[2] Du Bois estimated that over half the brick houses in or near Farmville were built by this gentleman, who also succeeded in driving white competitors out of business. Du Bois also gave special mention to an area two miles west of Farmville known as Israel Hill. Legend has it that when former Congressman John Randolph of Roanoke went away to college, a black man accompanied him as an aide. Randolph eventually grew so close to the man that he treated him almost like a family member, contributing to Randolph's decision to free his slaves as soon as he could afford to. Randolph was a descendant of one of the First Families of Virginia, who came over with the original colonists from England and helped settle Jamestown in the early 1600s. The First Families' ties to English aristocracy helped them garner land grants, which they used to gain wealth through planting and farming via slave labor. In 1833 Randolph died before he could carry out his promise to his black aide, but decreed in his will that his slaves were to be set free. After Randolph's brother contested the will due to Randolph's apparent insanity, it took over a decade for the courts to uphold it. They were given Israel Hill, which was considered fertile and could be used to promote farming. The free blacks also became blacksmiths, carpenters, and the like. Du Bois' conclusion about the Farmville Negro was mixed, yet he may have walked away with the "true" value of emancipation – the hope that the black race would some day prosper in America:

> After an impartial study of Farmville conditions, the industrious and property accumulating class of the Negro citizens best represents, on the whole, the general tendencies of the group . . . Finally it remains to be noted that the whole group life of Farmville Negroes is pervaded by a peculiar hopefulness on the part of the people themselves. No one of them doubts in the least that one day black people will have all rights they are now striving for, and that the Negro will be recognized among the earth's great peoples. Perhaps this simple faith is, of all products of emancipation, the one of the greatest social and economic value. [3]

Well, there is one other thing Prince Edward was known for. By age five or six I knew there was a deep, dark secret that adults only spoke about in hushed tones. I grew up in a family where "adult conversations" did not take place in front of children. But there was something about them closing down R.R. Moton. I assumed Moton was a school in some far-off land because the school I attended was called Prince Edward. My older cousins knew the secret, but whenever they discussed the subject in my presence they would start speaking in code so I could not follow along. Whenever I asked my parents about it the room would go silent and suddenly they would give me a list of chores to do. From what I could gather both my parents attended other schools for a few years but eventually graduated from Prince Edward. I never pressed the matter because it would put them in a bad mood for the rest of the day. Sometimes a high school teacher would try to broach the subject, but we would be like Sergeant Schultz from the sitcom, *Hogan's Heroes*: "I know nothing . . . I hear nothing . . . I see nothiiiing!" Around my sophomore year a classmate made a presentation on the school closing in history class. It was an excellent presentation but it made everybody, black and white, uncomfortable. We were pretty mad at her for even raising the issue. I was proud of my family and always carried myself as if I had a regal sort of background. By my sophomore year I knew the schools were closed a few years and the people in the town were helpless to stop it. If however, you had an inkling that black people did not matter in this country, the school closing was a constant reminder. I was also afraid that if I was reminded of this in class, I would get pissed and show my true colors, jeopardizing the "safe Negro" status I had built up amongst the white students. Darryl Johnson actually brought a picture of his mother and my mother as teenagers, mouths wide open, screaming at a protest to reopen the schools. I was proud that my mother stood up for blacks and did not take that nonsense lying down. Overall, I was in denial and pretended it never even happened. Besides, the school closing had taken place almost 25 years earlier – ancient history. I simply tabled the subject until I was ready to handle the material and its implications.

My first year at the Darden School of Business, University of Virginia (UVA), I finally opened that door. It was Cid Scallet's rhetoric class and he wanted everyone to write an essay that included something personal about the writer. Cid was extremely popular amongst the students and mentioned in *Businessweek's Top 25 Business Schools*. I wrote the paper about the school closing and how it impacted my life. I wanted to write a very technical article so I walked over to the UVA Law School library and started with the actual legal case. This is what I found.

Prince Edward Makes History

Prince Edward County had a segregated school system, which was condoned by the government as long as the schools were "separate but equal." However, in April 1951, all 450 students at Robert Russa Moton High School walked out to protest what they deemed to be an inferior education at inferior facilities. The school buildings were made of tar paper and plywood and had no indoor plumbing. Prior attempts by Moton's principal and concerned parents to build a better school for blacks were met with silence from the Prince Edward County school board:

> The trouble had begun on the morning of April 23, 1951, at Farmville's R.R. Moton High School (named for Booker T. Washington's aide and successor), when the school's principal was informed by telephone that the police were about to arrest two of his students down at the bus station. Failing to recognize the call was a ruse, he had dashed off for town. Shortly thereafter, a note from the principal was delivered to each classroom, summoning the whole school to a general assembly. All 450 students and twenty-five teachers filed into the auditorium, and the buzz of gossip gave way to shocked silence the instant the stage curtain opened to reveal not the principal but a sixteen-year-old junior named Barbara Johns. She announced that this was a special student meeting to discuss the wretched conditions of the school.[4]

Barbara Johns was the niece of Vernon Johns, a famous preacher at the Dexter Avenue Baptist Church in Montgomery, Alabama. Johns also hailed from Prince Edward County and was considered one of the top African-American preachers of his day. Johns was branded a radical, as he was staunchly opposed to segregation. I guess he came by it honestly; Johns' paternal grandfather was hanged for cutting his slave master in two with a scythe. After being kicked out of Virginia Seminary for radicalism, Johns graduated from Oberlin College in 1918 and later attended the University of Chicago's graduate school of theology. By the late 1940s Johns was pastor at Dexter Avenue, where his radicalism again got him into trouble. Sermons like "It's Safe to Murder Negroes in Montgomery," a failed protest against blacks having to sit in the back of the bus and an attempt to eat at a "whites only" restaurant caused angst amongst the members of Dexter Avenue. After four years, Johns and Dexter Avenue parted ways. Afterward, the church sought a less-established and less-controversial preacher. It eventually settled on Martin Luther King, Jr. Though King gained notoriety for his bus boycotts and nonviolent marches, he credited Johns for having prepared his congregation for those events. Moreover, Johns is considered the "father of desegregation."

While Johns was in Montgomery during the school walkout, he advised his niece over the telephone. Lawyers from the Virginia Chapter of the NAACP, along with the students and the townspeople, filed a legal case to end segregation altogether. In May of 1951 they filed *Davis, et al. v. County School Board of Prince Edward County* in the federal district court of Richmond, asking that the state law requiring segregated schools to be overturned. In 1952 the U.S. District Court decided in favor of the school board. On appeal, the case was bundled with four other cases that collectively made up the 1954 landmark case of *Brown v. Board of Education of Topeka*, overturning segregated schools in the U.S. The other four cases arose in Delaware, Washington, D.C., South Carolina and Topeka, Kansas, of course. However, Prince Edward was the only case led by students. Though African-Americans were ecstatic about the *Brown* decision, the actual timing of school integration was left up to the states. The red herring in *Brown* was the language "with all deliberate speed," describing the manner in which school integration was to occur. This language could be interpreted differently and used as an excuse to delay compliance with *Brown*. Virginia, led by Senator Harry F. Byrd and his policy of "mass resistance," would be one of those states.

The Byrd "Machine"

Harry F. Byrd was a conservative Democratic senator of Virginia when the *Brown* decision was rendered. His father was a wealthy apple planter in the Shenandoah Valley section of the state and publisher of the *Winchester Star*, which Byrd later inherited. At the time, the *Winchester Star* was heavily in debt. To save the paper, Byrd repaid indebtedness out of cash flow from operations. As state senator (1915-1925), he upgraded many of Virginia's secondary roads paid for by cash receipts generated by the state or new taxes levied to cover such construction. In addition, Byrd served as governor (1926-1930), and U.S. Senator (1933-1965). Prior to the Conservative Democrats gaining favor in the late 1880s, Virginia politics was controlled by the Readjuster Party, co-founded by Confederate General Robert William Mahone and Harrison Riddleberger, a lawyer from Woodstock, Virginia. After the Civil War, Virginia was left with debt of approximately $50 million. The majority of that indebtedness was incurred from infrastructure investments like roads and railroads. After West Virginia seceded from the state, "Readjusters" felt the debt should be readjusted downward and West Virginia should pay its fair share of the debt burden. Mahone and Riddleberger formed coalitions with progressive thinking factions and took advantage of blacks' growing political power. William E. Cameron was elected governor from the Readjuster Party in 1882. At the time, three state senators and 11 delegates were black. Cameron's administration passed progressive legislation like the abolition of anti-black voting regulations, the establishment of Virginia State University, and increased funding for public schools. Both Republicans and Democrats alike wanted to quell black advancement, which meant destroying the Readjuster Party. By 1883 the Readjusters had lost majority control of the state legislature and the governorship to the Conservative Democrats. By 1902 the state legislature passed laws which eliminated the voting rights of blacks, and stated for the first time that the races were to be educated at separate schools.

During Byrd's rise to power in the 1920s, he used his web of connections, mainly in rural areas of the state, to control Virginia politics for over 40 years and vigorously maintain racial segregation. Elected officials in counties throughout the state would recommend candidates to Byrd who they thought were suitable for statewide office. Without Byrd's approval, potential candidates stood no chance of getting elected. For example, the state of Virginia has the distinction of being the only state that does not allow the governor to serve consecutive terms, yet a former governor may campaign in subsequent elections. To control the governorship, Byrd would have someone from his organization elected governor and after his four-year term, replace him with another member of the Byrd Machine . . . in sort of a human shell game. This allowed Byrd to maintain his lock on the U.S. Senate and control the policies made by the governor, as well as elected officials, in several rural counties. In the spirit of maintaining Jim Crow laws which kept the races separate, Byrd vehemently resisted the *Brown* decision. He implemented a campaign of massive resistance designed to form a coalition of Southern states to render the *Brown* decision powerless. Furthermore, the density of African Americans in Southside Virginia, as high as 60% of the population in some areas, made white residents in the Southside viscerally opposed to school integration. The very thing that made Prince Edward County a place of interest to Du Bois – a large, prosperous African-American community – made it a target of those who wanted the public schools and races to remain separate.

> The loudest voices defending the overturned separate-but-equal policy came from the Southside, the heartland of the Byrd machine, where the black percentage of the population was highest and where fears of race mixing were strongest . . . He [Byrd] could not afford to antagonize his rural power base, and this gave the region and its racism an influence on policy making out of proportion to its population in the state. As Lindsay Almond said years later, 'There would have been no hard, unyielding core of massive resistance in Virginia if there were no Southside. Virginia as a whole was opposed to race mixing in the public schools, but outside of the Southside the state evinced more of a willingness to face reality.'[5]

Byrd's mass resistance circumvented the federal law by (i) creating tuition grants allowing students to attend a private school of their choice and (ii) forbidding municipalities from raising state funds for integrated schools. For the 1959-1960 school year, Prince Edward County refused to raise taxes to support public schools. The county's public schools did not open in 1959 and remained closed until 1964. A private school, Prince Edward Academy, was built for the white students in the county during this time. County officials offered African-Americans a private school of their own; however, the parents rejected this proposal as nothing more than what had existed previously – a separate school for whites and blacks. Fifty years after the lockout, Mignon Griffin framed the matter: "A private school 'went against everything *Brown v. Board* stood for,' says Mignon Griffin, whose father, L. Francis Griffin, led the black community from his pulpit at Farmville's First Baptist Church during the long closing. 'We knew we'd be second-class again in that school.'"[6]

Impact of School Closing

Whether you attended a school outside Prince Edward or left the county to live with relatives or friends was pretty much the luck of the draw. If you were an only child your parents may have been able to afford to send you away. For those kids born into large families, the parents most likely sent the youngest kids away to attend school, while the older kids missed out or went to work to help maintain the home. Or they decided that no one would attend school. Sending kids to surrounding school districts was no easy task either, as those districts did not want interlopers using county facilities if they did not pay taxes there. During the lockout my mother attended school in Charlotte County, where she lived with a lady named Ms. Edmunds. She and her younger brother later graduated from Prince Edward County High after the schools were reopened. Of her other four siblings, one graduated high school in Washington, D.C., where he lived with an aunt. The other three made their homes in the Washington, D.C. area, but the conversation of high school was never mentioned and I never asked. My father graduated from Prince Edward as well. Whenever I asked what school he attended during the lockout, I was met with complete silence. His siblings mostly moved to the Long Island section of New York where they finished high school. Members of my father's extended family who were affected by the lockout left Prince Edward and vowed never to return to the state of Virginia.

Why Farmville?

The prevailing question remains, "Why Farmville?" Why did the student boycott which set up the landmark *Brown* decision happen there and why did parents refuse a private school for blacks when it was offered five years later? Defying Senator Byrd and the entire state of Virginia was considered extremely radical and a losing proposition. Many believe it was the presence of free blacks who had built successful businesses on Israel Hill decades before emancipation. Or maybe it was Prince Edward's status relative to surrounding counties. My guess is that it goes back to Prince Edward's "peculiar hopefulness" described by Du Bois over 60 years earlier. Not debatable is that the five-year war of attrition between black students in Prince Edward and the state of Virginia broke the Byrd Machine. By the early 1960s state and federal courts had rendered many of Byrd's mass resistance laws "null and void." Byrd retired from the U.S. Senate in 1965 and died one year later.

MY FARMVILLE – FAMILY, GOD, AND PRINCE EDWARD COUNTY HIGH

The Farmville I remember was just how Du Bois had described it. Every Saturday the size of the town grew about three-fold as residents from surrounding counties came to shop and do business. There were special events that happened annually like the Heart of Virginia Festival, the Five County Fair or the Christmas parade, where local businessmen and town officials would be on display. But the big draw was the school band, which came down the street last. I can vividly remember standing in the cold to hear the Prince Edward Marching Band, the baddest high school band in the state . . . the majorettes, the drum major high-stepping and the drumline with its trademarked cadence. Outside of those special occasions, it was family, God and Prince Edward County High.

Family Life

Family was the most important aspect of my hometown. My father was from Farmville and my mother, who spent her early years in Washington, D.C., was raised by her maternal grandmother there as a teenager. Everyone I came into contact with was either related to me or knew my family. You needed a linear programming model to keep track of who was related to whom or who was married to whom. For those you were unsure were related to, you simply called them cousin or uncle "so and so." The bigger picture was that family stuck together and there was strength in numbers.

Gramma and Grandpa

The hierarchy of power went from top to bottom. My grandparents had the most juice, then my parents. My parents, I and my three siblings (Mark, Sharmane and Dwayne) lived with my father's parents until we moved into our own house when I was in the fourth grade. My father had spent a tour of duty in Vietnam, so my grandparents pitched in while he was away and after he returned home. My grandmother, Ana Mae, was probably the sweetest person I have ever known. She was a tall, slim, light-skinned lady who never had an unkind word to say about anybody. Even when you tried to bait her into saying something negative, she would refrain. She spent her life pretty much taking care of others. She worked as a housekeeper for a few families in Farmville and the Hampden-Sydney area – the Marks and the Newmans to name a few. Gramma talked about these families and their kids so much that we felt like we knew them personally. We did not like sharing her with other people and expected her to always be there for us . . . to listen to our problems, put a Band-Aid on our wounds or bake us a cake for our birthdays. She had five children: Ralph and Frances resided in Farmville and Josephine, Barbara and Shirley lived on the Long Island section of New York. But her 19 grandchildren were her heart, that and the Mercy Seat Baptist Church just down the street. She sang on the church choir and was always discussing church business. I never remember her happier than when she had all of her kids and grandkids at her house at the same time . . . kids running through the house, acting crazy and vying for her attention. It seemed as if we were the examples of how she had spent her time here on earth.

She was always bragging about us and showing off our pictures, report cards, etc. Whenever anyone came by to visit, mainly Ms. Bertha Jenkins or some of the other church ladies, she would call us from outside playing. We would have to tell the ladies our names, ages and what our interests were. On cue they would reply, "Annie Mae, you sure have some well-mannered grandchildren." We knew this routine well; it was impossible to screw it up because we rehearsed it year-round. She ruled more with the "carrot" than the "stick." It was not just what she did, but the precision with which she did it. First of all, she would always make us peanut butter and jelly sandwiches for lunch. She always bought the crunchy peanut butter because that's what we liked. She would then cut the sandwiches diagonally across the corners, making two triangles. For your birthday she would bake you a cake in any style you liked; she had 11 grandchildren in Farmville, which equated to 11 birthday cakes a year. And whenever you would cut your leg or hand from playing outside or falling off your bike, she would put hydrogen peroxide on it instead of alcohol because peroxide did not sting. It seems insignificant now but to a kid stuff like that was important. You would never play with reckless abandon if you knew that the alcohol was waiting for you. The only pet peeves we had with Annie Mae were her living room and the Kool-Aid. She was adamant that no one walk through her living room, breathe in there or even look at it. And the more she fussed about it, the more we wanted to do it. The carpet was all plush, and the furniture looked like it hadn't been moved in decades. But the Kool-Aid was another story. Gramma must have had to ration sugar during the Great Depression or something because she went real light on it when making Kool-Aid. We would frown up our faces even before we drank it. The tartness paralyzed your tongue and sent the rest of your body into a spasm, twisting and turning, looking down at the floor trying to avoid making eye contact with her. We would complain in private to my mother, hoping that she would break the bad news. Yet, even my mother "chickened out" and kept quiet. For years "Annie Mae's sour Kool-Aid" was a must-have whenever you visited.

And if you thought Annie Mae was weak, you thought wrong. She held all the power – access to my grandfather, Joe Baker. If anybody wanted anything from Joe, they would broach the idea with Gramma and she would give her take on (i) the likelihood that Joe would go for it and (ii) how she could help. Joe would mull it over, give Annie Mae his answer and she would deliver the news to the requesting party (my mother, father, Aunt Frances). The trick was to get Gramma to become an advocate for your proposal; then it would sort of become her idea. And she knew Joe's weakness – peace and quiet. If there was something Annie Mae wanted that Grandpa had left undone, we knew there would be no peace. She would nag him unmercifully. It was like a siren that would not shut off; she would have the entire house running around trying to fix whatever was ailing her. We would rather take a beating (and we took lots of 'em too) than to see Annie Mae upset about something. It was the least we could do since she took care of everybody. I can still remember Grandpa lying in bed in the middle of the night begging, "Come on Ana Mae, can I go to sleep please? I heard you now. I'm gonna do it." We would joke about how the U.S. had the

10

secret weapon to end the Cold War with Russia – Annie Mae's nagging – yet refused to use it. After a few minutes of listening to her, KGB agents would have given away all the Russians' secrets.

As a kid, Joe Baker was probably the meanest black man I had ever met. The funny thing is that he never raised his voice to us or laid a hand on us. The closest thing he ever came to beating one of us was when Dwayne did something he had no business doing. I had never seen Grandpa so mad before. He had the impression that Dwayne "didn't think fire burned." Grandpa went into the attic (I think) and pulled out a bullwhip; it was made of leather and had creases in it that could leave some serious scars. Grandpa grabbed Dwayne and that fool was crying and screaming like Grandpa was gonna kill him, which was funnier and did more harm than actually beating him. For the next few days Dwayne walked around in a trance as if he had seen a ghost. But you could sense a dark side in how Grandpa carried himself . . . a real mysterious side, as if he was a different person in a previous life. I always attributed his persona to a hard life he may have had growing up. He was the total opposite of Gramma. She was tall. He was short, about 5'5". She was sweet as pie and he was mean as a rattlesnake. I would look at them two and for the life of me I could not see the attraction. The man rarely spoke to us. Maybe we would get a grunt here or there. When he did speak, usually a complaint about something we were doing, Annie Mae relayed the message – "Junior, your grandpa said please quit throwing the ball against the house . . . Would ya'll please turn the T.V. down? Your grandpa is trying to sleep. You know he has to go to work tonight." By all accounts the dude was a killjoy, and I think he reveled in that distinction. He worked the night shift in the boiler room at Longwood College. He slept during the day, which meant we had to either turn the volume down on the T.V. or not watch it at all. We had to tiptoe around the house all evening like a bunch of burglars. As soon as he awoke, Mark, Dwayne, my cousin Thomas and I turned the T.V. off, lights off, and hopped into bed before anyone could find who the culprit was. When we heard him snoring again we would turn the T.V. back on, with Annie Mae on "pins and needles." This ritual – us tiptoeing, Joe waking up, Annie Mae whining and us with a quizzical look on our faces like, "Who us?" would go on for over a decade.

Since Joe was king of his castle, we had to follow his rules. Whenever he came home from work Sharmane usually met him in the driveway before he could get out of the car. When Joe entered the house, everything immediately took on a more serious tone. We had to gauge Grandpa's mood before we knew how to proceed. If he was in a good mood, the recklessness could continue. If he had had a hard day at work or if his back ached, we had to tone it down. During supper Grandpa always ate first; he would taste the food, then give feedback on whether something was too hot, too cold, or too salty. And Gramma only cooked what Joe liked, which was pretty much anything. But Joe did not have to eat it, even if it was good for him. However, we had to eat everything that was good for us (squash, turnips, cabbage, etc.). But the double standard was few and far between because Joe was never around. Grandpa was seemingly in three states –

going to work, at work, or coming from work. We never saw him except on weekends. He worked the night shift for decades and I never once heard the man complain. He did whatever he had to do in order to provide for his family. As much as he was a killjoy, he definitely had our respect. He worked hard and was a man of means. He had a tractor, an antique truck, a pickup truck and a "Deuce and a Quarter," or what the rest of America affectionately referred to as an Electra 225. Back in the day, a black man with a Cadillac or Deuce and a Quarter commanded respect. He kept it so clean that we didn't even want to put our feet on the floor for fear we would leave a speck of dirt. Grandpa would drive us into town on Saturdays and we would love to run into our friends from school or people from the neighborhood. The car gave us status. It was the first car I had ever seen with electric windows, and when he took his foot off the gas pedal the car kept going. We thought it was magic but the official name for it was "cruise control."

Before we left for town, Joe would put his "stuff"on and slick his hair back with some of that Vitalis he kept on the bathroom counter. He would be cleaner than the Board of Health. We would go to some of the department stores and then take Annie Mae grocery shopping. Our last stop would always be the ABC store where Grandpa would buy a supply of liquor. Virginia is a "blue law" state that prohibits the sale of alcohol on Sunday. The ABC store closed at 5 p.m. and at 4:59 p.m. there would be a mass of people running to beat the closing – a Saturday ritual. And like clockwork, starting around 9 p.m. and into the wee hours of the night, there would be a knock at Joe's door. Grandpa would answer, go into his stash and sell some of his inventory. We would see all kinds of people from the community, some from Mercy Seat, Hampden-Sydney, Darlington Heights, etc., looking like they were in dire straits. If he didn't know the person, then Grandpa miraculously was out of liquor. We kids saw this take place for years and never once mentioned it, not even amongst ourselves; we knew better. If it was to be done then Joe Baker did it, including loan sharking. He sort of embodied the Southern expression of, "Always have more than you show, and always speak less than you know."

Grandma

My mother's parents were deceased by the time I was born so I never met them. She was raised from her teenage years by her maternal grandmother, Ola Layne Allen, whom we affectionately called "Grandma." We pronounced it differently from "Gramma" so people could distinguish her from Annie Mae. Farmville was the type of place where people came over uninvited; your hosts got offended if they offered you something to eat and you refused. And everybody had a picture of Jesus, the two white guys and the black guy hanging on their wall. Grandma said that Jesus died to save us humans on earth and the two white guys were the Kennedys and the black guy was Martin Luther King, Jr. They died trying to help black folks. Grandma and I shared as strong a bond as a great-grandmother and great-grandson could share. According to my cousins I was her "pick." I was pretty rambunctious as a toddler and apparently was so out of control that they had to tie my stroller to a table leg to keep me from getting away. Well that rambunctiousness caught up with me eventually. When I was around two years old my mother was in Charlotte County helping out Ms. Edmunds, the lady she had stayed with during the school lockout. Ms. Edmunds had gotten up in age and my mother was there to support her for a few weeks. One day after cooking dinner, she poured the leftover grease into a canister and placed it on a shelf above the stove. She then left the room to wash clothes. I had seen her put the hot grease into this canister several times and was curious as to what it was. Seizing my opportunity, I grabbed a chair, tiptoed high enough to reach the canister and accidentally tipped it over onto myself, hot grease and all. My mother came running from the next room but it was too late. I remember events before and after the incident, but not the incident itself. The grease scalded about three-fifths of my entire body – the right side of my face, neck, most of my chest and the side of my right leg. I was in the hospital for a few weeks and cocoa butter would become my new best friend. On the doctor's orders, my mother religiously placed it over my scars every morning. Daily I had to show my stomach to my mother and grandparents so they could see the progress. It got to the point where friends of the family (mostly women) would inquire about my scars. I hated showing my body to some stranger but never complained to my mother about it. Looking back, the more the scars went away the less guilt she felt for not doing a better job of protecting me. Around age 9, a strange car pulled into Grandma's driveway. A lady got out and walked inside. About 10 minutes later my mother called me inside from playing basketball with the other kids. When she summoned only me I knew what was about to take place. I walked into the family room where the lady, my mother, Grandma, and a few aunts were talking. The lady asked to see my chest, to which I obliged. She gave the obligatory "what a miracle it was" and so on and so forth. I then asked, "Now can I see yours?" There was dead silence. My mother was about to light my rear end up, but I did not care. I had had enough. Grandma and my aunts were grinning from ear to ear though. Grandma intervened with, "Don't beat him Suzie." She knew it had gotten old. I never had to show my chest to strangers again after that.

When I came home from the hospital after the scalding Grandma had a party for me "Up the House," the name we gave her 20-plus-acre establishment. All of my aunts and cousins were there and a few people from the neighborhood. They made a cake for me, fruit punch, the works. Of course I was thinking like, "Maybe I should darn near kill myself on a monthly basis." I could not figure out what the big deal was. But when people started making a big fuss, I played it up. This was the first time everybody had seen me since the accident. After seeing the burns all over my body, my cousins felt a bit sorry for me. Grandma marveled at the fact that though I was weak, and sickly, I still tried to play with the bigger kids. At that point I became her "pick." And from then on Grandma had a rule, "If that boy don't play, nobody plays!"

Demon Child

To this day my cousins describe me as the "demon" who could do no wrong. Grandma had about 20 grandkids, 17 great-grandkids and kept two or three foster kids from time to time. Add in some additional kids from the neighborhood and there was an army of us. The activities took place around the clock. And whatever games were going on, all you heard was, "Let that boy play." If there was a basketball game going on and my older cousins blew me off, I ran into the house to tell Grandma. She would come outside and take the ball away until they let me shoot a few times, or let me stand on the court and give the illusion as if I was actually playing. We also played softball or "tennisball." And of course I had to play. At two or three years old I could barely hold a bat but they had to stand there and pitch to me until I finally connected. Then I cried if I got out. Grandma would come outside and tell my cousins to put me back on base. They would put me on base to give the illusion as if I was "safe" when I was really "out." When we played football I had to be "Number 43" for Larry Brown, the All-Pro running back for the Washington Redskins. Larry Brown was my hero and if I could not be #43 then I was not playing. And if I wasn't playing, nobody was going to play. I would hold up games for 15-20 minutes at a time with my nonsense. Twenty or so kids in the yard and everybody had to cater to one kid. It was no wonder I cried to go up there, then cried when it was time to leave. When my mother pulled into Grandma's driveway, we would open the car doors before the car stopped and race to the house like it was the Kentucky Derby. While Ana Mae and Joe had clearly defined rules in place, I was untouchable Up the House. My rambunctiousness sometimes crossed the line and my mother made a concerted effort to put me back in line. I tested boundaries and saw just how much I could get away with without getting a beating. My mother was from the school of "spare the rod, spoil the child," and she seemed to purposely try to undo all of the good work Grandma had created. While most kids loved summer vacation, I had mixed feelings about it. I knew I could play all day but there was also a lot of time to spark my mother's ire. During summer break I literally got a beating every day . . . usually something involving a ball or having "too much mouth." I broke too many storm doors and windows at Grandma's for me to count. All that land Grandma had and I had to play "catch" near the house. Maybe it was the danger of it all that I enjoyed.

After I had broken something I had to wait around all day for my mother to come home. Suzie worked at Leggett's Department Store and got off at 5:30 p.m. Around 5 p.m. my cousins would laugh about how it was time for me to get my "tea." When my mother pulled into the driveway and got out of the car, you could tell by how fast she was walking whether or not she had heard about what I had done. She would take my belt and wear my rear end out. The beatings would go on for a little while and then Grandma would step in with, "Don't kill that boy Suzie!" Then my mother would stop. I pretty much had it timed. I would yell a little bit in the beginning and after about 15-20 seconds I would be thinking, "Alright Grandma where are you? Grandma, come on now!" And with her extrasensory perception, Grandma would step in and save my life. Since I was the oldest child, Suzie wanted to make an example out of me for the other three. When my own son Ralphie was around 7 years old I was doing some painting around the house and I asked him to bring me a new paintbrush. Instead of walking the paintbrush over to me, the kid threw it and accidentally smashed the window. I never said a word. I just had this sheepish grin on my face. He could not believe he was not going to get in trouble for it. I simply told him that as a kid I had gotten enough beatings for the both of us.

Us Against the World

Grandma was the matriarch of the family and pretty much all-powerful in my eyes. She never laid a hand on me, Mark, Dwayne or Sharmane. She did not have to. We were literally scared to death of her. We had also witnessed some of the beatings she delivered to my older cousins. She did not tolerate laziness, or insubordination. She also had a thing about lying and "putting your hands on something that didn't belong to you." She would threaten my cousins, one in particular, that "You going to the pen." I'm thinking like, "What pen . . . the pig pen? And why would you be sent to the pig pen for being a big liar?" I was too young to understand but she was fixated on keeping her grandchildren "out the pen." Whenever someone broke one of her rules you knew the penalty – the switch. She would make you go into the woods and pick your own. Now there was a strategy to this. The bigger the switch, the more stable it was, the more it would hurt, and the longer the beating would last. However, if you did not get a big enough switch Grandma would have Mr. Allen, the man she remarried later in life, go get one. And he would come back with an entire tree branch. Once my cousin returned with the switch, Grandma would examine it for length, thickness, and flexibility. Mr. Allen would add his two cents and no matter how long or thick the switch was, he always felt it was inadequate. Once the switch had passed inspection, the beating would begin. After hearing (never seeing) what took place next, that was the best advertisement Grandma needed as to what happened when you crossed her.

One way to avoid the switch was to keep Grandma in a good mood. One of her passions was professional wrestling, or "the rasslin'" as she called it. The wrestling came on every Saturday at 3:30 p.m. on Channel 6 (CBS), and she watched it religiously. The chores stopped when the wrestling was on and if you were about to get the switch, Grandma miraculously forgot all about it. This thing had more drama than any soap opera on television. And the characters – Rufus R. "Freight Train" Jones, "Black Jack" Mulligan, "Supafly" Jimmy Snuka, Tony Atlas, The "Iron" Sheik – had their own wrestling styles. The most despised, dastardly performers were Gene and Ole Anderson (The Minnesota Wrecking Crew) and "The Nature Boy" Ric Flair. The Andersons were cold, calculating, unfeeling assassins. They would apply the "screwdriver" to a guy's head or knee him while he was down. They were not in it for the sport; they were in it to inflict pain. And Flair was always pulling victory from the jaws of defeat. It was bad enough that he always won, but he had to tell you about it. He bragged about his long-flowing blond hair, his expensive robes, his beautiful girlfriend ("Baby Doll"), and generally how much better he was living compared to you. Grandma made us keep the television on Channel 6 all day until the wrestling went off. That meant that we only watched the cartoons that CBS showed, even the reruns. Some of the most frightening moments Up the House occurred when the wrestling was not shown. We would try to explain to

Grandma that "it didn't come on today" but that would make her even madder. We would scramble around to find the local *T.V. Guide*, else we would walk to the store and buy one. But 46-50 Saturdays out of the year, we screamed and yelled at the television in the hopes that our guy would win.

Grandma's other infatuation was *The Price Is Right*. We would shout out the prices for the products as if the contestants could actually hear us. Whenever a woman won, she would run onstage and give the host, Bob Barker, a kiss. Grandma would then exclaim, "Look at her running up there to kiss Bob! That's probably all she wanted to begin with." We would all freeze and look around at each other in amazement. Years later when I was in business school, a breaking news story flashed across the television. Bob Barker was embroiled in a lawsuit concerning an inappropriate relationship with one of the models on the show. My roommate, as well as the public, was in disbelief. But I found the story very credible; I was certain that the model was not telling the whole story and that Bob's affections had not gone unrequited. My roommate asked what made me so certain. I simply chuckled to myself and changed the subject. Grandma also had a very serious side, however. Keeping the family together was very serious business. She told us stories of the hardships she had to overcome raising her family . . . how they had to hunt, cut pulp wood and pull tobacco, else they went hungry. Real estate developers offered to build her a "turnkey" house with minimal debt. However, she was dead set against going into hock; instead, she built her home in stages as the family earned the money. She was proud of her commonsense approach to building her house, and loved how I hung on her every word. I envisioned how things might have been different had she gone with the turnkey option and shuddered at the thought.

Her farm was a real working farm too. Every day my cousins fed the hogs and the chickens. The chickens ate mainly corn, corn, and more corn. Grandma kept them in a wooden coop covered with mesh wire. There was usually a dominant male who would fly around the coop and make everyone else move out of the way. Sometimes they would fight when the dominant male wanted to remind everybody who was in charge or a younger upstart wanted to issue a challenge. This was *Animal Planet* prior to the History Channel. Two chickens trying to kill one another and the rest of them trying to stay out of harm's way – it was both scary and comical at the same time. My cousins would even give these fools names. I never got too attached to them because I knew that eventually . . . sooner or later . . . all good things must come to an end. Then the day finally arrived when Grandma reminded my cousin Ricky to get ready. Ricky was about 6'2", 190 pounds and pretty deft with an axe. He walked down to the chicken coop with Grandma and the rest of us in tow. First Grandma discussed the strategy for chopping off the chicken's head (apparently there was an art to this). At around 8 years old I was brave enough to watch but too scared to stare death in the face, so I kept my distance. Ricky reached into the chicken coop and the first chicken came willingly. He then placed the chicken's head on top of a tree stump (the chop block). There was complete silence as Ricky measured the chicken's head with the axe. Then whack! Down went the axe, off came the chicken's head and utter pandemonium. The body of the headless chicken ran around the yard flapping its wings like crazy. The little kids and I ran for our lives, with the headless chicken right on our trail. We zigzagged, but we could not shake the headless beast. We ran around in a circle and the chicken seemingly ran in the same pattern. Meanwhile, the rest of the chickens, having now come to the conclusion that "this is real," started cackling and flying around the chicken coop. Eventually the headless chicken ran out of energy and collapsed. Grandma collected it and pointed out which one was next. Ricky reached into the coop and literally had the fight of his life, as the rest of the flock would not go quietly. But eventually, the cackling and flying around the coop came to an end. It was our first lesson about the pecking order amongst the living and the eventuality of death.

There was always something going on Up the House, like some big-time family gathering or activity. For Mother's Day the boys took on the girls in a family softball game. The boys won of course, but this nonsense was a spectacle. You always knew whose mother was at bat because the kid would stare at the ground out of embarrassment or try to hide behind a tree. First of all, my mother hit from the left side of the plate. I mean, who does that? Then she pulled her right leg out before swinging, as if she was afraid to get hit by the ball. You were supposed to step toward the pitcher; that way you generate more power when swinging through the ball. Who didn't know that? Then she couldn't make contact with the ball . . . embarrassing! It took her about 10 swings before she could ever put the ball in play and that was usually a weak ground ball. We would pretend to misplay the ball so she could get on base. Every year the boys would destroy the girls. But I did have one aunt (who shall remain nameless) who was a powerhouse. She had us backing way back into the field and she still hit the ball over our heads. The outcome was scripted but overall, it was lots of fun and the day we probably looked most forward to.

And to break into my family, you had a better chance of breaking into Fort Knox. There were a lot of teenage girls in my family. The caveat was that for the local boys to get anywhere near them, they had to make the trek Up the House and pass inspection from Grandma, my mother, and my aunts. Whenever a boy was coming over, everybody vied for a front-row seat. There would be about seven or eight women and six or seven of my cousins on the front porch. Everybody would extend pleasantries and Grandma would ask, "Aren't you so and so's boy? How's she doing? Isn't so and so your uncle?" If she didn't know anything about the boy she would ask who his people were, where they lived and worked. The women would then put the guy through a catechism of questions. The entire setup was designed to make the guy unsettled. If he buckled under the pressure, my aunts would eat him alive. The boy would be seated in the center of the porch with women to his right, women seated directly in front of him and Grandma always on the couch to his left. And you could hear a pin drop it was so quiet. I would bet that there have been board meetings at General Motors that were not this intense. Once I was allowed to see the goings-on. I saw my aunts asking the questions while Grandma sat back and observed. They played a version of "good cop, bad cop," with one aunt acting hostile to unnerve the young fella and Grandma coming to the boy's rescue when one of my aunt's had crossed the line. The women fired questions from all angles. While one aunt asked a question, another was preparing one. They also asked similar questions, but worded them differently. Only if the boy was telling the truth could he give the same answer to four or five similar questions. If he hesitated, that was a sure sign of a lie. Lack of eye contact was another dead giveaway. Offering up one-word answers to serious questions, or something as seemingly trivial as a lack of a firm handshake would send red flags.

When the meeting with the suitor was over, the guy would come down to the basketball court. After making small talk, my cousin Skippy and I would break into our little two-man ruse. Skippy would challenge him to a game of "H-O-R-S-E" against me. Now the entire time I would be standing around playing the "shy kid." At age 10 or 11, I was small for my age so I looked like I was around 7 or 8. My first five or six shots were always scripted. I would start the game off with lay-ups with either hand, or a shot from behind the backboard. After a series of warm-up shots it was on to the serious stuff. I would walk outside to about 18-20 feet away and I could see dude's eyes widen, like he was in disbelief. My cousins would scream out "set shot from the top of the key," "jump hook from the wing" or "sky hook from the corner." Like a cold-blooded assassin, I would start burying shots. It was like a human video game . . . my cousins Skippy, Kim, and Chucky calling out shots and me responding. The guy would look all incredulous because it seemed as if the shots were luck, like I was simply throwing the ball at the basket. If he refused to go quietly, my cousins would scream out "all net," which meant the shot had to go straight in without hitting the rim. After it was all over, I would just walk off, never making eye contact with the suitor. The guy would pay Skippy, who would have a Cheshire cat grin affixed to his face. Everyone would remain quiet, like this was an uncommon occurrence or something. And of course, the boy would beg for a rematch. Five games and 50 cents later, the guy would acquiesce and admit to having "an off day." After the suitor pulled out of the driveway, and the coast was clear, we would all roll around on the ground from laughing so hard. The mere thought that some fool could actually beat me in a game of H-O-R-S-E, in my own backyard no less, had us in hysterics. Skippy and I would walk to the store with our winnings and buy a bag full of candy. We would come back to Grandma's and share it with the rest of the kids. But it was all good with the suitors though. Although it was hard to break into our family, it was nearly impossible to get out. Once they had been vetted by the process they were our boyfriends from then on.

Suzie and My Daddy

My parents were Angela and Ralph Baker, but that is not how my siblings and I referred to them. The story goes that when we were toddlers, Mark and I would ask our mother for something and she would say, "Go ask your daddy." Of course he would tell us to go bother "Suzie." From then on we referred to them as "Suzie" and "My Daddy." Suzie and her four siblings (the Neversons) were born in Washington, D.C. and lived in the Georgetown section there. They fell on hard times after their parents died and were taken in by Grandma when she was a teenager. When they became adults, my uncles and aunt all moved back to D.C. but Suzie remained in Farmville, got married and started a family. She never really spoke about Washington that much, other than the fact that she preferred country living. She pushed us to be proud of who we were and how we grew up, and not to let anyone talk down to us. She was always trying to help people and took a special interest in children who she thought were less fortunate. It was a quirk that we had to deal with and we hoped that ultimately, it would get her into heaven or something. However, she lived for her own children; we were her world. Her main worry was who was going to take care of her kids if something happened to her. She would query different family members from time to time to ensure someone would step in if need be. It got to the point where it was almost an obsession. Suzie was about 5'7" with a large frame. When she stood over top of one of us she could literally block out the sun. It was almost laughable to us that something could happen to our mother. The quintessential "strong" black woman, she could bend but never break. Even if she died we figured she would find a way to come back to life. Yet, there were times when she put a scare into us. If she was not home from work by 6:30 p.m. we ran in the house and sat real still. Then we would call just about every relative we had, inquiring of her whereabouts. Grandpa had a police blotter where he could hear about emergencies, car accidents, fires, and police chases. We would listen to that for a while to see if there were any reported car accidents in the neighborhood. By 7:30 p.m. if she was not home and had not called, all hell would break loose. Life in my Farmville was very predictable – there were set times for certain things to occur and for people to be certain places. But there was also a level of fragility; if some misfortune had befallen our mother, we would never have recovered.

Not only was she our safety net, but Suzie pushed us constantly. She instilled in us to be "go-getters" and that we could accomplish whatever we wanted in life. There were boundless opportunities for blacks growing up in the '70s and '80s (unlike in her day), and there was no excuse not to pursue your dreams. The only caveat was that we had to try our best and finish what we started. In retrospect, we ran the poor woman ragged. We played every sport and were in every activity imaginable. At Prince Edward, Dwayne and I played football, basketball and baseball. Mark was in the band and Sharmane was a cheerleader and played basketball and softball. She never said "no" to anything we wanted to do; My Daddy thought we were a bunch of ingrates and that she did too much for us. It never really dawned on me how indestructible she must have been until I had a son of my own. My wife and I were exhausted from trying to keep up with his schedule – piano lessons, soccer, basketball, chess, etc. And that was simply weekend duty. For Suzie, there were four of us, seven days a week. She became a fixture at athletic events, hollering and screaming during the games. But of course my brother Mark and I tried to take advantage of the situation. Sometimes we would attend dances after games. Before I received my driver's license Suzie had to pick us up. The dances would last until around 1 a.m. and they were heavily chaperoned with teachers and parents. Suzie would tell us to be ready by 11:30 p.m., at least an hour before it was over. This was problematic because Mark and I had convinced the rest of the school that we were grown. Having to leave the dance early was a clear sign that you were on a short leash and you would lose cool points with your peers. We nodded in agreement to whatever she said, but had no intention of leaving before midnight. We would have to get our tea when we got home, but under no circumstance were we going to look bad in front of our friends. Suzie would have to go home from the game, get some shut eye, wake up out of her warm bed and drive back down to the school to pick us up. By 11:45 p.m. some crazed parent would be flashing her car lights outside. Five minutes later one of the teachers would come inside to find us (in the dark) and tell us our mother was outside. We still blew her off. Ten minutes later Mrs. Scott Brown would come over the loud speaker: "Ralph Baker, Mark Baker, ya'll mama here to pick ya'll up and she said to come to the car right now!" Busted! We would lower our heads and slither out like two slinkies. We would traipse past the teachers and chaperones with our eyes averted toward the floor. Mrs. Scott Brown would give us that speech, "Why didn't you all come on the first time your mama called you? You know how your mama is."

By the time we reached high school it had been well documented how "our mama was." My third grade social studies teacher, Ms. Bell, gave me a "D" during one of the marking periods and wrote some nonsense like, "Ralph spends too much time in class talking to Lee Taylor." I didn't even know what a "D" looked like. It only added insult to injury that Ms. Bell was telling stories on me for no apparent reason. A few weeks later I was in the back of social studies class hamming it up with Lee. Suddenly, in mid-sentence, Lee stopped talking. He seemed fixated on something behind me. I reacted like "Lee, are you okay? What's wrong man?" Lee never said a word, just pointed upward behind me. When I turned around, the room sort of got dark. I didn't know if it was Godzilla or Megalon . . . I'm still not sure to this day. But Godzilla/Megalon told Lee to never speak to her son again in class. She then grabbed me by the back of my collar and marched me to the front of the room. She instructed Ms. Bell that I was to sit in the front row from then on and for the rest of the students not to speak to her son in class anymore. She gave Ms. Bell her phone number and advised Ms. Bell to call her at work if she had any more problems out of me. I sat there with my head down, shocked that I had so far survived the attack and prayed it would be over soon. The rest of the class was stone-faced. First of all, we had never witnessed a parent enter the classroom like that. Even Ms. Bell was taken aback . . . she sat back in her chair, mouth wide open, not realizing she was nearly an accessory to murder. Secondly, no one could believe that I was actually afraid of anybody. I was one of the littlest kids in class and also had the most mouth. The kids were part happy to see somebody finally silence me, and part happy I was still alive.

Yet, when we were in the right Suzie was the first to come to our defense. My freshman year in high school, we were required to maintain class notes for an introductory Spanish course. Most of the learning took place from the interaction between Ms. Black and the students, which you were supposed to capture in your notes. Each nine weeks Ms. Black checked the notebook; not submitting it would result in an automatic "F." No one in his right mind would maintain the notebook each day for nine weeks and not turn it in. However, Ms. Black was absent from school the day the notebooks were due for inspection. I told the substitute I would rather hand it in to Ms. Black personally, to which the substitute agreed. The following Monday I recounted the exchange I had with the substitute teacher. But Ms. Black would not accept the notebook late – an automatic "F" for the class. Deep down I never expected to actually fail the class. I had done the work, and by golly my grade was going to reflect it, somehow. When I received my report card weeks later, I opened it before football practice and lo and behold, there it was – a big fat "F" in Spanish. I had been in denial for weeks but now I had to deal with it. I confided in my cousin Wayne; when I told him about the "F" he yelled to the rest of the team, "Ya'll aren't gonna believe this. The bookworm got an 'F' on his report card!" About five of our teammates came running over to see the spectacle. They responded half-jokingly, "Boy your mama gon' get you. She ain't gon' like this at all . . . hard to play football after your mama kills you." I had to spell it out to Wayne that if he ever wanted to see me alive again he would have to help me out of this situation. He paused and said, "Man, just tell her. She's going to find out eventually anyway. Tell Suzie it wasn't your fault, simple as that." The entire time I was looking at Wayne with my mouth agape, awaiting the "real" plan of action. I mean dude was two years older than me, and "tell the truth" was the best he could come up with? When I got home I sat Suzie down and told her about the "F." I showed her the notebook and explained that I had been keeping copious notes all along. The grade did not reflect the work I had put into the class and she needed to do something about it. Surprisingly, she agreed and decided to meet with the principal, Mr. Townes, and "that teacher."

My mother and I worked down dual paths. She set up the meeting with Mr. Townes and I performed some high-level due diligence on Ms. Black. I spoke to a few upperclassmen who had taken her Spanish class before; they each described Ms. Black as hard, but fair and a very nice lady, but "no-nonsense." To a man they said the notebook was one of her pet peeves and the "F" was ironclad. Furthermore, the idea of my mother meeting with her and Mr. Townes was a complete waste of time and to "forget it." On the afternoon of the meeting, Suzie passed me in the hallway with a serious look on her face. The meeting seemed to take forever, lasting a few hours. I didn't hear any screaming so I took that as a good sign. Then right after school ended she walked up to me in the hallway and whispered "You got a 'C'" and returned to work. A few of the upperclassmen badgered me about the outcome. When I told them I was getting a "C" they thought I was lying. After I showed them the actual grade on my revised report card they retorted, "Yo' mama must be one bad lady."

While Suzie was hands on, My Daddy was never around. During the weekdays he was always working. He had lots of jobs when I was growing up, but the job I remembered most was when he worked in construction in Richmond. Suzie would drive him to meet his carpool at 6 a.m. when we were still in the bed sleep. When he got home at 10 p.m. or later, we were in the bed sleep. He was like a ghost . . . we could hear footsteps from time to time but never really saw him. And on the weekends he was always out with his cousin Larry; the two were inseparable. When you mentioned one you had to mention the other – "Ralph and Larry" or "Larry and Ralph." I always had the impression that My Daddy could not have cared less about us, since he was never around. And we sort of liked it that way because when he was around he was always barking orders; he was either giving orders or critiquing the orders we were supposed to carry out. Suzie said he never used to be that way. Before he went to Vietnam he was a cool dude, real happy-go-lucky and known for his sense of humor. I simply took her word for it. In general, I could not see what the attraction between them was. Whenever they went out Suzie would be looking all fine and everything and My Daddy would look like Helen Keller had dressed him – looking all wild and crazy with plaid pants and polka dot shirts. Having served in Vietnam after being drafted into the Navy at age 19, My Daddy tried to run our house like the military. And the war stories . . . I have never physically been to Vietnam but my father took us there thousands of times. His buddies from basic training, mostly teenagers, became his best friends. Their primary job was to keep each other alive. That plan did not work out too well because the first month after entering Vietnam, half his company was killed. He would tell us about the encounters with the Vietnamese ad nauseam, and how he never thought he would make it home alive. Sharmane would go to her room. Dwayne would suddenly become tired and Mark would have to go to the bathroom, leaving me to sit there alone for hours on end. For some odd reason it was important to him for us to know what he went through in Vietnam, but it went clearly over our heads. The Vietnam War was ancient history to a 10-year-old. Secondly, the U.S. was the mightiest country in the world, and the thought of losing a war to a small country like Vietnam was pretty hard for me to comprehend. At the end of his hours-long diatribes I would always ask, "Why not just drop a bomb and go home?" But My Daddy said the war was a little more complicated than that.

When My Daddy was not barking orders or telling war stories, he was pretty much a killjoy. First of all, he made us go to bed at 9 p.m. on weeknights unless we had homework to do. Granted, I was not a morning person but a 9 p.m. bedtime was darn near criminal. That also meant I had to miss *Monday Night Football*. Tuesday morning I would sit next to Wayne on the school bus to get the scoop on the game. One day Wayne played a joke and told me the wrong names of the teams and the wrong outcome. Kicking it with my boys prior to homeroom, they were discussing the actual game while I was discussing something else. After they figured out that the game lasted past my bedtime, I became the butt of a lot of jokes. And when he was not embarrassing us, My Daddy was working us half to death. If there was an easy way to do something and a hard way, he chose the latter. We used oil to heat our house but he installed a wood stove in the basement which we used instead. My Daddy and Larry would go into the woods, chop down trees with a power saw and deliver the wood to our house. Mark, Dwayne and I had to split the wood into pieces and pile it up against the house in June, though winter didn't hit Virginia until mid-December. Then we had to stack the wood a certain way, so that the triangular pieces fit together. We would be so pissed off that we stacked it the way we wanted. Don't you know the first thing that man did when came home was inspect that wood? He would point out the pieces that were not stacked properly and make us tear it down and stack it the way he said. This required another two full days of work. We thought he was crazy. To give you a sense of how serious My Daddy was about those chores, my junior year in high school I didn't get my share of the wood in. Instead, I went to basketball practice and blew it off. We played Goochland the following night and I had 30 points. After it started sleeting, a 45-minute bus ride lasted hours. When I finally got home I crashed. At 3 a.m., in the middle of REM sleep, My Daddy woke me up like we were in Vietnam. I was scared to death because I thought there was an emergency. Apparently there was – I had to get in my share of the wood. This fool had me outside splitting wood under the porch light in a foot of snow. I was out there for four hours while everybody else stood around laughing.

When I was in the fifth grade My Daddy thought I needed to learn about the stock market. He was working as an insurance salesman at the time and had to keep abreast of the economy and the market. Each day he would make me read something called *The Wall Street Journal*; he would simply give it to me and say, "Read it." I was convinced he lay awake at night thinking of new ways to torture me. I had to actually stop playing basketball and watch the 6 o'clock news to get the recap on the market. By 7 p.m. My Daddy would be home to quiz me. *The Journal* made me feel sort of dyslexic with all these words, charts and graphs leading to nowhere. I would regurgitate what I had heard on the news or read in the paper – "the *Dow Jones Industrial Average* dropped because of concerns over inflation," or "the transportation index fell because of increasing gas prices." But of course, this was not good enough for My Daddy. "Why?" he would ask. He would make me comb *The Journal* until I found a sufficient answer, which could take hours. Suzie would look on with a smirk on her face. To shut My Daddy's mouth up, I cross-referenced various news sources to create my own story, and referenced previous versions of *The Journal* to prove that prices were indeed going up, and how it was affecting the Dow. Heck, everybody knew that high prices were a bad thing. My Daddy would try to argue but I had my evidence, and that was all I needed. He would give up after I showed him the research I had done. I actually liked learning about the market. It was very competitive, there were winners and losers, and you could make a lot of money if you invested correctly. But to this day, I refuse to follow the market on a daily basis. I have known since fifth grade that the "so-called" experts use canned language to explain that on certain days there are more buyers than sellers, and vice versa.

And so it went. My Daddy spent most of his summers and weekends devising ways to torture me, and I devised ways to get out of it. He was pretty much a Jack of all trades. He could build houses, repair cars, and fix things around the house. I tried to hammer something once and missed the nail and hit my thumb.

I never picked up another hammer again. He taught me how to drive a car and was so darn overbearing that even Grandpa felt sorry for me. We had to learn how to change the oil, change a flat tire, etc. He tried to show me some other things but working on a car was not my forte. All I wanted to do was drive the thing and look cool. Some of my most painful childhood memories involve looking for a screwdriver or a wrench My Daddy needed when he was working on one of the cars. He would send me into the basement for a 5/8" wrench and I (i) could not find it, (ii) brought something other than what he had asked for or (iii) brought the entire toolbox. Either way I got yelled at. I would beg Dwayne to help me find said wrench or screwdriver, and he would retrieve it and run tell My Daddy what he had accomplished . . . what an apple polisher. In Farmville if you could not build a house or take a car apart, you were considered a geek. My Daddy would tell me all the time, "Boy, I hope you make a lot of money when you get grown because you're gonna have to pay 'The Man' every time you need something done." I would laugh it off. Once when I was 16 he had me help him work on my mother's car and instead of paying attention, I was dribbling my basketball. He paused, and I will never forget the look on his face – the look of defeat. He just said, "Go on up the road and play boy." I couldn't believe it! Victory was mine! After all those years, I had finally beaten him down.

At age 30 I bought a brownstone in Brooklyn that had incurred fire damage and needed a total rehabilitation. It was located in the Fort Greene section, a chic neighborhood with a lot of African Americans and near all of the trains. I thought it was a great time to move in before the rest of the city discovered it. I researched everything, calculated the costs and hired a contractor recommended to me. About a month into the project I met with the contractor and the architect to discuss potential cost overruns. During the walk-through, the architect pointed out 16 new wooden beams that needed to be replaced. Days later, I visited the site and saw that the contractor had inserted over 90 new beams. He said the additional cost would be around $32,000 – nothing close to what we had discussed. The man kept going on about how they needed to be replaced and how the homeowner across the street, a structural engineer, had concurred. The contractor was speaking to me like it was his project and he had the carte blanche to do whatever he wanted. I stopped the job and set up another meeting with him and the architect. At the second meeting, it was clear that this guy was a loose cannon and since I knew nothing about houses, he had taken the liberty to do whatever was in his best interest. The entire time I was thinking, "I sure wish My Daddy and Larry were here. My Daddy would have been here every day, overseeing what the contractor was doing and making sure I did not get taken." I fired the guy on the spot. He placed something called a "contractor's lien" on my house for some exorbitant amount, and the bank refused additional funding until it was removed. Three years, three contractors and over $150,000 in cost overruns later, I decided to get a handyman and complete the house myself. It was 85% completed and I needed to finish the rest in order to get the certificate of occupancy (C of O) from the City of New York. Meanwhile, the mortgage was still accumulating and with no C of O, I would either have to sell the building or file for bankruptcy.

I went to work during the day and met the handyman as soon as I got home. We worked every night from about 7 p.m. until 1 o'clock in the morning. I remember putting up some sheetrock and thinking after 30 some-odd years of running from that hammer, there it was staring me right back in the face. I held the nail in place between my thumb and my pointing finger and tried to hammer it as straight as I could, just like I had seen My Daddy do it. Yeah, I thought about My Daddy every night and his prognostications about having to pay "The Man" – now "The Man" was trying to bury me. Leading up to the final building inspection I got on my hands and knees and prayed for that C of O. I was literally out of money and out of options. When it was finally authorized, I gave a sigh of relief that my ordeal was over. It was then that I understand that he was not trying to make me a mechanic, or a contractor, but simply teaching me how to protect myself and to be self-sufficient.

Mercy Seat

The black church is one of the most important parts of the African-American existence in this country. We were actually affiliated with three churches – New Hope, Mercy Seat and Triumph. From my earliest recollection I was always in church. Mark and I sang at Mercy Seat on behalf of Ms. Cleveland, one of the upstanding members of the congregation, during certain evening programs. Ms. Cleveland would offer to pay us for it but Suzie turned it down because "it was our responsibility." We were no older than 4 and 5. People made such a big deal over our singing that we sort of enjoyed the attention. The church permeates almost every aspect of black culture. You learned how to dress in church. We always wore our Sunday best and took cues from the deacons and the minister who wore suits from the '50s and '60s; they didn't make bad suits in those days. You learned how to conduct yourself in church. Mark and I were required to sit up straight, remain quiet and pay attention to the sermon. However, Sharmane and Dwayne would cry and show off in the presence of Annie Mae, thinking she would save them. A hard-headed child was embarrassing to a parent and you were not going to make Suzie look bad in public. When they persisted, she would walk them outside and when they came back in, they were really calm. Mark and I never had to go outside. There was nothing out there for us.

We even debated in school over whose church was better. The arguments were mainly with the kids from the town of Farmville, who attended Race Street or First Baptist. Race Street was made up of working-class African Americans while First Baptist was more for the upper class. The Reverend Francis L. Griffin, the famous civil rights activist who helped fight for school integration in Prince Edward, was the minister at First Baptist. It was blasphemous to even speak his name in a manner that could be construed as negative, so when the First Baptist contingency spoke up, I shut up. Nonetheless, I was extremely proud of Mercy Seat. It stood apart from other churches, from the way it was built to the style of the place. It had the look and feel of a Methodist church. Most black churches were made of brick, but Mercy Seat was all wooden. It was not a holy-roller type of church either. If you fell out and got "happy" you were on your own. If you had a confession to make then you had better make it brief or the congregation would look at you with consternation. Furthermore, if the minister or the choir received an "amen" during the service then they were doing well. To outsiders the congregation may have appeared dead, but we were just orderly. The church could have been on fire and everyone would have lined up in single file, and marched out in an orderly fashion. The congregation was full of educators, businessmen and movers and shakers in Prince Edward County and that was just the way it was.

Attending Mercy Seat was a rite of passage. Uncle Jesse (Gramma's brother) picked us up every Sunday at 9:45 a.m. for 10 o'clock Sunday school. I was always glued to the television watching Paul Hornung and Vin Scully narrate Notre Dame's football games. I had to race out of the house at the last minute behind Mark and Thomas. Mercy Seat was full of experts who could apply lessons from the Bible to everyday life. Any difficult questions that came out of Sunday school could be taken up with Reverend Spragues just before church started at 11 a.m. "Doris Day" taught Sunday school for the kids. We went over the usual lessons of Adam and Eve, Cain and Abel, Noah's Ark, and Samson and Delilah. It was in Sunday school that people in the community knew I was pretty smart. In second grade I was probably on a sixth grade reading level already. I prided myself on understanding the meaning of words and being able to spell correctly. Of all the Sunday school lessons, the one that vexed me the most was the crucifixion of Jesus Christ. I loved to read about the miracles Jesus had performed. If he could perform miracles like healing the sick, helping blind men see and feeding 40 people with a fish and a loaf of bread, that was a good thing right? Then why was he so hated upon? I asked these questions of Doris Day repeatedly and would not let it go. I also asked Reginald Smith (deacon) and Grandma. No answer was satisfactory. How someone as good as Jesus could be crucified vexed me throughout my childhood.

Suzie had always envisioned that her kids would be a prominent part of Mercy Seat. Besides, Annie Mae expected it. In fourth grade Suzie asked me and Mark to join the junior choir. Annie Mae sang on the senior choir so it was only fitting that her grandchildren sing as well, but singing once a month and practicing beforehand seemed too confining and uncool. Besides, I could never picture Shaft (black movie hero) singing on a church choir. Suzie and I did this little dance for months where she broached the idea like it was optional, and I suddenly became tone deaf. Annie Mae tried to intervene, but to no avail. What made matters worse is that Thomas, Mark and two other kids our age, Vincent Crawley and Keith White, were already involved in the church. They looked real mature and got praise from other members of Mercy Seat. Those "do-gooders" were putting the pressure on me. Eventually Suzie gave me a choice to either sing or get a whippin', to which I replied, "Where's my robe?" There were the so-called "professional" singers on the choir who had to sing every solo, and then there were the rest of us. Thomas and I held up the rear. They would throw us a bone every once in a while and let us sing "Trouble in My Way" . . . all off-key. The best part was watching Annie Mae and Aunt Nannie (Gramma's sister) beaming with pride. To make a long story short, I sang throughout high school, never missing a Sunday. In retrospect, a church is just a building. It's the people inside who truly make it what it is.

Prince Edward County High

School was all anyone talked about. One of the compromises after the school was reopened was that it would no longer be called R.R. Moton. When my big day came to start school, it was a complete disaster. It rained heavily and while running to the school bus, I slipped and fell in a puddle of water and got mud all over my new outfit. Then I left my lunch in the bathroom and somebody stole it. Other than my first day, I took to school like a fish to water. I had heard stories of how Prince Edward was a free-for-all when it reopened, but the school I encountered in 1972 was pretty orderly and disciplined. For the black kids in the county, attending the public school was not up for debate. For the white kids, the school you attended had political implications. The majority of the Caucasian students attended Prince Edward Academy. Those who could not afford to attend it, attended Prince Edward; then there were white families who actually wanted to send their kids to the public school. And that is saying a lot because Prince Edward was all black. I actually thought blacks ran the world. Just about everybody I came into contact with at church, at school, and in the neighborhood was black. It wasn't until I was in sixth grade social studies class that I learned how Martin Luther King, Jr. died, and that African Americans were actually in the minority. I nearly lost my mind. That said, the few white kids in elementary school were pioneers in their own way. I remember the boys in my class, especially. Kenny Meade, Michael Roach, Wesley Hackney, "John W." and I were in the same class throughout elementary school. John and I became really good friends. He was a pretty smart guy and we would always do school projects together; we made a pretty good team. I thought of myself as the creative, sort of "ideas" person. Working with John, you knew the project was going to get done on time and you would get no less than B+, regardless of what you did. So I guess he was the "time management" and "quality control" guy. Little did we know that we were the "test cases" for integration in Prince Edward. Ironically, our true test came after leaving high school.

I attended Hampden-Sydney, where I was one of two African Americans in my freshman class, and John attended UVA. In 1985 UVA experienced some turmoil between the African-American students and the college as a whole. I came across a few articles of the tensions there but never really followed it closely. John visited me during one of his school breaks and explained how the UVA campus was pretty divided. The whites did not venture into the black section and vice versa. We laughed out loud at how for the first time in my life I was an actual minority, and for the first time in his life, the kid who had grown up in an all-black school system did not feel welcomed around African Americans. The last time I saw John was at my bachelor party in Washington, D.C. a decade later. When he showed up all of the other attendees thought he was in the wrong place. Little did they know he had attended the blackest high school in the country. Everybody was in a pretty festive mood and determined to send me out with a bang. I was never a drinker, but I was drinking that night.

We ended up getting kicked out of three nightclubs. At the first establishment, I was on the dance floor by myself for a complete hour performing every *Soul Train* dance ever created. The dance floor was packed, but there was nobody within 10 feet of me. When I went to the men's room, everybody waited for me to come out before they entered. And when I exited, the bouncer asked us nicely, "Ya'll ready to go?" and followed us to the door. At the last "establishment" I was so exhausted that I just sat in the back of the room; the room was spinning like one of those Spike Lee movies. As you entered the place, there was a clear sign that said "Don't Touch the Women or Tiny Will Have to Come From the Back." We were there for about all of 90 minutes when I noticed a member of our entourage was getting closer and closer to one of the women. I was unconcerned because in his lifetime, this guy had probably never even jaywalked before. But of course, he picked this night to get gully. He made what I would describe as "inappropriate contact" and like Carl Lewis I got to it. It looked like the 4x100 relay up in there – 15 guys sprinting for the exit. The drivers of vans we had rented pulled off without ensuring everyone had made it out. We ended up at an IHOP in Northern Virginia at 6 a.m. trying to piece together what had actually occurred the previous night. I just remember John and I staring at each other in disbelief. And for one more moment in time, we were in the fifth grade again . . . in his parents' living room with a blank poster board trying to figure out how we were going to meet a deadline on a project we had known about for weeks. Neither of us said a word. It was understood that we would never speak of this night to anyone.

Prince Edward had been a start-up operation just eight years before I started school. Admittedly, the public schools did not receive the full resources of the county since the kids of those who controlled the purse strings did not attend them. Yet, Prince Edward was a nurturing place. It not only taught reading, writing and arithmetic, but it also taught us what it meant to be black in America. During Black History Month they would describe a famous African American over the loud speaker and the first person who got to the principal's office with the answer received recognition. Weeks prior, we would research every black person known to man; we knew the stories of Crispus Attucks (first martyr of the Revolutionary War), Matthew Henson (first to reach the North Pole), Charles Drew (pioneered research for blood transfusions), Lewis Latimer (inventor), and George Washington Carver (agriculturist, inventor) by heart. And if you could not recite their contributions then your classmates assumed you were an idiot. Just before special school events we didn't sing the national anthem. We sang the black national anthem, "Lift Every Voice and Sing," written by James Weldon Johnson in 1900. If you missed a word or sang off-key, the teachers would stare at you disapprovingly. And in high school, we read works from all the famous black writers like Alex Haley, Alice Walker, Richard Wright, and James Baldwin. It was required reading. Since, I have encountered some African Americans who never received any schooling in black history until they got to college or beyond. They always seemed odd to me, like the spotted owl.

The majority of the teachers were black too and they pushed us beyond our limits. Mind you, we are talking about a time when teaching was one of the most respected professions; teachers were spoken of with extreme reverence. It was a small school and Prince Edward tracked each of us. The teachers knew your parents, siblings, friends, and neighbors. Some like Ms. Smith, Ms. Gibson, and Ms. Whitehead were very well-known because they had taught for so long. Others like Ms. Coles (now Mrs. Barksdale) and Mrs. Scott-Brown were just starting their careers. We were fortunate to have them so early in their careers when they still had the fire in the belly. They were young, hip, dressed like us and spoke our language. Ms. Coles was my favorite teacher in elementary school. She was one of the first teachers to identify that I could excel in the classroom. She recommended that I get skipped from the second grade into the third grade. However, Suzie vetoed the idea. My friend Darryl Johnson and I were later selected to be in the school's Gifted and Talented Program when we were in the fifth grade. It is funny how you can affect a child at an early age by putting the notion into his head that he is highly intelligent. Years later when I worked in corporate America these guys would try to convince me that I was not in their exact words, "as smart as I thought I was." I could hardly contain my laughter at something so ludicrous. Mrs. Scott-Brown, my sixth grade physical education teacher, told us so often that we could do anything and achieve anything in life that it became a known fact – sort of like "the sky is blue." She went beyond the physical education curriculum and made us look at the world in black and white and our place in it. She had us follow the 1979 NCAA tournament and track two players in particular – Magic Johnson and Larry Bird. She had us cut out magazine and newspaper articles and point out the differences in how the media portrayed the two players. Apparently, she knew then what we would all know decades later, that the Bird vs. Magic game would have everybody in a frenzy and split the nation down the middle – one black, one white. To this day, it is still the most watched NCAA basketball game in history. Assignments like those had us literally running each other over to get to her class.

Prince Edward was nurturing, but if you got out of line you quickly saw another side. The administration did not play. If you got into trouble you would have to go see Mr. Trumbull, the principal. He had this big ol' paddle; I saw it a few times in his office. The teachers would warn the so-called tough kids about "going to see Mr. Trumbull." When that didn't work, they would pimp into his office and come out with a noticeable limp. I got into trouble twice in elementary school. The first time was when Skippy accidentally cut a plug in my head and had to cut my entire Afro off. I wore a hat to school and the teacher told me to either remove it or go see the assistant principal (Mrs. Morton). I got up and walked to the principal's office. She took one look at my bald head and immediately started laughing, and tried to convince me that I looked just like Isaac Hayes. The second time was in fifth grade math class. The teacher, Ms. Carnett, had left the room and immediately all of the boys started acting up – throwing paper airplanes and switching seats. By the time she got back, everybody was back in place but the girl who sat in front of me dropped a dime

29

on me. Ms. Carnett called me up to her desk and the usual suspects – Johnson, Lee Taylor and Wesley Hackney – gave me a look like, "Don't do it Baker. Don't tell." She took out a stack of rulers held together by rubber bands and paddled my hand with it. Suddenly the acronym "ROY G. BIV" took on an entirely new meaning. My hand must have turned every color of the spectrum – red, orange, yellow, green, blue, indigo and violet. The tattletale started laughing and then she got paddled for teasing me. Now that was funny. It made my year.

Elementary school was competitive, but once we reached eight grade it was more strategic to work together. We were the low guys on the totem pole and the rest of the high school labeled us "sub-freshmen." Recognition for me came on the gridiron. All I ever wanted to do was wear the mighty purple and gold. There was one small problem, however. I was puny. I was 4'11" and weighed 84 pounds. There were only two kids in the entire school shorter than me – Charles Saunders and Willie Simmons. I would love to see them coming down the hallway so people could see how tall I was in comparison. There were no cuts in football. If you were brave enough to go out there then they gave you a uniform. Practice started in August, about four weeks before school opened. We practiced twice a day in that Virginia heat. Then you could not get water until Coach Armwood (JV Coach) told you to. The heat, no water, getting tackled, run over, stepped on and yelled at, cut the wheat from the chaff pretty quickly. By the time school started I was still standing and earned the nickname "Shortcake" and a reputation for having a big heart. On the night of our first game the coach gave me jersey number 99. The thing fit me like a dress. Secondly, I played defensive back and I was wearing a defensive lineman's number which only meant one thing – I was not going to play. While the rest of the guys charged out of the locker room hollering and screaming, Wesley Hackney and I charged out carrying the water cooler filled with some new drink called "Gatorade." It tasted good too. When the starters came off the field the benchwarmers got chewed out for drinking all the Gatorade. I spent my first year of high school football trying to keep bad stuff from happening. Do not get lit up in practice. Do not drink all the Gatorade. Huddle together with the other benchwarmers to avoid frostbite on the sidelines. And if by a miracle I did play and happened to get jacked up, do not let my mama come onto the field. I had given Suzie strict instructions that no matter what, she was to keep her behind in the stands; I never would have lived down the embarrassment of being called a "Mama's boy."

After my success in football (on my terms) I tried out for the basketball team. The student body thought it was some kind of joke because I was so short. But after football season, all of the coaches knew I was a serious athlete. I had never missed a game or practice, never complained, and I had something you could not measure – heart. During tryouts I played excellent defense, brought a lot of energy and displayed an uncanny ability to get my shot off over bigger people. In any other year I would have been a shoe-in to make the team. However, the school had just gotten rid of the eighth grade and freshman basketball teams, so JV was my only option. It had been unheard of for an eighth grader to play JV but Don White, Luther White, Rodney Vaughan and I set out to change that. The last day of tryouts Coach Scott said he would come by our classroom to inform us if we got cut. If you did not see him then you knew you made the team. The next morning, the kids swore that Coach Scott had asked me to come by his office to talk about something. I ignored them. By sixth period I was on pins and needles; Mrs. Faggins' English class seemed to last five hours. I stared at the door awaiting the axe, but still no Scott. When the bell rang to signal the end of school, about 40 students were lined up outside the gym door to see who had made the team. I came back 30 minutes later when no one else was around so I would not be embarrassed if my name was not listed. I made the team but had to run sprints for being late to practice.

Coach Scott kept 16 kids and I was the 15th name on the list. During practice, a few of the sophomores – Mitchell Smith, Ed Jennings and Michael Jordan (not that "Michael Jordan") established themselves as leaders of the team. Mike had a crazy handle and I copied all of his moves. We had a lot of fun and the team was full of characters. All the other kids had taken nicknames like "Doc" and "Ice" so I chose the only name left – "Silk." This was the moniker given Jamaal Wilkes of the L.A. Lakers. My classmates thought I was a clown. They knew I would not get much playing time so why the nickname? They could not stop laughing at me. I had Suzie go down to the local sporting goods store and monogram "Silk" on all my basketball gear. Sometimes the "S" would fall off and it would just say "ilk," but I still wore it. Suzie and My Daddy started becoming concerned about me, and hoped it was just some type of phase. The night before our first game I slept in my uniform. I refused to take the thing off. Mike, Mitchell and Ed showed off and we beat the living daylights out of some poor team. We were up by about 30 points late in the fourth quarter when Coach Scott called my name. I pretended like I did not hear him. Another player had to grab me and march me to the scorer's table. I checked into the game with my wrinkled uniform and the crowd gave me a standing ovation. Here I was the smallest guy in school trying to play with the big boys.

I spent most of my eighth grade season riding the pine and ingratiating myself with the veteran players. During games I would identify the prettiest girls in the stands, get their phone numbers and pass the information along to Mitch, Ed and Mike. I was acting as a middleman of sorts . . . I had to add value somehow. Though I did not play that much I, as well as Don, Lou and Rodney, showed lots of promise. It was a forgone conclusion that we would eventually lead Prince Edward back to the state tournament. By freshman year I had worked my way up to seventh man – the second guy off the bench. I carved out a niche for myself as a lockdown defender. Coach Finney, then the JV coach, would sic me on the opposing team's best guard and I would put the clamps on him. The kids called me Finney's "whipping boy" because he always rode me in practice for seemingly minor mistakes. Sophomore year I remained on JV. Still a lockdown defender, I had the green light to do whatever I wanted on offense. My set shot had morphed into a jumper and I could pull from anywhere on the court. I was pretty tricky with the basketball and could put guys on skates with a plethora of crossovers, stutter steps and hesitation moves. If a teammate wasn't paying attention, I would hit him in the head with a "no look" pass on purpose, and then laugh about it after the game. That was what Ron Orr saw when he approached me about playing pickup with the Longwood basketball team. Then when I referred to myself as "Silk" my classmates didn't think it was funny anymore – they started calling me cocky.

Academics

Prior to high school I had specifically heard how hard Marcella Rigby (algebra), Gerald Roach (general business), and Lydia Peale (world civilization, american civilization) were. I made a mental note to avoid these teachers. I had planned on an easy five years of high school and then killing myself in college. However, the road to college led through them, amongst others. Ms. Rigby was pretty much true to form. She was very serious, intimidating and no-nonsense. She took algebra seriously and expected her students to as well. If you didn't know high school was official before taking algebra, then you knew it afterward. She handed you the syllabus, your homework assignments and that was that. She moved along pretty quickly and could tell who was keeping up with the material by the quality of the questions you asked. Based on her experience, she probably even expected you to struggle at certain sections of the class. And when you least expected it, she hit you with a pop quiz to remove all doubt. Algebra was the first subject I struggled in and I spent many nights solving for "X." Of all the classes I had in high school, I probably worked hardest in hers. I did not like Ms. Rigby . . . I mean nobody did. But I respected her and I killed myself in her class. She had a reputation for being unwavering. Your grade was your grade and she did not care how it impacted your G.P.A., what college you were "destined" to attend, or who your mama and daddy were. I had heard through the grapevine that this did not sit well with certain parents. I never received an "A" in her class, but I learned algebra though. Ms. Rigby would later save my career several times over. On one job, after the managing director and senior vice president encountered some conundrum on a deal, they would "assign" a section of the project to me. After everyone had gone home, I would spend a few hours solving for "X" and have the answer waiting for them the next morning. After walking them through my thought process and shooting down their arguments, they would eventually give up. I would leave their offices thanking Ms. Rigby under my breath. A decade after having graduated from Prince Edward I heard she left the school. I was livid; not only was Ms. Rigby a good teacher, but she was preparing kids for the real world when solving for "X" could be the difference between keeping one's job or not.

Mr. Roach was the resident killjoy at the school. I had him for eighth grade homeroom and later for general business, typing and computer science. You had to be in class and in your seat when the homeroom bell rang or he would mark you as "late." He was always talking about how things were done in college or in the real world. "But this is high school," I thought. "We can cross those other bridges when we get there." And when you were about to do something you had no business doing, like loitering in the hallway without a hall pass or using foul language, the man multiplied. He was always there to catch you. It was like there were seven or eight Gerald Roachs. At one point he was the athletic director and then the assistant varsity basketball coach, so you always wanted to stay on his good side. And he was a walking, talking paradox. For all the grief he gave you, deep down you knew he was a necessary evil because he got things done. He was one of our eighth grade advisors and was diligent about helping us fund our senior trip to the Bahamas. He laid out a plan for us to raise money selling everything from candy to flower bulbs. He monitored each of our sales goals and kept the funds raised in the bank. By our senior year, we had funded the entire trip and had enough extra money to leave the school $4,000. We couldn't have done it without Mr. Roach's help. And legend has it that dude had paper as long as train smoke. My freshman year we took a trip to New York City as part of our world civilization class. Someone, I cannot quite remember who, lost the tickets to the New York Mets game. The entire class was standing outside Shea Stadium all amped up. But before a minor issue grew larger, Mr. Roach paid for the tickets (30 students and a few adults) with traveler's checks he had with him. We were standing around trying to do the quick math. How much did the tickets cost and if Mr. Roach had a few stacks on him as walking around money, how much could he have stashed away somewhere? The non-incident simply added to his legend. And he was always available to open the gym for me in the summertime when I wanted to work out. In fact, he was at the school most of the time. I would drive past the school years after I had graduated and there was Mr. Roach's car parked outside the school, making sure everything was running properly. The guy bled purple and gold.

Where Mr. Roach was a necessary evil, Mrs. Peale was the one teacher you did not want to disappoint. She ran the advanced english and history program. Her husband was a professor at Longwood College and she sort of had a professorial way about her as well. Her father-in-law was Dr. Norman Vincent Peale of *The Power of Positive Thinking* fame and she had the fortune, or misfortune, of teaching her three kids at the school. I was in the same grade with her daughter Lacy, who we teased unmercifully about "thinking positive thoughts" whenever something did not exactly go her way. I had every intention of avoiding world civilization freshman year. I had signed up for another class when Mrs. Peale accosted me in the hallway and told me she thought it would be a good idea to take her class. She also ran the Gifted and Talented Program so she remembered me, Johnson and John from way back in elementary school. Her "suggestions" were the same as another teacher's twisting your arm. I thought I was going to coast through high school but Mrs. Peale fixed that for me. My first assignment was a book report. I did mine on the autobiography of former Redskin running back, Larry Brown. But somehow Mrs. Peale was not very impressed. I had to choose books from her predetermined reading list from then on. My second assignment was a book report on Ralph Ellison's *Invisible Man*. This was going to be a lay-up. The gist was obvious; Ellison was talking about how blacks did not matter and were invisible to mainstream America. Secondly, I purposely picked a book I figured Mrs. Peale had not read before. I could make up whatever I wanted and she would be none the wiser. I dug into *Invisible Man* and soon realized it was thicker than I had assumed, and the phrasing was so advanced that I had to use a thesaurus to understand many of the words. On top of that, I could only follow half of what Ellison was trying to say. I found one scene so repugnant that I stopped reading. The protagonist is assigned by his school's headmaster to pick up one of the trustees visiting from out of town. Instead of taking the trustee on the "safe" route to the school, the boy takes him via a back route through the poor section of town. There they run across a black farmer who had committed a heinous act – apparently "in his sleep" – that resulted in both his wife and daughter becoming impregnated at the same time. His penchant for "sleepwalking" made him a celebrity amongst the white community in town and the scorn of blacks, to the farmer's consternation. The farmer tells the boy and the trustee how the local sheriff came to check on his crops (something he had never done before), and even had a journalist take down his story and "put his picture in a magazine and everything." I literally started screaming, "Doesn't this fool know they're making fun of him?" I was appalled, so I "winged" the book report as only I could. Mrs. Peale questioned me about key scenes I had excluded from my report, wondered aloud which book I had actually read and made me do it over. At that moment I realized that the woman had read every book on her "predetermined" list and knew them by heart.

And so it went. I spent several nights up until 1 a.m. - 2 a.m. with a book, a thesaurus and a flashlight (so not to wake up Dwayne and Mark). I went lindy hopping with Malcolm Little, tried to remake myself with Jay Gatsby, and screamed "run black boy run!" at Bigger Thomas. Mrs. Peale knew we would need a thesaurus to understand the material. That was mainly the point – to help increase our vocabulary and include it in our writing. Sometimes she would harp on certain themes like a pit bull chewing on a steak. For instance, in Arthur Miller's *The Crucible*, Abigail Williams accused Elizabeth Proctor of being a witch. Okay, Lady A (Abigail) was in love with Lady B's (Elizabeth) husband so she tried to have Lady B removed from the equation. What was the big deal? But Mrs. Peale would not let it go. She looked at the tension between the two women from multiple angles and went on for what I thought to be ad nauseam. I never got her obsession with Abigail and Elizabeth. But nothing frustrated me more than Bigger Thomas, the jarhead from Richard Wright's *Native Son*. Bigger is hired as a driver by a white family (the Daltons), partial to blacks, in 1930s Chicago. One night while driving the Daltons' daughter, Mary, home after she had gotten wasted, Bigger helps the girl upstairs. Instead of leaving her in the middle of the floor, this fool decides to help Mary to her room. While he is in the bedroom alone with Mary, her blind mother stands in the hallway listening in. Trying not to be discovered, Bigger places a pillow over Mary's mouth and accidentally smothers her. He later disposes of the body and flees with the police on his trail. The very next day, Ms. Justice, who taught the history section of the class, turned to the passage where the girl had gotten smothered. She called on a few students for their thoughts but got no response. Everybody just stared down at their desks. She called on me and of course, I had to say what all of the other black students were thinking. I frankly did not think Wright's Bigger character was realistic because no black person could have possibly been that dumb. Every black person I knew would have left her drunk behind on the floor and gone back to work. The man was hired as a driver only. Helping his employer's drunken daughter to her room was not a part of the job description. Then Ms. Justice wanted to know if I were in Bigger's position, would I have confessed to accidentally murdering the girl instead of fleeing. Frankly, I was insulted. I thought the woman was trying to call me an idiot on the sly. My response was, "That could never happen to me because I am not a fool. If there was a commotion in the West Wing, then I would have been in the East Wing with Sue Ellen and J.R. If there was a commotion in the East Wing, then I would have been in the West Wing with Pam and Bobby. I would have made it my business not to be where trouble was brewing." Interestingly enough, the class was split along racial lines. The white students thought Bigger should have turned himself in because Mary's death was an accident. The African-American students thought the situation was hopeless and Bigger was as good as dead. I opted for "run black boy run!" I developed a hatred for Richard Wright for making up that scenario that could never happen in real life. I especially hated him for putting me on the spot like that in class.

Over four years, Mrs. Peale and I had our battles. To her, writing had a specific structure. You had your opening statement, presented your facts, and concluded with what you wanted your reader to walk away with. Of course, I tried things my way and red mark after red mark, by my junior year I was a beaten man. I eventually took her three parameters and created within them. At one point I got so good I could flip them – start with the conclusion and pick and choose the facts to support my argument, or make the reader believe whatever I wanted, based on my mood at the time. But I mainly preferred to let the facts lead to wherever and let the chips fall. I think it was Galileo who once said, "You can't teach a man anything. You can only help him find it within himself." From that perspective, Mrs. Peale never really taught us anything, she simply gave us the framework to help us find our own voices.

Senior Year

The summer after my sophomore year I worked my behind off. I practically lived Up the House. I played basketball every day, rain or shine. I shot in the morning and took a break around noon. I came back out at 5:30 p.m. and played with whoever from the neighborhood showed up. The only way guys could stop me was to foul me. Then I would play two, sometimes three kids at once. By 8 p.m. everybody had cleared out, but I would keep shooting until it got dark. That was less efficient because I first had to shoot the ball, and then go find it. Eventually Grandma put up a street light so I wouldn't have to shoot in the dark anymore . . . bless her heart! I then shot until 1 a.m., sometimes 2 a.m. in the morning. People in the neighborhood thought I was crazy. They would drive to work in the morning while I was shooting and then return home in the afternoon while I was shooting. They would go out in the evening while I was shooting and around midnight or so, a car would slow down and then come to a complete stop. The driver would watch in amazement at me still shooting. People originally thought I was peculiar, but it soon became odd when I was not out there. Suzie would call Up the House at 9 p.m., then midnight to check on my whereabouts. Heck, I thought *she* was peculiar, for where else would a teenage boy be at midnight during summer vacation? By 1 a.m. she would tell me to come home but I would stay an extra hour anyway.

Our junior season was pretty much a wash. We were a young team and we took our lumps. However, we all knew that senior year was our year. Personally, I had to make it to the state tournament in order to get some exposure. That was where all of the college coaches could see you play. We started our senior year at 5-0 and generated some serious buzz, capped by a 44-point performance I had against Charles City. Those fools tried to play me straight up . . . no double or triple teams. I was like a human video game out there. But we got a quick dose of reality when we lost to Cumberland, the favorites to win the state title. That set off a three-game losing skid that we could not seem to shake. Toward the beginning of the season Suzie mentioned that Coach Don Thompson from H-SC had inquired about me. I pretty much ignored her. I thought it was some kind of joke. I mean the school was Division III, all white, all-male and get this – a mile from my house. To make matters worse, by then Suzie worked in the school's dining hall, so I would be under her watchful eye for another four years. I immediately began covert operation "Do not go to Hampden-Sydney," though deep down I knew it was the obvious choice. I met Coach Thompson at a few of my games. He seemed like a straight shooter and we hit it off pretty well. I also got recruited to play football at Randolph-Macon College, H-SC's archrival. By my senior year Shortcake had turned into a decent football player. I rode the pine until my junior year, but I stuck with it. On my recruiting trip I met with Macon's basketball coach also. However, he did not think I was good enough to play there, which I found pretty laughable. James Madison told me I could try to walk on, but that sounded a little too open-ended. Mr. Roach and I sent a few game tapes to Longwood but the coach wouldn't even return my phone calls. And here I thought I was doing them a favor. I always had mixed emotions about the place anyway. Jerome Kersey and those guys brought us a lot of fond memories. However, I was perturbed that Longwood never recruited any players from the area. They preferred players from larger areas like Richmond, Hampton Roads, or D.C. Years later I found out they were hesitant to recruit local kids due to added pressure from the townspeople. The coaches did not want thousands of locals hounding them with, "How come little Bobby's not playing?" Their logic made a lot more sense to me as an adult.

Midway through my senior year I had made up my mind to attend H-SC. If asked, I would tell any high school player to "go where they love you and not where they like you." On Suzie's suggestion I spoke to a few of the African-American students at the College – Maurice Jones, Willie Fobbs and Frank Carr. Suzie had talked about Maurice on occasion as some kid who had a 4.0 GPA and was really going places. I recognized him from having played varsity basketball at Central Lunenburg High – a school in our district. He talked about the academic environment and how a Hampden-Sydney degree could take you anywhere you wanted to go in life. As a handful of African Americans, I would later find Maurice to be a tough act to follow. Frank and Willie were like celebrities to us – "those two brothers from Highland Springs." Highland Springs was a football powerhouse in Richmond and Channel 6 always showed their highlights. They gave the black community in Hampden-Sydney extra incentive to watch the football games on Saturday afternoons. They talked to me about the workload, and about their plans after graduation. They treated me more as a little brother and told me I could visit anytime. I was accepted at H-SC, Macon and James Madison, but H-SC was my first and only choice. I knew it was an excellent school academically, and seeing all those BMWs and Mercedes-Benzs on campus did not hurt either. Who knew, with an H-SC degree maybe I could afford one someday. The news reverberated throughout the community. Reginald Smith and a few other church members worked at the College and were excited for me. That is practically all they and Reverend Spragues ever talked about. It was a source of pride that one of "us" would be attending. Suzie put the icing on the cake with "Annie Mae would be so proud of you too." Gramma had died of heart failure my sophomore year in high school; she probably would have baked the biggest cake in the world for the occasion. My classmates, however, gave me the serious "side eye." I noticed how people who normally rushed me in the hallway began to watch me from a distance. I figured they were trying to ascertain whether I was still in my right mind. Most of the African-American students attended historically black colleges, Longwood, or large popular state schools like Virginia Tech and Virginia Commonwealth. At the time they viewed H-SC like it was some type of punishment. Since, the College has become one of the more popular schools for Prince Edward grads. As far as my senior basketball season, we righted the ship, but lost to Fluvanna in the second round of the playoffs. Don, Rodney, Lou and I never spoke of it, but we felt that we had let the school down in not winning the state title like everyone had predicted back in eighth grade. Nonetheless, I looked forward to attending H-SC, determined to earn small college All-America status by my junior year. I thought I was that good.

Year From Hell

Suzie, Dwayne, Sharmane, and Mark helped me pack everything I owned for the mile-long trip to college. Suzie attended the meetings where they talked about the expectations of the students, the needs of the parents and their communication with the faculty and administration. There was no hiding at H-SC. There were about 900 students with a student to teacher ratio of 10 to 1. All of the professors had their doctorate degrees, and if you had a problem you could always meet with the professor after class. If there was an emergency you could reach the professor at home. The professors took attendance each day and if you missed class, he or she took it as a personal affront. If you missed three classes during a semester they sent a pink slip home to your parents. The faculty, dean, etc. made sure your parents knew exactly how their money was being spent. After a few hours my family left and though I lived merely a mile up the road, college felt like the furthest I had ever been away from home. The students later gathered at Johns auditorium where they gave us a pep talk about what a fine college choice we had made and the expectations of a "Hampden-Sydney Gentleman." A Hampden-Sydney Gentleman was a man of honor and everyone took a pledge not to "lie, cheat or steal, or tolerate anyone who does." The College was dead serious about that Honor Code. You could get suspended simply for writing a bad check. The majority of the Honor Code violations was a result of procrastination. If you waited until the last minute on an assignment, you were prone to take shortcuts. I knew a guy who procrastinated on a research paper. He went into his fraternity's files to find a paper written in that same professor's class. First he merely got an idea for a subject to write about. He then borrowed a paragraph or two, and that paragraph turned into three or four paragraphs. He got an "A" on the assignment and afterward the professor inquired about his sources. The professor had remembered the original paper and the student who had written it from over a decade earlier. Naturally, he suspected the student of plagiarism. After doing some digging, the professor discovered that one of the books the student had cited as a source was not even located in the state of Virginia; the book's nearest location was in the library at the University of North Carolina. The professor immediately brought him up on Honor Code charges. The incident happened at the very end of our junior year and the Honor Court was not scheduled to meet until the first semester of the following year. The student knew he was a goner so he transferred to another school over the summer.

Another quality of a Hampden-Sydney Man was the ability to communicate orally and in written form – half your grade was based on class participation. And with an average class size of around 15 students, there was no place to hide. I once had a rhetoric class with Dr. Brinkley, the College's first Rhodes Scholar, with as few as six students. Once it snowed so hard that the school had to suspend classes for the first time in over 20 years; heck, Brinkley called all six of us in our dorm rooms and told us we were still having class. You had to come prepared to class every day because Brinkley was going to call on you at least five or six times. Otherwise, you had to sit there and look foolish for the entire period. And if you did speak without having a command over the material, the other students made you look foolish. The professors had a way of pitting students against one another and making them take the opposite side of an argument. The art was being able to argue without being argumentative. When the discussion did not involve a clear-cut answer, you could possibly sway your classmates with your delivery or the confidence in your voice. The classroom was like a cauldron that forced your command for the material, or lack thereof, to bubble to the top. This went on every day for four years. Spanish (Wilson), biology (Crawford), history (Heinemann), psychology (DeWolfe) in addition to my economics major and the required rhetoric courses helped me meet the "well-roundedness" test of a Hampden-Sydney Man. The College took communications skills so seriously that you had to pass a writing exam just to graduate. You took the exam at the end of your freshman year and they graded you on the structure of your essay, the quality of your argument, and whether or not it was grammatically correct. The process sounded like the same one that Mrs. Peale had browbeat me with in high school. You either passed the exam in three attempts or you were asked to leave the school.

When I wasn't grinding in the classroom, I was grinding on the basketball court. I played pick-up basketball with the team on an informal basis each day. It was war every day, and I couldn't dominate guys like I had in high school. I played good defense and played hard but I couldn't buy a jump shot to save my life. I would actually go to the gym early and stare at the basket to make sure it was the same height as the ones we used in high school. Consisting mostly of juniors and seniors, the team was predicted to win the Old Dominion Athletic Conference (ODAC). I figured the players had heard some exciting things about me, but I could tell by their facial expressions they thought I was pretty underwhelming. The "Silk 32" license plates (you could not make this up) on my 1974 Datsun did not help my cause either. The running joke was that people had seen another car driving around town with the license plates "Silk 23," and were wondering who the real Silk was. I actually knew the guy and though how he was portraying himself may not have been illegal, it was definitely unethical. I figured it had to have been some sort of copyright infringement. My adjustment to college, and the fact that the college game was more physical, added to my woes. There was a sophomore point guard named Charlie who was built like a fire hydrant. We were on an unavoidable collision course and everybody sat back and enjoyed the show. I was a little quicker than he was but whenever I tried to drive to the basket, he had a way of tying me up. It frustrated me to no end, resulting in a few shoving matches. I thought he was fouling me; however, this type of extra-physical play was allowed in college. Years later I started a youth basketball team. To teach the kids defensive techniques, I constructed the "Charlie Pain" drill, which I got a taste of my freshman year.

Shoving matches, smack talking, and guys having to be separated were common occurrences amongst the team; it became pretty clear to me that these guys didn't like each other very much. The animosity revolved around an off-season workout program. Apparently Thompson, whom the veterans affectionately referred to as "DT", had given assurances that only those who completed the workout program would play. There were cliques within the squad and cliques within the cliques. I couldn't keep track of who were friends with whom so I stayed neutral. I was playing so poorly (in my own mind) that I grew paranoid about getting cut from the team. Whenever I saw Coach Thompson, he always had this Cheshire cat grin on his face like he had the winning Powerball ticket. I ascertained that he also knew what I had kept secret – that I was a Division I caliber player on the Division III level. Not one to leave anything to chance, I would try to engage him to see what the other guys were saying, and if I was still going to make the team. During our first formal inter-squad scrimmage, it was clear why we were picked to win the ODAC. We had size, good guard play and were athletic at the forward positions. One guy scored 43 points. He was raining jumpers from at least six feet beyond what is now the 3-point line. And when you tried to guard him out in space, he simply drove around you. After that display, all the grumbling and jockeying for position ended. We won our first game of the season against a team I had never heard of. My whole family was there and a bunch of people from the neighborhood. I came off the bench and scored two points. I played good defense and got the ball into the hands of our playmakers. It was not a great debut but I didn't exactly embarrass myself either. We lost our next game by 10 points to a team we should have blown out. We literally missed about 17 lay-ups. What struck me as odd was that none of the players felt any remorse; everything was somebody else's fault. And when they had exhausted that excuse it was, "The coach can't coach." After two more losses we were set to play Christopher Newport at their place.

When Thompson went over the game plan, he kept mentioning Newport's All-American candidate, Buck Moore. Apparently the guy was athletic, unstoppable in the midrange and a great rebounder at 6'4". I was barely even paying attention. To stop Christopher Newport, we had to stop Buck Moore. The entire time I was thinking, "Wait 'til Buck Moore sees me . . . I'll show him an All-American." During the game I did not see anyone who I thought was "all that." About seven minutes in, they passed the ball to the small forward on my side of the floor. From about 17 feet away, he rose to shoot and I simultaneously jumped to block his shot. I landed and looked up – the guy was still suspended in air. All I saw was the bottom of the dude's Converse. He kissed the shot off the glass very softly and the crowd went wild. I was running down the floor shaking my head like, "That must be Buck Moore right there." The guy scored about 30 points and made it look easy. It was a seesaw game but we ended up losing by two points. On the ride home one of the guys stood up and yelled, "Look ya'll. Ralph got Buck Moore's autograph!" He held up a Christopher Newport basketball program promoting Buck's candidacy for All-American; it included a picture of Moore and a signed autograph. They rode me the entire way home. I just sat in the back with my head down. Playing Division III was a little harder than I had expected. A few years later, Michael Jordan, my old high school teammate, had landed at Christopher Newport. We beat them my senior year when they had Lamont Strothers, a high flier who later had a brief stint with the

Portland Trailblazers. After the game, Jordan told me that their coach had been singing my praises for weeks, saying that, "in order to beat Hampden-Sydney they had to stop Ralph Baker." I cracked up at the irony of it all.

The low point of the season came after our loss to Randolph-Macon. Though Macon was D-II, they were still our archrivals and we could not lose. We were despondent; it seemed like everybody was looking for the next guy to make a play. I personally did not do much. I could get to the basket seemingly at will but was unable to finish. We lost 48-40 in an uninspiring performance. That ODAC prediction was an albatross around our necks. The Macon football players whom I had met a year earlier were in the front row, in hysterics. My uncles had come down from D.C. to surprise me, but I surprised them with a mere six points. Lee Taylor, who was attending Virginia Union at the time, came by for support. He and my family thought something was physically wrong with me because I didn't look like the same person from high school. The only explanation I could muster was that I was in a slump, which would eventually pass. It had to. The players were livid at our performance; furthermore, our disappointing 1-6 start was all "DT's fault" and "something needed to be done about it." We lost to Macon on December 9th and by December 18th when we were scheduled to face Bridgewater College, Coach Thompson would be fired.

Following the Macon game, Thompson and one of the team captains got into a verbal altercation during practice. Friday of that week Thompson called a team meeting. The mood in the locker room was "solemn." Thompson informed us that the two captains had been kicked off the team; they had gone to President Bunting to seek his dismissal and he was not going to tolerate such insubordination. That set off a chain of events that made my head spin. I honestly thought the coach would reinstate the captains after a couple of weeks. Two of the players exclaimed, "If the captains are gone then we're out too." The veterans called a "players only" meeting on Sunday to discuss matters involving the team. A few players began stating their grievances with DT, most of which had occurred the previous year. Someone pulled out a petition that would be presented to President Bunting to have Coach Thompson fired. It already had about six signatures on it. The moderator of the meeting passed it around and guys started signing it for reasons that ranged from lack of playing time, to peer pressure, to the belief that it was for the "good of the program." When the petition came to me I passed on it. I was one of three freshmen on the team and nobody expected us to take a position anyway. It was after this meeting that I realized the two captains had not acted alone – they had the backing of several others. Just as Thompson had to dismiss the co-captains for insubordination, the veteran players had to quit because they too were party to the coup on Thompson. It had all the makings of a Shakespearean drama. About seven original players were at practice later on that night. I was shaking my head because I had seen a couple of them sign the petition to have Thompson fired; and here they were playing "both sides of the fence." I made a mental note never to turn my back to those guys. I figured we would get blown out the rest of the season but I would probably average at least 40 points per game. Coach

41

Thompson had spread the word around campus that we were looking for players and three football players showed up to join the team. The football players were good friends with some of the "petitioners" so they had a big falling out, earning the nickname "scabs." However, it was a moot point because in a matter of days, Thompson was dismissed and the assistant coach, Joe Lammay, was named the interim coach. The petitioners returned and the two leading scorers from the previous year quit, out of loyalty to Thompson. The team decided that there would be no talking to the press. The captains sat me and the other two freshmen down separately and made sure it was crystal clear – no talking to the press under any circumstances – to which we all agreed. The very next morning the phone rang in Cushing Hall around 8 a.m. I crawled out of bed, half sleep, to answer it. It was a woman, yet not the one I was hoping for.

> Claudia Perry: "Hi Ralph. This is Claudia Perry from the *Richmond-Times Dispatch.*"

> Me: "I'm sorry Ms. Perry but I'm not allowed to speak to the press. The team captains gave us specific instructions."

> Claudia Perry: "I understand that Don Thompson was fired after the team signed a petition Sunday night."

> Me: "Sorry Ma'am, the team captains don't want us speaking to the press. I gotta go."

> Claudia Perry: "Ralph, I already know what happened. I've spoken to Coach Thompson and a few of the players. I'm just trying to confirm some facts."

> Me: "I'm sorry Ma'am, I've got to go!"

Before I could hang up, she just started talking. She was speaking in so much detail – dates, times, people, and places – about what had taken place that I thought she had actually been present during the goings on. She told me things about the team that even I was not privy to. It was clear that she had already spoken to a lot of players, and maybe even Thompson himself. I surmised that there would not be any harm in confirming things she already knew. All I said was "Yes Ma'am" or "No Ma'am" or "I'm not sure." She thanked me for my time and hung up. The next morning I went to Kirby Fieldhouse to shoot around before the Bridgewater game. As soon as I entered the locker room the upper classmen blasted me with, "Ralph didn't we tell you not to talk to the press? What in the world were you talking to Claudia Perry for?" I did not have a clue what they were talking about. "Yes," "No" and "I'm not sure" did not qualify as a conversation. They then showed me the morning newspaper:

> Hampden-Sydney College basketball coach Don Thompson was relieved of his post yesterday, effective immediately . . . Thompson told the *Times-Dispatch* last night that eight of his players had signed a petition that was presented to President

Josiah Bunting III Sunday . . . Hampden-Sydney was the preseason favorite to win the Old Dominion Athletic Conference championship. The team's record is 0-1 in conference play, 1-6 overall . . . The petitioners did not attend Sunday's basketball practice, freshman guard Ralph Baker told a *Times-Dispatch* reporter before the players voted not to speak to the press. Baker said he was one of five players who did not sign the petition . . . Three Hampden-Sydney football players volunteered to help the team if the petitioners did not return, Baker said. Baker said one of the team captains told him yesterday that Thompson was no longer the coach. Baker also said the petitioners have rejoined the team.[1]

I was speechless. I hadn't told Claudia Perry any of those things. Somebody else was the leak and she used my name to give her story credibility. In hindsight, "confirming facts" and then making the "confirmer" the source for the story is an age-old trick used by reporters. The entire team was visibly upset and turned cold toward me. I tried to plead my case but nobody wanted to hear it. I had betrayed the team and now I could no longer be trusted. The article simply confirmed what everybody had suspected anyway – I was partial to Thompson. I was Thompson's boy; like most freshmen, I could do no wrong in the coach's eyes. He played me a lot so I had a lot to lose by his dismissal. But the odd part was that even during my recruitment process, Thompson and I rarely spoke. He recruited Suzie and Reginald Smith and they recruited me – they were hell-bent on me attending H-SC. Even when the College hired a permanent coach there were undercurrents that I was still salty over Thompson's dismissal and would be hesitant to accept the new reality. But I also had nothing to gain by telling the newspaper details of closed-door meetings involving the team, and then having my name used as the source. Nor did I have a history of double-dealing. Decades later it would become clear to me that whoever leaked the story did not want his name mentioned publicly – someone who privately pushed to have Thompson fired, yet publicly wanted to give the appearance of having not been involved. It had to have been someone who enjoyed the confidence of both Thompson and the petitioners . . . someone privy to the inner workings of both camps – details he relayed to Perry. He then gave Perry my name and phone number and hid behind my skirt. It was a pure act of cowardice. The kind of cowardice that led to our 1-6 start and got Thompson fired in the first place.

We defeated a very young Bridgewater team that night but the news of the player revolt reverberated around the country. The *Washington Post* and *USA Today*, amongst others, bombarded the College with calls in order to get this incredible story straight. The basketball program had taken center stage at a school devoted to academic pursuits and to add insult to injury, the publicity was unflattering at that. Needless to say, the faculty was beside itself. Just two days before the article about Thompson's firing, the *Times-Dispatch* had run a story with the caption "H-SC Student Gets Rhodes Scholarship." Below the caption was a picture of senior Maurice Jones flashing a smile that could have lit up Tiger Stadium. That was the type of publicity the faculty and administration coveted; yet the spotlight was being hogged by a bunch of underachieving ballplayers. There were all kinds of rumors floating around. We were concerned the school would shut the basketball program down or turn it into an intramural sport. In addition to the two players who quit, a few others checked out emotionally. I was afraid we would be an embarrassment to the school if we kept playing. But the most scorn was held by the other ODAC coaches. They hated us with a passion. Not only were they friends with Thompson but they privately worried that if a "firing by petition" could happen at H-SC, it could happen at their institutions also. And they went through pains to prevent it. We heard stories of coaches having closed-door meetings to reemphasize (i) that what happened to Thompson would never happen to them and (ii) to make an example of us. They thought we were a bunch of spoiled brats who needed to be taught a lesson. A good man had lost his job and now somebody had to pay – the rest of the teams in the conference showed no mercy. During a 23-point drubbing at Emory & Henry, the fans held up a giant-sized petition with each of our names signed to it. After the game, one of their players walked into our locker room and asked, "Hey, ya'll got another one of those petitions?" His coach, a former U.S. marine, dragged him out of there cursing and screaming.

From then on we knew we would not be conference champs and simply played with nothing to lose. We went 8-10 the rest of the way with some special moments here and there. Our biggest win was over Roanoke College, a perennial conference powerhouse, by two points at home. I finished as the team's leading scorer, though the points were evenly distributed. I had a 27-point performance against Mary Washington College, where I went straight "Silk-mode," giving the fans a taste of what was to come. After the season the next order of business was the search for a new coach. Weeks later I heard the search committee was enamored with Tony Shaver, a high school coach from Northern Virginia who had played at North Carolina under Dean Smith. When the process had gotten further along, a few of the other players and I had lunch with Shaver. I was struck by how young and "nice" the guy seemed. He could not have been much older than I was. I wondered if he had what it took to handle this crew here. I also was a pitcher for the H-SC baseball team after basketball season finished up. We were playing an away game at Lynchburg College when our junior slugger, Guy Vilardi, finally broke out of a slump. Guy would literally hit tape-measure shots in practice. By the seventh inning Vilardi had already hit a home run and two doubles. Out of nowhere the school chaplain entered the dugout where I and three other pitchers were. I told him how sad it was that he had just missed the fireworks, compliments of Vilardi. He walked past the other three players without speaking and approached me directly, which I found rather odd. My first thought was "my mother." He informed me that My Daddy had been killed in an accident at our home and I had to come back immediately. The entire situation felt sort of surreal. By my junior year in high school, the man who was never around was suddenly always around . . . and now he was gone forever. During the funeral the church was packed with almost as many Caucasians (mostly from the College) as African Americans. After the service was over and people started to head home, I noticed Tony Shaver standing in the distance. In the decades since, I don't quite remember the wins or losses or how he used to run us like dogs after practice, but I remember vividly how he drove three hours to support someone he had met only once before. He had nothing to gain from it. I was not even sure if I was going to return to school the following year. I didn't want to be a burden to my mother so I was prepared to quit school and get a full-time job, at least for a year. She was dead set against it though. President Bunting told Suzie that the College would help in any way to ensure I was able to stay in school. I always felt indebted to Hampden-Sydney after that; deep down I knew that if I had not returned for my sophomore year I never would have finished college.

People Are Rational

By the end of my sophomore year I was required to choose a major. I had always assumed a light bulb would go off and lead me in the right decision. With the deadline fast approaching, I chose economics because it sounded sophisticated and like something one needed to know in order to be successful in business. My first course, Economics 101, was with Dr. Hendley who headed the Economics department. The first day of class everybody sat quietly. Hendley walked up to the board and wrote, "People are Rational." Then he turned around and looked at us like he had just solved the cure for the common cold. The class looked at Hendley and then looked around at one another with a "So what?" expression. Hendley enlightened us that everything he would teach us was based on (i) what a "rational individual" would do and (ii) a rational individual would always maximize his self-interest. Furthermore, if you did not believe that people were rational then you should leave the room immediately because you would not understand the other economic principals he was about to teach. A year after I graduated college, the famous Rodney King incident occurred. After a high-speed chase, King was pulled over and beaten down by several members of the LAPD. The incident was captured on video; the footage was shocking to watch and television stations around the country replayed it for weeks. California has always had an image as being the "Sunshine State," offering limitless possibilities. However, I had also heard rumblings of police brutality and racial profiling. Former Oakland Raiders running back, Marcus Allen, had gotten stopped so often while driving his Lamborghini that he had to get a special license plate. That way, the LAPD would recognize him in advance. African Americans in Southern California had complained publicly for years about police brutality, but their complaints had fallen on deaf ears. A year after the King incident, a jury found the members of the LAPD "not guilty" of police brutality. The controversial verdict set off a week of rioting in Southern California that resulted in 50 deaths and property damage of around $1 billion. The media and the general public thought the rioters had lost their minds. Their sentiment was, "Why would they destroy buildings in their own neighborhood? They're cutting their own throats." I believed the rioters, many of them African Americans from low-income areas, not only to be rational, but if the television pundits were in their shoes they would have rioted also. The riots prompted world leaders to wonder aloud, "If democracy cannot work in the U.S. then how can it work our countries?" The images also caught the attention of President George H. W. Bush, who had a Eureka moment! – "Hey I think the country has a problem in Southern California." President H. W. Bush engaged local leaders, found out what their issues were and went about addressing them. The dialogue resulted in

45

a change in the policing of black neighborhoods in Southern California. The government created what became known as "enterprise zones" where it encouraged investment in inner-city communities throughout the country; it also offered tax breaks as additional incentives. The investments provided quality grocery stores, and drugstores in areas where businesses had been reluctant to build. In retrospect, the Rodney King riots brought the world to a standstill and was a catalyst for positive change . . . sounded "rational" to me. Of all the economic concepts drilled into us, I applied the following concepts the most:

Law of Supply and Demand

The "Law of Supply and Demand" explains that given a certain level of supply and demand for a product, say widgets, the price of widgets will be set at the point where the "supply curve" and "demand curve" intersect. Once supply and demand are at equilibrium, an increase in supply would cause a decrease in price to generate the same level of demand and vice versa. Whenever Hendley called on me I had a penchant for making a reference to basketball. The other students found this rather amusing and over time, they became disappointed when I didn't make a tie-in between basketball and economics. Let's see if I still have it. The following supply/demand curves illustrate the supply of NBA teams, quantity of players, and the league's price of entry as measured in "tools," or the level of skill demanded by NBA teams. The five tools are as follows: (i) shooting ability, (ii) "basketball IQ," (iii) defense, (iv) ball handling or rebounding, depending on the position, and (v) professionalism.

With 23 NBA teams, the quantity of players is 276 (12 "core" players per team). Demand for jobs, as defined by individuals interested in playing and having demonstrated a certain level of proficiency, is 431. I derived at this figure as follows: (i) 276 "core" NBA players, (ii) the previous four McDonald's All-American classes (100), (iii) 25 players from the CBA (NBA farm system), and (iv) 30 or so European players. The point where the supply curve and demand curve intersect – the "price" – is 4.5 tools. Another way to interpret the chart is that in 1987, players were required to have between four and five of the tools previously discussed in order to play in the NBA. The following supply/demand curve illustrates the NBA at equilibrium with 276 core players and price of entry at 4.5 tools.

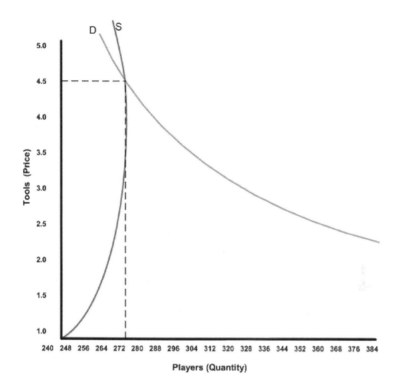

In 2010 the NBA expanded to 30 teams and approximately 360 core players. Given the increased supply of jobs, the owners lowered the price to around "2.5 tools" in order to fill the additional roster spots. The second supply/demand curve illustrates this. The line of demarcation was drawn in 1995 when the NBA expanded to Toronto and Vancouver, creating 27 teams, 324 core jobs and resulting in a "run on the bank" (NCAA). Not coincidentally, Kevin Garnett jumped from high school straight to the NBA, the first player to do so in over 20 years. The next year, Kobe Bryant and Jermaine O'Neal went to the league from high school; Allen Iverson, Shareef Abdur-Rahim and Antoine Walker entered the league after their sophomore years of college; Stephon Marbury entered after his freshman year. Since the 1980s, only Isaiah Thomas and Magic Johnson had entered the league after only two years of college but they (i) were both consensus 1st Team All-Americans and (ii) had led their respective colleges to the NCAA title. None of the aforementioned players had earned Magic's or Isaiah's level of success prior to entering the NBA draft. Basketball experts and pundits cited the higher skill level and athleticism for the increase in underclassmen entering the league. But the "economist" in me saw the phenomenon for what it was – an increase in the supply of jobs.

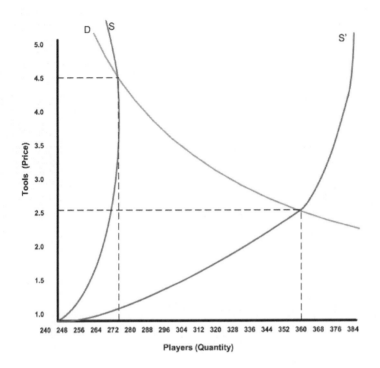

The NBA's lower price of entry is also reflected in the average points scored per season. For the 11 years from 1995 to 2006 (I picked these dates because the data was readily available) the mean and median scores for an NBA game were 96.1 and 96.3, respectively. For the previous 11 years the mean and median were 107.1 and 107.5, respectively. In 1998, the average score of an NBA game was as low as 91.6. The last time the league average was that low was in the 1953-54 season at 79.3 points/game, reflecting that the NBA post-1995 was "The Gang Who Couldn't Shoot Straight." The "Kool-Aid Drinkers" credited lower scores to the fact that players in the new era were quicker, could jump higher and were more athletic, which led to better defensive play. However, it became apparent that the NBA had become "watered down" when Team USA finished in sixth place in the 2002 FIBA World Championship, where they lost to the likes of Argentina, Yugoslavia and Spain. These new-era players followed up the FIBA loss with a bronze medal in the 2004 Olympics, suffering losses to Puerto Rico, Lithuania and Argentina. The so-called experts blamed the individual players and AAU basketball for their lack of skill. The economist in me again pointed to the fact that many of these players were not four- and five-tool guys in the tradition of the NBA. By definition, pre-expansion, about 85 of these so-called professionals would have still been in college, the CBA, playing in Europe or somewhere bagging groceries.

Other clues that reiterate my point are (i) Allen Iverson's famous exclamations about not wanting to attend practice (ii) Rafer Alston's questioning "whether the league was for him" after being fined by his coach for unprofessional conduct,

(iii) Gilbert Arenas and Javaris Crittenton playing "Cowboys and Indians" in the Washington Wizards' locker room, (iv) critics exclaiming that the 2011 NBA draft with Kyrie Irving and Derrick Williams going number one and number two was the worst draft in NBA history, and (v) an October 2011 interview where Lakers Pau Gasol told a French publication, *L'Equipe*, that he preferred the European game to the NBA because basketball is a team sport and more beautiful to watch when the players pass the ball.[2] The NBA has since tried to synthetically create a quality product and the parity of 1987 through (i) rules on age limits and (ii) clauses in the new collective bargaining agreement to prevent teams from stockpiling four- and five-tool players like the 2011 Miami Heat. But as economists, we know that such interventions create market inefficiencies. I have ideas on other ways the NBA could improve itself, but you will have to read my next book for that.

Old School Baller Explains Economics to SLAM Magazine Readers

The "Law of Supply and Demand" was applied to the NBA on *SLAM* Magazine's online website in April 2009 when "Old School Baller" argued that the NBA's expansion had killed the league. He was later attacked by the likes of AllenP, The Baconator, Ciolkstar, Jukai, Z, and STATUS. However, Old School held his own. Below are excerpts of his argument.

> As quiet as it's kept, smart kids and less intelligent kids who can ball should thank the NBA for expanding. Since Jordan, Bird, Magic were in their prime, the NBA has expanded by at least 5 more teams which equates to about 75 more jobs. Without the expansion at least 75 kids would either be (i) in college, (ii) in Europe, (iii) in the CBA . . . er I forgot the CBA disbanded because the NBA took all their players after the expansion, or (iv) bagging groceries. I dissect the NBA into (i) pre-expansion and (ii) post-expansion . . . That said, many of the guys who left early and flamed out could have made it had they gone to college and developed their skills and gained maturity. In the pre-expansion world, nobody left early until they had already dominated the collegiate ranks. Give me the flame out rate on guys like Isaiah, Doc Rivers, Magic, Worthy, Jordan, Mark Aguirre, Chris Webber, etc. These guys were so dominant that in most cases, their college coaches advised them to go early, and in the case of Aguirre, he had to go early just to give his teammates a chance to develop. Flame out rate on these guys – 0%. The post-expansion league is "watered down" with apprentices trying to learn the game. It's almost criminal to compare the accomplishments of Isaiah, Jordan, etc. to current players building their reps against high school kids, 6'8" centers, apprentices, European players, and 38-40 year [old] point guards 5 years past their prime.
>
> It still took KG, Kobe, and Dwight a few years to develop their basketball IQ. Even Amare admitted that his bball IQ would have been higher had he gone to college . . . seeing the catch 22 of going early . . . You think the NBA is requiring kids to spend a year in college in order to be obstructionists? How are diamonds made? Through centuries of heat, light, pressure, heat, light, pressure, etc. If you skip a step, the best you can ever be is a cubic zirconia. College is a ball player's version of "heat, light, pressure." The NBA doesn't want to hand out guaranteed contracts to cubic zirconias. And if kids keep trying to "game" the system, the

league will respond-in-kind again to get the results they want . . . I speak more as a fan who does not want to watch guys who either physically or mentally cannot play at the pro level, and then calling it pro basketball. Nor, do I want to pay someone who has never finished law school to represent me in a court of law. If you look at my earlier posts, the expansion of the NBA, not improved skill levels, created demand for HS and college underclassmen. It's naive to think [GMs] will keep investing guaranteed money in HS players when so many never earn the money. The definition of a pro player in my silly mind is a five-tool guy (handle, shot, defense, rebounding/passing depending on the position, and character/maturity). The NBA has lost die-hard fans like me who no longer want to pay $50+ to see two- and three-tool guys. I'd rather pay $10 to see them play in college. Otherwise, to draw fans the NBA will have to resort to gimmicks like handing out free toasters or forcing players to wear suits to games.[3]

Do NBA's David Stern and Ben Osborne Read SLAM Magazine?

In October 2007 NBA commissioner David Stern was talking about expanding even further. Stern was in Macau, China at an exhibition game where he tested the waters for expansion into China and other Asian markets. "'What we would like to contemplate in cooperation of our friends in the CBA [China Basketball Association] and the Sports Ministry is the possibility of an NBA-CBA venture that brings the NBA to China,' Stern said. 'Sort of an NBA China.' Meanwhile, this isn't the only Asian country Stern has his eye on. He also left open the possibility of going to the Philippines, which, under the radar, has become a very promising market."[4] As late as February 2008 Stern was considering five new NBA franchises in Europe over the following decade. Then seemingly overnight, he did an about face. During heated negotiations with the NBA's labor union in 2011, Stern decided that the NBA had too many teams and needed to "contract," i.e. reduce the number of teams. "According to Commissioner David Stern, there's a possibility that there will be fewer teams when play resumes. On an ESPN podcast, he indicated that there is interest in contraction on both the players' and owners' sides, although a collective bargaining agreement will be completed first. '[Contraction] is not a subject that we're against,' Stern said . . . 'The players actually have been heard to suggest that as well, which was interesting because that means they are suggesting that we eliminate 30 jobs.'"[5]

When Old School previously argued his case, Ben Osborne, *SLAM* editor-in-chief, noted that the discussion was "interesting." However, three years later, Osborne was echoing Old School; in a February 2012 article on how to fix the NBA, Osborne made the case to reduce the NBA down to 26 teams. "Yes, a case could be made that the League would have better competitive and financial balance with 26 teams, but that would require three existing owners to give up their teams, cost the players more than 50 jobs, and run some really talented players out of the League which we don't want to see. But cutting a team that is currently owned by the League [New Orleans Hornets] and based in its smallest TV market would create relatively few headaches."[6]

The Black Tax

Certain tenets of economics seem like foregone conclusions today, but they sent me into a spasm when Hendley first divulged them. First, there was no such thing as "full employment." The target unemployment rate in the U.S. was around 5%. The costs to the government of seeking full employment – inflation, high levels of government spending – were too taxing on those already employed. Secondly, the unemployment rate only included those both unemployed and actively looking for jobs; there was a certain population in America that did not want to work. But what I heard were "black people and welfare." In the mid-'80s "welfare" was a hot-button topic. President Reagan had politicized it during his presidential campaign by implying that welfare was dragging the country down and linking it with the image of a black woman with five kids by three different men. Even in the black community it was seen as persona non grata. Uncle Jesse railed against it on the way to Sunday school, during Sunday school, and on the way home from Sunday school. Thomas, Mark and I had heard that "welfare speech" so many times that we could recite it by heart. Today we joke about how Uncle Jesse "ain't never lied" about anything he ever told us. He knew then what all African Americans know now – welfare is like a pacifier. Once you get on it, it's almost impossible to wean yourself off. And that was the argument I made to Hendley; after the civil rights movement, blacks wanted jobs but the government gave us welfare. Furthermore, the theory about people not wanting to work was the darnedest thing I had ever heard and a complete folly. My arguing was the equivalent of "taking a knife into a gun fight." I had emotion on my side but Hendley had me outgunned – a few hundred years of economic theory and data on human behavior. Oddly enough, he was not the least bit intimidated by that intellectual beat down he was about to get. He actually seemed pretty amused by it all.

The other epiphany came when Hendley told us that the unemployment rate for African Americans has historically been 4%-5% higher than our white counterparts. The classroom turned silent. I could feel steam coming from my ears. Economists not only tell you how bad you are doing; they quantify it for you. There are a few ways to interpret the unemployment differential. But unlike Ms. Peale's way of letting the facts lead you to your conclusion, "the powers that be" tend to work backward and let the conclusion lead them to the facts. The obvious answer is that black men are shiftless, lazy, abusive and dysfunctional. One could also point to the success of other minorities as an example of how hard work pays off. The other way to drive the point home is through the use of black women. I always look askance when I see an African-American woman in the media bashing black men. While the mainstream media makes her think she is an intellectual, it also uses her words to explain the unemployment differential. The first time I ever saw the book *Waiting to Exhale* by Terry McMillan was at the University of Virginia. It seemed as if every African-American female undergrad at UVA was carrying it around. I had no firsthand knowledge about the book, but figured the author must have had a new twist on the theory of relativity. And when I moved to New York it seemed like required subway reading. I watched the movie to find out what all the fuss was about. All I could walk away with was "black men are dysfunctional." The book helped McMillan become one of the most celebrated authors of her era. I heard the local sheriff came to inquire about her crops and they even put her in a magazine and everything.

After business school I worked for GE Capital Corporation (GECC) in Stamford, Connecticut. Periodically the African Americans at the company got together informally. The corporate chatter of the day was who would become the first black CEO of a Fortune 500 company – Ken Chenault of American Express or A. Barry Rand of Xerox. Magazines described both as polished, accomplished and "patient." I thought the conversation was rather silly. Regardless of our talent, none of us was going to head GECC. One older gentleman joked how "if a lawyer misspelled a word, it was simply a misspelled word . . . if a black lawyer misspelled a word the conclusion was 'you can't spell.'" He labeled this double standard the "black tax" – the cost of being black in America. He would have me in tears from laughing so hard. Before quantifying the black tax – unemployment and incarceration – I would expect to see a sharp rise in unemployment starting in the late 1970s and early 1980s as the U.S. manufacturing base began to erode. Black men worked their way into middle class status by traveling to northern cities and California where manufacturing jobs were in abundance. The decline in U.S. manufacturing has hurt the economy overall, but African Americans especially. The inverse of this conclusion is that black men, for whatever reason, have been less successful in transitioning from the manufacturing sectors to the service sectors of the economy.

Unemployment Rates

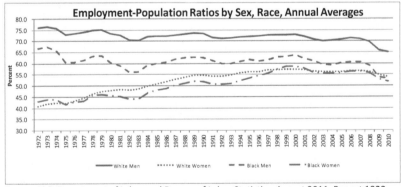

Source: U.S. Department of Labor and Bureau of Labor Statistics, August 2011, Report 1032

The above chart illustrates the employment-to-population ratio by sex and race, and measures the proportion of the population employed. This may be a better proxy for the true employment picture. The employment-to-population ratio for African-American men in 2010 was 53.1%, as compared to 65.1%, 67.5% and

68.0% for white, Asian and Hispanic men, respectively. Prior to seeing the data I would have expected a sharp decline in the ratio for black males starting in the mid-80s as the country's manufacturing base began to erode. However, the figures were relatively unchanged in 1980 (60.4%) and in 2000 (60.2%), yet fell precipitously by 2010. It reiterates the adage that "when America catches cold, black America catches pneumonia."

There was no noticeable difference in the employment-population ratio amongst women from different racial groups. The ratio for all women has increased since the early 1970s as more women have entered the workplace. Yet the differential in the ratio between black women and black men is the smallest vis-à-vis other ethnic groups. For instance, in 2010 the differential in the ratio between black men and black women (1.6%) was much less than that of whites (11.1%), Asians (14.5%) and Hispanics (10.4%). The differential may be symptomatic of a U.S. service economy more comfortable with black women in the workplace.

Incarceration Rates

The rate of incarceration also reflects the additional costs of being black in America. One could say that unemployment and incarceration rates are linked in that one (high unemployment) leads to crime and ultimately, incarceration. The abnormally high rate for African Americans is a known truth in the black community. After doing some research, I found that the U.S. has the highest incarceration rate of any country in the "free world."

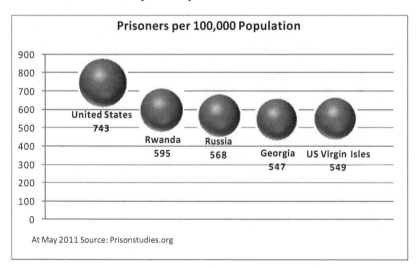

The U.S. incarceration rate has increased from 200 per 100,000 U.S. residents in the mid-90s to 743 per 100,000 residents in 2010. The incarceration rate is a function of admissions, times length of stay. Simply based on the number of admissions per capita, the U.S. would not be the world's largest jailor. The U.S. prison policy, highly affected by mandatory drug sentencing, has a higher length of stay relative to the rest of the world. Critics have also blamed the so-called "war on drugs" for the abnormally high incarceration rate of African-American males (4,797 per 100,000 U.S. residents) as compared to that of white males (708 per 100,000 U.S. residents). Even more damning is the fact that a high percentage of white males are incarcerated in local jails with shorter stays, causing less of a disruption for their families. In contrast, the majority of black males are jailed in federal prison with longer stays – a phenomenon that has practically ravaged the black family. Instead of reducing the level of violent crime in America, the war on drugs has resulted in a frequent number of arrests for low-level drug transactions and non-violent offenders; about 50% of the U.S. prison population represents non-violent crimes. Nor will it ever reduce drug trafficking. Senior year, Dr. Hendley presented us with a case involving a town with an exploding population of dogs. The town manager had a dilemma – to control the population by either spaying male dogs or female dogs. The logical answer would be to spay the male dogs, since they were the "obvious" culprits. However, if the ratio was 10 female dogs per 10 male dogs and he spayed as many as six male dogs, the remaining four could still service 10 female dogs. Instead, the town manager spayed the female dogs and the dog population decreased proportionately. To that point, attempting to "spay" drug dealers does not have the same impact on the drug trade as spaying the user through incarceration, treatment, or education. In no way am I attempting to dissect the criminal justice system, but simply presenting data that supports what Grandma always knew – if you are black in America, odds are you are going to the pen.

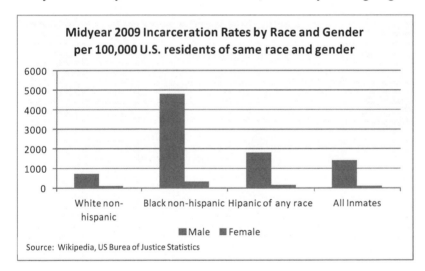

Marginal Propensity to Consume

President Kennedy was elected in 1960 with the campaign promise to spur the economy and improve employment. Kennedy and his economic advisors proposed tax cuts. During class discussions we learned about a concept called the "marginal propensity to consume" (MPC), or for each extra dollar one makes, the percentage one spends. The inverse of the MPC is the marginal propensity to save. The theory goes that lower-income Americans have "pent up demand" i.e., their demand is constrained by a lack of money. If they had extra income they would spend it immediately on clothes, appliances, or food. In contrast, wealthy individuals who already own three automobiles, a main house and a stone mansion in the Hamptons are not constrained by money, so their spending would not increase dramatically with more income. For each additional dollar in income received, if lower-income individuals spent 90%, economists would say they have an MPC of 90%. Kennedy's dilemma was whether to cut taxes for lower-income individuals or for corporations and the wealthy. Throughout history, when Republican presidents offer tax cuts to the wealthy, Democrats chastise the act as a ploy "to support their political base." When Democrats offer a tax cut to lower-income Americans, Republicans counter with claims of "redistribution of wealth."

Housing and Autos Drive the Economy

We learned several concepts in isolation, like the MPC, MPS, "Law of Supply and Demand" and the "crowding out" effect of government spending. But Dr. Townsend tied them all together with his "Townsend Econometric Model." Townsend's model illustrated how interest rates impacted housing starts, or how government spending spurred demand and then caused inflationary expectations, driving up interest rates and choking off future demand. I memorized this model and dreamt about it in my sleep. However, for me to fully grasp something I have to be able to actually touch it, feel it or see it happen before my eyes. Almost a decade later I attempted to predict future movements in the economy by sketching out the econometric model from memory. Embarrassingly enough, I could not remember all of the components of Townsend's concentric circles and my notes were stacked away in my parents' basement. I then took the two largest components of the model (housing and autos) and developed a short-form conclusion – housing and autos drive the economy. After the renovation on my house I saw the economy move firsthand. Below is the original estimate of the renovation and its components.

Gut Rehablitation Project - Sample	
Permits	$ 2,000
Demolition & Disposal	10,000
Wood Joists	4,000
New Wood Strip Floor	14,000
New Wall	14,000
Insulation - Outside Wall	2,000
Insulation - Any Floor	4,000
New Windows	8,000
New Apartment Doors	4,000
New Interior Doors	6,000
New Complete Baths	15,000
New Complete Kitchen	19,000
Electrical	10,000
Plumbing	16,000
Paint	4,000
Total	**$ 132,000**

About three years and three contractors later I got my house finished. Now replicate this estimated rehab project about 100,000 times every month and you would get an indication of how housing starts move the U.S. economy. Apparently Dr. Townsend knew what he was talking about.

In Volcker We Trust

Paul Volcker was appointed Chairman of the Federal Reserve by President Jimmy Carter in 1979 and served until he retired under Reagan in 1987. Volcker not only defined the primary role of the Fed Chairman – to fight inflation – he accomplished it amid heavy criticism from the public and the presidents under which he served. Volcker inherited the Fed chairmanship amid 13% inflation. The public responded by demanding higher wages and investing in assets they thought would appreciate faster than inflation. Volcker slowed the economy by raising the federal funds rate (rate at which banks borrow from one another) to 19% in 1981, causing lending rates and credit card rates to exceed 20%. By 1982 Volcker had halved inflation to 6.5% and slowed the economy. Despite overtures from both the Carter and Reagan camps to spur the economy through fiscal stimulus, Volcker stuck to his principals and maintained the independence of the Fed. Hence, he is the standard by which all Federal Reserve chairmen are measured.

The Real World

From my junior year on, I planned on making a career in retail banking. I was acquainted with a local banker named Jay Fulton who worked at Central Fidelity Bank. I liked the way he was in a position to help people in the community so I thought a job like that would be pretty rewarding. I often told people that I wanted to go into banking because "that's where the money is." During my senior year I interviewed with several banks including Sovran, the largest bank in Virginia. I'm not certain if it is legal today, but applicants for Sovran's 1989 management training program submitted to psychological testing. I scored the highest of anybody in the management training class that year and the bank made me an offer on the spot. On the basketball court we won the ODAC championship my senior year and made it to the NCAA tournament. It felt pretty fulfilling after all the grief we took my freshman year. I also scored 33 points in an overtime victory over William & Mary that year. Afterward their coach was quoted as saying something to the effect that "after Curtis Pride (Detroit Tigers, New York Yankees) got hurt they did not have anyone quick enough to guard me, and I was a Division I caliber player on the Division III level." I actually felt vindicated for not receiving a D-I scholarship. The summer after my freshmen year I lived in the weight room and Coach Shaver also helped me correct a flaw in my jump shot. I had been shooting the ball with my palm instead of my fingertips, limiting my shot's rotation. With the correction and 1,000 jump shots per day in the off-season, I didn't miss too many open jumpers after that. I never reached my goal of All-America status by my junior year – I didn't make it until my senior year. I left the basketball program in the hands of some very capable underclassmen that made NCAA tournament appearances a common occurrence.

Still, I exited college just as I had entered it – amid controversy. Though I was recognized as one of the best players in the country, a kid from Washington and Lee won ODAC Player of the Year. The scuttlebutt was that Bill Leatherman, the Bridgewater coach, did not vote for me for first team or second team all-conference, leaving me without enough voting points to win Player of the Year. The newspaper quoted Leatherman as saying that he let his players decide who should make all-conference and they left my name off the list. I laughed it off, thinking it was Leatherman's poor attempt at humor. It was so blatantly racist that it made the guy look like an imbecile and gave the ODAC a black eye. Whenever I return to the College, one of the trustees always reminds me of how Leatherman treated me and what a travesty it was; it's sort of an inside story between us. My family was excited at my graduation. Ms. Bertha Jenkins was there too, so I guess Annie Mae was there in spirit if not in body. However, Suzie spoiled my mood with the cryptic statement, "So I guess it's time for graduate school now." The thought had never entered my mind, actually. I had stared down Heinneman, Rogers, Hendley, DeWolfe, Wilson, Brinkley, Townsend, and Angresano amongst others, for four years and I had no intention of entering another classroom ever again. I left the College with a B.A. in economics, pretty much ready to bite the ass off a bear.

MR. DRYSDALE

I started with Sovran Bank in Lynchburg, Virginia, commuting from my parents' house every day, 51 miles one way. The first assignment from the branch manager was to memorize something called the Community Reinvestment Act (CRA). I sifted through some banking policy manuals on CRA and expected to be bored to death. What I uncovered totally blew my mind. The act came about after a group of African-American customers in Illinois complained about discrimination in their local bank's lending practices. Year after year residents complained that they deposited money with said bank but could not secure a loan. In the mind of the declined customers, the one common denominator amongst them was not low credit scores, limited work history, or inability to repay the loan – it was race. They complained so much that local regulators reviewed the bank's lending policies. Their review process was as follows – (i) secure a map of the bank's lending area(s), (ii) review all loan applications, (iii) match up the zip codes of all declined loan applicants and (iv) color in red the areas on the map where the declined loan applicants lived. After this process was over, regulators had drawn a red line through the neighborhoods where only African Americans lived – hence the term "redlining" was coined. Based on the dispersion of the loan declines, it appeared that the bank's loan officers had predetermined to decline all loans from African-American neighborhoods. This was not true of course, but the bank's lending practices had the same effect as if it were true. As a result, CRA was enacted that legally required banks to prove they served the needs of the community, including the need for credit.

I worked directly with a personal banker named Jean, the sister-in-law of Jerry Falwell, the famous Baptist preacher who founded Liberty University (1971) and the Moral Majority (1979). Jean had a "high valued customer" (HVC) list that was not only long, but deep; some HVCs had been doing business with her for decades. She showed me everything involving bank products, from checking accounts to certificates of deposit (CDs). I mostly watched how she interacted with customers though. Her customers were pretty wealthy and most of their questions focused on the direction of interest rates. Each branch received information on rates for CDs, savings accounts, fixed rate mortgages, adjustable rate mortgages (ARMs), and prime loans each Monday morning before the office opened. The rates were then posted in the office where they would be easily visible to customers. Interest rates were driven by either the federal funds rate or U.S. treasury rate. For instance, the federal funds rate is the rate at which banks charge other banks for overnight loans. This in turn drove the prime lending rate charged to customers. The U.S. treasury rate is the rate at which the government borrows money from the public. The theory goes that the U.S. will never default on its loan obligations so no individual could ever be more creditworthy than the U.S. government. If the 10-year U.S. treasury has a yield of 6.00% then a 30-year mortgage to a fairly creditworthy borrower would be 2.00% to 2.50% higher at 8.00% - 8.50%.

Sovran taught me quickly about how the "real world" works. At one of the branches I was responsible for the overdrafts and the following decisions: (i) pay the check with (a) no fee or (b) a $25 overdraft fee or (ii) return the check with (a) no fee or (b) a $25 overdraft charge. When I thought the accumulation of fees were excessive, particularly for lower-income customers, I cut them a break. Besides, the money was not going into my pocket. I never charged an HVC an overdraft fee. However, there was one customer whose husband owned a local car dealership. She had six or seven personal accounts totaling about a half a million dollars, yet one of her accounts was overdrawn at least four times a week. I always paid the check and never charged a fee. This went on for weeks until I finally had had enough and continued to pay her overdrawn checks, yet charged a fee for the nuisance. She visited the branch manager one day to talk business and everything was pretty jovial. At the end of the meeting she mentioned some odd overdraft fees she had been getting and asked him to "take care of them." What seemed like a good idea at the time turned into pure naïveté. From then on instead of focusing on helping people, I decided to "help" myself and took pains to placate all customers, especially the more affluent ones. At that moment I understood how the world worked, and morphed into "Mr. Drysdale" – the nickname my family gave me. Affluent people received perks like frequent flier miles and zero banking fees, while those who needed them the most – lower-income people – received nothing. After all, one could argue that affluent customers either paid the bills or had the financial resources that companies offering the perks wanted access to.

Training Program

Sovran's true appeal was its vaunted training program – the envy of banks throughout the region. We learned every aspect of both the bank's retail and corporate operations. We traveled to training sessions throughout Virginia and Washington, D.C. We discussed the bank's financial statements, the quality of its loan portfolio, its acquisition strategy and national ambitions. We also networked with corporate executives within key divisions. Regional banking was about to change dramatically and Sovran had the capital and the ambition to lead it. It did not take me long to figure out that I did not fit your typical "corporate" description; the other trainees explained it to me, albeit in a roundabout way. Our first training session was in Virginia Beach. I rolled up in my Mazda GLC with the "Silk 32" license plates. When I got out, all of the African-American trainees started laughing. I think I even heard someone say under her breath, "He needs to wash his car." I remember a lot of faces from the program, but the African Americans stick out most in my memory. There were these two guys running around talking about where they went to school, who they knew, and how large they were living. They put me in the mind of "Carlton Banks" of the television show *The Fresh Prince of Bel-Air* and Mr. Bentley, the former man-servant for music mogul, Sean "P-Diddy" Combs. I had no interest in selling myself to the rest of the group. However, several trainees managed their image amongst their peers and executives who ran the training program, as they jockeyed for full-time assignments. If nothing else, at least the guys spoke to me. The African-American women treated me like I was "dangerous," the second coming of Attila the Hun. After meetings were finished, the training class would have dinner together and socialize as a group. Then everybody would break off into smaller groups and do whatever. The black women would plan their soirees and would include everyone except me. Sometimes I would walk by when they were in the midst of discussing their plans for the evening; they would either start whispering or wait until I had passed to resume speaking. Instead, I would simply hang out by myself. I would ask the concierge for directions to where all the black nightclubs were and then head out. The next day the head of the training program would give us tips on the dangerous areas in town to avoid. Everybody would write this information down feverishly and after a few seconds I would realize, "Hey, that's the area I was hanging out in last night." Regardless of what city we were in, this was always the case.

Sovran was the biggest and the best bank in the state of Virginia. We also had a presence in North Carolina and Washington, D.C. and before long our brand would be national. Part and parcel of that, Sovran executives wanted to repeal interstate banking laws, enter the insurance industry and mimic the success and business model of Citicorp ("Citi"). These three things were pretty much all they ever talked about.

Interstate Banking

The National Banking Act of 1863 created a national banking system, but it did not allow interstate banking. Several arguments had been made for banks to operate across state lines but there were more factions against the idea than for it. Of the three distinct interest groups – the big New York City Banks, the Midwestern city banks and the country banks – only the Midwestern city banks were interested in positive structural reform. "The New York banks were interested in maintaining their supremacy (the status quo) by preventing schemes that would give more importance to Midwestern banks – especially in Chicago – that were threatening that supremacy. The country banks, on the other hand, wanted to prevent any branch-banking scheme that would put them in direct competition with the city banks."[1] However, proponents would receive two gifts in the form of the S&L debacle and the rise of Japan to superpower status. Both occurrences would make the interstate banking argument more palatable to Congress.

Savings & Loan Debacle

The S&L debacle of the 1980s made it practical for bank regulators to allow takeovers of out-of-state banks in order to protect deposit holders. It also mitigated the potential moral hazard on taxpayers who would ultimately bear the cost of the debacle. "In 1982, the Garn-St. Germain Act officially permitted out-of-state emergency takeovers under specific conditions, while also encouraging other kinds of interstate activity."[2] Each state was allowed to establish its own policies on whether to allow outside banks to enter its states. State exceptions ranged from allowing reciprocal interstate banking agreements with other states, to not allowing interstate banking at all.

"Japan Threat"

By the late '80s Japan had become the next superpower and America's primary global economic threat. They not only dominated the U.S. auto industry by producing high-quality autos with fewer defects, but they were more efficient and customer-focused as well. Japan's just-in-time inventory manufacturing concept, considered "best-in-class," left U.S. auto manufacturers scrambling to catch up. Their dominance of the auto industry chipped away at the American psyche, and their acquisition of U.S. trophy properties like golf resorts in California, office buildings in New York, and hotels in Hawaii only exacerbated the situation. When I heard that Japan's Mitsubishi Estate Company purchased the landmark Rockefeller Center in 1989, heck, even I wanted to go out and fight somebody. By 1989, the world's 10 largest banks and 23 of the world's 50 largest banks resided in Japan; from the U.S., only Citicorp, Chase Manhattan, Bank of America, and J.P. Morgan cracked the top 50. Sovran's regional manager reminded us of this fact constantly. She also noted that Japan's banks had lower regulatory capital requirements than we did so they could hold more assets per dollar of capital. Given their thin capitalization, we knew that if Japan's banks made any huge missteps, they would have a banking crisis never before seen. That said, the U.S. banking industry played on the Japan fears. They lobbied regulators that interstate banking laws created inefficiencies. Furthermore, for U.S. banks to compete globally with the Japanese, we needed size. Else, the U.S. banking industry would go the way of the U.S. auto industry. The "Japan threat," real or imagined, probably motivated regulators to allow interstate banking more than anything else.

Combine Banking and Insurance

Sovran executives also wanted to marry banking and insurance. The bank was already selling credit life and credit disability insurance attached to loans. After reviewing several loan applications it became clear that of all the variables (term, rate, etc.), the profit on loans was most sensitive to whether credit life or credit disability insurance was included. I had overheard some bankers pushing the product. However, I always mentioned the benefit to customers casually and let them decide if they needed it. Though the premiums were not very large, credit life/disability insurance carried a high profit margin; the profit potential was enormous. The fixed cost branch network was already in place. Any insurance products sold would only incur a small variable cost, and the rest of the revenue would fall directly to the bank's bottom line. In addition, in mid-tier towns across the country, customers relied on bankers like Jean (Lynchburg) for advice on all financial services products. They valued her counsel and if banks could have added insurance to its product mix, they could have put an untold amount of insurance agents out of business. Lastly, the insurance industry would unlikely be able to replicate banks' entrenched branch networks or the valued counsel of their personal bankers. Therefore, banks lobbied Congress vigorously for the right to sell additional insurance products, and insurance agents lobbied vigorously against it.

Citicorp, Citicorp, Citicorp

Of the eight money center banks, Citi was the largest. It was also the most respected, boldest and most innovative. It did the largest and most innovative real estate transactions; it made loans to Latin American countries; its credit card portfolio was the envy of the industry; it had the only global consumer bank in the U.S., generating cash flow from Europe, Latin America, Asia, etc. The Citi brand was one of the most recognized and most respected in all of financial services. Citi seemed limited only by the imagination of its CEO, John Reed. Everything we did was in relation to Citi – our size, the quality of our loan portfolio, the number of branches, and size of our credit card portfolio. After interstate banking laws were repealed, it would be a race to determine where the next major banking center would be located – Virginia or North Carolina. North Carolina had three high-quality banks in NCNB, First Union and Wachovia, all with national ambitions. NCNB and its CEO, Hugh McColl, the former marine, appeared to be the most aggressive of the three. It was pretty clear to me that the future of Sovran was going to be (i) a steady march toward rivaling Citi, or (ii) a subsidiary of one of the North Carolina banks. Eventually Citi would be punished for its boldness in every product, in every market. In 1987 it established loss reserves of $3.3 billion for its less-developed-country (LDC) debt – more than 30% of its total LDC exposure. By 1989, the average money-center bank had total reserves of almost 50 percent of total LDC loans outstanding.[3] After the commercial real estate crisis materialized in 1990, rating agencies downgraded the company to junk status. It was sitting on $13 billion of commercial real estate, 43% of which was nonperforming. It had made large bets to developers like Donald Trump (Taj Mahal) and the Reichmann Brothers (Canary Wharf) who could not service their loans. The company was also heavily exposed to LBO loans, which by the end of the 1980s had become riskier just as the economy was about to thaw. By the end of 1991, Citi's stock price had hit lows not seen since the 1960s, and considered technically insolvent. I imagined the "fix" we would be in if every U.S. bank imitated Citi.

Washington, D.C. – Trial by Fire

In the fourth quarter of 1989 the bank's area manager asked the trainees in the Lynchburg area to cut back on expenses, whether that meant carpooling, or eating at cheaper restaurants. He mentioned that the bank was worried about the economy. I also spoke to my former classmate, Rory Perkins, then in his third year at H-SC. He said the economy was so bad that many of the companies like Sovran that used to interview at the school had now cancelled. Students were scrambling to secure a job before graduation. I breathed a sigh of relief that I had graduated the previous May, or I would have been jobless. That said, Sovran jettisoned its two-year training program after only nine months. All of the interns then had to decide what part of the bank they wanted to work in permanently. The retail side (branch banking) offered me the managerial skills I coveted but not the finance training, and vice versa. And therein lied the quandary. My dream job was in the real estate finance department located in Northern Virginia, just outside Washington, D.C. The thought of doing large real estate deals not only excited me, but the analytical training and the opportunity to negotiate with developers would have been valuable experience. However, there was a woman in the training program who already worked in the Northern Virginia office; she had been lobbying for that position for months. The executives in the real estate finance department liked her as well, so the opportunity had been decided long before the training program was even over.

There were also openings for an assistant manager position in Suitland, Maryland and Waldorf, Maryland, both near Washington. I was offered both jobs and the regional manager told me I could have my pick. The Waldorf office was very calm. The staff was very experienced and the customer base was stable which meant "repeat business." The Suitland office, on the other hand, had been full of turmoil. It had been robbed three times in the previous five years, and the rumor was that at least two of the robberies had been inside jobs. In one of the incidences, the bad guys robbed the place from the drive-through window, which was bulletproof. The story sounded so ridiculous that it had to have been an inside job. Sovran removed the drive-through and replaced it with a "walk-up" window. That way, if someone robbed the place they couldn't drive off – they had to run off. Turning around the Suitland office sounded like more of a challenge so I chose to go there. When the manager from Waldorf heard about my decision she thought I had lost my mind. Suzie had finagled a deal where I would move in with my Aunt Jackie and Uncle Maurice and the money I saved on rent I could send to her. This worked out pretty well because I didn't know a soul in D.C. My commute from Silver Spring, Maryland to Suitland was about 35 minutes with no traffic. The walk-up window opened at 7 a.m. so I had to be there by 6:45 a.m. each morning. The full branch was open from 9 a.m. to 4 p.m. Monday through Friday and reopened again on Friday from 5 p.m. to 8 p.m. During office hours we had a security guard. I heard through the grapevine that an assistant manager at an office in the area had been shot and killed. Since then the bank installed security guards at certain offices. In one office, the managers even had bulletproof glass separating them and the customers. You had to ring a bell in order to gain access . . . a little different from what I had experienced in Lynchburg.

The manager, Rochelle, and I were responsible for Suitland and a satellite office within the U.S. Census Bureau across the street. The Census Bureau had two tellers and a customer service representative (CSR) who had been at the bank seemingly forever. They had a captive customer base of Census Bureau employees; most importantly, they brought in a lot of money without creating any problems. We enjoyed "managing" them because they made us look good. The Suitland office had five tellers, two CSRs, the manager and me. I met everyone and the first thing that stood out was that they were all women and all black. I figured we would make a lot of money for the bank and have a lot of fun in the process. Rochelle was insistent that I meet one more person – Mrs. Green, the area manager and the person Rochelle reported to. All she said was "Mrs. Green does not play." She worked over at the Seat Pleasant office, the area more well-known now because NBA star Kevin Durant grew up near there. I thought the meeting with Mrs. Green went well. I just tried to remain composed and sound confident. In retrospect, I was probably a little too confident for my own good. I was 23 years old and looked like I was around 19. Some of the employees I would be managing had been at the bank longer than I had been alive.

In my second month there I experienced the "dye-pack tester" incident. Each of the tellers kept an electronic dye-pack in their drawer covered with $20 bills. To put it succinctly, the dye pack is battery operated and the batteries need to be tested monthly to ensure they are still operable. Afterward, I returned the tester back to the vault. During the month in question, I went to test the dye packs and guess what? The tester was missing. I told the manager and we looked all over for that darn thing. Then Diane (CSR) said sort of cryptically, "Ralph was the last one to have it," implying that I may have lost it. I just smirked. How complicated was it to walk a dye-pack tester from the vault and then back to the vault? The manager then erupted with, "I want that dye-pack tester immediately. Someone knows who has it!" I was wondering what the big deal was. We could always get another one. After hours she told the staff that if the dye-pack tester did not reappear by the next day she was calling "Internal Controls" to investigate. The next morning the head teller, also Diane's sister-in-law (you could not make this up), said Diane had a confession to make. Diane admitted to everyone that it was she who threw the dye-pack tester away. My "country" behind still did not get it. I breathed a sigh of relief. "It was obviously an accident so we can all go back to work," I said. Diane then admitted that she did it on purpose in order to get me into trouble. She had been at the bank 17 years and had applied for the assistant manager's position. She was mad when I got the job so she decided to sabotage me. My eyes got as big as silver dollars. That was not quite the answer I was looking for. What I found most disturbing was that the entire staff had known about it all along. Rochelle reprimanded Diane and put her on six months' probation. The news reverberated throughout the branches; even some of the customers found out. Diane was so embarrassed that she resigned three weeks later.

The following month was the "telephone pole" incident. One morning a car ran into a telephone pole, knocking out all of the lights on our side of the street. We used flashlights and candles for lighting in the meantime. The employees thought we should go home because we couldn't serve customers in the dark. I decided to keep the office open and direct customers to the walk-up window. One of the CSRs, Carol, started getting hysterical because with all of the security cameras inoperable, she felt unsafe. I tried to calm her down, but to no avail. Besides, even with lights, if you got shot and killed, the security cameras were not going to bring you back to life. They may have been instrumental in helping us catch the robber though. Carol decided to go home anyway because apparently, I was incompetent. About two hours later I received a call from Mrs. Green:

    Mrs. Green: "Ralph, what's going on over there?"

Me: (Oh Lawd I'm 'bout to get fired) "Nothing much Mrs. Green. A car hit the power lines outside the office this morning so all of our lights went out. I kept the office open and just directed customers to the walk-up window. Those customers with more complicated needs will have to wait until the lights are back on."

Mrs. Green: "I just received a phone call from Carol saying, 'Mrs. Green, I know Ralph told you already but I left the office. The lights are out. We have no security cameras and it's just not safe. Ralph told everyone to stay but I left.' Is that true?"

Me: (This girl did what? Now she's got us both inside the lion's den.) "Yes ma'am."

Mrs. Green: "So you told her to stay and she left anyway?"

Me: (Oh Lawd, I'm 'bout to get fired twice now. She's going to fire me, then give me my job back so she can fire me again.) "Yes ma'am."

Mrs. Green: "She's being insubordinate and I want her written up immediately."

Me: (If I write her up and she quits then that means more work for me.) "Mrs. Green, Carol did seem genuinely hysterical and she has been a model employee."

Mrs. Green: "Ralph I want her written up immediately . . . you understand?"

Me: "Yes Ma'am Mrs. Green."

Carol, nor I, knew that the higher-ups thought our office was a case of inmates trying to run the asylum. Carol thought I was going to run and tell Mrs. Green "what had happened" so she tried to beat me to the punch. I couldn't run to my boss's boss every two seconds because it would have made me look weak. Mrs. Green also knew that if I let Carol's insubordination go, it would have made me look even weaker. She let me know in a polite manner that "it was either them or me . . . pick your choice." I reprimanded Carol, put her on probation and within a month she resigned. Weeks after resigning she visited the office; I thought it was pretty nervy of her to come back and grin in my face after trying to blindside me. We made some small talk and then I turned off all the lights. After a few seconds I turned them back on and glared at her. The look on her face was priceless. The other employees, who had gotten used to my sarcasm by now, were in hysterics. She never called or visited again after that.

I was inexperienced, but still pretty resourceful. My first order of business was to account for everything in the office that could be used as money. I took inventory of treasurer's checks, CDs, etc. and created a log whereby someone had to sign for every item removed from the register. I also embraced change.

Sovran was going through the process of automating every function in the bank. Many of the older employees were intimidated by computers, so there was a lot of hand-holding during training sessions. I had been at the bank barely a year when Sovran introduced its new 401(k) plan. The bank would no longer manage your money or offer you a guaranteed payout post-retirement. With 401(k) plans, employees contributed a certain amount each pay period and the employer "matched" a portion of that contribution. This way, the actual liability to the employer was always known and the performance of the retirement plan was the employee's responsibility. Sovran sent a lady from the retirement savings area to explain the new investment plan. You almost felt dyslexic trying to decipher the long-winded descriptions of each of the investment options – short-term bond fund, long-term bond fund, blue chip fund, or aggressive growth fund. The implications were pretty daunting. Based on your knowledge of the stock and bond markets, or lack thereof, your retirement plan could grow at an attractive rate or get wiped out altogether. After she left, the staff berated me with questions. I never gave advice. I just gave an indication of where I was putting my money, what little I had. Nor did I trust the stock market; it had crashed just three years earlier, and I had received signs that the economy was headed for a fall. I also knew that the long-term bonds were most sensitive to interest rates so I parked everything into short-term bonds. Any time I read an article about the direction of the stock market or interest rates, I distributed it to the staff.

After the incident with Carol, I wondered when the next shoe was going to drop. Around this time I received a call from "Carlton" of the training program. He inquired about how I was doing after hearing I was down in the "trenches." He also lamented my fate given that he was working in the bank's division that bought and sold securities – his dream job. Carlton informed me that "Bentley" was working in the trust department, which managed money for wealthy individuals and estates. Bank trust departments were the precursor to mutual funds and one of the last bastions of "disintermediation" where mutual fund companies and investment banks began to cherry-pick banks' most profitable products. Carlton went down the list of former trainees, where they were and how they were doing. I found out that the woman who went into the real estate finance group was not fairing so well. The group was not financing any new real estate transactions and she was relegated to working deals that had gone belly-up. Sovran had laid off several people in the department and another round of layoffs was expected. I breathed a sigh of relief from having dodged that bullet. The Suitland office was looking really good right about now. I put a happy spin on everything and told Carlton how much I was enjoying D.C. I actually found his pleasantries rather amusing.

I must have spoken too soon because things at the office soon turned ominous. The manager and I were at a monthly meeting with the higher-ups when all of a sudden, the music stopped. We received word that there was an emergency at our office and we had to leave immediately. The head teller, Edwina, had attempted to settle her drawer for the day and was short $5,000. We looked everywhere for it. We had her retrace her steps and all we could make out was that she must have accidentally sat a stack down somewhere. She was adamant that someone had taken the money and certain that it was Tracey, her bitter rival. The rivalry (dating back to the old regime) centered around who made the most money or whom the manager doted on the most. Though the inmates banded together against management, they also had their own petty squabbles. Tracey, sensing she was being accused, turned into a drama queen. She opened her pocketbook, urged us to search her car, and feigned indignation. The next day "Internal Controls" investigated the matter. Since we never found the money, the incident was recorded as an "exceptional loss" and Edwina was terminated. She was one of the few employees who did not appear to be disloyal. Also, it made no sense that Edwina would steal from herself. Moreover, the thief was still at large and that kept me awake at night. I too suspected Tracey and decided to get rid of her . . . by any means necessary.

Simultaneously the bank made sweeping changes within the branches. Sovran bi-furcated the retail functions into sales managers and operations managers. The sales manager would be responsible for generating revenue and the operations manager (me) would ensure the bank ran smoothly. It also meant that I had to report directly to Mrs. Green, which terrified me to no end. She had been at the bank for 17 years and had forgotten more about retail banking than I would ever know. She wanted her area to be the best, which meant no mistakes. What made matters worse was that I hated the woman with a passion. Oddly enough, she had never actually done anything to warrant my disdain. Everything she had told me was for my own good. It was the kind of hate that Christians have for Jehovah's Witnesses. There is a running joke in the black community about how pushy Jehovah's Witnesses are, and how they are always trying to convert you to their religion. Sometimes they would drive up to our house on Saturdays when our parents were gone; we would literally turn off the television and pretend no one was home. The real reason for the hatred is that Jehovah's Witnesses know the Bible better than Christians do. Once you started debating with them they would immediately cite passages from the Bible and get you all tongue-tied and confused to the point where you doubted your own religion. It was much easier to make up a reason not to like them.

On top of that I had no social life. When I was not poring through bank manuals to come up to speed at work, I was studying for the GMATs for business school. Suzie would not give the issue up so I went back to the career services center at H-SC to research the best programs. The plan was to get the finance experience in business school that I did not get at Sovran. For some odd reason all signs kept pointing to the Darden School at the University of Virginia. Warren Thompson (H-SC 1982) was an executive at the Marriott in the D.C. area and he spoke glowingly about the place. Hugo Rodriguez and Rob Citrone, who were a few years ahead of me in college, were attending Darden at the time, which was another big endorsement. Regardless of where I landed after graduate school, I wanted to return to Virginia so a degree from Darden would carry more weight than one from another top school. Lastly, of all that I had read, it was considered the toughest business school in the country, which I liked. After a liberal arts degree in college, I wanted the toughest business school experience I could get. Everybody from the College was excited to know I was applying; Coach Shaver and a few of the professors volunteered to write recommendations. However, my application was not complete until Dr. Rogers, who was an advisor to the African-American students at the College, reviewed it. He was not at home when I called so I waited around all day. Even after we had graduated we were still encroaching on the man's time. After Dr. Rogers gave the "okay," I sent in the application and interviewed several months later. I killed the interview – I talked about my experience at Sovran, how I was responsible for the integrity of the bank and how I made decisions on a daily basis that I was held accountable for.

Business school or not, the only way I would be successful in my new assignment was with the undivided attention of the staff. Instead, I got more shenanigans. One Monday Tracey called in sick because she had a hangover from the previous weekend. She had gone out partying with her boyfriend on her birthday and had gotten a bit carried away. Monday morning was one of the busiest times of the week and we needed everybody. I suggested that she change her mind but she swore she was too hung over. She also had a penchant for getting away with stuff and bragging to the rest of the staff about it. When she requested use of her last vacation day later on that summer, I informed her that when she called in sick due to a hangover, I reported it as a "vacation day." She let out a shriek that could be heard at the end of the block, and went into a rampage that lasted weeks. She even threatened me with, "Wait 'til my boyfriend hears about this." She claimed that her boyfriend was the cousin of Rayful Edmond, the D.C. drug kingpin. Edmond was a mythical figure; I am not sure how the mainstream media portrayed him but locally, he had that "Robin Hood motif" working for him. I became friends with one of the customers who came to the bank from time to time. She enjoyed the finer things in life and made sure I knew it, which I found rather comical. She showed me around D.C. and often referred to Edmond – "Rayful Edmond has a car like that" or "Rayful Edmond's car has rims like that." Once I inquired, "Isn't he a drug dealer?" The woman went on a 10-minute explanation in defense of the guy. It dawned on me that if a young college graduate was enamored with Edmond, then this guy could probably sell ice to an Eskimo. The fact that he sold drugs instead was probably due more to circumstance. I looked up from my desk one morning and Edmond's supposed cousin was standing right in front of me. I informed him that Sovran business was not up for discussion and if he did not have an account then he should leave. I made sure to keep my distance and not let him "crowd" me. My older cousins Up the House taught me that as soon as a guy enters your personal space, let your hands go and ask questions later. However, he left without incident; I told Tracey that if her boyfriend ever came to the office again she was fired. She exclaimed, "I'm leaving anyway!" I asked her for a date and she replied, "By the end of the month." I called Sovran's headquarters and requested a replacement. To my surprise, the woman in charge of staffing knew exactly who Tracey was and sounded relieved she was on her way out.

After three weeks had passed, I pressed her for a formal resignation. The fact that I had to keep bothering her about it struck me as odd. Where she had once been sarcastic, she now became combative when I broached the subject. The week of Tracey's exit came and still no resignation letter. I was livid, and saw it as another attempt at insubordination. On Tracey's supposed last day at the bank, I requested a closed-door meeting with her and the manager. I never came to the meeting. "Joe Baker" showed up instead. Joe demanded Tracey's resignation and she tried to stall for time. About five minutes went by when she began to beg to keep her job. Rochelle felt that Tracey was genuinely sorry and would shape up, to which Joe replied, "Tracey, if you won't type your resignation then I'll type it for you." He walked over to the typewriter, typed the resignation and placed it in front of her. Instead of breathing fire as expected, Tracey broke down and started crying uncontrollably and begged for her job. Joe just glared at her, motioned for her to sign the resignation letter and escorted her off the premises. Of course the news reverberated throughout the bank. I even got a call from the regional manager, who inquired about the details and reminded me of the fine job I was doing. From then on, the staff thought I was "crazy and unpredictable," which was just the way I liked it.

To my surprise, the woman could not stay away from the office. I heard she had started coming to the walk-up window with one of the bank's elderly customers after hours. "How nice" I thought. Weeks later, the customer's daughter and son-and-law paid us a visit from Ohio. They alerted us to some suspicious activity in their mother's account; someone had withdrawn about $3,500 that had not been requested. Apparently Tracey would bring the lady to the bank where she would request say, $500. Tracey would write the check for $1,000, give the customer $500 and keep the rest. She did this a few times a week for about a month. We had to reimburse the customer and advised her to steer clear of Tracey. Previously when someone left the bank we would receive a new employee right away. After Tracey resigned we were told that due to the economy, Sovran was cutting back on staff and we would have to make do. After two other employees left to work for the previous managers at the Suitland office, we were severely understaffed. In my first six months on the job seven of the original eight employees I started with were gone. Some were terminated and others, no longer able to run the asylum, left on their own accord. Yet the short supply of staff meant I had to pull double duty. I worked the teller window in the mornings when it was busiest and worked the desk in the afternoon. After the bank closed I spent a few hours performing paperwork. The workload left me contemplating the drivers of the declining economy and when the slowdown would exacerbate.

Persian Gulf War

The Gulf War was triggered by an invasion of Kuwait by Iraqi troops in August 1990. The U.S. condemned the actions of the Iraqi leader, Saddam Hussein, and sent U.S. troops to Saudi Arabia, which was used as a base from which to attack. Troops from the United Nations and coalition forces representing over 30 different countries combined to prevent Iraq from annexing Kuwait, and taking a step closer to creating one Arab nation. Crude oil prices spiked immediately due to a decline in Iraqi oil production. The stagflation that resulted from rising unemployment and rising gas prices crippled the economy. The public originally thought the war would last a few months but as it waged on into the following year, there was talk of reinstituting a military draft. There was concern within the black community over the high percentage of African Americans on the front lines. I had not formed my own opinion of the war but one observation stood out to me – it had just been a little over a decade ago that the U.S. was at odds with Iran during the hostage crisis. We even tried to get Iraq to help us in our fight against Iran. Then just when we started hating Iran, the government was now trying to get Iran to help us fight against Iraq. From what I could tell, the one constant in the entire chain of events was the United States. I later researched our dealings with both countries and it all came down to oil – our need to control it and ensure that we always had a steady supply of it. Regardless of the fact pattern, when the U.S. sends troops into a foreign country that country more often than not has some type of natural resource (oil, zinc, cobalt, diamonds, etc.) that we covet. Nonetheless, when the Gulf War ended in February 1991, President Bush's expertise in international affairs was solidified and his approval rating so high that the media thought it foolhardy to oppose him when he sought reelection.

Commercial Real Estate Debacle

Commercial real estate prices cratered in 1990. The debacle started in New England, hit New York, Washington, D.C. and then touched down in Texas. At least twice a week *The Washington Post* wrote a scathing article about a real estate developer that had just gone bankrupt, and listed the banks he owed and the amount of the loans in default. And each time I would see Sovran named as one of the lenders. I figured it would not take long before we would feel the impact at the branch level. Sovran merged with C&S National Bank of Atlanta in September 1989; it was dubbed "a merger of equals." It was really designed to thwart a takeover of C&S by NCNB, which had made a hostile attempt during the spring of 1989. In the second quarter of 1990, Sovran's "nonperforming" real estate loans increased from $130 million to $250 million. By year-end they were $400 million and by the first quarter of 1991, they had climbed to $1.1 billion. Enraged at the hit to earnings, management from C&S took control of the merged entity and carved out a separate group in the bank to deal solely with loan workouts. Also during the first quarter of 1991, a bank executive informed us that there would be branch closings and a potential impact on employees. I had suspected it for some time, but the staff was horrified. A few branches had already been shut down, and each day brought new rumors about who was next on the chop block. After the bank executive's presentation, I asked him how he could expect us to be penalized for the mistakes of the real estate finance group. It was my first introduction into how corporations work – the mistakes roll downhill. The following factors led to the crisis and caused the failures of banks and S&Ls throughout the country.

Blind Optimism

The credo of the 1980s real estate developer was "build it and they will come." Meanwhile, S&Ls made commercial real estate loans up to 100% of a property's asset value, and banks made millions in loans to developers without requiring the property as collateral. Such high-risk, no-money-down, or no-collateral loans prompted S&L regulator, William K. Black, to tell Congress it was easier to secure a $50 million speculative loan than a $50,000 mortgage. In the Washington, D.C. area, real estate developers were building strip malls next to other strip malls that had not been fully rented. Maybe a *Washington Post* article best summed up the blind optimism that led to the real estate debacle of the '80s:

> Those who failed to realize that retail developers were adding too much space to the marketplace either were naïve or relied too heavily on unrealistic growth projections. In either case, it's obvious that all market studies weren't based on economic trends that began to emerge after 1986 . . . They put too much stock in the self-congratulatory fodder that was being fed into the area's promotional machinery during the 1980s . . . The retail market is a casualty of the same syndrome that produced the massive oversupply of office space: blind optimism and too much space for demand.[4]

Bank of New England Failure

In 1989 bank regulators raided the Bank of New England due to its alarming overconcentration of real estate loans. By the end of the fourth quarter its chairman, Walter Connolly, was forced to resign and the bank later posted a staggering $1.2 billion quarterly loss. "Under the gun for their belated handling of BNE, regulators came down like gangbusters on institutions throughout the country, virtually cutting off bank credit for real estate transactions. 'That just killed the market,' said [John] Reed. 'From then on you couldn't sell buildings for love or money.' If the credit crunch and the recession that it triggered needed a starting date, the 1989 examination of the Bank of New England was it. Reed would later describe the downturn as a 'regulatory recession.'"[5] The credit crunch that ensued from the commercial real estate debacle suppressed future lending, and helped choke off economic growth. The financial losses realized by banks and S&Ls resulted in hundreds of thousands of job losses, adding to the unemployment rate.

Leverage Buyout Craze

The 1980s saw the biggest corporate takeover boom in the history of the U.S. William Simon's (former Secretary of the Treasury) 1981 acquisition of Gibson Greetings in which he acquired the company and sold it a few years later at multiples of his investment, sparked envy and invited competition. The strategy was to acquire a company by investing 20%-30% equity and borrowing the rest. Post-transaction, you could cut expenses by selling the corporate jets, laying off employees, and removing the water coolers. Once you increased cash flow, you could sell the company years later at a higher price, pay off debt and earn an attractive return on your investment. The fuel that drove corporate takeovers was high-yield debt ("junk bonds") revolutionized by Michael Milken of Drexel

Burnham Lambert. Milken popularized the theory that a diversified portfolio of high-risk, low-rated bonds could deliver a higher return than a portfolio of blue-chip bonds. The attractive gains from a diversified portfolio could more than offset the losses on one or two of the junk bonds. Milken tested his theory by selling high-yield bonds used to fund LBOs to insurance companies, S&Ls and other investors in search of high-yielding assets. For all his ambition and genius, Milken will probably be remembered more for his greed and disregard for U.S. securities laws. In 1989 Milken was indicted on 98 counts of racketeering and stock manipulation charges related to insider trading. The end of Milken's career on Wall Street marked the beginning of the political career of Rudy Giuliani – the young, ambitious lawyer for the Department of Justice who led the investigation. Nonetheless, Milken's prosecution left a void in the high-yield bond market which could best be described as "directionless."

By the late 1980s, LBOs became larger, more complex and more poorly structured than the Gibson Greetings transaction. They also became less about making corporations more efficient – the emphasis turned to generating fee income for bankers who structured them. Gibson Greetings may have defined the beginning of the LBO craze, but Campeau Corporation and "The Burning Bed" marked the end of it. Campeau was comprised of Allied Stores and Federation Department Stores – owner of Bloomingdale's. In September 1989 Campeau was unable to make payments on the debt obligations it incurred pursuant to the LBOs of the department stores; it was also unable to buy Christmas merchandise and was looking to obtain financing elsewhere. The announcement drove down junk bond prices further and was an embarrassment to First Boston, the firm that underwrote Campeau's junk bond transaction. Prior to the Campeau disclosure, First Boston had withdrawn a $475 million junk bond offering for Ohio Mattress Co. because of lukewarm interest, and had twice extended the offering deadline for AMI International's junk bonds.[6] In March 1990 First Boston sold to its French parent company, CS Holding, half its $450 million short-term loan ("bridge loan") to Ohio Mattress. The bridge loan was designed to facilitate the Ohio Mattress LBO, and was to be repaid later from a high-yield debt issuance. The high-yield issuance never occurred after the junk bond market cratered, resulting in a "hung deal." Afterward, bond traders affectionately named the Ohio Mattress transaction "The Burning Bed." Once the LBO market cratered, companies saddled with debt laid off thousands of employees to make those highly leveraged transactions work. Banks, saddled with high-risk paper they were unable to unload onto investors, experienced billions in charge-offs. This led to more lay-offs and accelerated the credit-crunch that followed.

The Perfect Storm
I sat at my desk contemplating the slowdown in the U.S. economy and how it would eventually become intractable. Declining GDP, rising unemployment and rising gasoline prices resulting from the Gulf War had created the "perfect storm" – stagflation. I had learned about stagflation in Townsend's economics class but never imagined I would experience it firsthand.

Vital Signs

I examined the 10-year period between 1986 and 1995 to illustrate the deterioration in the economy's vital signs. I chose big-ticket items that drive the economy like housing starts and auto sales, and compared them to the real growth in GDP in 2005. "Real GDP" in this example, measures the price of a collection of goods and services in each given year as compared to the price of a similar collection of goods and services in the 2005 reference year. I then illustrated the impact real GDP growth had on unemployment.

Housing Starts-to-GDP

Though 1990 was the year businesses acknowledged the recession, the economy started on a downward spiral in 1987. Housing starts (single and multi-family) declined a little over 10% from 1.8 million in 1986 to 1.6 million in 1987. They hit a trough of 1.0 million in 1991 and trended upward to 1.4 million in 1995. The Federal Reserve began lowering interest rates in 1991, which may have helped starts. That said, housing starts still never dipped below 1.0 million during the review period.

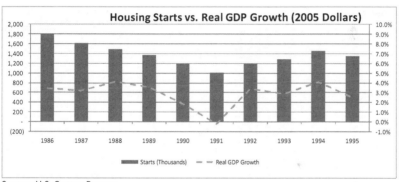

Source: U.S. Census Bureau
Real GDP from World Bank Development Indicators and IMF at 1/26/2012

Automobile Sales

Auto sales declined from 16.2 million in 1987 to 15.3 million in 1988. Though they increased in 1989, auto sales never reached their 1987 peak during the period. They hit a trough in 1991 of 12.5 million and ramped up from there. The trajectory of auto sales during the period seemed to mirror that of housing starts.

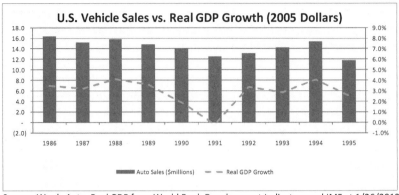

Source: Wards Auto, Real GDP from World Bank Development Indicators and IMF at 1/26/2012

Unemployment

The unemployment rate declined gradually from 7.0% in 1986 to 5.6% in 1990. It ticked up to 6.8% and 7.5% in 1991 and 1992, respectively. The rate seemed to lag the decline in real GDP growth. 1990 (1.9%) and 1991 (-0.2%) were the years with the lowest GDP growth, and 1991 (6.8%) and 1992 (7.5%) were the years with the highest unemployment percentage during the period.

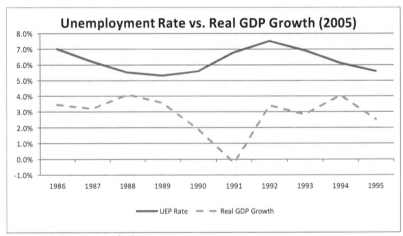

Source: U.S. Department of Labor
Real GDP from World Bank Development Indicators and IMF at 1/26/2012

Real GDP Growth

Real GDP growth was flat from 1986 to 1989 and declined precipitously in 1990 and 1991, consistent with declines in housing starts. This would make sense being that housing starts and auto sales are large components of GDP.

Oil Prices

Amplifying the pain of the recession were the oil shocks caused by the Gulf War, and the corresponding increases in gasoline prices. Average U.S. crude oil prices increased from $18.33 per barrel in 1989 to $23.19 per barrel in 1990. Gulf tensions may have actually been priced in by 1989 because in the prior year, average U.S. crude oil prices were only $14.87 per barrel. That said, the average retail gasoline price, just $0.91 per gallon in 1988, spiked to $1.13 per gallon in 1990 and never declined below $1.07 per gallon again during the review period (1986 to 1995).

I tried to understand the culprit of the uncertainty and pain the American public was experiencing. The stagflation of 1991-1992 would ultimately cost President George W. Bush his job, regardless of his initial approval ratings. All signs for the "perfect storm" kept pointing back to one man – Ronald Reagan.

Reagan Revolution

I watched the 1980 presidential election in the living room with my mother. We watched as the states rolled in – Reagan was defeating President Jimmy Carter by a landslide. But there was still hope. Up next was Virginia, which has always been a Republican state. When the screen showed Reagan had taken Virginia by a huge margin and it was clear that he was going to be the next president, Suzie exclaimed "Black folks are going to catch hell now!" I slid over out of arms' reach and asked, "Why?" Never even turning to look at her smart-aleck teenaged son, she said cryptically, "Just wait and see." Suzie was a Democrat, just like every other black person I had ever met, but I was ecstatic that Reagan had won. Reagan's victory speech on November 4, 1979 was exactly one year after the Iran hostage crisis in which students took over the American embassy in Iran, and held 52 American diplomats hostage (November 4, 1978). When I first learned about the hostage crisis, my reaction was, "Who would be foolish enough to pick a fight with the United States?" News reports showed an Islamic cleric named Ayatollah Khomeini screaming and chanting about the U.S. He had what seemed like millions of Iranians hovered around him in a frenzied state. Physically the Ayatollah looked old and feeble; he had a long gray beard, clearly no match for Carter. I figured Jimmy Carter would flex U.S. military muscle, get the hostages back and the Ayatollah would be sorry he ever messed with us.

However, it never happened. Days turned into weeks and weeks turned into months, with no action. Carter tried diplomacy – no deal. He applied economic sanctions on Iran, refusing to buy their oil. Nothing worked. And the longer it went on the more powerful Khomeini appeared and the more inept Carter looked. Then to add insult to injury, in April 1980 Carter attempted a rescue mission, Operation Desert One, which failed miserably. Two of the eight helicopters used for the mission malfunctioned in a sandstorm. . . Unbelievable! In all our infinite wisdom, my classmates and I would sit around and pontificate about what Carter "should have done" to free the hostages. I loved Jimmy Carter. We all did. When he rationed out gasoline to combat rising gasoline prices, it was an inconvenience but we stayed the course. I can still remember (i) how cars with odd-numbered license plates could buy gas on certain days and even-numbered plates on others and (ii) news reports of cars in miles-long lines out in California waiting to buy gas. But it did not matter though. We had to persevere for the good of the country and because Jimmy Carter asked us to. However, this failed attempt to free the hostages had embarrassed the country and made us look weak. For that, Carter had to go!

Besides, Reagan had a plan. He was going to balance the budget, which I thought was very responsible. And he was going to get people off welfare and make them get a job. This message resonated with seemingly all of White America, but it resonated with a lot of blacks also. Reagan made the term "Welfare Queen" famous during his campaign and referred to her at every stop.

> There's a woman in Chicago . . . She has 80 names, 30 addresses, 12 Social Security cards and is collecting veterans' benefits on four nonexisting deceased husbands . . . And she's collecting Social Security on her cards. She's got Medicaid, getting food stamps and she is collecting welfare under each of her names. Her tax-free cash income alone is over $150,000.[7]

We know today that Reagan totally sensationalized a story about Susan Taylor, who was discovered by the chairman of a committee investigating welfare abuses. Ms. Taylor had used only four aliases and the fraud was more like $8,000 – not the $150,000 that had been alleged. The image of the "Welfare Queen" dragging down the country had been brandished in the American psyche, right next to the image of the Iranian hostages. Minutes after Reagan's acceptance speech, the Ayatollah released the hostages. Reagan was like a modern-day John Wayne – he talked tough and he could back it up. Khomeini was clearly afraid of what Reagan would have done to him. At least that was how it appeared to me. We know now that the timing of the hostage release had nothing to do with Reagan, and everything to do with the Iranians wanting to further punish and embarrass Carter.

What Reagan Said Would Happen

30% Across-the-Board Personal Income Tax Cut
During the presidential campaign, Reagan proposed a reduction in the federal income tax rate of 30% over three years and a liberalization of corporate depreciation allowances that would allow companies to depreciate property, plant and equipment faster, reducing their taxable income. In earlier speeches, Reagan had originally stated the tax cuts would generate enough revenue to pay for themselves, but later estimated that "tax cuts, amounting to $172 billion by 1985, would stimulate economic growth only enough to bring in $39 billion in additional tax revenue."[8] Carter predicted Reagan's tax cut was a mistake and that Reagan would eventually abandon the plan. He also predicted that Reagan's plan for cutting taxes and increasing military spending would lead to a reduction in social programs. In order to balance the budget, Reagan had to reduce entitlements if he delivered on the other two promises (tax cuts, military spending). However, Carter was assuming that Reagan planned to actually balance the budget once in office. Even Republican congressmen thought Reagan was using "smoke and mirrors."[9]

No Reduction in Entitlement Spending

Boxed in by Carter's claims that his tax cuts to the wealthy and increased military spending would come at the expense of social programs, Reagan promised not to reduce entitlement spending. However, he promised savings from (i) tighter administration of eligibility requirements for welfare and unemployment compensation and (ii) savings from military spending where there was a lot of waste.[10]

A Balanced Budget by 1985

Based on budget projections, Reagan promised the following once elected: (i) a $27 billion deficit in 1981 with the possibility of it falling to $23 billion if aggressive cost cuts were achieved, and (ii) a budget surplus of $93 billion by 1985.

What Actually Happened

Reduction in Taxes

Reagan introduced a tax bill that included (i) an across-the-board cut in personal income taxes of 25%, (ii) accelerated depreciation for businesses which lowered taxable income and ultimately, taxes payable to the government. His tax reduction lowered revenue from 1982 to 1990 by approximately $1.9 trillion.[11]

$0 Additional Revenue From the Tax Cuts

Reagan had become a disciple of "supply-side economics" whereby (i) you provided tax cuts to businesses and the wealthy and (ii) the additional spending and investing provided by the tax cuts would create additional tax revenue in the future. The theory that the tax cuts would pay for themselves was put forth by Professor Art Laffer, the father of supply-side economics. However, Reagan's budget director, David Stockman, admitted the theory was pure folly, albeit after the fact:

> Laffer and [Jude] Wanniski, the two high priests of supply side, sometimes argued that the tax cuts would pay for themselves. They implied the Treasury would take in *more* after the tax cuts than before. I never bought that literally and didn't think they did, either. I put it down to salesmanship.[12]

The Democrats had lobbied for a one-year tax cut only, limited to those making $50,000 or less. However, Stockman rejected the proposal outright saying it was counter to the tenets of the Reagan Revolution and represented a "redistribution of wealth."

Bait and Switch

The tax cuts and economic growth that were below Reagan's original budget projections had some economists predicting a budget deficit of up to $70 billion in 1982. To offset this, Reagan proposed budget cuts of $16 billion which included, but were not limited to (i) $7 billion in "discretionary" funding appropriated annually for government programs and operations, (ii) $5 billion by delaying cost-of-living increases in entitlement programs, (iii) $1.5 billion in

77

reductions in Medicare, Medicaid and aid to low-income families with dependent children, and (iv) $300 million by reducing the federal work force.

Increase in Military Spending

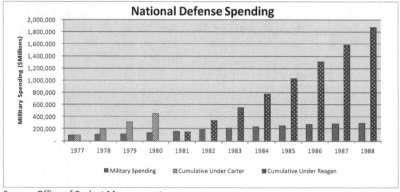

Source: Office of Budget Management

The Cold War with Russia was at a fever pitch, leading to a military arms race. Cumulative military spending during the Carter years was $452 billion. Reagan almost doubled this amount during his first four years to $780.1 billion; he spent nearly $1.9 trillion during his two terms. Runaway military spending was partly the result of a budgeting error by David Stockman, Reagan's budget director. When submitting the fiscal year 1983 five-year budget projections, Stockman made a calculation error that budgeted $1.46 trillion for Department of Defense ("DOD") spending. Stockman naively assumed the DOD would adjust the projections downward, saying "For the moment, however, I was eager and ready for a new budget blitz, and getting the defense numbers back into line would be the first order of business. The professional defense staff at OMB was delighted at the prospect. They had been shocked and incredulous in February when we handed over $1.46 trillion to the DOD . . . It was obvious that the numbers we had in the budget were flagrantly excessive as a matter of pure fiscal responsibility."[13] Once Caspar ("Cap") Weinberger, Secretary of Defense, saw the budgeted numbers, he and his military generals conveniently found ways to spend it. During a showdown between Stockman and Weinberger over the best way to trim the defense budget, Cap dug in; he implied that a reduction would cause us to fall behind Russia in the arms race. Not wanting to give the impression of backing down on the defense build-up, Reagan sided with Cap. Of the $1.9 trillion in military spending during the Reagan era, over $1.5 trillion was spent during his last five years in office – all due to a budgeting error.

Nearly Three-fold Increase in Federal Debt

Reagan's eight-year tenure was marked by cumulative deficit spending of over $1.3 trillion. In addition, the federal debt increased almost three-fold from $994.8 billion (36.6% of GDP) to $2.6 trillion (51.9% of GDP). While the arms race with Russia may not have broken the U.S., it definitely brought the domestic economy to the brink. Reagan's massive deficit spending mortgaged the country's future, prompting Stockman to deride him publicly. Widely thought of as one of the authors of Reagan's economic policy, Stockman backtracked – "Yet here he was telling the Atlantic that 'none of us really understands' the numbers in the budget . . . This time Stockman told *Fortune* magazine that the president was wrong to expect to cut nondefense spending any further in an effort to reduce the deficit, which he thinks should be done. He thinks the way is to cut defense spending and consider tax increases, both of which the president opposes."[14] By 1984 Suzie's ominous words, "Just wait and see," seemed rather prescient. Disillusioned with the "Reagan Revolution" that was not, Stockman resigned as director of OMB in August of 1985. The federal debt in relation to GDP during Reagan's tenure is below.

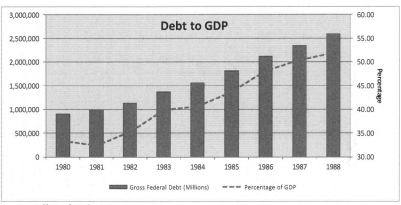

Source: Office of Budget Management

Savings & Loan Scandal

Savings & Loans (S&Ls), also known as "thrifts," specialized in taking deposits and using the funds to make mortgages and consumer loans. Their ownership was usually mutually held, i.e. depositors and borrowers had voting rights and made financial and managerial decisions. In this way, S&Ls existed for the benefit of the depositors and borrowers. By law, 65% of their loans was required to be in mortgages and consumer loans. They essentially took in demand deposits on a short-term basis and loaned it out for long-term 30-year mortgages. In accordance with Regulation Q of the Glass-Steagall Act of 1933, S&Ls were also prohibited from offering interest rates on deposits above a certain limit. Such low deposit rates allowed them to offer low-rate mortgages and still earn "net interest income" (interest income on loans less interest expense on deposits). This arrangement existed fine until the high interest rate environment during the Carter Administration prevailed. Other financial institutions were able to offer market rates to savers that exceeded those offered by S&Ls. This led to rapid disintermediation as former S&L depositors moved assets to money market accounts tied to higher-paying treasury securities. In response, Congress deregulated interest rates in 1980 to prevent a "run on the bank." However, while S&Ls increased their cost of funds by paying higher savings rates, they could not increase their interest income in unison – they were locked into long-term mortgages.

Because most S&L mortgage-loan portfolios still were laden with long-term loans fixed at old, low rates, the average yield on S&L loans rose much slower than their average savings rate. To help S&Ls transition their loan portfolios to higher yielding products in the immediate term, Congress passed the Garn-St. Germain Act of 1982 to broaden their investment options and encourage them to sell their low fixed rate mortgage portfolios at deep discounts. Hundreds of S&Ls were driven into insolvency and the Federal Home Loan Bank Board ("FHLBB"), which regulated federally chartered thrifts, allowed healthy S&Ls to acquire those that had failed. Over 1,000 S&Ls were eventually closed, at a cost to taxpayers of approximately $520 billion.[15] In addition, incentives to spur commercial real estate development added to the frothiness of the commercial real estate market and lax underwriting standards. High-yield bonds were the other investments of choice for many S&Ls. First Executive and Columbia Savings poured so much money into high-yield bonds sold by Drexel that they became puppets of Milken. At times, they ceded control to Milken and allowed him to act as buyer and seller of securities on their behalf and invest in high-yield issues doomed to fail. S&Ls' insatiable appetite for junk bonds helped fuel the greatest takeover boom in the history of the country and lined Milken's pockets – in one year he earned $550 million on fees from junk bond issuance.

Attack African Americans

Reagan's so-called war on drugs turned out to be nothing more than a war on African Americans. The increase in incarceration for low-level drug offenders and mandatory sentencing led to black men becoming the most incarcerated group in the world. The policy has eradicated entire families and has threatened to eliminate the African-American race as we know it. In September 2011, *The Wall Street Journal* was so "concerned" that it even had a forum where experts advised African-American women to seek out white males for marriage partners. On the surface, Reagan's rhetoric on reducing "big government" appeared sound. Yet, even Stockman acknowledged that, "We weren't going to solve a $60 to $100 billion deficit problem by dumping a few thousand useless federal employees, which would reduce the federal payroll by only $3 billion. There just weren't enough of them to amount to serious dollar savings."[16] The lion's share of those government jobs was filled by African Americans and for them, a "good government job" was the only avenue to middle-class status. The poet, Langston Hughes, once said, "The post office killed a lot of dreams." He worked in the post office in Topeka, Kansas; his family thought he was crazy at the mere thought of leaving his "good government job" and suggested that he forget about poetry. He eventually moved to Harlem, and became part of the Harlem Renaissance. When Reagan said "big government was bad," what African Americans heard was "Reagan wants to put us out of work."

Fallout

The fallout from the Reagan era of deficit spending, Laffer Curves and blind optimism was failed banks, layoffs, and a deteriorating economy. C&S/Sovran, the merger designed to thwart the hostile takeover of C&S by NCNB, was hampered by over $1 billion of failed commercial real estate loans. To survive,

C&S/Sovran was paired with a healthy NCNB to form NationsBank, the second largest bank in the country; in effect, Hugh McColl essentially acquired both banks in one fell swoop. At the time, banking experts thought the country had too many banks. With over 12,000 banks, the U.S. had 50 banks per one million people, while Britain and pre-unification Germany had six each, and France had eight.[17] However, the fragmentation in the banking industry allowed regulators to merge failing banks with participants that avoided the concentration in commercial real estate loans and LBOs.

On one afternoon in January 1991 I received a phone call at my desk. I just stared at the phone, wondering if it was Mrs. Green, the draft board, or a bank executive with news of our office being closed. I picked it up and took a deep breath. The voice on the other end said, "Hi Ralph this is Jon Megibow from the Darden School. I just wanted to congratulate you on being accepted to the Darden class of 1993." I was so excited that I dropped the phone and jumped about 10 feet into the air. When I collected myself, Megibow (head of admissions) quipped, "Does that mean you accept?" Thereafter, whenever we crossed paths at Darden Megibow would point at me and start chuckling. The next month I was at home hanging out. My cousin Roger happened to be back in town so I made a beeline Up the House. He was now in the military and I had not seen him in a few years. When we were kids he used to toss me around like a rag doll, but I was grown man now. I knew he would eventually challenge me to a game of basketball. He wanted to know what a small college All-American looked like up close, so I showed him. Worn out from all that physical activity, we just relaxed for the rest of the evening and talked about old times and about the future. Around 8 p.m. Grandma was complaining about pains in her chest. She was rushed to the hospital and that was the last time we saw her alive. The following Saturday, the morning of Grandma's funeral, I was awakened to my sister screaming and my cousin Pattie trying to console her. I never moved. It was clear to me that Suzie's premonition had come true. I was happy that at least she had lived long enough to see her kids grow into young adults. I knew exactly what to do; she had been preparing us for this all of our lives. I just became more resolute in fulfilling the promise I had made about business school. I took some time off and returned to the bank pretty much numb. In two years it was the first time I had ever missed a day from work.

I eventually solved the bottleneck at the Suitland Office – I simply had the employees over at the Census Bureau help out. The offices had always operated separately as "us" and "them." However, we were there to serve customers and their needs came first. Once I had gotten the Census Bureau on board, everything else fell into place. Employees from both offices were operating as a team – something no one could have envisioned beforehand. Mrs. Green even praised me for the great job I had done in turning the place around and lamented that after all I been through and all I had learned, I was about to leave. Shortly before departing, I received a call from Carlton. He told me how well he was doing in the sales and trading area, to which I congratulated him. He also told me some crazy news about Mr. Bentley. The guy had befriended an elderly

Caucasian woman – a customer of the trust department. This fool moved into the woman's house and was living rent-free. I shuddered to think of what benefits she was getting out of the arrangement, and of what state of mind Bentley had to have been in to think he would ever get away with it. The woman's children complained to the bank's higher-ups that Bentley had taken advantage of her, and pilfered tens of thousands of dollars from her trust account. All I could say was, "This boy wants to go to the pen, doesn't he?" I just started cracking up at how he had been running around the training program blowing his own horn – I never bought that nonsense for a minute. I told Carlton that all was okay in the D.C. area and cut the conversation short. The last time I ever saw him was about a year and a half later. I was leaving class during my second year at Darden and bumped into him as he was entering the building. He ran up like I was a lighthouse in stormy seas – "Hey Ralph! It's Carlton from Sovran! How's it going man? I just had my first interview. I'm still with the bank . . . but I want to come to Darden. Can you put in a good word for me with the people in admissions?" I was startled for a second. I listened briefly and feigned interest. I walked off wondering to myself how funny life was. "Mr. Corporate" who had lamented about my having been shipped off to the "Russian Front" now needed my help. Let's just put it this way, I don't think he got accepted.

TOP GUN

I sold my BMW, packed up everything I owned and headed down to Charlottesville. The first week we had a few social gatherings with fellow classmates and professors. The atmosphere was what I would describe as "electric." There were students from MIT, Harvard, UVA, Howard, UNC, and William & Mary with type "A" personalities and interesting backgrounds. It reminded me somewhat of the movie *Top Gun* where Maverick's superior officer laments over having to send him to train at the Navy's flight weapons school. I may have accidentally contributed to the *Top Gun* motif. The first day of class the professor asked us to write whatever name you wanted to be called (nicknames included) on our nametags. I was stiff and official at the bank and used Darden as a chance to learn and have fun; I wrote "Silk" on my nametag. By the end of the first week I was chatting with a second-year black student who informed me that "somebody was running around calling himself 'Silk.'" I quickly changed the subject and walked off. Darden was small and intimate with less than 500 students, half the size of other business schools. The school operated via the case method that involved real-world dilemmas (cases). Where Wharton is the oldest business school in the country, Darden differentiated itself by working us half to death. It didn't just talk about providing a rigorous MBA experience; it gave us 14 cases a week – we had to work in teams just to complete the assignments. My daily routine was class from around 8:30 a.m. to 1 p.m. I worked on cases from 1:30 p.m. to 6:30 p.m. and met my study group at 8 p.m. The team included two finance guys, a statistician and a former soldier from the Swedish army. Nobody knew who to follow but since the statistician spoke the most forcefully and convinced us of his world-renown quantitative skills, we usually listened to him. The meetings went late into the night as we tried to get our analysis perfect. I would hit the bed around midnight, get to class at 8 p.m. and start the routine all over again. *SportsCenter* was my only vice during the week, while my roommate was hooked on *Star Trek: The Next Generation*. I used to laugh at how utterly ridiculous it was. By the end of the year, he had me hooked on it too. During the first two weeks about six people left school, citing "The intensity of the program and the workload were not what they had signed up for." As the news of the departures reverberated, it just made everybody more determined to finish the program.

Half our grade was based on class participation, so the strategy was to contribute to the discussion early and often. That way, you could avoid getting "cold-called," a process where the professor randomly called on you to present your analysis. Once you were cold-called in corporate finance or accounting, there would be an investment banker or a CPA who could potentially pick you apart. The professors would coax students into taking opposite sides of an argument and then watch the battle royal ensue. You could always tell when someone was winning an argument because classmates would join in to agree with his or her point of view. I enjoyed these types of discussions because it was the same format as at Hampden-Sydney. The "real world" dilemmas added more weight to the discussions. Sometimes the case writers attended class and told us how they actually handled situations presented to them. We met a corporate raider whose job was to deliver pink slips to employees being laid off at the takeover target. Buying companies, breaking them up, or laying off workers to make the "numbers work," sounded sexy in concept. However, decades of having to face laid-off workers prompted him to walk away from the deal business altogether. The guest speaker I remembered most was a former Procter & Gamble product manager who had left his job to develop a market for children's deodorant. The product was a sell to parents and kids – it promoted good hygiene at an early age. He secured financial backing to manufacture the product and get it onto grocery store shelves – half the battle. In response, larger competitors copied his idea and used their marketing clout to secure the majority of the shelf space in supermarkets. They let him use his blood, sweat and tears to create this new market, then they came in and crowded him out. After years of living a Spartan lifestyle, then conceding defeat to the competition, he came home one day and saw that his wife had packed up all of her belongings and left . . . no note, no explanation. She had signed on to marry a Procter & Gamble product manager with a steady paycheck, not some maverick with a pipe dream. The manner in which he described her stealing away in the middle of the night was pretty hilarious, yet the point had been made. The majority of stories of entrepreneurship you hear about are the successes. You rarely hear about the failures and the personal tolls they take on peoples' lives.

Our entire world consisted of cases. Whenever my girlfriend came to visit I felt sorry for her. She would mention the goings on outside of Darden and we would all look dumbfounded. At the time, the psyche of U.S. business had been bludgeoned. We trailed the Japanese in every known metric and many of the cases involved understanding their management style and business practices. We particularly chafed over Japan's dominance of the global auto industry. The irony was that the tools Japan used to outperform us had been created in the U.S., yet ignored by U.S. auto manufacturers. Bored as a financial analyst at Ford in the 1950s, James D. Power III left the company to pursue his passion for consumer marketing. His J.D. Power and Associates ("J.D. Power") conducted customer surveys for various products, including automobiles. Ignored by U.S. automakers, J.D. Power's Customer Satisfaction Index ("CSI") was used by Toyota and other Japanese firms as a rough measure of the problems customers encountered with their cars, how customers were treated by dealers, and customer preferences.[1] Power pitched his CSI to the "Big Three" automakers but they gave him the cold shoulder. Detroit's cold reception to outsiders was not new. It "was eerily similar to the reception W. Edwards Deming got in Detroit decades earlier when he tried to teach statistical methods for the factory and the impact of management theory on product quality. The men of Detroit disregarded Deming even while Japanese industrialists were embracing his methods and continuously improving quality."[2] The oil shock of the late 1980s created a need for compact, fuel-efficient cars that could travel farther on a gallon of gas than U.S. autos. While high gas prices were a lucky accident for the likes of Toyota, Honda and Datsun, the customer satisfaction and loyalty they generated were not. For over a decade they had focused on improving customer satisfaction and reducing defects. American consumers gave these cars a try for their fuel efficiency, but were pleasantly surprised by how well made they were. After constantly hearing about Japan's dominance and America's ineptness during class discussions, I had had enough. A classmate who had previously worked in Japan was going on again about how they "do it in Japan." Speaking solely on emotion, I suggested that Japan would eventually get its comeuppance; its economy could not maintain its current trajectory and would eventually overheat due to hubris or a buying spree gone amok. Its economy has been in a period of deflation ever since. I practically willed it so.

Yet our own country's deteriorating economic condition also crept into the class discussions. In Mark Eaker's economics class we discussed a historic period of "stagflation" – rising unemployment and rising costs – not felt since the Nixon administration. It was also imperative to understand the economic cycle we were experiencing in order to help guide our business decisions post-Darden. Bob Conroy, finance professor, brought in an article describing the credit crunch the business community was experiencing. Reeling from their recent loan loss experience, banks thought it was a better business decision to invest in treasury securities than to make loans. This phenomenon (i) further exacerbated the recession because companies could not secure loans to grow their businesses and (ii) had the potential to create future losses if rising interest rates caused banks' cost of funds to exceed the yield on their treasury securities. Some banks were in such dire straits that they were more than willing to take that risk. The real world implications of a dire economy hit us in the face after the first semester – we had to find summer jobs. The three to four job offers that MBAs enjoyed during the "go-go '80s" were no more. There was a near mutiny after the class of 1992 faced the stark reality of leaving business school unemployed. The career services department was under tremendous pressure to deliver the equivalent of life rafts to passengers on a sinking Titanic. While my mission was to learn as much as I could in my two years in Charlottesville, others had planned ahead and built relationships with the decision makers at companies prior to Darden. I decided that corporate finance/mergers & acquisitions would be the path, with the hopes that one day I could put my own deal together.

AMF Sewn Products

I interviewed with several investment banks and commercial banks prior to landing a job with AMF Companies for the summer. The incessant interviews paid off. I met with Bill Goodwin, one of the heads of the investor group that purchased AMF Bowling and the AMF name from Irwin Jacobs, a well-known LBO investor. The bowling alleys generated substantial cash flow that AMF used to invest elsewhere. AMF had a Sewn Products unit that made sewing machines used for stitching high-end clothing. AMF salespeople were required to stay abreast of the needs of its customer base, the competition and industry trends. The newest talk of the apparel industry involved cumulative trauma disorders (CTDs) suffered by workers from repetitive motion within the sewing operations; CTDs had come on the radar of the Occupational Safety and Health Administration (OSHA). In response, apparel companies were making huge investments in ergonomic equipment, tables and chairs, in particular, to decrease the number of stress-related injuries. Ergonomic equipment commanded premium prices – $1,500 to $3,000 per worker – yet represented huge savings when weighed against the cost of workers' compensation claims, losses in productivity, and OSHA fines. AMF Sewn Products thought the ergonomic equipment market would be a high growth, "add-on" product for the company. The CEO, a Harvard Business School grad, wanted me to determine the best way for them to enter the marketplace – via acquisition or by building the equipment themselves. He gave me an open-ended assignment and said to "go figure it out."

The AMF sales force and engineers brought me up to speed on the apparel industry and AMF's major competitors. I called every major ergonomic equipment manufacturer and told them I was student performing industry research – you would be surprised at how much information companies give to students. They loved to talk about themselves and gave me more information than I asked for – sales figures and price points. I then built some high-level valuation models to determine how much it would cost to acquire each of the entities. For most of the targets, I only had revenue figures so I had to make assumptions for operating income. The next step was to determine the cost to build the equipment internally. I met with the sales and engineering departments again to ascertain the unit costs and price points that we could market the equipment for. I backed into the number of units we had to sell in order to recoup our up-front investment. The units sold equated to a certain "rate of penetration," i.e. the percentage of the installed base of customers expected to adopt the equipment. In comparing the merits of a "buy" versus "build" scenario, I met with the CEO and CFO directly; they helped fine-tune the analysis. I finished the project with a presentation to AMF senior management on a "wish list" of about 10 acquisition targets ranked by (i) potential synergies with AMF, (ii) product differentiation, and (iii) size. It was a very rewarding project and a precursor of what was to come.

Wall Street or Bust
When I was not reading trade magazines from the apparel industry, I was reading books to help me learn more about Wall Street. I did not just read them; I devoured them – *Greed and Glory on Wall Street: The Fall of the House of Lehman, Our Crowd, The Predators' Ball, Liar's Poker, Barbarians at the Gate, Den of Thieves* and the history of Salomon Brothers. But my favorite was *The House of Morgan*, written by Ron Chernow in 1990. It chronicled John Pierpont Morgan's rise to captain of the American finance industry. Chernow traced J.P. Morgan's history from its roots as a merchant bank in the mid-1800s. He captured how events leading up to the stock market crash of 1929 and the Great Depression in the 1930s shaped U.S. securities laws that still last today. By the 1930s the public saw Wall Street as a giant casino rigged by professional traders, bankers and other insiders. Wall Street firms also developed a penchant for fleecing the public whenever its own investments turned sour. When Morgan's investment in railroad bonds deteriorated and depleted the firm's capital base, it

pawned stocks to the public via initial public offerings (IPOs). Morgan used the much-needed fee income it earned from the IPOs to offset the losses on its railroad bonds. Many of the companies it took public had weak business prospects; needless to say, the equity offerings performed poorly and Morgan was accused of "betraying the public trust." National City Company was even more brazen. It packaged its bad Latin American debt into bonds and sold them to small investors through its securities affiliates. Adding insult to injury, National City assured investors of the bonds' safety. "Bankers took on the image of garrulous hucksters. Among these men, there was a fad for foreign bonds, especially from Latin America, with small investors assured of their safety. The pitfalls were not exposed until later on, when it became known that Wall Street banks had taken their Latin American debt and packaged it in bonds that were sold through their securities affiliates. This would be a major motivating factor behind the Glass-Steagall Act's separation of the banking and securities businesses."[3]

In the early 1930s, Herbert Hoover waged war on Wall Street and what he saw as excessive speculation. During the presidential debates between Hoover and Franklin D. Roosevelt, Roosevelt blamed Hoover for creating a climate of recklessness on Wall Street that led to the stock market crash of 1929. Hoover countered by suggesting the separation of commercial banking and investment banking – "ring fencing" speculation on stocks and bonds. The public outrage against bankers drew to such a fever pitch that Carter Glass, a senator from Lynchburg, Virginia quipped: "One banker in my state attempted to marry a white woman and they lynched him."[3] Senator Glass and Representative Harry Steagall of Alabama formally introduced a bill to separate commercial and investment banking and the famous Glass-Steagall Act was signed in 1933, ushering in the "modern age" of commercial and investment banking.

I met with firms at the end of the summer and spoke to anybody who would listen to my story. I spent the majority of my second year in business school strapped to a plane seat going from interview to interview. I made it to the final round of interviews with Kidder, Peabody and Lehman Brothers. Kidder was a small, niche firm that had built an expertise in specific areas like oil and gas, and retailing. Lehman was known for its entrepreneurial spirit and M&A prowess. There was one other company that I had targeted as well – GECC. GECC was very active in LBO lending and financed the Gibson Greetings transaction mentioned earlier. Its training program and manufacturing approach to due diligence offered me the opportunity to learn the deal business from the ground up. Ultimately, I accepted an offer from them. I went out and bought me a Ford Festiva (the cheapest car I could find), packed up my belongings and headed to Stamford, Connecticut.

GE CAPITAL

My first week in Stamford a policeman stopped me while driving through town. I saw the officer in my rear view and tried to smoke him out with a few right turns when he finally pulled me over in my $3,500 Festiva. He asked me, "What are you doing in the state of Connecticut?" I surmised he was suspicious of my Virginia license plates. I told him I had just graduated from the top business school in the country and was starting a job with GE Capital in a few days. This was probably the last answer he had expected to hear. He paused for a moment, and clearly at a loss words, gave me back my license and drove off. I stayed temporarily in the cheapest motel I could find. About two doors down from my motel room was a bunch of activity, 24 hours a day. Whenever I walked past the room in question, the lodgers gave me the evil eye. The only reason I noticed is because they acted so suspiciously whenever they saw me, like I was the police or something. Imagine that – the police thought I was a criminal and the criminals thought I was the police. And just when I found an apartment I liked, that went awry too. A local real estate broker found one-half of a house for $675/month. I saw the place and wanted to move forward as quickly as possible. The only caveat was that the owner wanted to meet me first. We set up the meeting and the broker and I drove over. A lady came to the window and told us the owner was not there. We waited for about an hour when the broker offered to help me find another apartment. When I asked her, "Why, what's wrong with this one?" she looked at me like I was from outer space. It took me about six months to fully grasp why the owner never showed up. And that was my indoctrination to the Northeast.

Financial Institutions Group

GECC had a two-year training program and my first rotation was in the Financial Institutions Group ("FIG") in Stamford, Connecticut. FIG began its roots financing LBOs in the insurance sector. The highly leveraged transactions often allowed FIG to take a warrant position, i.e. the option to secure an equity stake at a point in the future. The group was so successful that it convinced Gary Wendt, GECC's CEO, to enter the insurance industry. The industry was going through a fair amount of upheaval at the time. The traditional multi-line insurance model where companies tried to be everything to everybody no longer worked. Attempting to sell life insurance, property and casualty, disability, and healthcare without the necessary economies of scale left many multi-line insurers questioning their expertise. GECC liked the asset management component of the insurance business and it had the capital and core competency in M&A to add scale across product lines and distribution channels. Insurance effectively represents a "promise to pay," so insurers must maintain the necessary capital to provide future benefit payouts. Many insurers still had high exposures to commercial real estate and new regulatory requirements were forcing them to disclose their true market values. In 1993 interest rates were the lowest they had been in decades and resulted in reduced sales for annuities and certain life insurance products with a savings component. To quote the group's Managing Director, "Rates can't fall from the floor." I had actually expected Alan

Greenspan, Federal Reserve Chairman, to raise rates that summer. General Electric's price-to-earnings ratio was above 23x, the highest in the company's history. The internal debate at the time was (i) should we use more of GE's stock for acquisitions since the price was so robust and (ii) the best way to expand into variable annuities and mutual funds given the public's appetite for equity investments.

FIG Strategy

GECC's insurance operations consisted of GNA Corporation, which it acquired from Weyerhaeuser in January 1993 for $525 million in stock. GNA gave GECC the opportunity to participate in the pre-retirement savings market – it was one of the largest marketers of tax-deferred annuities and proprietary mutual funds through banks and other financial institutions. Using GNA as a platform for consolidating acquisitions of annuity companies, FIG acquired United Pacific Life ("UPL") from Reliance Group Holdings in April 1993 for $550 million. UPL was a run-off block that had sold single premium deferred annuities through banks, S&Ls and independent agents. I quickly distinguished between buyers like GECC and advisors like Lehman or Kidder – the buyer had to live with the results. My first project was to analyze the actual financial performance of GNA as compared to the projections used to justify the deal. For my second assignment, I had to put together the top 300 insurance companies sorted by assets, capital, investment style and product line. I had to pour through reams of A.M. Best (insurance rating agency) books to compile the information. But it taught me a lot about the products, industry participants and their strategy. Though the GNA and UPL deals were successful, FIG knew it had to diversify the product line, expand the distribution channels and add back office scale. The senior deal guys used the screen to determine which companies fit the acquisition profile they were seeking.

A major issue I faced was the knowledge gap between me and the rest of the team. FIG had two managing directors, two vice presidents and an assistant vice president who in addition to the two acquisitions, had worked on the LBOs for GECC's Corporate Finance Group. I pored through A.M. Best books after hours, read every article I could get my hands on, and studied the differences in the accounting rules for statutory (used by insurance regulators) and GAAP (used by publicly traded companies). And the in-house financial models they used to analyze acquisitions were pretty hard to describe – 60-70 pages of income statements and balance sheets, by product line, in both statutory and GAAP accounting formats. The transactions had to meet GECC's internal hurdles of returns-on-equity after taking into account the company's funding costs. GECC was one of only two financial services companies rated "AAA" (J.P. Morgan was the other). Such a high credit rating allowed the company to issue commercial paper – short-term borrowings at rates well below rivals'. All acquisitions had to meet GECC's internal hurdle rates which imposed a certain level of discipline on the deal process. Yet the "art of the deal" was determining which assumptions the model were most sensitive to (interest rates, synergies, revenue growth), and how realistic they were. That said, the financial modeling was the lifeblood of the group. All of the senior members had gone through their own rite of passage, so to speak. That thing was humongous. All I saw were Lotus cells coming at me. The vice president I worked with was what I would describe as "unforgiving." He literally flogged me every day. He caught every shortcut I tried. He would take one look at the darn thing, call me into his office and say "fix it." And whenever I asked him a question he wouldn't answer me directly. Instead, he would ask me a series of questions that led me to the answer – sort of like in the movie *The Paper Chase* starring John Houseman. Not only did the numbers have to be correct but the presentation had to be perfect as well. I would crawl into bed sometimes as late as midnight, and wonder what I had just gotten myself into.

The upside was that you got to work on some interesting projects that were meaningful to the company. During "Project Calvary" GECC launched a proxy fight in order to pressure Calvary to accept its $2.2 billion ($55/share) bid. The negotiating tactic, known as the "bear hug," was all over *The Wall Street Journal*. Calvary's CEO accused GECC of being a corporate raider and suggested that we mind our own business. Calvary was an insurance, brokerage and asset management conglomerate. Its stock price had been depressed due to losses in its real estate portfolio and underperforming brokerage business. The jewel was its asset management company with $70 billion in assets management (AUM), which alone was probably worth $2.2 billion. The proxy was led by GECC's Strategic Planning Group, yet some of the senior FIG members were also asked to assist. In true Shakespearean fashion, Conseco, an insurer and former GECC LBO client, trumped GECC's offer with a $67/share bid. One of its senior executives had actually run FIG a few years earlier. The media was none the wiser but there were undertones of the student (Conseco) trying to teach the teacher (GECC). Then there was Project Big Red, which involved the potential acquisition of one of the largest multi-line insurers in the country. Big Red's strategic partner had announced its intention to increase its ownership from around 20% to 100% at an advantageous price. GECC's higher-ups asked us to analyze a third party bid, taking advantage of the fact that Big Red was already "in play." The caveat was that we only had one week to complete the analysis of the $1 billion transaction. The entire team worked day and night and pulled together some good work on short notice, but senior management decided not to pull the trigger. The size of the transactions we analyzed was mind-numbing. The publicity surrounding our work made it all the more exciting.

Outside Events
My time in Stamford was interesting in several respects. The political climate was one that would shape the country for decades to come, and events outside of FIG would have an impact on my personal and professional outlook as well.

Race Baiting of America
After the Gulf War ended in March 1991, President H. W. Bush enjoyed a record-high approval rating of 89% and was hailed for his expertise in foreign affairs. As the U.S. unemployment rate reached 7.8%, he seemed oblivious to

the pain stagflation was inflicting on the country. Previously, Bush had made overtures to Alan Greenspan to lower interest rates to jumpstart the economy. After a January 1991 jobs report showed a loss of 232,000 jobs – a bigger loss than economists and the Fed had expected – Greenspan finally lowered the federal funds rate by 50 basis points. However, there was a lag period before banks reduced rates for prime loans and mortgages. President Bush's deemed apathy toward the recession opened the door for Bill Clinton to unseat him in the 1992 presidential election. Clinton's oratory skills and vision for America stoked memories of Kennedy's "Camelot." With Clinton's victory, the Democrats controlled Congress and the White House. The recession left many white-collar workers unemployed. Americans were used to blue-collar workers needing to retrain themselves or simply being out of work. However, the high level of unemployed white-collar workers was something new. The media inundated the public with stories of executives who, afraid the neighbors would find out they were unemployed, were too ashamed to check the mail during the day. The movie *Falling Down*, which captured the travails of William Foster (Michael Douglas), a divorced, unemployed defense contractor, was number one at the box office. Corporations' push for diversity left many white men feeling ostracized and gave credence to the myth of the "angry white male."

Republican Senator, Bob Dole, a leading candidate for the party's presidential nomination, played on the angry white male sentiment with repeated attacks against affirmative action. A regular on the evening news, Dole explained how minority set asides were making America inefficient. It was as if Dole was putting the recession, S&L crisis, budget deficits, real estate debacle, and busted LBOs at the feet of African Americans. He assumed affirmative action could drive a wedge through the Democratic Party by pitting white voters against African Americans – the party's staunchest constituency.[1] Dole introduced a bill to abolish affirmative action and eliminate all preferences for minorities and women. Attempting to one-up Dole, Republican Senator Phil Gramm vowed that as President, his first executive order would be to abolish affirmative action. Never ones to let the facts get in the way of a good argument, neither Dole nor Gramm ever pointed out that though white males made up only 15% of the country, they held over 95% of the corporate jobs. Seeing the danger in dividing the country between black and white, male and female, their Republican cohorts voted against the initiative.

A rising GOP star and congressman from Pennsylvania, Newt Gingrich had his own plan to overtake Congress. He crafted the famous "Contract With America," which outlined 10 initiatives Republicans would take if elected to Congress. The "contract" included but was not limited to (i) $45 billion in spending cuts for food stamps, Medicaid, Aid to Families with Dependent Children and other programs aimed at the poor, (ii) removing recipients off welfare after two years, (iii) $190 billion in tax cuts over five years, and (iv) a balanced budget. Gingrich said the contract had received a favorable response rate from the focus groups and that 300 or so congressional candidates had signed it. Yet the contract Gingrich claimed to have "co-authored" was not at all original; critics argued it was taken from excerpts of Reagan's 1985 presidential acceptance speech. Gingrich introduced the contract about six weeks prior to the midterm elections of November 1994 and it was successful beyond anyone's expectations. In the Senate, Republicans won eight additional seats and prompted Democratic Senator Richard Shelby of Alabama to switch parties. Meanwhile, they added 54 seats in Congress, resulting in Republican control of both Congress and the Senate for the first time in over 40 years. Gingrich was named Speaker of the House and lauded a "visionary" for his efforts.

Repeal of Glass-Steagall Act

After the Republicans' historic victory in November 1994, the question remained, "Could they govern effectively?" The revolution prompted Clinton White House Secretary, Dee Dee Myers, to exclaim, "The burden of government is now on them."[2] The Republicans immediately hedged on their ability to deliver on all of their campaign promises. The House candidates also admitted that the Senate, which had not signed onto the contract, would have changes. By 1999 the GOP was drunk with its own power; it also had its coffers filled with hundreds of millions raised from business interests looking to repeal Glass-Steagall. During the 1997-1998 election cycle, the financial services industry which lobbied for its repeal gave more than $15 million to the members of the House Banking, House Commerce and Senate Banking committees and more than $58 million to political parties.[3] In the six years prior to 1997, the industry spent over $100 million on such lobbying efforts. Wall Street's lobbying the House Banking Committee to repeal Glass-Steagall had become an annual ritual; the Republicans' control of the House of Representatives made its repeal more likely. Some of the biggest proponents of its repeal were executives from Citigroup and Travelers, Inc. who had just agreed to the largest merger in history ($76 billion). A repeal of Glass-Steagall would have allowed the merged entity to maintain operations in banking, brokerage, and insurance. When I heard the repeal was gaining traction I starting pacing around my house cursing under my breath. "Why tear the fence down before finding out why it had been erected in the first place?" was my main question. Proponents argued that Glass-Steagall was a Depression-era act that was no longer relevant. Times had changed, and the vertical integration of financial services companies would create efficiencies in the marketplace that would ultimately benefit consumers. I countered that "the Bible says, 'What's in a man's gut is who he is.' Though the Depression had occurred sixty years earlier, what was in an investment banker's gut in the 1930s – the desire to fleece the public – was still there."

In November 1999 President Clinton signed into law an overhaul of Glass-Steagall – the Gramm-Leach-Bliley Act. The bill was approved in the Senate by a 90 to 8 vote and in Congress by a 362 to 57 vote. Lawmakers received a resounding response from Wall Street as the stocks of banks and insurance companies rose due to speculation from the pending wave of mergers in those industries. Treasury Secretary Lawrence Summers was quoted as saying, "With this bill, the American financial system takes a major step toward the 21st Century – one that will benefit American consumers, business and the national economy."[4] The previous Treasury Secretary, Robert Rubin, who had resigned from his post in May 1999, also had a hand in repealing Glass-Steagall. Less than a week after its repeal he became one of the chairmen of Citigroup. President Clinton cited the legislation as "truly historic" and claimed, "'We have done right by the American people.'"[5] Little did he know that lawmakers had just set in motion the beginning of the next financial crisis, rivaled only by the Great Depression.

Stamford Express

I played basketball a few times a week with GECC's intramural team against other corporations in the area like Pitney Bowes and Xerox. I was still in pretty good shape and was like a one-man wrecking crew out there. One of my teammates was Warren Spann, a Wharton grad who worked in GECC's division that provided capital for infrastructure deals. Dave Cooks, also of GECC's infrastructure group had just started a travel team, the Stamford Express, affiliated with the Amateur Athletic Union ("AAU"). While receiving his MBA at Duke, Dave was a volunteer assistant on Mike Kryzhewski's staff. Warren and I contributed money to the program, but the lion's share of the fundraising was done by Dave. I always wanted to give back somehow and this seemed like a fun way to do it. Dave pretty much took kids who nobody wanted or knew about and worked them half to death. The practices were brutal – lots of conditioning drills and instruction. The kids came with a varying degree of skill level, ranging from "pretty good" to "developmental." They competed hard, which raised everybody's level of play. They seemed appreciative and absolutely idolized Cooks. I had forgotten what high school was like, but after a weekend with those kids my memory quickly returned. They nicknamed me "Coach Starks" due to my resemblance to John Starks of the New York Knicks. And I did look like John Starks, until I went to the bank. And while they idolized Cooks, they constantly gave me the "business." They would start with my clothes, move on to my haircut and end with jokes about my Ford Festiva. When I defended myself with jokes of my own they would look bewildered, as if I had never been a teenager with too much mouth for my own good. They questioned us constantly – where we were from, where we went to school, and what we did for a living. We just preached that college was attainable for each of them if they applied themselves. If they were lucky enough to get a scholarship they could attend college for free, but also have a chance to be their own "brand." Their classmates would remember them from having represented the school on the basketball court and would be the first ones to patronize whatever business they went into after college. While we provided them with positive role models, they taught us the latest slang like "true dat," hipped us to the hottest rapper (some guy named "Nas"), and updated us on the best high school players in the country – Stephon Marbury from Brooklyn and Kevin Garnett from Chicago.

We dragged those kids everywhere. We played throughout the state of Connecticut, traveled as far north as Albany, New York and as far south as Virginia Beach, Virginia. We got destroyed the first year but over time the kids gave as good as they got. I got a chance to see the top players in the country up close – Luke Recker (Indiana), Bobby Simmons (DePaul, NJ Nets), Majestic Mapp (Virginia), Dan Gadzuric (UCLA, NJ Nets), Ronald Curry (UNC, Oakland Raiders), Jay Williams (Duke, Chicago Bulls) and Gary Payton's little brother, Brandon, out of Oakland. We played against a McDonald's American candidate named Shane Battier out of Detroit Country Day School who was rumored to have committed to Duke. I thought he had a basic, fundamental game. However, at one point, he rose up for a dunk and one of our guys came over late for the block. It was like a pending train wreck that you could not avert your eyes from. Battier "groined" our player and for the rest of the summer the kid was affectionately known as "Battier Breath." I missed the trip to Chicago where we played against Ronnie Fields (high school teammate of Kevin Garnett) whom Spann described as electrifying. They also told me about a kid named Quentin Richardson (DePaul, NY Knicks) who was upset because he had to sit out due to an ankle injury.

The trips to New York City were always interesting. We made the annual pilgrimage for a showcase event called "Rumble in the Bronx." The first year we faced an Eddie Griffin-led New Jersey Playaz. I swear the kid must have blocked about 20 shots. Griffin was 6'9" and ran the floor like a deer, covering about five yards with every stride. We were screaming at our guys to quit "shooting the ball at his hand." Two years later Griffin was playing in the NBA. But the star of the event was Dajuan Wagner, a 6'2" shooting guard out of Camden, New Jersey who was so good he had contemplated entering the NBA draft after his junior year in high school. Everywhere he went there was an entourage and cameramen in tow. The rapper "Fat Joe" and NBA players Allen Iverson and Rod Strickland sat right behind me in the stands – it was like a scene out of a movie. And the kid did not disappoint. He displayed a crazy handle, a soft touch from beyond the arc and the "athletic arrogance" to make a play on anybody at any time. To this day Wagner is still the best high school player I have ever seen in person. But watching the kids succeed was the most rewarding part. Kids who were once unknown were landing scholarships to St. Peters, American International, Iona, Drake, and Texas Tech. There were a few dual athletes too – one kid played lacrosse at Johns Hopkins and two played football at University of North Carolina and Boston College, respectively. As time has passed my respect for Cooks and Spann grew due to their hard work and dedication. They embodied the true meaning of community involvement. I promised that if I ever had a son I would start something similar for him.

Bigger Thomas Is Real
One evening in April 1994 the FIG managing director had a look of consternation on his face. He said there had been a big blow-up at Kidder and the problem was "huge." The announcement shook me to the core. Investment banks like Kidder had sizeable investment portfolios; the term "blow-up" could

range from a couple hundred million dollar loss, to taking down all of General Electric. I was not sure if I would have a job to come to the next day. I left the office thinking "Some white guy is going to get it now!" The next day when I opened *The Wall Street Journal* there was one small problem – the culprit looked black! I assumed it must have been a misprint. The paper mentioned that Joseph Jett was a managing director and one of the most powerful African Americans on the Street. First of all, I could never have imagined a black man rising to such a high position at Kidder; secondly, assuming Kidder would give an African American that type of power, it was unfathomable that he would be stupid enough to blow it by making a huge trading loss. All I could think was, "Run black boy, run!" According to Jett, even the throng of reporters in the lobby of his apartment building was looking for a white guy:

> I picked up the phone, surprised to hear one of my neighbors. 'Joseph, I just wanted to tell you there's a crowd of reporters downstairs. When I walked out of the building they thought I was you and asked for comments.' I'd forgotten there was an outside world. A few minutes later my apartment buzzer started ringing; shouting came over the intercom: 'Mr. Jett! We know you're up there! Come down and talk to us! It's for your own good! The buzzer rang every few minutes, the same loud male voice shouting the same demands . . . From the lobby I could hear the voice of the guy shouting into the intercom as I paused to calm myself. Taking a deep breath, I pulled the door open. A blaze of lights erupted, blinding me . . . For a second or two I couldn't see anything but the glare. My vision cleared in time to see the group begin to relax, break up and retreat. Directly in front of me the face and hair of a young blond woman emerged from a silhouette as the lights dimmed. She was thrusting a large microphone toward my face. Suddenly it fell limp in her hand, the metal stem dangling for a second from its cord as she looked at me blankly, slightly exasperated. Then she, too, turned away. All the lights were off, no one was looking at me anymore, and I heard the now familiar voice resume shouting. Behind me, the guy was wedged behind the lobby doors, pressing again on the buzzer, 'Mr. Jett, Mr. Jett! We know you're in there! Come down and talk to us!' I pushed through what was left of the milling crowd and started walking toward the corner, shaking with the rage rising in my chest . . . I wanted to turn around and bellow: 'I *am* Joe Jett!' Instead I kept walking . . . They were looking for Joseph Jett, Harvard graduate and multimillionaire Wall Street bond trader. They weren't looking for a black man.[6]

Jett was the head government bond trader at Kidder and had incurred a $350 million loss on a trading scheme involving government strips – instruments that represented the bonds' interest payments. The newspaper went into detail about how Jett had a Harvard MBA, worked out religiously, quoted Nietzsche and was a disciple of Shaolin Kung Fu. My first reaction was, "One of those huh? One of those African Americans who attended an Ivy League school and presented himself to white America as being different from other blacks, yet at the first sign of trouble was the first to run to the NAACP for help." Stories began to surface from his Harvard classmates that he was a devout Republican, against affirmative action, and during case discussions involving race, he always sided with his white classmates. The fact that he read Nietzsche was not an issue for me, but the fact that he broadcasted it would prompt Shakespeare to say, "Thou doth protest too much." To me, Jett appeared to have been trying too hard to differentiate himself from other African Americans. And just like Bigger Thomas, I figured he was about to get exactly what he deserved.

Kidder had been breaking the bonds into interest and principal payments and making a market in them separately. Jett entered into forward contracts where the strips of bonds would be exchanged at a later date. However, the exchange never took place as Jett rolled them forward. The quirk in Kidder's accounting system was that "it allowed him to capture the profit on the price of the strip – the interest portion of the bond – before it was 'reconstituted,' or turned back into the original bond."[7] It was these bogus profits, generated from thousands of trades, upon which Jett's annual bonus was based. Jett had earned a $9 million bonus in 1993 and received the "chairman's award" as Kidder's star employee at a meeting of Kidder senior executives that same year. His acceptance speech was made for Hollywood – "This is war . . . You do anything to win. You make money at all costs."[8] However, it was not until the bonds' interest and principal strips were reconstituted that one could ascertain whether profits had been made. In Kidder's haste to make a market in the interest-only bonds, Kidder's clients left them holding long-dated strips, which were the most volatile to movements in interest rates. On February 4, 1994, the Federal Reserve finally raised short-term interest rates to preempt inflation. The move sent bond prices lower and caused the Dow Jones to drop 96.24 (2.4%) to 3871.42 – the largest single-day decline in the previous two years. With Jett holding long-dated strips that declined in value as rates increased, the Federal Reserve action marked the beginning of the end for Kidder.

Once Kidder attempted to reconstitute its government strips, it realized Jett's trades were masking losses in the hundreds of millions of dollars. GE's CEO, Jack Welch, was livid, not only because of the sizeable losses, but due to the fact that GE was not made aware of them prior to its quarterly earnings report. GE had reported increases in quarterly earnings for over a decade; the losses at Kidder broke that string. GE positioned Jett as a "rogue trader" who acted alone in an attempt to maximize his bonuses. It retained Gary Lynch to lead an investigation into what went wrong. Lynch was the former SEC enforcement chief who helped take down Michael Milken and Drexel. GE had a vaunted reputation for management processes and controls; the trading scandal exposed Kidder's, and ultimately GE's, lack of internal controls. GE had to save face and the outcome of the Lynch investigation was predetermined to exonerate Kidder. They froze Jett's personal securities account totaling almost $5 million and held back another $3.4 million in deferred compensation. GE said it was entitled to keep the money as security in light of Jett's sizeable losses. In isolating Jett, Kidder CEO, Michael Carpenter, was in effect exonerating Kidder – "Mr. Carpenter says Wall Street suggestions that Kidder 'has loose controls and is run by a bunch of bozos' are also nonsense. Ticking off two years' worth of initiatives to tighten the securities firm's controls, Carpenter says, 'I will tell you categorically that we have been extremely diligent with respect to compliance, controls, and risk management.' The alleged phantom trades were so well hidden, he adds, that it could have happened 'to anybody – anybody' on Wall Street."[9]

The irony was that while Kidder was part of GECC on GE's organizational chart, Carpenter reported directly to GE CEO, Jack Welch. As a former GECC executive vice president, Carpenter did not get along with Gary Wendt. One GE official described Wendt as one who wants to "control very closely" and Carpenter as one who "doesn't like to be controlled."[10] It was that lack of control – Kidder could not even calculate the size of Jett's true trading losses – that had gotten Kidder into hot water. According to Jett, Kidder was so out of control that it had kept two sets of books – one set that it reported to GE and a separate set that documented the amount of GE's capital it was really using. Jett was trading $30 billion of GE's money, not the $18 billion that the press had reported. It was all a part of a grand plan by Edward Cerullo, Jett's immediate boss, to wrest Kidder away from GE and operate as a separate company.

Jett was investigated by the Manhattan U.S. attorney's office, the New York Stock Exchange, the National Association of Stock Dealers (NASD) and the Securities and Exchange Commission (SEC); there was a strong possibility he would be banned from the securities industry for life. GE played the "rogue trader" angle to the hilt, and the more articles surfaced about Jett, the more shame the African-American employees at GECC felt. We felt like we were all on trial. I was usually pretty jovial, but after the Jett fiasco I kept a low profile. I almost started to apologize to the group on Jett's behalf. FIG's reaction was simply, "Kidder again." They mentioned something about $750 million in Kidder bridge loans that GECC ultimately had to pay for after the high-yield bond market cratered (1990). Kidder had been a problem for GE from the very beginning. When a white-shoe firm like Morgan Stanley was unavailable, GE "settled" on buying 80% of Kidder for $600 million in 1986. To celebrate the consummation of the deal, GE planned a dinner with Kidder executives. On the day of the planned celebration, Martin Siegel pleaded guilty to insider trading within Kidder's arbitrage group.[11] Including the $25 million SEC fine for Siegel's misdeeds, the $750 million in bad bridge loans and cash infusion for the Jett fiasco, GE pumped a total of $1.4 billion into Kidder. Its investment paled in comparison to the $200 million Kidder earned under GE's ownership.[12]

After the barrage of articles crucifying Jett, I became more sympathetic to his predicament. Was he a terrible trader? Of course he was. How could someone be so reckless as to carry an $18 billion bond portfolio when the Fed was about to raise interest rates? He should have been fired and his bonuses clawed back. The absurd scenario from Richard Wright's *Native Son* had struck again. Where the world was strictly black and white as a high school freshman, I could now see the "gray." Jett was incompetent but it was asinine to think that Kidder executives were unaware of what he was doing. Everybody on the Street knew Kidder was using its balance sheet to earn profits from principal trading. While Jett's salary totaled $11 million from 1993 to 1994, Cerullo made approximately $28 million during that time. In 1993 the fixed-income department headed by

Cerullo generated the lion's share of the firm's annual income; Jett alone accounted for 20% of the fixed income group's profit, second only to Michael Vranos, who traded mortgage-backed securities (MBS). While Wall Street may have found the argument far-fetched, it played very well on "main street." People in Des Moines, IA probably wanted to believe that Jett had acted alone. However, I was torn internally. Other traders had incurred huge losses during the Fed's rate increases. Hedge fund, Askin Capital Management, imploded – losing all of its $600 million in investments on MBS and principal-only strips; famed hedge fund investor, Michael Steinhardt, who had used leverage to invest in European bonds, lost $800 million of clients' money in just four days; Kidder's Neil Margolin was fired for hiding a $10 million loss on a bond derivatives transaction; Vranos' MBS losses led to Kidder posting a net operating loss for the second quarter of 1994 of nearly $30 million; Bob Citron, the Treasurer of Orange County California, lost $1.6 billion from exposure to inverse floaters which bankrupt the county. While these investors had made "honest mistakes," GE and the media portrayed Jett as "cunning" and "nefarious." I chafed at the fact that Jett's portrayal seemed all the more credible since he was African American. However, after reading excerpts from Jett's childhood friend, Harold Massey, another side of me thoroughly enjoyed watching GE twist the proverbial knife – ". . . Mr. Jett has been further isolated by not supporting traditional black social issues or socializing with other blacks. 'He's put himself in a position that makes him marginal . . . He's not a guy the NAACP is rushing to defend, and his white co-workers at Kidder have hung him out to dry.'"[13] Nonetheless, GE set an important legal precedent in dealing with incompetent traders: (i) claw back their bonuses; (ii) determine if their negligence was due to fraud or incompetence; (iii) have them investigated by the NYSE, NASD, and SEC; and (iv) if warranted, have them barred from the securities industry and incarcerated.

Project Farmer

In April 1994 FIG received news of a life insurance company being sold through an auction process by one of the bulge bracket investment banks. The bank sent over a sales memorandum describing the company's strategy, products, distribution and earnings. Located in Orlando, Florida, "Farmer" was a non-strategic subsidiary of a publishing and retailing company. Farmer sold single premium deferred annuities, structured settlements, credit life and Medicare supplement plans through 7,500 agents. There are over a thousand ways to sell insurance, but this company's distribution system had to be one of the most unique. It had an exclusive 25-year relationship with over 20 farm publications, representing over 1 million subscribers. The publications provided leads for the agents to sell insurance. From a product and distribution perspective, Farmer fit perfectly with GNA. We crafted a list of information (due diligence request list) we needed to better understand the company and a vice president and I flew down to Orlando to gather the materials. The documents were voluminous but the vice president knew exactly what he was looking for. We had to compare our list to the materials Farmer and the bankers provided, and put together a second request for what was missing. They gave us enough information to make a preliminary bid, yet not enough that a competitor could poach key employees or understand how Farmer priced its products.

We were there for two days and after our work was finished, I hit up a popular Orlando nightclub. The place was packed. I walked up to one of the finest sisters in there and struck up a conversation. I was like the Rifleman I was firing so much game at this girl. I made a veiled reference to my basketball exploits in college and figured it would be a wrap. We were partying it up when suddenly everybody headed for the exits. I went to see what the commotion was about and there was Shaquille O'Neal parked outside the front steps in what looked like a black '67 Chevy convertible. In his second season with the Orlando Magic, O'Neal was the future of the NBA. Throngs of women ran over to his car and begged for his autograph. O'Neal hogged the spotlight for a bit, and then the guy in the passenger's seat got out of the car and made a beeline to the young lady I had been talking to. He whispered something and she followed him to O'Neal's car. Shaq and the young lady made eye contact; she hopped in the backseat and the three of them drove off. It all happened in the blink of an eye – "blocked" by Shaquille O'Neal! I had never seen anything quite like it. Shaq never moved. His "man servant" did his bidding for him. "What a coward," I thought. The next time I saw Spann and Cooks I told them about seeing Shaq on my trip to Orlando and what a cool ride he had. The part about how he "snuffed" me, I conveniently omitted.

You Only Get What You "Inspect" Not What You "Expect"

We ran a few high-level financial models for Farmer and the managing director decided that something around $340 - $350 million was the right bid; anything higher would have been overpaying. We discussed it with GNA's management team who would operate the company post-transaction. I listened in on the conference call and it appeared to be a good system of checks and balances. The M&A team looked at how well the transaction fit strategically, but was disciplined when it came to meeting our financial hurdle rates. Management was focused on how well Farmer's product line and distribution would complement GNA's. However, our bid was not high enough to get us into the second round of the auction process. Farmer had piqued the interest of some of the largest names in life insurance, so the auction was hotly contested. I was excited about working on my first live deal but understood the need to be disciplined. A week later, I was working out in the company gym when I received a call from the managing director that miraculously, the deal was back on and we were headed to Orlando. We descended on Orlando on a Sunday night like a bunch of piranha. The due diligence team included FIG, GNA, actuaries, lawyers, internal auditors, and investment portfolio experts. I sat in on a presentation from Farmer's CEO on Monday morning and that was the only break I got the whole week. I was holed up in the "war room" – a huge conference room where we kept our files and worked independently between meetings. I updated the financial projections as we uncovered new information. I quickly realized that a lot of the information in Farmer's offering memo was either stale or simply untrue. The offering memo showed the company in the best possible light. It was our job to determine what the company's actual experience was in various areas like product pricing and investment returns. I sat with the managing director and GNA's chief actuary and listened as they vetted our assumptions about the crediting rate on Farmer's $2 billion annuity block, or the implications of structuring the transaction as a sale of stock or a sale of assets. This is where the "art of the deal" came in.

Around 7 p.m. everyone met for a recap of the day's meetings. Each group delivered its findings for the day and divulged any potential "deal breakers." Meetings with the seller's employees were a real eye-opener. The employees wanted to remain with the company so they were eager to impress potential buyers and divulge Farmer's true drawbacks. We went to dinner from 8:30 p.m. to 9:30 p.m. and went back to the war room to model out more scenarios from 9:30 p.m. to midnight. On Tuesday morning we started our work at 8 a.m. The work schedule felt a lot like Darden's.

After a week of due diligence we returned to Stamford, completed our analysis and lobbed in a $385 million offer. The bankers later thanked us for our efforts but confirmed that Farmer was in exclusive negotiations with another buyer. The thought that our bid would not succeed had never even crossed my mind. After weeks of hard work, preparation and envisioning how the marriage between Farmer and GNA would work, the transaction had taken on a life of its own. I was in pure "deal heat" and was willing to pay whatever the seller wanted, regardless of what the model suggested. Apparently others within FIG felt the same way; on Friday of that week, one of the vice presidents wanted me to run more scenarios to see if there was anything we had missed. However, the Stamford Express had a tournament in Albany, New York that weekend. I had not seen the team in over a month, having devoted all my time to Farmer. We met internally and everybody decided that Farmer was officially dead and that the Albany trip was a "go." Spann and I got settled into the hotel room, turned on the television and on every channel was live footage of O.J. Simpson and A.C. Cowlings driving down the California freeway with the LAPD in hot pursuit. Apparently O.J.'s ex-wife, Nicole, had been found murdered a few days earlier and O.J. was the prime suspect. The LAPD had given O.J. a chance to turn himself in but he tried to flee instead. His lawyer, Robert Kardashian, had earlier read a note from O.J. claiming his innocence and the ominous statement that "he has had a great life." Killing one's ex-wife was not something Hall of Fame football players did. There had to be some good explanation for this nonsense, right? Though the LAPD had him surrounded and motioned for him to pull over, O.J. refused. I was certain we were going to see O.J. gunned down on live television. My mind was racing a hundred miles per minute. First Farmer was dead and now O.J. What a week!

Ain't Over 'Til It's Over

The following Friday night I was in the office alone combing through the model, trying to find a nugget of information that could change things. At 11:30 p.m. I received a call from the CEO of GNA. He wanted to know what the returns would look like at a $400 million purchase price. The financial buyer that had won the auction process was having trouble securing financing. Farmer was willing to let GECC pre-empt the other buyer with an all-cash bid. The only caveat was that we had to come in at $400 million. I ran the returns and faxed them over to GNA's management team. I called the vice president from our team, who then phoned the managing director with the good news. The details were finalized over the weekend and I had my first deal. From that point on, I never gave up on transactions that appeared hopeless. I finished my rotation in Stamford in August of that year and transferred to Commercial Finance (CF) in New York. The credit department, which approved and documented all of the transactions for CF wanted me to work in their group in Norwalk, Connecticut. However, I was determined on going to the New York office. Someone (erroneously) had put the idea in my head that I had to be in New York if I wanted to be successful long-term. I was warned to avoid a certain senior vice president there because he was a jerk. I nicknamed the guy the "Third Rail" – the rail on the New York City subway system known for carrying an electric current. A decade later, I looked up the vice president who used to flog me and thanked him for what he did for me – making me learn those financial models the correct way. He saved my career a thousand times over. I hadn't realized it at the time but he actually gave a darn.

Finding the "Mullet"

On my second day in the New York office everybody was excited about the annual softball game in Central Park. I tried to avoid it but the rest of the group insisted that I attend. They thought it would be a great way to meet everyone informally. My first turn at bat, I launched a rocket over the centerfielder's head for a home run. My next turn at bat, the pitcher stopped the game so the centerfielder could back up another 30 or so yards. This time I hit the first pitch over his head and into the trees. He came charging out of the woods about five minutes later as if there was going to be a play at the plate. The next morning I heard everybody was saying things like, "You see that black guy hit that ball?" Being known for my athletic prowess was the main reason I tried to beg off the event to begin with. And that was my introduction to the New York office. My other introduction was to the different ethnic groups the city had. In Virginia everyone was either black or white. In New York people made distinctions amongst Caucasians – Polish, Italian, Irish, Jewish, etc. They schooled me on these distinctions in order to make me more aware of my surroundings. One group in particular was run by all Italians. They did everything together – ate together, arrived at the office together and left together. They traveled in a pack. When you saw one you saw them all.

CF was a vestige of GECC's LBO lending group. I was assigned to the financial sponsors group, which worked with buyout shops and coincidentally, included the Third Rail. I was also in a pool of associates that any of the groups could utilize when they needed help on deals. The key to getting ahead was to get a senior person to "champion you" – lobby for you to get promoted and placed on high-profile assignments. My strategy was simply to do good work. And by "work" I mean financial models. The models were pretty pedestrian compared to the ones I worked on in FIG. CF's models were 15-20 pages long with full income statements, cash flow statements, balance sheets and product line information. The work was easy, but the people . . . well that was another matter. The first thing I noticed was the morale of the place. There was this ridiculous story floating around about a former employee who arrived in the office around 5:30 a.m. He sent a fax to Gary Wendt about the terrible job Wendt and the executives in the LBO group were doing, and how they were tarnishing the GECC brand in the marketplace. You had to swipe an electronic card before entering the office. A record of everyone's entry was logged electronically. The managing director and security simply pulled the logs, found out who was in the office at 5:30 a.m. (at least two hours before the next visitor) and summarily fired the culprit. Whenever I heard this story I would go into hysterics.

GECC had written off about $1.3 billion in loans made in the late 1980s at the height of the market. While GECC was scaling back its appetite for leveraged deals, several insurers and non-financial services companies ceased funding LBOs altogether. Based on the ratio of approved deals, it was clear that GECC favored more asset-based deals secured by accounts receivable and inventory, as compared to loans to be repaid from a company's cash flows. In a bankruptcy scenario one could liquidate the assets to repay the loan. There were certain industries the credit guys would not even consider doing deals for. GECC had in its portfolio wholly-owned companies like shoe stores and cable companies, where the LBOs had gone belly-up. Where transactions in the early to mid-80s may have been done at debt multiples of four to five times operating income, minus capital expenditures – an internal measure of a transaction's indebtedness – by the late 1980s GECC was lending at 10-12 times this metric. And while buyout firms were investing 25% - 30% equity for deals, by the late '80s the purchase price was driven more by how much debt a buyer could raise.

Every day a group of guys would sit in the lunchroom and gossip about what deals were occurring in the marketplace. Most of their vitriol was directed at one person – the Queen Bee. She must have possessed a special kind of pixie dust because all of her deals seemed to get done. She completed asset-based deals, cash flow deals and hybrids with cash flow and asset-based components. She was a rainmaker and was pretty much carrying the group, which left some of the other deal generators smarting. Meanwhile, she floated around the office with a perpetual smirk on her face. Some threw rocks, saying she underpriced transactions and was essentially providing "mullet money." Others claimed that she would lift an offering memo from a colleague's desk, call her industry contacts to get the same book, and lobby the managing director to let her lead it. There were rumors that she had stolen a colleague's client with insinuations that the colleague was "too junior" to lead a deal and had gotten fired from a rival firm. Sometimes junior people would engage in this sort of gossip or pick sides in turf wars; they would have their careers ended for picking the wrong side. I stayed neutral, avoided that lunchroom like the plague and tended to my own business.

On a typical day a vice president or SVP would toss a deal book on my desk; my job was to build a financial model projecting the target's cash flows and how much debt it could support. The buyout shop needed a quick turnaround so the model had to be completed within two days. I would go back to the project leader with three scenarios (Management Case, Base Case, and Downside Case) modeled out. The Base Case would illustrate what I thought could happen realistically post-transaction while the Downside Case was used to determine how much debt the deal could support if cash flow hit rock bottom. This was sort of tricky in that you had to first find the games the management team was playing within the projections and insert a level of realism. The obvious assumptions that impacted the projections were a shift to higher margin products, a reduction of capital expenditures or better management of working capital, i.e. collecting on accounts receivable quicker or paying bills slower. Each of these modifications would impact a company's cash flow.

The Mullet

The team leader and I would present the financial model and a short description of the deal to the managing director for a quick read. He would reel off questions about the entire transaction, including how the senior debt was priced and the internal rates of return (IRR) on the subordinated debt and common equity. If he thought the interest rate on the senior debt was underpriced he would exclaim, "This is mullet money!" Sometimes he accused the sub-debt investors of being "mullets" or the common equity investors of being greedy. He would send us back to the client with a Chinese menu of (i) better terms on the senior debt or (ii) maintain the current terms on the senior debt and allow us to participate in the common equity. I later found out that a mullet was a "dumb" fish that sat at the bottom of the ocean. If fish swam into its mouth then it ate. If not, then it starved to death. The mullet did not have sense enough to go where the food was. In GECC parlance, a mullet was a lender or investor that did not get paid adequately for the risk it took. In LBOs at least one tranche of the capital structure was mispriced; being accused of providing mullet money, or dumb money, was the kiss of death. That is when I realized what my true role was – finding the mullet and structuring around him.

Caught Between Chemical and "A Hard Place"

CF also faced concerns outside of its own return hurdles. The biggest concern was the LBO industry's 800-pound gorilla known as Chemical Bank. Chemical's client base included some of the top private equity shops in the country. It "circled the deal," issuing commitments for all levels of the capital structure so that the private equity firm only had to deal with one lender. This created a certain ease of use that clients enjoyed. While the lead time from receiving the deal book to delivering a commitment letter was weeks at some firms, Chemical could get there in days. Chemical's other competitive advantage was its vaunted syndications ability. On a multibillion-dollar loan, Chemical would "syndicate" or sell down 80% - 85% to other lenders, holding only 15% - 20% of the risk for itself. It would also maintain a higher share (25% - 30%) of the up-front fees on the loan than its share of the risk – known as "skimming." This allowed Chemical to enhance the returns on the loan vis-à-vis other members of the syndicate. It had a stronghold on the most prestigious private equity firms in the business; if other banks wanted access to those quality loans, they had to agree to Chemical's terms, or else: "Given the bank's choke hold on the big time loan business, Mr. Lee [James B. Lee, Jr.] has the ability to 'jam' other lenders – threatening to cut them out of future syndications if they decline to participate when he needs their help."[14] In effect, Chemical had taken Drexel's business model and applied it to leveraged lending. Its early stage "commitment letter" was similar to Drexel's "Highly Confident Letter," which was almost as good as a guarantee. And Chemical's loan syndications chief, "Jimmy" Lee, held as much sway over his banking syndicate as Milken held over buyers of his high-yield bonds. Milken once said that he and his corporate takeover machine would strike fear in the hearts of blue chip corporations like GM, Ford and IBM, and that he would tee them up.[15] In a similar vein, Jimmy Lee appeared on the cover of *Forbes* magazine in 2000 with a list of takeover targets and a promise to clients, to "write them a check." His star within his company's investment banking group fell immediately after the article was published.

CIT

On the other end of the spectrum was CIT, the largest factoring business in the country. It purchased nearly $8 billion in receivables annually by the 1990s. Factoring involved buying a company's accounts receivable at a discount and realizing a profit after fully collecting on them. Its factoring expertise dovetailed into asset-based lending to middle-market clients. The loans were typically made to borrowers who did not have the most pristine credit. In the event of a default, the lender could liquidate the assets to repay the loan. The skills necessary to succeed in asset-based lending – constantly monitoring the assets and the ability to liquidate those assets if needed – were the same skills that factoring companies possessed. Its approval process for lending decisions was streamlined, and it was as aggressive in its niche as Chemical was in cash flow lending. If GECC tried to go upstream (cash-flow lending) it faced Chemical, yet downstream, (asset-based lending) it had to contend with CIT.

Project Graphite

In late 1994 we were members of a syndicate in a $585 million Chemical senior debt facility to recapitalize "Graphite," a leading manufacturer of graphite electrodes. Graphite electrodes were used in the production of steel in electric furnaces (EAF). EAF penetration of worldwide steel production had doubled to 31% from 1973 to 1993. Industry experts were predicting it would increase to at least 36% by the year 2000. The Third Rail sourced the transaction for GECC; I had worked with him twice before. On one of the deals we flew to Dayton, Ohio for two days of due diligence. It was an hour's drive from the airport to the company and the guy did not say a word. And when he did speak all he did was complain. He also had a serious issue with the Dillon Read analyst representing the target company. The analyst had worn a double-breasted suit during the meetings, which the Third Rail thought was a serious faux pas. He fumed something to the effect of, "Did you see that kid with that double-breasted suit? You must be at least a managing director before you can wear a double-breasted suit. Is he arrogant or what?" He then threatened to take the matter to the guy's boss. I thought he was preposterous, like a caricature out of a movie. We worked out of a conference room in Norwalk, Connecticut to prepare a presentation for the deal. A few women had just gotten promoted to managing director and he complained about how unqualified they were, included the woman who was the co-managing director of FIG in Stamford. He never gave any empirical evidence as to why they were unqualified; I guess people were supposed to take his word for it. He probably would have complained about African Americans if there had actually been any in the company. I kept my mouth shut and stayed busy. He lamented about GECC's sudden lack of appetite for unsecured loans and how when he was at my level, senior deal guys were paid big bonuses. He had "fallen on the sword" for GECC, awaiting his turn. Now that he was senior guy the punch bowl had been taken away. The Third Rail sounded similar to the angry white male described in the press. He was feeling encroached upon by the gains of women in the workplace, and frustrated by being a cash flow lender in the new asset-based world.

The assistant vice president and I attended a meeting of the Graphite bank syndicate. We were in a huge auditorium with a few hundred other people, including bankers and lawyers. Thirty minutes later, in walked the main attraction – Jimmy Lee. It was the dead of winter and Jimmy Lee was fully tanned. We couldn't figure out if he had just flown in from vacationing in Bermuda or if he had been sitting under a sun lamp all day. He started his presentation with, "To my friends in the industry" and talked up the merits of the transaction, and the value-added of the bank syndicate. He finished to a standing ovation. Afterward, we presented our case to the credit group. A major part of the analysis involved predicting the future price of graphite electrodes and sales volume. We had consulting reports but needed to hear the story firsthand from the private equity group, so we set up a meeting. The private equity partners met with us for about 20 minutes, and then marched us into a conference room to meet with the resident expert on the steel industry. There, I found myself sitting directly across the table from the legendary David Stockman, Reagan's former budget director. He had on his banker uniform – Hermes tie and double-vented suit – and immediately started talking. He gave us his prognostications of worldwide steel volume and EAF's expected share of it. The guy went on nonstop for about an hour, but all I heard were "marginal propensity to consume," "trickle-down theory," and "Laffer Curve." If the Third Rail had not been sitting there I would have gone at Stockman . . . tested his assumptions about the worldwide steel industry, and why his calculations would bear a different result than his budget estimates of the early '80s. On the train ride back to Norwalk, the Third Rail went on about how we had just met Reagan's former budget chief and how brilliant he was. I bit my tongue. To get the credit guys comfortable with our projections of worldwide steel prices and production, the Rail invoked Stockman's name – "Because David Stockman said so." Our $50 million participation eventually got completed and everybody seemed happy. It was easy work in my opinion.

Third Rail Gets Electrocuted

Shortly after Project Graphite was completed I received a visit from a woman in human resources (HR). The Third Rail had complained about my work. She could not say what his issue was specifically so I requested that we meet with him, the head of HR, and the managing director. The game of "possum" I had been playing had turned into a high-stakes game of poker. I was actually looking forward to it. I was in a pool of associates and the managing director did not know me from a can of paint. This would be my chance to show him what I knew firsthand. I had remembered the Third Rail from that softball game earlier that summer. He had struck out repeatedly . . . even my mother could put a softball into play. But when he thought the odds were in his favor, he feigned himself a tough guy. The entire time Mrs. Green's voice played in my head, "It's either them or you." The meeting took place a few weeks later, but I wasn't there. Joe Baker, bullwhip and all, went in my stead. Joe actually led the meeting. He walked the managing director and HR executive through the financial model, line by line. He demonstrated his command of Graphite's business, the projections and the different tranches of the capital structure. Compared to the work I had done in Stamford, Joe told them the models in CF were "pedestrian," at best. The Third Rail appeared nervous and unsure of himself, and stuttered a lot. He mentioned that I had not modeled the returns on the preferred stock correctly, but Joe walked everybody through that calculation as well. The guy's argument then pretty much boiled down to "because I said so." Though the managing director showed a good poker face, it was clear that the Rail was outclassed and didn't have a clue what he was talking about.

The Third Rail was also unaware that I had been warned about him before leaving Stamford. I kept all models, presentations, and meeting notes on each one of his deals. He also didn't know about Tracey, Diane and Carol from Sovran, and my penchant for making people disappear. I had been preparing for the meeting months in advance, coming in on weekends to organize my files in case anyone inquired. I chalked it up to the black tax. I could not simply go to work and do my job like everyone else. I had to prove my competence beyond a reasonable doubt. GE had a concept called "kiss up and kick down," a culture in which employees kissed up to those who outranked them and attacked subordinates. I had purposely played possum, knowing he would underestimate me; shortly after our meeting, he disappeared. I resigned from GECC two years later but before I left, a few people in the group had a confession to make. They said the Third Rail had inquired why I wanted to meet with him and the managing director. He also pleaded with them to co-sign the lie he had told HR about me; however, they refused. Unbeknownst to me, the entire office was aware of our showdown and anxiously awaited the outcome. I sat there in stunned silence.

KEY TRANSACTIONS

I have worked on so many transactions that I cannot remember them all. The deals all seem pretty fuzzy and have started to run together. Other than Project Farmer, two transactions stand out due to their complexity and how they shaped my outlook on the U.S. capital markets.

Project Scope

In August 1994 a manufacturer of medical analytical equipment sought to acquire the clinical diagnostics division of a Fortune 500 company for $750 million. GECC was acting as co-agent on $475 million of senior debt. Kidder and the buyer were to provide $350 of subordinated debt and $150 million in equity, respectively. The buyer and "Scope" had complimentary product lines in the worldwide market for In Vitro Diagnostics. The $750 million purchase price, refinancing of $90 million of existing client debt, transaction fees and excess debt capacity available at closing totaled $975 million. Management projections demonstrated that the new company could comfortably repay indebtedness. However, our client's $750 million bid was not high enough to win the competitive auction process for Scope. Either the client had to increase its equity in the deal or GECC had to increase the amount it was willing to lend. Kidder's solution was to increase the subordinated debt component of the structure. However, Kidder expected GECC to "bridge" the sub-debt, i.e. fund the sub-debt for a period of time until Kidder could sell it to high-yield investors. We met with Kidder's investment bankers who were adamant they could sell the sub-debt. Apparently, the terms of the debt were favorable vis-à-vis high-yield issues in the marketplace. We countered that at a $750 million purchase price, the transaction was pushing the limits of how much debt it could support. And since the client was not willing to inject more equity, the transaction was likely dead. Yet the Kidder bankers would not let it go; they decided to put together their own set of projections. It was like talking to a bunch of crazy people. If they could sell the sub-debt to high-yield investors, the Kidder team would have received an upfront fee. However, if they could not, GECC would be left with $350 million of paper that could not be repaid, and we would surely lose our jobs. We tried to convey the lack of risk/reward on our end but Kidder appeared tone deaf.

Heart of an Investment Banker

At the next meeting Kidder showed us the "Rosetta Stone," their financial model that would solve the Scope conundrum. To my surprise, their projections were more aggressive than management's. Now I knew they were crazy! To even suggest that we move forward based on those numbers would have prompted screams of "mullet money." It was then that I understood the "heart of an investment banker" – GECC, the public, etc. only existed for bankers' personal gain. If the transaction was successful for both us and them then fine. If we got fired in the process then that was fine too, as long as they got their upfront fees. Steve Joseph, former Chairman of Drexel, experienced this phenomenon when he asked Drexel employees to forgo part of their bonuses to help save the firm:

> Amazingly Joseph had misunderstood the ethic of the Drexel culture, the mindset
> fostered by the firm and embodied in Milken: Drexel was nothing but a corporate
> vehicle for personal gain. When Joseph asked his stars to accept lower bonuses,
> howls of protest rose from [Leon] Black and his allies . . . Joseph took all of his
> own $2.5 million bonus in preferred stock. Still, he could get his people, on
> average, to accept only 18% of their bonuses in stock. Drexel saved only $64
> million in cash, as it paid out over $200 million of its desperately needed capital.[1]

Undeterred, the Kidder deal team pled its case to Dennis Dammerman, the former top financial officer at GE. Dammerman had just replaced Michael Carpenter as head of Kidder. Carpenter could not survive the Joe Jett fiasco, especially after the NASD revealed that during the majority of his tenure, Carpenter did not have the license required to manage a securities business. We heard that once Kidder presented Dammerman their financial projections for Scope, which the word "reckless" would be too kind to describe, it sent him into an uncontrollable fury. Scope was eventually sold to another bidder for approximately $1 billion, a mere $250 million higher than our client's bid. It was public knowledge that GE was weighing whether to keep Kidder or sell it to a competitor. Kidder's recommendation on Scope brandished its reputation as a bunch of cowboys willing to take outsized risks; however, when those risks did not pay off, it expected to leave someone else holding the bag. It also accelerated its own sale. Two months later, GE sold Kidder to Paine Webber for $670 million in common and preferred stock, retaining a 25% stake.

Project Joseon

In 2000 I worked on Project Joseon, the acquisition of the sixth largest investment trust manager in South Korea with $8 billion in AUM. After combing through its financial statements, I quickly realized Joseon was technically insolvent; it was undercapitalized by a few hundred million dollars. I inserted the historical financials into an internal financial model I had built and ran some high-level projections. Joseon had accumulated losses from funds sold to investors with guaranteed returns. Yet it had invested the funds in equity securities whose performance was anything but guaranteed. To the extent the actual performance of the funds was less than the returns promised to investors, Joseon had to make up the difference or redeem investors with funds secured from new investors. In an attempt to build a nascent asset management industry, the Korean government encouraged the practice of offering guaranteed or "suggested" returns.

Due Diligence

The Korean business industry was dominated by "chaebols" – industrial conglomerates that usually included a bank, an asset manager, and businesses ranging from electronics to automobiles to manufacturers of heavy machinery. The Korean investment trust industry was burgeoning until the financial crisis of 1997-1998 crippled the Korean economy. The crisis was caused by the collapse of Daewoo, Korea's second largest chaebol behind Hyundai Group. Due to mismanagement and unbridled expansion, Daewoo could not repay its debt. In July 1999 creditors agreed to roll over Daewoo's bonds and commercial paper, and extend it $3.6 billion in additional credit. Of the $3.6 billion in new loans, $2.2 billion was contributed by the investment trust sector; the loans were parked in funds sold to investors with guaranteed returns. Joseon's exposure to Daewoo was around $255 million. The deal team landed in Seoul, South Korea after a 17-hour flight from New York. We left on a Sunday night and by the time I awoke for breakfast, it was already Tuesday morning in Seoul. I was taken aback by how cosmopolitan the city was. It felt a lot like New York, London or Paris with the skyscrapers, corporate offices and hustle and bustle in the atmosphere. I ate quickly and headed over to Joseon's headquarters, which was about a 15-minute walk away. I went to cross the street and once I got midway, traffic took off. I walked at a moderate pace, yet the cars actually sped up. I then took off into a full sprint, carrying a computer and a leather bag with binders full of due diligence material. I barely made it across to the other side. It looked like they were trying to run me over on purpose. I was out of breath, thinking, "Haven't these people ever seen a black man before?" Around noon I went to lunch with the rest of the team, which included some accountants who worked in Seoul. I was ready to make a mad dash across the street again when they directed us through a tunnel leading to the other side. There were tunnels throughout downtown that were used for crossing the street and allowed traffic to flow more smoothly. I never told them about my near-death experience earlier – and that was how my trip to Korea began.

My phase of the due diligence involved understanding Joseon's financials. The majority of Joseon's staff spoke very good English and all of the financial statements had been translated prior to our arrival. I went through the income statement line by line and took notes on how each revenue item was generated. I went through each line of the balance sheet with the financial management team as well, to determine what the amounts represented and potential impairment issues. The bond funds were valued separately by an internal fixed income expert. We had to ensure that the business activities Joseon undertook were consistent with those described in company presentations. Ironically, U.S. investors were reeling from losses incurred from the stocks of Adelphia Cable, WorldCom and Enron, who had misrepresented their financial status. Joseon's financial statements were lucid compared to the statements of many U.S. publicly-traded companies, yet we looked askance on them. Then to add insult to injury, the 2000 presidential election, which had been previously awarded to Texas Governor George W. Bush was contested because the votes in Florida were not counted properly. The employees from Joseon got a big kick out of "electiongate" and questioned Americans' ability to add and subtract. Their sentiment was, "Even third graders could decide an election for class president with more accuracy." After the grief we had given them over the transparency of their financial statements, all I could say was "touché."

The spirit of the negotiations was to find a solution to Joseon's capital hole, via an acquisition or a strategic investment, whichever worked for both sides. Dinner with the Joseon team was an excellent way to get to know our future partners. The CEO suggested the restaurant, ordered for us and explained exactly what it was we were eating. Out of respect I ate every morsel, and smiled incessantly. I found the kimchi a bit spicy but other than that, I enjoyed the food. The CEO was rather engaging and an excellent storyteller. His reaffirmation, almost verbatim, of what we had heard during the diligence process gave us comfort around Joseon's business processes. Over a year after our initial meetings, we, Joseon's parent company and a third party co-invested $165 million in the form of convertible preferred stock and debt securities. This allowed the company to continue its operations while insulating us from estimated losses ($260 million) in Joseon's investment portfolio. The agreements gave us the option of converting our securities into common equity in the future, or redeeming the securities with accumulated interest. I spent a total of six weeks in South Korea. On weekends I visited landmarks to learn more about the country and its culture. I gained the following insights:

Tensions With Japan

I visited Gyeongbok Palace, probably the most well-known of the five grand palaces built during the Joseon Dynasty, which lasted from 1392 to 1910. The tour guide walked us through the entire complex, from the gardens, to the king's sleeping quarters to a description of the architecture. Most interesting was the description of Korea's historical tensions with Japan. Japan invaded Korea in the late 1500s. Strategically, Japan saw Korea as a window into the rest of Asia. Its proximity to Japan made it a natural target for Japan's imperialistic ambitions. With assistance from China, Korea was able to beat back the invasion. Japan attacked again in the early 1900s and ruled Korea until 1945 when it surrendered to Allied Forces at the end of World War II. After World War II, Russia and the U.S. divided the peninsula into North Korea and South Korea. During my time to South Korea, the U.S. still had about 33,000 soldiers stationed there. At the time, it was the largest U.S. military presence on foreign soil, signaling that the U.S. too values Korea as "a window into the rest of Asia."

They Know Us Better Than We Know Them

I had several conversations with Joseon's CEO; he also used it as a chance to maximize his role as de facto ambassador for South Korea. He conveyed the national pride that Koreans have and the sacrifices they make to help their country prosper, such as working long hours and supporting products from domestic manufacturers. Most of the cars I saw were made by Daewoo or Hyundai; I saw very few American-made cars. Another sacrifice was living apart from his family for extended periods of time. His wife lived with his two teenage sons in Northern Virginia where they attended high school. They returned to Korea during summer breaks and holidays. Fairfax County, Virginia is known for having the best public schools in the U.S. However, the real estate prices and the cost of living are extremely high in the county, making it difficult for Virginia residents to live there and enjoy the educational benefits – the "crowding out" effect of international demand. It also dawned on me that Joseon's negotiating team knew us much better than we knew them. In that sense, they enjoyed a marked advantage during negotiations. Once we came upon a thorny issue with Joseon's financial results during due diligence. My Joseon counterpart struggled to explain the issue in English so we had to table the discussion for later. At the end of the week the counterpart spoke briefly about his background and divulged that he had just graduated from UCLA – "touché" again.

Excellent Traders

Korea was known for its open-air markets, where you could buy quality goods at a fraction of the cost in the U.S. The price was based upon your negotiation skills. Its most famous market, Namdaemun Market, had been around since the 1400s and was the center of furious trading for food and clothing. The thought that the Korean culture of bargaining would transfer to the boardroom had never occurred to me. In hindsight, Joseon's CEO was an excellent negotiator. His company was technically insolvent, yet the guy fought tooth and nail for over a year to cut the best deal possible. I got the sense that he could have negotiated for another year if he had to. Joseon's concept of time was a lot different from ours. At one juncture, our parent company assumed the transaction was close to completion and prepared a press release announcing the deal. With Joseon still hanging tough on terms, our senior management wondered what was taking so long. Management then pressured the deal team to speed the process up because we had already overrun the deadline originally promised. It was as if the press release had taken precedent over our agreeing to a transaction that best reflected our negotiating position. Joseon sensed our impatience and used it to its advantage. The CEO also had a penchant for "retrading" terms that both parties had previously agreed to. In our culture this would have been seen as unethical, but he acted as if the tactic was done in the normal course of business. That said, Joseon walked away with the best bargain possible, given its negotiating position.

Investment Management Industry – Linchpin to Industrialization

South Korea's status as a developed nation by the late 1980s was impressive given that Japan's occupation had ended just four decades earlier. However, the government knew it was missing the one item necessary to make it fully industrialized – a system of investing. South Korea considered its investment trust industry the linchpin to industrialization. This explains the government's eagerness to stabilize the investment trust industry amid the Daewoo collapse. A sophisticated system of investing was also dependent upon the "public trust" – something Americans take for granted. Because Koreans did not fully trust the vagaries of the stock market, investment trust companies marketed their funds with guaranteed returns, despite the fact that the funds' underlying securities were not "risk free." The burden of meeting suggested returns may have been necessary to build Korea's nascent investment trust industry.

THE CORPORATE GAME

Nearly a decade after Darden, I was working on a transaction in Geneva, Switzerland. I finished up my work and planned to meet my wife in Paris in a few days. To kill time, the concierge at my hotel suggested I attend a jazz festival in Montreux – a four-hour train ride away. Within five minutes of the train's departure, Lake Geneva appeared, and it got wider and wider, longer and longer. The sun began to set and I understood what the big deal was all about. It was literally the most beautiful sight I had ever seen. There was a woman and her young son sitting next to me. The kid was whining and would not keep still. I stayed quiet but thought to myself, "Boy you had better calm down before you get some tea." I suddenly realized what a long way from home I was and wondered, "How in the heck did I get here?" I also wondered if I would ever see Farmville again. Yet the Farmville I longed for was that of my youth – softball games on Mother's Day or singing at Mercy Seat while Annie Mae looked on approvingly. The little boy was still crying and acting up while the mother shouted something in a foreign language. The Swiss speak about five different languages, but whatever she was saying, I was certain it involved some "tea." Lake Geneva seemed as if it would go on forever. I thought what a shame it was that everybody from Farmville did not get the opportunity to see the sun set over Lake Geneva. And then it happened! The little boy received his tea and in an instant, I was back in Farmville, waiting for Grandma to save me from Suzie.

I began to see images of my parents, grandparents and teachers. I wondered if they really knew I was doing the "corporate shuffle" – trying to get recognition for my contributions and simultaneously trying to avoid taking the blame for the screw-ups of others – what they would really think. My thoughts turned to Mrs. Scott-Brown and how it was partly her fault I was now all by myself, about a million miles from home. She told us we could do anything we wanted, yet skipped the part about how difficult it would be. I thought about my son, then about 7 years old. This boy had the nerve to tell my brother Mark, "My daddy doesn't care anything about me. He's never around," which ironically, was the same thing I said about my own father. I figured it was time for me to get off of the corporate treadmill and build my own brand somehow; maybe it was time to quit procrastinating on that travel basketball team I had promised to start. But the trick was to make it educational somehow. I had tried teaching my son about the stock market but I was away from home too much to be consistent with it. If I fused the two together – basketball and investing, I thought it would be a fun way to spend a lot of time together and formally teach him and other kids about the fundamentals of investing. In thinking of harnessing my entrepreneurial side, I also began to reflect on what I had learned working in corporate America. I had never wanted to work in an environment where everybody looked alike, shared the same religion or politics. I only wanted to do deals. Then my mind raced back to the time I was a pain in the rear to my Sunday school teacher . . . badgering her nonstop about how if Jesus was such a good guy why did the Pharisees turn on him. By now it was crystal clear why Jesus was the most despised and hated on man on the planet – he had made the folly of performing real miracles in a land of false prophets.

The Pharisees

Years after I had started with FIG I worked for a nascent group that had not completed any transactions and had no in-house financial models – that mission was left up to me. I built the models from scratch. I nicknamed the managing director "Leatherman II" after the Bridgewater College coach due to his penchant for coming up with the most specious arguments to explain the "obvious." He also had one standard for everyone else and a completely different one for me. The guy not only wanted me to build the acquisition models, he actually timed me on it. After a few days, the guy demanded to see my progress so I gave it to him, not even halfway complete. When I walked by his office later, his jaws were tight, like he was disappointed or something. I thought the guy had a lot of nerve, badgering me about something he was incapable of doing. I finished the model to my satisfaction by the end of the week – an LBO-type model that could be used for any industry. Leatherman II then questioned me about it incessantly. I explained to him that regulated businesses had to maintain a minimum level of capital, and the market measured them on how efficiently they employed that capital. Therefore, we should measure our acquisitions based on a return on total invested capital. I quickly realized that during our conversations, he was asking all the questions and I was delivering the answers even though he was my boss. He was picking my brain but trying to give the appearance that he was actually managing me. He then took the model to the company's CEO to explain how the acquisitions would work financially; however, he never allowed me to attend the meetings.

During the group's first acquisition attempt Leatherman II requested about 3 million changes to the projections, with multiple scenarios. I made it look easy. After the project was finished, he requested that I send the model to one of the top investment banks in the world. He wanted to ascertain if it was technically correct. I was hesitant and thought to myself, "Why in the world would I do that? He had never sent his work for an external review so why was he sending mine?" I was miffed that sinse the guy was my boss, why did he not know the details of the financial model? For some reason this guy was trying to "get me got" and did not want to believe I was as good as I was. After I sent it, he never broached the issue again nor mentioned the feedback from the investment bank. I assumed they told him something he didn't like – the model was perfect. If they had found a mistake I never would have heard the end of it. About a year after I had started with this new group we hired a senior deal guy onto the team. The new guy had some very interesting views about African Americans. I called him "Campanis" because he reminded me of the former general manager of the Los Angeles Dodgers – Al Campanis – who thought blacks did not possess the mental capacity to manage a ball club. I showed the model to the guy and he simply stared at it as if it was written in Greek. We went through it in a tremendous amount of detail . . . how I projected regulatory capital requirements and the IRR on the deal. Campanis had supposedly graduated from a top business school, yet I had to explain how an IRR was calculated – something we learned in our first two weeks at Darden. He took it back to his office and perused it for days. Periodically he would come back and challenge me on something and I would explain to him why it was correct. He eventually had to admit, almost disappointingly, "This is an excellent model."

Campanis and I worked on several proposals together, which raised my suspicions about the guy. We would write sections of a specific proposal and then review each other's work. I would check his section for errors, concepts that did not make sense and areas where his written explanation were not consistent with the financial projections. I would point them out to him and ensure he made the necessary changes. However, if he found a mistake or what he perceived to be a mistake in my work, he would run to Leatherman II to show his value-added. After one proposal he called me into his office to discuss the model, for seemingly the 500th time. He had circled in red ink the depreciation expense on the income statement – he was so excited. I showed him a separate page of fixed assets and details of how they were depreciated. He explained to me why I was wrong and tried to bait me into a philosophical discussion – the equivalent of arguing over how to tie one's shoes. I had modeled this over a thousand times and knew I had experience on my side. He then threatened to send the model to a partner at one of the Big Five accounting firms for review. I told him to do as he pleased and left. I was embarrassed to have to work around somebody so incompetent that he had to have an accounting firm do his work for him. He never mentioned the conversation again, which meant the accountants agreed with me. If they had not, he would have run to Leatherman II to brag about how he had found a mistake in my work.

Once I told Leatherman II and Campanis that I needed to take a half-day off while my roof was being inspected. I was clear as to my whereabouts and what time I would be in the office. Around 10 a.m. I received a call from the administrative assistant. It was odd because she never stated what she wanted. When I pressed her on it, she simply said, "Campanis told me to call you." I had her transfer the call to Campanis, who started mumbling something and eventually said he didn't want anything. I was livid! The guy had simply called to ensure that I was at home like I said I would be – as if he was an overseer on a plantation. When everybody else took time off, they were simply taking time off. When the black guy took time off he was up to something nefarious. When I returned to the office I walked right into Leatherman II's office and asked if he needed something. He was mum, yet he had this smirk on his face. For some reason he had enjoyed getting under my skin. I then approached Campanis and asked him what he needed and he feigned innocence, responding, "I didn't want anything. I just didn't know where you were." It was clear that he had been running to Leatherman II and bad-mouthing me. Like Mrs. Green, I was now the Jehovah's Witness who everybody was intimidated by and had to be kept in my place. It had gotten silly, too. Instead of working harder to close the knowledge gap, Campanis started hoarding information from me. He would keep me uninformed about important meetings and then tell Leatherman I didn't add much during the meeting. He would also receive updated information about a deal and not share it with me; that way he could sound more intelligent during meetings with management. During my annual review Leatherman II admitted "off the record" what I had already known – they thought I was interviewing for another job. The notion had obviously been put into his head by Campanis; he had been poisoning Leatherman II against me in order to hide his own incompetence and remove someone he saw as a threat. I was now in the land of the Pharisees. I had come in confident and sure of myself, and decided I was leaving the same way.

It's All Subjective

During this particular annual review, Leatherman II also described me as "fortunate." It was a veiled reference to the fact the group had completed two transactions that year, both of which I had worked on. He was implying the transactions were successful by luck or happenstance, not because of anything I had done. Politically he could not talk me up because his mentee, "Miscellaneous," had not completed any deals. Miscellaneous had started in the group after me and had no prior M&A experience. My work, including the financial models, had become the standard for the group. Whenever Miscellaneous had any questions about the model, he would never ask me directly; he would ask Leatherman II or Campanis and they would broach the subject with me. They would then tell Miscellaneous what I had said – this way, it would not appear that an African American was smarter than him or was bossing him around. It was their way of protecting him. The entire time Leatherman II and Campanis were trying to undermine me and get me to doubt my work, they were coaching Miscellaneous, and trying to instill confidence in him. The only problem with Leatherman II's "you're fortunate" quip was that I had been told from the time I was born how intelligent I was, and no one was going to convince me otherwise. Leatherman finished the meeting by saying "it was all subjective" and based solely on his opinion. "This was a technical job," I thought. "Leatherman II is operating his group like a social fraternity."

Matthew Henson, Anyone?

One Sunday afternoon I received a call from an executive at one of the business units; we were working with his division on a potential acquisition. The executive struck me as a Bernie Madoff type figure. He had a reputation for being smart, yet I couldn't ascertain that from having worked with him. We had finished our due diligence and it was time to decide whether or not to move forward with the transaction. The seller was disappointed with our offer and could not understand why the returns did not justify paying his asking price. So of course "Fake Madoff" decided there must have been some mistake with the model. He wanted me to come into the office to go over the numbers with him and the representative from the other side. Why the seller had a say in how we analyzed deals was beyond me. I had to break plans with my family to figure out what Fake Madoff was whining about.

When I arrived at the office Fake Madoff was never specific as to what was wrong with the model. He simply complained that it was not giving him the answer he wanted. During conversations with him and the seller, Fake Madoff made a request that I had never heard of in all my days – he wanted me to email the actual excel model to him and the seller so they could review the calculations themselves. I was incredulous. That was the equivalent of the Redskins sending the Dallas Cowboys their playbook for review. Fake Madoff simply confirmed what I had already suspected – he was trying to look smart and sound smart but in actuality, he was as "dumb as a bag of hammers." His stupidity was compounded by the "deal heat" he was experiencing. An idiot in heat – imagine that combination. I refused to send them the excel spreadsheet; instead, I faxed to them the "key drivers" – a set of assumptions underpinning the projections. The phone conversations, emails and faxes tied me up from around noon until 11 p.m. At the same time I had to attempt to have a productive conversation with an idiot who did not realize he was an idiot. I didn't inform Leatherman II or Campanis (who was supposedly leading the deal) about the goings on because they would have just gotten in the way and created more work and more confusion.

The next day you would have thought all hell had broken loose. Fake Madoff left Leatherman II a voicemail where he wondered if "I understood my own modeling." He also wanted to go through the model with the seller and the entire deal team that afternoon. We got on the conference call and Fake Madoff was still going on about "not understanding our own modeling" again. It was all I could do to keep from laughing. I was on vacation in Paris when an analyst had originally been assigned to the deal. He had been having trouble with the numbers so Leatherman II called me in the middle of my vacation to help out. He described the situation as "imperative." What Fake Madoff did not know was that I had built all of the company's acquisition models. His questioning my competence was the equivalent of questioning Bill Gates' knowledge of the Microsoft operating system. The seller then started in on the estimate of the current year's earnings – the starting point for the projections. He felt we were being too conservative. The first issue was that I only had results through March, which was not enough information to estimate full-year results. It was a herculean effort on my part to even come up with something that appeared credible; instead of being praised, I was getting beaten up on. Secondly, since Fake Madoff's division was buying the company, it was his responsibility to estimate the full year's earnings, not mine. In effect, the guy was trying to fob off his responsibility onto me. We walked through the components of the target company's year-to-date results, line by line. I had simply taken certain line items through March and annualized them. For those revenue and expense items that appeared abnormal, I removed any "one-time" events that would not be recurring post-transaction. Though the transaction had appeared dead at one point, I still reviewed each of these items with the accounting firm helping us with the due diligence. I also documented, in tremendous detail, how the revenue and expense items were derived and how year-end results were estimated. When Fake Madoff saw the details and how they had been confirmed by the accountants, there was complete silence on the other end of the phone. Then the seller started in on why he thought the year-end results would be better than our forecast. This fool thought we were going to take three months of information to estimate the rest of the year. I asked that since it was now July, why not take June results and estimate year-end from there? Again there was stunned silence. It now became clear to Fake Madoff what the seller and I already knew – the target company was not on track to meet its year-end projections. June results would have shown this and that is why the seller wanted to focus solely on March.

What made the conference call even more incredulous was that Leatherman II was not keen on doing the deal. Campanis and I both knew what that meant – it was not going to happen. There was a strange correlation between deals Leatherman II was not keen on and the rate in which senior management did not approve them. While Leatherman II pretended to support the transaction and listen to Fake Madoff's reservations about the modeling, behind the scenes he was trying to kill the deal. I sat there amazed by this wussified way of managing. Instead of telling the guy up-front that he did not support the transaction and the reasons why, Leatherman II simply hid behind my skirt. The guys on my end of the phone were all thinking what a clown Fake Madoff was. Leatherman II was not his friend, nor was the seller. The seller's valuation was unrealistic and if Fake Madoff had acquired the company based on aggressive projections, he would have been called on the carpet by senior management a year later. Pressed as to why the acquisition was underperforming, he then would have positioned himself so that our group took the fall; there was no way we were going to be the mullet in that chain of events. With Fake Madoff and the seller quieted, we ended the call acknowledging that the model was perfect.

My work had been sent to the world's leading investment bank, the top accounting firm and now vetted by the target company's management team. No one in the history of M&A had ever been held to this level of scrutiny. A few years later I read an analyst report which hailed how the company's acquisitions had improved earnings and brought it back from the brink of disaster. It also praised the "unique way in which it analyzed acquisitions based on total capital employed." The ironic part was that the name "Ralph Baker" was never mentioned. Leatherman II had played me like Matthew Henson, running around the company trumpeting a model I had built. We were taught in school that Henson was the first African American to reach the North Pole; in actuality, he was the first person of any race to reach it. The public acknowledged Commander Robert Peary, leader of the North Pole expedition, as the first to reach the North Pole. However, during the journey Peary took ill and sent Henson ahead. Once reaching the Pole, Henson planted the U.S. flag. Only 40 years later did Congress acknowledge Henson's accomplishment and give him equal status with Peary.

Take Credit for Work of Others
A major part of the corporate game is what you can convince people to believe. If you broached an idea during a meeting it would often get shot down or people

would remain quiet, as if they did not approve of it. A few weeks later someone would present that exact same idea, with a slight twist, as if it was his or her own. The issue was never the idea, but that in acknowledging someone else publicly, that person could get some exposure vis-à-vis the rest of the group. And if you continually tried to be a jerk by presenting ideas and making yourself seem smarter than everyone else, you made yourself a target. In particular, Leatherman II would actually take something I had taught him, get into a meeting with senior management and explain it back to me as if he was the teacher. Several times he would explain concepts about the model – the one I had built – to me in front of others. I would simply play along to make him feel smarter than he actually was. After we lost the bid for a company in a hotly contested auction process, I decided to put together a list of acquisition targets in the niche industry the target operated in. The acquisition screen was similar to the first assignment I had worked on at GECC years earlier. I worked independently with an executive of one of the business units, and together we fine-tuned it. We were prepared to inquire about partnering with the more attractive companies on the list; then seemingly out of nowhere, Campanis started calling the business unit executive to introduce himself and discuss his new role with the group. He also wanted to discuss the acquisition screen I had created. The executive was obviously confused as to why he was getting phone calls from Campanis about a project he and I had been working on for months. Campanis had sat on his rear end, and once he saw the project was gaining traction, decided to take it over. Both he and Leatherman II were in agreement; he never made a decision unless he first had Leatherman II's approval. Together they decided Campanis would lead my project and eventually I would get the hint. My work led to an acquisition called "Project Edsel." No one in the group had ever done an acquisition screen, but it later became all the rage. Leatherman II created screens for all of the business units. But of course, he made it seem like it was his idea and he was teaching me something new.

Even more annoying was while Campanis was attempting to take over my project(s), the guy couldn't do his own work. As I was about to leave work around 5:30 p.m. one afternoon, Leatherman II and Campanis asked me to write a review of the company's brokerage operations. The review had to be finished by the following morning in advance of a meeting with management. They were gassing me up, telling me how I knew the business and what value I could add to the project. Leatherman II's jaws were tight – he looked this way when he was upset or about to do something unethical. I had read every article and trade journal about investment banks and brokerage houses since my days at Darden. I read the background on our business and literally made up something on the fly. I mentioned that despite the business' poor financial results, the research team was top tier; it was the true jewel of the business and needed to be salvaged. I made several high-level observations but made it clear that if the research guys left, the value of the firm would decline precipitously. It took me until about 3 a.m. to finish it. They took the work, presented it to senior management and never mentioned it again. I found out later that Campanis had been working on the presentation for over a week. At the last minute he and Leatherman II dumped it onto my plate. Because Campanis was incapable of doing the work, I had to stay up all night to do it for him. A few years later while having dinner with Fake Madoff on his failed acquisition, he started chirping about the brokerage business and the impact on research if we tried to shop it around the Street. I guess he was trying to impress us with his knowledge. His comments were what I had written earlier, verbatim. I sat there in disbelief – my work had been circulated around the company as the gospel and Leatherman II and Campanis had taken credit for it.

For Mistakes, Position Yourself So Someone Else Takes the Fall

From the outside it appears as if people rise through the ranks in corporate America based on talent, drive and business acumen. The true reason is due to their mastery of office politics. The first step in this mastery is to take credit for the ideas of others. The second step is to position yourself so that others take the blame for your mistakes. A year after completing the first acquisition in Leatherman II's group, the CEO wanted to know why the actual results had fallen short of the projections. During due diligence, the business unit executive was afraid the CEO would not approve the deal, so he made the projections more aggressive. I pointed out to Leatherman II that accelerating the revenue growth would not have much of an impact on the returns because in regulated businesses, the higher the revenue, the more capital the company required. The increase in required capital would drag down the returns. The anomaly was that regulated businesses actually made more money once they stopped growing. He brushed me off and gave me a look as if, "This black guy thinks he's smarter than me." After the fallout, instead of blaming the executive from the business unit, Leatherman II went combing through the model in hopes of finding an error so he could blame me. Everybody knew the business unit executive had pushed for those projections and now that he couldn't produce, he was trying to position himself so that someone else would take the fall. It also became clear that given a choice between subordinates and his internal client, Leatherman II would be quick to throw us under the bus.

When it came to mistakes "it was always somebody else's fault." It seemed like Leatherman II assigned blame based not upon reality, but upon who he did not like personally. Whenever a mishap occurred the senior guys in the group would go behind closed doors and discuss who was going to take the blame – it was ingrained in the culture. Once, Leatherman II called me into his office and asked what I knew about a particular deal. He had this grave look on his face. I hadn't the slightest idea what he was referring to. Someone had dropped the ball on something and he was determined to hand me the "shit end of the stick." This was the part of high finance that they didn't teach you in business school. When he found out it was not my fault, he never mentioned it again. Even GECC, with its so-called "best management practices" engaged in this behavior. There was an executive whom they referred to internally as "Teflon" because "nothing sticks to him." For those LBOs that resulted in $1.3 billion write-offs, the story went that Teflon used his clout to personally get many of those deals approved, at the height of the market. When the deals did not work out, hundreds of people lost their jobs – everybody but him. In fact, Teflon rose up the corporate ladder to the level of executive vice president. When I first heard the story it went totally over my head. I found it incredulous. Years later, after having witnessed this phenomenon firsthand, I believed. I also began to understand why the morale of the employees in the New York office had been so dismal. Moreover, corporate America is littered with hundreds of thousands of Teflons.

Butt Kissers and "Yes Men"

When Campanis was not trying to poison Leatherman II against me, he was kissing his rear end. As soon as Campanis joined the group he became Leatherman II's shadow. When Leatherman II went to lunch, Campanis followed. When we went on group outings, Campanis sat under him the entire time and refused to move, staring at him incessantly and laughing extra hard at all his jokes. Whenever he saw someone else in the group speaking to Leatherman II, Campanis would frown disapprovingly, like a jealous lover. He had a way of always complimenting Leatherman II to his face, about how smart he was or what a great leader he was. Campanis' constant praise must have been intoxicating – Leatherman II would sit in Campanis' office chatting for hours, while they gazed into each other's eyes. Then there was the parroting. If you wanted Campanis' opinion on a subject, all you had to do was ask Leatherman II . . . Campanis always agreed. No matter the subject, Leatherman II was always right. If Leatherman II liked golf then Campanis took lessons. Leatherman II was a Duke Blue Devil fan and when Duke won the NCAA national championship, Campanis was the happiest person in the office, despite never having shown an interest in basketball. Nonetheless, Leatherman II's true love was Miscellaneous. Experts say love is less about how you feel about someone, and more about how that person makes you feel about yourself. If Leatherman II thought he was brilliant, then Miscellaneous reinforced it by referring to him as "sensei," a reference to the famed master/student bond from the movie *The Karate Kid*. In turn, Leatherman II referenced how he had "saved Miscellaneous" from a dead-end career when he let him join our group; he seemed to retrieve some sense of power from this fact. Even famed John Pierpont Morgan, the father of the modern-day U.S. capital markets, was not immune to office romances:

> Pierpont doted on [Robert] Bacon and wanted him constantly by his side. It was said Morgan had 'fallen in love' with Bacon and 'rejoiced in his presence.' Bacon's elevation in the bank signaled a problem with the Morgan empire: Bacon, a charming lightweight, reflected Pierpont's fear of hiring commanding figures. That Bacon was second in command spoke poorly of his boss's managerial judgment. Art critic Roger Fry saw Morgan as a vain, insecure despot who 'likes to be in a position of being surrounded by people he has in his power to make and unmake.'[1]

I saw the roles within the group as technical jobs that few in the world were capable of performing. You could not simply hire or reward people based solely on who shared your politics, your religion or favorite college basketball team. I wondered how many other corporations operated this way, and how long it would take before corporate America crumbled from placing people in decision-making positions based solely on who always agreed or referred to the boss as "sensei."

NEW YORK SHOCK EXCHANGE

In 2004 I began coaching my son's 9U basketball team in a recreational league in Brooklyn. He was incredulous and questioned my credentials as a coach. I begged my cousin Tommy to help me. I told him I would only do it if he would be the assistant coach. The league ranked the kids based on skill level. The coaches then drafted the players they wanted. I was excited to be working with kids and sharing my love of the game with my son. The team was not very good though. The talent level ranged from pretty good to "tabula rasa." I was amazed at how 9-year-old boys could not make a lay-up or did not know the rules. I quickly learned that this new generation spent more time playing video games than playing real basketball. The team literally got destroyed. Though the draft process was supposedly fair, some teams were stacked with talent. However, as the season went on, we actually won a few games and ended up making the playoffs. The parents liked how we encouraged the kids and the intensity Tommy and I brought. The other coaches loved us because we "worked so well with the kids." The following year when the league held the draft I didn't rely on the ratings; I already knew which kids I wanted from having seen them play. I also noticed how coaches "gamed" the system by having highly-skilled players purposely perform poorly during the tryouts to get a low rating. The coaches then drafted the players whose ratings were lower than their skill levels implied. We began the season by having fun and creating controversy. After we defeated the so-called "team to beat" in the final seconds, the opposing coach complained to the league commissioner. By midway through the season we were still undefeated; the opposing coaches complained about me so much that the commissioner sat behind our bench just to monitor my coaching style. He would stare at me as if I was the black Rasputin, employing some type of magic. I understood their issue had nothing to do with basketball and more to do with destroying their assumptions. Of the 10 teams, only two were coached by African Americans. And of African-American kids who participated, the majority was accompanied by the mother. You rarely saw the dad. The mere thought of black men involved with their kids must have been a foreign concept. Then we had the nerve to win the championship; we weren't supposed to know anything about basketball strategy or tactics. Little did they know that I had competed in college and Tommy had been a high school teammate of Billy Donovan's, the coach for the University of Florida.

Dream Big Dreams

In 2006 I finally started an 11U AAU team like I had promised. I recruited the better players from the recreational league because those were the only kids I knew. The only problem was no one really wanted to do it. What else would 11-year-old boys do in the summertime? I didn't want players from other AAU teams because I wanted to give new kids a chance to play. Some of the parents and coaches from the recreational league were still salty and told kids not to play for me. After weeks of begging, I rounded up about eight players. I couldn't find any 11-year-olds so I formed a 12U team and my son had to play up. We met with all of the kids and parents about the concept of travel basketball and then it got weirder. I named the team "New York Shock Exchange" and we were also going to teach the kids the fundamentals of investing. I got a lot of blank stares and questions as to how it would work. I explained that investing was a life skill they would need to master. If you relied solely on a broker for investment advice then you would get taken for a ride, the same with auto mechanics and contractors. The world where employers offered a pension plan to last throughout your retirement no longer existed; the burden of saving for retirement now rested with employees. The investment ideas would come from the kids and I would help them narrow down the list based upon investment fundamentals. Ralphie told me he thought it was the dumbest idea he had ever heard of and if I did not change the team's name he was going to quit.

Season One

I modeled the program after the Stamford Express. We practiced twice a week, ran drills and did a lot of skill development. The kids seemed like they were really into it and were dying to play some live competition. After each practice I asked them to think about what products they used the most and which companies manufactured them. I told them about Peter Lynch, the famous investor from Fidelity who had outperformed the stock market for 10 consecutive years. Lynch felt that the best investments were companies that made products that you understood and used on a regular basis. That said, the kids probably knew as much, if not more than professional investors like Lynch and myself. We played our first tournament in north Jersey about three weeks after we started. I had no idea how the team would perform but was cautiously optimistic. I watched a few of the games prior to ours and it did nothing to shore up my confidence. I saw kids taking the ball the full length of the floor and finishing with either hand. About 30 minutes prior to our game, some big kids walked past, somebody's 14U team, I thought. I envisioned that whoever we played, the difference would come down to my coaching acumen.

We stepped on the court and my son screamed, "Look at 'em!"

I replied, "Look at who?" I could not see what the big deal was.

Then he screamed again, "Look at 'em Dad!"

Annoyed, I replied, "Look at who?" I did not see the team we were playing anywhere around. Maybe they were running late or afraid to show up. They surely must have heard about my level of intensity and coaching acumen.

Ralphie, now agitated, screamed again, "Look at them!" But this time he pointed directly at the 14U team that had walked by earlier. For some reason they were warming up on the other side of the court, which I thought was extremely rude. Trying to hold back my laughter I countered, "You didn't think we were playing them did you? Don't be so silly. They must be playing after us."

Those boys proceeded to beat the living daylights out of us. We got out to an early lead and that just made them madder. They started pressing and fast-breaking and it was a wrap after that. The other team looked like a bunch of "little LeBrons" – point forwards who could handle the ball, shoot from outside and play about four different positions. To a man, they were bigger and stronger than every one of my players. When the smoke cleared the score was 72-13. The entire experience was pretty surreal. When we shook the other team's hands I noticed that they had at least five players over six feet tall. The parents commented that the kids on the other team were aged 13 and 14, if not older. All I could think was, "Why would they do that? What does a coach get out of putting older kids in a basketball tournament and why would the parents allow it?" I was actually tickled to death to be hanging out with my son. As far as getting blown out, I figured it could not get any worse. But it did. The next tournament was in Philadelphia, Pennsylvania at Temple University. Our first game was against a team from Baltimore – they were huge. One of their forwards had muscles as big as mine. We got blown out again and I got excited over our simply making a basket. They were too big, too fast, and too strong for us to realistically compete. What made it worse was that we had this catchy name – "New York Shock Exchange." If our name had been something more nondescript like the "Tigers" or "Lions," no one would have remembered us. I started telling people we were from Rhode Island. I told so many lies I couldn't keep up with them all. One of the spectators said, "I thought you said you all were from Vermont." Sheepishly I replied "Yeah. We live on the border of those two states."

In between games I stood apart from the team – not too far where I could not keep an eye on them, but far enough where no one could tell we were together. I was too embarrassed. Someone asked Ralphie about the coach and he said, "My Dad's the coach." This boy proceeded to walk the guy down the hall to where I was standing, pointed and said, "Here he is right here. That's my dad." Bless his heart. He was so proud. Meanwhile, I had this look of horror on my face like I had just committed a crime and was about to be found out. When the guy questioned me about the team I told him, "I don't know. You have to ask the head coach but he didn't make the trip. I'm only the part-time volunteer assistant coach, on an interim basis." At our next tournament at Fordham University, we faced a team that was even bigger than the last. A few kids were at least 6'4" playing 12U. It was crazy. After the game, one of the parents on the opposing team suggested that we participate in an outdoor tournament in Fort Greene called *Hoop Connection*; that would be more our speed. We joined their 12U/13U bracket and got blown out consistently by 25 to 30 points every game. This was worse because now we were the laughingstock of the neighborhood. People would just show up to see how badly we would lose. After the games we discussed the economy and the stocks the kids were most bullish about. The whole park would look at us like we had two heads. The kids picked a group of stocks and narrowed the list to GameStop and Apple Computer. However, I tried to talk them out of it. I had never even heard of GameStop and I thought Apple Computer was overvalued. Eventually, Microsoft's Zune would run Apple and the iPod out of business, as usual. I picked Phoenix Insurance Companies, not based on fundamentals, but because it would soon be taken over. The kids were howling and complaining that the process was not fair since I was an expert.

Some of the local kids would approach us about playing; we needed the help so we let them join. The new kids never came to practice so I had to make a Faustian bargain – draw a hard line and continue to get blown out or let them play. I chose the latter and an amazing thing happened – we started winning. The new kids added some size and talent and the original crew got a lot better. Not only were we scrappy, but we were more organized than the local teams. We made the playoffs and our luck kept getting better – the number one seed did not make our game in time and had to forfeit. That put us in the championship game. One of the new kids, Darryl, was our best player. I called this kid every day to remind him of Saturday's championship game. I usually picked him up but he swore to me he had a ride and would be there on time. Come Saturday morning, there was no Darryl. I called the kid's house about 20 times and no one answered. We played another team from Brooklyn that was stacked with talent. We outplayed them in the first half but wore down late and lost by about eight points. It was our best game. The kids got second place trophies, which were well-deserved.

At the end of the summer I set about building a website (www.newyorkshockexchange.com) to chronicle the kids' accomplishments and document our thoughts on the economy and stock market. In retrospect, it was a pretty ambitious mission. I struggled to perfect what exactly our philosophy was. I created a concept that I thought was rather hokey at first, but decided to include it anyway:

> To challenge student athletes to "dream big dreams" on the basketball court as well as in the business world. The Shock Exchange is a big proponent of visualization – before you can achieve something you must first visualize it."

I'm From Marcy Son!
Darryl, who had previously bailed on us, had bragged about what great players his friends were. I decided to go meet these kids and try to build a relationship. Darryl had relatives he sometimes stayed with in the famed Marcy Housing Projects in Brooklyn where his boys also lived. They had raw talent but were pretty undisciplined and talked a lot of trash. I told them when tryouts were and the requirements. I needed more players and they needed a team so it appeared to be a match made in heaven. We practiced a few times and that was an adventure. Once they found out they were on the team they went hog wild. They clowned around the entire practice and I had to tell them five times to do something. When I tried to teach them the "motion offense" they started running around and shooting the ball from half court. When some of the kids who played the previous summer saw them, they quit immediately. I put the team in a holiday tournament hosted by the Brooklyn Bears. The first hurdle was getting the kids from Marcy to the game, which was only a mile from where they lived.

I had to pile everyone into my car, drop them off and then circle back to get the rest of them. None of the parents showed up, which I thought was odd. When we finally played it was the same story – every team was bigger, stronger, faster and older than my team. Nonetheless, the kids actually played very well. A lot of it was a freelance style of play. We needed to be more organized to win the tournament, but overall, I was impressed. The second night of the tournament I surprised the team with a new set of uniforms that had arrived that morning. We played well, plus I got a chance to meet other people in the Brooklyn basketball community. Some of the kids decided to walk home afterward, though they had insisted on riding with me before. On the way back to Marcy, Charlie, the point guard, said he had just gotten "recruited." The Bears' coach had asked him for his phone number after one of the games. He wanted Charlie to play with his team from then on since they were winning. I remained silent but literally could not believe that the guy would do that. Here I was supporting his event and he was using it as an opportunity to steal one of my players. After I got home one of the players called and said, "Coach, You may want to check your uniforms. I think those kids from Marcy stole 'em. Don't tell 'em I told you because I don't want a problem with them. You left the uniforms with Charlie when you went inside the gym. He told the other kids to take the uniforms. He said, 'What's that punk gonna do?' They all stuffed the uniforms in their bags and under their coats. Coach you can't tell'em I told you. Those dudes are a bunch of thugs."

I checked the box of uniforms and sure enough, eight were missing. I called the ringleader, DaJuan, and inquired about the uniforms, to which he replied, "I don't know." I pulled a page out of Rochelle's (Sovran Bank) playbook and said, "My man, I know you all have my uniforms and I want 'em back. I don't care who took them. I don't care how you get them back, but I am coming down to Marcy in the morning and you all had better have them." I called each of the kids and their parents with the same message. The next morning I retrieved all of the uniforms except for a pair of shorts. Let's just put this way, I didn't go back down there again. I just charged it to "the game." I asked the ringleader why they stole from me and all he could say was, "I don't know." I never had any contact with the kids from Marcy after that. Whenever I saw the Bears coach there was always an awkward silence. In every conversation he never failed to mention Charlie. He would start with something to the effect of, "You know Charlie sure is unreliable. We had a tournament in Vegas and I couldn't get the kid out of bed. Does the boy wanna play ball or what?" After a few of these encounters I realized that he thought I held a grudge over the incident. Here he was focused on a 13-year-old kid I would not trust alone with my uniforms, while I was probably daydreaming about the reunification of North Korea and South Korea. In actuality, I had forgotten all about the kid; I only wanted to coach my son. However, I did run into Charlie about three years later at Brower Park in Brooklyn. He saw me first and tried to duck away. I barely recognized him. He had grown about two inches to around 5'6" and had a potbelly. I had heard he stopped playing ball and was running around Marcy pulling capers, trying to play "stick up kid."

Season Two

In the summer of 2007 I was determined to make the Shock Exchange a household name. I watched a lot of youth league games over the winter and tried to recruit the best players I could find. I had caught basketball fever and was gung ho about expanding to three different age groups – 12U, 13U and 16U. I got three coaches to help out as well. I visited several recreational centers in Brooklyn; for those centers that did not have teams during the summer, I asked them to encourage their kids to play with us. My marketing efforts worked too. The tryouts were packed with about 60 or so kids. We selected the kids we wanted and waited a month for the season to get started. I figured it would be an interesting summer.

Crabs in a Basket?

Our first game was in the famed Brower Park tournament in the Crown Heights section of Brooklyn. Our 12U team was about to tip off against a youth center out of Brownsville. Out of nowhere the opposing coach starting yelling, "I know he ain't playing! He's too old! We know him!" The entire park stopped and looked over at the commotion. I hadn't the slightest idea what he was talking about, but he was looking directly at a kid named Brian, our power forward from Brownsville. I was pissed. I had not yet received a copy of everyone's birth certificate before the game. However, I had gotten a verbal assurance from the better players and their parents that they were the correct age. The shady coaches in these streetball events were known to request the birth certificates of kids who were doing damage. Brian was what the kids called "bralic" – 6'1" and 185 lbs. He looked like a 12-year-old George McGinnis, the former pro for the Indiana Pacers and Philadelphia 76'ers. I was salivating. I asked Brian again was he 12 years old and he said "yes." I told the referee to start the game. But the opposing coach, who was built like a construction worker, would not let it go. He kept harping on the kid being too old and some of his players were nodding their heads in agreement. Brian then pulled out a copy of his birth certificate and showed it to the official. The coach then started yelling, "I don't care. That birth certificate could be a fake. How I know that's the right birth certificate?" Now I knew he was crazy!

I had promised our parents that the kids would learn the game of basketball in a safe environment; this did not appear safe. I made sure I kept my distance, but warned him not to talk to any more of my players. When play resumed Brian was putting in work – grabbing rebounds, blocking shots, etc. The opposing coach kept woofing and I asked the official to give him a technical foul for unsportsmanlike conduct . . . he was trying to take the game away from the kids. Nobody wanted to hear that nonsense. The coach then went on about, "We know him. He gotta come back to the neighborhood eventually!" And that's when I erupted! This was clearly a veiled threat aimed at the kid. The referee stopped play for the third time and called us both to center court. I told the official, "If this ex-con makes another reference to any of my players, we're leaving." I then looked right at the coach and challenged him, "I know who I am. I'm the All-American out here Hoss . . . And who might you be again?" He never said another word after that. But the damage had been done. Brian was shook. He was totally despondent, and his body language signaled that he wanted to be someplace else. The opposing team was actually pretty organized and well coached. They calmed down after they started winning and eventually defeated us by eight points. Admittedly, I was taken aback by their sense of entitlement. Since they were from the 'hood and we were from the suburbs (at least that's what they assumed), we weren't supposed to win. The next year when we faced off again in Brower, Brian was playing with them – exactly what the ex-con had wanted all along. Suddenly Brian's age was no longer a problem. The last time I saw Brian would be at another outdoor tournament in 2010. He walked right by me to grab a drink of water and I didn't even recognize him. He was skinny and his teeth were rotted out. He looked like a 25-year-old man but he could not have been any older than age 15. He had also lost all of his basketball skill – the real reason I didn't notice him. I later ran into one of Brian's classmates who said he had been using drugs heavily, of which crystal meth was one.

And that was pretty much how the entire summer went. I was the catalyst for about six teams that summer – the two additional age groups for the Shock Exchange and the four teams the recreational leagues started simply to keep the kids away from me. They decided, "Why let them play for this guy when we can do what he does?" Several of the kids who came to my tryouts quit due to pressure from their local recreational centers. We even had kids playing on two different teams, and when we played those teams in the same event the kid was pressured to pick one. Right before one game, a coach took my uniform off of a kid and made the boy wear his. Some of the coaches for these new teams were prepared for some beef with us, but I never said a word. I sat back and let them have their wish, and they got absolutely "cooked." I knew they were unorganized and would face tougher competition than they were used to. When the losses mounted, I saw their teams give up during games, a lot of crying, and pouting. A few of the teams quit and did not come back. In actuality the coaches were not there for the kids. They wanted to win for the benefit of their own egos. When they realized it would take time to develop a winning team, they didn't want to be bothered. One team was getting cooked so badly that the kids walked off the court in the middle of the game claiming, "The coach can't coach." The parents asked for their money back but the coach refused. One of the parents, from a notorious housing project in Brooklyn, sent her goons to retrieve her $75 fee. When the coach recanted this story to me I simply shook my head.

However, these new teams did accomplish one goal – they kept their best players away from the Shock Exchange. They were behaving like crabs in a barrel, the analogy Carter G. Woodson used to describe African Americans in his book, *The Miseducation of the Negro*. For all their complaints about "The Man," in many ways African Americans are their own worst enemies. Whenever you put a bunch of crabs in a basket, as one tries to escape the others pull him back so he can share the fate of the rest of them. Woodson coined the phrase to describe the behavior of African Americans who undermine each other's attempts to become successful. To make matters worse, the two coaches who had volunteered to participate had to beg off because of increased commitments at work. So now I was stuck coaching three teams. I did get one of the parents to help coach the 12U team though. Believe it or not the guy, William, attended Prince Edward with me. His son played on the team too and was also affiliated with another team – the Pelicans. Coach William came off somewhat like a caricature – he was always plotting something. He would constantly tell me about which players he could steal from the Pelicans, but I would quickly change the subject. First of all, I did not want that type of program, nor I did want a war with the Pelicans. I preferred to stay under the radar. Secondly, if he was plotting to steal players from the Pelicans I suspected he would try to steal from the Shock Exchange as well. I also noticed how he took a special interest in the best players, constantly complimenting them. However, I had my hands full with two other teams and did not have time to manage the guy.

I could not be three places at once so I scheduled all of the games at Brower Park and Wingate Park, less than a mile apart. The first hurdle was getting the kids to the games. There were about 24 kids and four parents. I would give the kids and their parents the exact directions to the park – driving and by subway. And every Saturday, without fail, some of the players got lost. There was one kid on the 12U team from the Ukraine; his mother could not understand English but she was at every game at least 20 minutes early. Meanwhile, the black folks who had grown up in Brooklyn couldn't get their kids to the games on time. And of course it was my fault because I didn't give them good directions. If the kids and parents had low expectations off the court, then what could I expect from them on it? We practiced one day per week, ran plays, performed shooting drills and defensive drills, etc. Most of the kids on the older teams would simply freelance and revert to streetball. Whenever I tried to hold them accountable for what we learned in practice, they resisted. If they could run faster and jump higher than the other team then we won. If not, we lost. Taking them out of their comfort zone was like pulling teeth. Out of three teams only four of the kids had family members there to support them. So I knew no one was working with them at home on their weaknesses. A few of the parents questioned me whenever the team lost as if it was my fault. I could hardly hold back my laughter at the thought, as if I were competing.

At the end of the summer one of the players had an older brother who was gunned down in broad daylight. The incident was in all of the newspapers. The kids said the guy was standing on the street corner minding his own business when a member of a gang shot him at close range. At that point I realized, "I wasn't in Kansas anymore." While I was preaching basketball many of these kids were trying to survive. I stopped being so hard on them after that. Besides, the basketball fever I had developed earlier had started to fade and begun to feel more like work. Every Sunday around 6 p.m., I would skip dinner and curl up in the bed in the fetal position. I would not wake up until the next morning just in time for work. However, the kids were eager to participate in the investment meetings, which I was pleased with. After all, that was what the program was all about, right? My cousin, David Neverson, was now running the meetings and I would chime in from time to time. I would give him an outline of what I wanted to cover and get out of his way. Dave was working at a private equity firm and the kids and parents were mesmerized by him. He would start the meetings by discussing how the economy was slowing and give statistics on dismal housing starts, declining automobile sales and home prices. Then we would drill down on the price-to-earnings ratios and expected growth rates of the stocks we owned. In August I was updating the website with the performance of each of the stocks when I did a double take. The returns I was deriving could not have been accurate. I spent a while proofing the numbers and started to question whether or not I could add and subtract anymore. I shot Dave an email to take a look at my analysis. There was no way I was going to post those results onto the website; nobody would have believed it. Dave called back and confirmed my calculations – the stocks of GameStop and Apple Computer had achieved returns of 82% and 112%, respectively. Phoenix Companies, the stock I had picked, had a return of negative 1%. Those kids were smarter than me and any other investment manager on the planet. I leaned back in my chair and scratched my head.

Season Three

In 2008 I scaled the program back and focused on the 13U team only. I was amped up and had a lot of news to share with the kids. We were hosting "Shock Exchange Comes to Harlem" – our first AAU tournament – March 21-22 at City College. *Black Enterprise* magazine had heard about the exciting things we were doing off the court and wanted to profile us. But there was only one problem – nobody wanted to play. I could only round up three kids from the previous year's team. My two best players, Calvin and Shane, were nowhere to be found. I spoke to Calvin and he admitted that he was leaving to play for the Pelicans – he cited that he wanted to win more and the Pelicans offered him more exposure. Over the winter, Coach William called several times for Calvin's phone number and those of a few other kids. He wanted them to play for some CYO team he was coaching. I had my reservations, but if the parents didn't mind then I was fine with it. I later found out he had been bringing Calvin and Shane, the two best players, over to his house for dinner, helping them with their homework, etc. And overnight they were also best friends with William's son. I was livid. Not only was Coach William trying to steal my players, but he had them over to his house without my knowing about it. Two of the top programs in New York City had been shut down due to inappropriate relationships with the boys on the team. If William had some ulterior motive for bringing grade school boys to his house, then I did not want my name associated with it. Now Shane, Calvin and William's son were playing for the Pelicans, where they made William an assistant coach due to his ability to "recruit" elite players. I called him up and read him the riot act. It turned my stomach that some "desperate crab," unable to make his high school basketball team, was trying to eat off my plate. The following year the Pelicans' program was shut down. Instead of using the parents' team fees to pay for tournaments, the head coach ran off with their money – I had seen this coming from a mile away. Shane's mother later called me out of the blue about letting him play with us in the second annual "Shock Exchange Comes to Harlem." William had put the notion in her head that Shane was the second coming of Nate "Tiny" Archibald, but I quickly brought her back to reality. I told her, "Your son will never wear my uniform again . . . in this lifetime or the next."

Black Enterprise

In February of 2008 I received a call from Jessica Jones, a freelance writer who had heard about the stock-picking prowess of the Shock Exchange. We spoke over the phone where she asked a lot about my background and the rationale behind the program. I sent her a link to the website chronicling the stock picks and the due diligence done by the kids. I also sent the presentations on the meetings where we had predicted the looming recession. She wanted to attend our next investment meeting, which was scheduled for the second week in March, a week before "Shock Exchange Comes to Harlem." I tried to steer the conversation away from the tournament because I was not sure if anybody would show up. I had a lot of teams interested, but only a few had actually paid. I told the parents and kids that *Black Enterprise* would be at our next investment meeting, so dress up and come prepared. They were giving me that look again, like, "Is this guy for real?" Nobody believed me. In fact, I didn't believe me. Jessica and a photographer actually did show up. If I had known they were coming for sure, I would have gotten a haircut. Anyway, the entire event was surreal, our most intense meeting ever. We discussed the performance of the investment portfolio and how our kids were actually smarter than professional stock pickers because (i) they could spot trends before adults could and (ii) we focused on products the kids used on a regular basis. I finished the meeting with my take on how the economy was experiencing stagflation and was in the worst shape since the Nixon Administration. Within six months everybody from the Senate, to the president to Wall Street analysts would quote me and the Shock Exchange verbatim. However, they would conveniently forget to cite the source. April and May went by with no *Black Enterprise* article. The kids and I waited with bated breath. The June issue showed Senator Barack Obama on the cover, with no mention of the Shock Exchange. I felt bad for the kids since they had gotten their hopes all up high. Then in the July issue the article ran. It was a five-page spread – the largest article in the entire magazine. It featured the team and our tournament, better than I had hoped for. The article also proved prescient – it went in depth into the need for financial literacy, which the entire nation would soon become overly concerned with.

Shock Exchange Comes to Harlem

In 2008 our budget was limited and I noticed that there were few AAU events in New York City; most were in New Jersey, Connecticut or down south. I thought it would be a cool idea to have a local event right in the city. The sell to local teams would be that you could play a top event in your own backyard, with no travel costs. I started marketing the March 2008 event in September 2007. The first person I reached out to was Jimmy Salmon of the NJ Playaz. I remembered his team from the Eddie Griffin days at "Rumble in the Bronx." In the email I told him we were just starting out and needed to partner with more established teams like the Playaz. I contacted every top team in the city – Gauchos, Riverside, Metrohawks, and New Heights. I kept calling and emailing until someone told me to stop. People had seen our website but nobody knew me from a can of paint. I called the director of the Metrohawks so many times that whenever he heard my voice, he would take a deep breath and sigh, "You again?"

I arranged to have the event with City College in Harlem due to its rich basketball tradition. I named it "Shock Exchange Comes to Harlem" after the '70s movie *Cotton Comes to Harlem*, which I was not supposed to watch. A month before the event, I had a lot of promises, some "maybes" and about four checks. I got my big break when Jimmy Salmon finally made a commitment to come about three weeks before the tournament. Then seemingly out of nowhere teams starting inquiring about the tournament, and would the Playaz be there? Teams who previously would not return my phone calls were now begging to get in. I got commitments from about 36 teams in a period of three weeks. I had to turn teams away due to lack of space. The day of the tournament, it was total madhouse – a lot of anxiousness coupled with the novelty of having an event in Harlem. Then throw in some drama, and it was an event to remember. One team didn't like the schedule so they walked out without even paying me. Their parents also demanded a return of their entry fee. On their way out, they made an odd comment to the effect of, "We know this is a big tournament and all." They were an elite team and the entire gym was watching to see if I would cater to their demands to get them to stay. I said "bye" and kept it moving.

The second day I was face-to-face with coaches I had only read about – Jimmy Salmon, Sandy Pyonin (NJ Roadrunners), Billy Council (Kips Bay), and Gary Sheares (Brooklyn Ballers). I didn't have a clue of what I was doing but it was competitive and exciting, so everyone gave me a pass. Behind the scenes, the giveaways for the winning teams (hoodies, t-shirts) were stuck at a UPS warehouse in Brooklyn that was closed on Saturdays. Tommy had to use his winning personality to retrieve my stuff. Had he not have, I am certain that some of those teams would have made me disappear. Three years later "Shock Exchange Comes to Harlem" has become one of the top events in the city, drawing teams like the Roadrunners, Brooklyn Ballers, Maryland Ruffriders, NY Falcons, Hudson Valley Hornets, Rockland Rockets, Boys Club of New York, New Heights, and Kendall Madison Playaz every year. We have had two McDonald's All-Americans (Doron Lamb, Jayvaughn Pinkston) attend and kids who have gone on to play at Kansas State, Maryland, Oregon State, George Mason, Kentucky, Villanova, Fordham, and Arizona, to name a few. The team that walked out that first year has never returned. However, they started their own tournament two years later just like ours. In fact, several other teams have since started high-profile events, bringing top teams to the city.

AAU Basketball – They a Witch!

AAU basketball has been around for decades. But after the expansion of the NBA accelerated the jump from high school to the pros, AAU coaches became almost as important as college coaches. It has also put AAU into the crosshairs of the NCAA. The NCAA used to maintain the services of elite players like Patrick Ewing, Michael Jordan, Mark Aguirre, Doc Rivers, and James Worthy anywhere from three to four years. Today they leave college after one year – the period in which the NBA's mandatory age requirement expires. In contrast, the AAU system controls them from age 8 to age 18. AAU has gotten so much bad publicity that everyone wants to know how to fix it. Just like Lydia Peale knew back in high school, if you have something that somebody else covets, you will be attacked. But when they attack you, it's never because (i) "You got my man and I want him back," (ii) "You control the lion's share of the world's oil supply and we want it," (iii) "You are an expert in financial services and have a wealth of deal experience and I'm threatened by you," or (iv) "You control the next Kevin Durant, LeBron, or Allen Iverson and we want to make money from their services." Instead, they accuse you of being a witch. Below are some of the loudest criticisms of travel basketball.

"Recruiting"

From the day I started the Shock Exchange other coaches have tried to "recruit" my players. The incident with the Brooklyn Bears and Coach William has been a common occurrence. I have always told my players not to speak to other coaches when they are wearing my uniform. Once, I received a call from a coach concerning my big man. He wanted to take the kid with them to the AAU Nationals in Hampton, Virginia but I told him "no." He sold the gesture as "excellent exposure for my big man." Again I told him "no." I knew that once he built a relationship with the kid I would never see him again. AAU coaches pride themselves on being able to recruit players from other programs. Not only does it improve their team's prospects, but it weakens a competitor. One night my 12U team was playing against an Under Armour-sponsored team – one of the best teams in the city. They were stacked with "grade exceptions" – kids 13 years or older but still in the 7th grade. Our forward, Steven, a 6'1" 12-year-old had the game of his life. He scored 35 points and was clearly the best player on the court. Our other top player was taken out of the game mentally. He was all emotional because kids from his former travel team were in the stands teasing him. Needless to say, we got blown out. As we were leaving the gym, Steven was surrounded by about four men in mink coats and gold chains. I asked them what they wanted and one of them responded, "We want to talk to your player." I literally saw my life flash before my eyes. You should have seen it. Steven gave them his name and phone number as they were gassing him up. The Under Armour-sponsored team offered him an embarrassment of riches and the opportunity to travel throughout the country for free. He had to call his parents to find out what his next move would be. I knew then that he was leaving the Shock Exchange but I never begged him to stay. "You can't steal a player that does not want to be stolen," I thought. He and his parents never said he was formally quitting. He simply stopped showing up. After that, I stopped trying to recruit and develop new players for other teams to steal. I just focused on the kids who remained loyal. We became less about winning and more like a family; the kids suggested that we change our name to the "New York Flip Floppers" because kids quit on us so much. I was spending time with my son and he still enjoyed playing. "That was the main thing," I reminded myself. I had no intention of getting into a street altercation over some 12-year-old kid. And just to think, no one knew or even wanted Steven before he played for us.

Three years later I saw Steven at an outdoor tournament with the Under Armour-sponsored team. By then he was a junior in high school but they had him "ringing" in tournaments for 10th graders. In my day a "ringer" was considered a highly skilled player. Today the term connotes a kid who is older than everyone else. He was 6'3", having grown merely two inches over the previous three years. He also had suspect ball-handling skills and an inconsistent jump shot – the exact same weaknesses when he played for us. His current team offered him free trips around the country and exposure, yet the kid had not gotten any better. Steven started the game but was benched for most of the second half after a ball-handling mistake. The kid replacing him was a sophomore being groomed for the future. They won the championship, but after the game I noticed how Steven left the court by himself, apart from the rest of the team. There were no scouts, hangers-on or sycophants plying him with compliments. That was reserved for his team's new superstar, one of the top sophomores in the country and New York City's next phenom. I too had seen this coming from a mile away.

Reclassification

The most popular trend among youth players today is what is known as "reclassification." AAU goes by grade instead of age, so if a kid is an 18-year-old high school junior and is expected to graduate in 2013, he can still play in the 11th grade division. The top scouting services like Rivals.com and Scout.com will classify his year as 2013, despite the fact that kids typically start their junior year of high school at age 16. When two highly skilled teams face one another, the team stacked with grade exceptions will usually dominate because they are older, bigger and stronger. And to the victor goes the spoils – exposure, wins, major shoe endorsements, the best players, and college scholarships.

Where Have All the Black Men Gone?

At one of my practices I criticized a kid for not running our motion offense correctly; he resorted to playground basketball, instead. I stopped play and demanded at least five passes before a shot. I had to point this out to the kid at just about every practice. Instead of taking the criticism in stride, the boy got frustrated and starting gesturing with his hands. I responded with, "You guys act like a bunch of drama queens. You all cry about every little thing." I paused, looked around at the team and realized that of the 10 kids, eight of them were being raised by women. I had never seen their fathers, nor had I ever heard mention of them. And that is when I had a Eureka moment! I had heard the statistics about the high level of incarceration among black males but to me they were just numbers. Once I got involved with kids in the community, the statistics took on new meaning. Nonetheless, these kids had been coddled by their mothers and were not used to having a man lay down the law.

The Coach Can't Coach

The fact that I was coaching a bunch of girls disguised as boys was one thing. The kids did not have a father or older brother at home to teach them the game, and it was killing the team. The only way they could get better was to have their fathers take them to the park and work with them on their weaknesses. Instead of taking my criticism to heart, I knew these kids would simply go home and cry to Mama. They would also whisper behind my back about how "the coach can't coach." As quiet as it is kept, the parent is the first coach. Without having a dad around I knew the game was not being passed down from generation to generation. I was simply a facilitator; if what I was teaching during practice was not being reinforced then the kids would not get better. I empathized with teachers in the inner cities. They have the good fortune of teaching the neediest kids. However, if no one is around to help little Johnny with his homework then little Johnny will not learn. Yet teachers are scapegoated constantly by parents, politicians, et al., that "the teacher can't teach."

The worst player I ever coached spent more time crying to his daddy than he did playing. The kid was lucky to even be on the team, yet his father was always calling and emailing me about something. We played a tournament in D.C. where I told him to "pass the ball to the open man" and I thought the boy was going to throw a bitch fit at center court. He took his jersey off and went into the locker room – this from the sorriest kid on the team. His father called me after the game and talked my ear off for about 20 minutes. As soon as we got home, I dropped him off and told his father never to contact me again. What I was witnessing was unbelievable – undisciplined kids, coaches stealing players, invisible parents – I figured I had to get it all on tape. I spoke to anybody in the entertainment industry who would listen. I eventually worked with some videographers out of Los Angeles to put together a docudrama. I got some great footage and thought I had an unbelievable storyline – the reluctant coach working with some inner-city youth. However, the industry "Pat Booned" me and started developing a similar concept with Mark Wahlberg as the authority figure. Walberg admitted that he and Justin Bieber will be making the movie together with Paramount. The storyline involves basketball and "a reluctant mentor in an inner-city environment."[1]

AAU Does Not Teach the Kids Anything

One of the biggest claims from the NCAA is that AAU coaches do not teach the kids basketball fundamentals. In a lot of ways that is true. However, I break the universe of travel teams into two camps – "managers" and "developers." Managers recruit the best players and have the funding to put them in showcase events where they play in front of top college coaches. They are also skilled at marketing players to get them ranked by the major scouting services. Developers like the Shock Exchange approach the game more from a teaching perspective. They run organized practices and teach basketball fundamentals. The one fact the critics miss is that the kids choose which programs they want to play for. Steven willingly left our program to go to an Under Armour-sponsored team. He never got much better but he received free sneakers, backpacks, hoodies and trips to Las Vegas. Both he and his parents bought the dream they were selling.

A few years ago I came across a *Wall Street Journal* article that quoted NBA player, Michael Beasley, saying something to the effect that, "If you want to learn defense then don't play AAU."[2] It was a veiled reference to Beasley's defensive woes as a member of the Miami Heat. What the article failed to mention was that Beasley attended five high schools. The last high school, Notre Dame Prep, specialized in basketball. He also spent one year at Kansas State. Out of all those schools, none of them taught him how to play defense? And if he really wanted to learn defense then why did he not stay at Kansas State instead of jumping to the NBA after one year of college? The article did nothing more than ride the wave of criticism of AAU coaches. Coincidentally, the majority of elite players in AAU, including Beasley, are coached by African Americans.

AAU Coaches Are Profiting Off the Kids

Nike changed the landscape of the summer basketball circuit when it started funding travel basketball teams in the 1980s. The goal was to build a relationship with youth basketball clubs in hopes of finding the next Michael Jordan to pitch its products. Reebok, Adidas, and now Under Armour have followed suit, offering travel teams six-figure stipends. However, the major shoe endorsements only go to the elite clubs. The majority of AAU clubs operates on shoestring budgets and is funded mainly by parents and friends of the program. Meanwhile, in 2011 the top 10 college coaches made from $7.5 million (Rick Pitino) to $2.1 million (Roy Williams), not including endorsement income from the major shoe companies. Kentucky's John Calipari has been one of the most vocal critics, accusing AAU coaching of "profiting off the kids." He has even suggested that the NCAA only allow recruiting during the high school basketball season to quell AAU's influence. Coincidentally, Calipari was also the second-highest paid college coach at $4.5 million.[3] The rationale is that an AAU coach who works with a kid from age 8 until age 18 should receive nothing. Meanwhile, a college coach who works with a kid for four years at most, should receive a multimillion-dollar salary.

iHoops . . . Running Black Men Off the Corner?

On season three of HBO's cult classic, *The Wire*, Baltimore's mayor tears down the towers – the housing projects ruled by drug kingpin Avon Barksdale. With his insulated customer base now gone, Barksdale branches out across West Baltimore and takes over the corner operations of lower-level drug organizations. One by one, they capitulate – except for Marlo Stanfield, and a turf war ensues. Stanfield's "moral high ground" versus Barksdale's "muscle," defines season three. The scenario could also be used to describe the grassroots basketball landscape. In 2009 the NBA and NCAA started a joint initiative called iHoops, with Nike and Adidas as founding partners. Its board members included Duke men's basketball coach, Mike Krzyzewski, NBA Deputy Commissioner Adam Silver, and NCAA Vice President of Basketball and Business Strategies, Greg

Shaheen. The iHoops website is owned by NBA Media Ventures LLC, whose chairman is NBA commissioner, David Stern.

iHoops CEO Kevin Weiberg stated iHoops "is to establish a structure and develop programs to improve the quality of youth basketball in America in order to enhance the athletic, educational and social experience of participants." The target market for iHoops is travel and club team basketball but they do not rule out venturing into recreational league basketball.[4] While iHoops' true mission remains unclear, the basketball community has had mixed reactions. Many suspect it is looking to control the recruitment of elite youth athletes and profit from their recruitment – from hosting tournaments to marketing them. A former high school coach was quoted as saying, "'iHoops is going to put control of high school players back in the hands of high school coaches all year round and get rid of these grassroots programs that take advantage of the kids. AAU basketball is in trouble.'"[5] Yet Jim Hart, head of the Albany City Rocks travel team, which operates the "Rumble in the Bronx" event, noted that the NBA and NCAA were expecting a return on their $50 million investment in iHoops. "They are a FOR-PROFIT company and have to be profitable after three years. [It] doesn't sound like they are there to clean things up. It's hard to be about the kids and for-profit at the same time."[6] Effectively, the NBA and NCAA have publicly criticized grassroots basketball clubs and then set up iHoops to do the same thing – profit off the kids.

Summer Basketball Should Be Controlled by High Schools, Not AAU
Since AAU teams only profit from the kids, the summer grassroots basketball circuit should be controlled by high school coaches instead. This argument is the proverbial sleight of hand and a veiled attempt to remove African-American coaches from grassroots basketball. Again, the fight with the NCAA is over elite players. Using the 2007 high school class as an example (the year Michael Beasley graduated high school), of the 24 McDonald's All-Americans that year, 18 (75%) were African-American. Those kids have been coached by men from their communities since they were in grade school – the African Americans coached by African American men and the Caucasians players coached by Caucasian men. However, the trend is for these elite players to attend prep schools with financial means that are coached by white men. During the recruiting process, if a college coach has to speak with an elite player's AAU coach, there will most likely be a black man on the other end of the phone. If AAU were controlled by high school coaches, the majority of the time college coaches would deal with a Caucasian on the other end of the phone. Moreover, "AAU" has become synonymous with "black."

The following table illustrates a sample of the 2007 McDonald's All-Americans, their AAU and high school coaches. Rather than chasing data by trying to craft this for all 24 players on the McDonald's list, I chose Beasley since he was the subject of the previously mentioned *Wall Street Journal* article. I chose his AAU teammates, Austin Freeman and Nolan Smith, and threw in Chris Wright for good measure since all four players hail from the Washington, D.C. area. Three of the four players suited up for the famed D.C. Assault AAU team, which behind the exploits of Beasley, won the AAU National Championship in 2007. Meanwhile Wright played for Boo Williams out of the Hampton Roads area. Both the D.C. Assault and Boo Williams (the "Dean" of Grassroots basketball) are headed by African-Americans. On the high school level, the trend has been for them to attend prep schools that specialize in basketball and play a national schedule. Most of the prep schools also have white coaches. That said, three of the four players – Beasley, Smith and Wright – played for high school programs where the head coach was Caucasian. The summer grassroots basketball circuit is where college recruiting is done today. Coaches can see hundreds of prospects at one AAU event instead of watching one or two prospects during a high school game. That said, putting grassroots under the control of high school coaches is the same as saying, "Let's exclude African-American coaches from grassroots basketball." When calling on these four kids, each time a college recruiter had to speak to an African American – Curtis Malone or Boo Williams. If college recruiting were controlled solely by the high school coaches, three out of four times the recruiter would have spoken with a Caucasian coach. By happenstance, the grassroots basketball landscape would also mirror that of the NCAA. The majority of the elite players would be African-American and the majority of the coaches, Caucasian.

		AAU			High School		
Player	Race	Team	Coach	Race	Team	Coach	Race
Mike Beasley	AA	DC Assault	Curtis Malone	AA	Notre Dame Prep	Ryan Hurd	C
Austin Freeman	AA	DC Assault	Curtis Malone	AA	Dematha	Mike Jones	AA
Nolan Smith	AA	DC Assault	Curtis Malone	AA	Oak Hill	Steve Smith	C
Chris Wright	AA	Boo Williams	Boo Williams	AA	St John's College HS	Paul DeStefano	C

Sample of 2007 McDonald's Americans

Note: "AA" connotes African-American and "C" connotes Causcasian

SHOCK EXCHANGE FUND

Investment Meeting – Summer 2006

We asked the team to select a list of their favorite stocks that they wanted to invest in. As you would expect, the list included the makers of those products that the kids use on a regular basis, the usual suspects: Microsoft, Sony, and Apple Computer. One company I had not heard of which was popular with the kids was GameStop. We eventually whittled the list down to three stocks – Apple, GameStop, and Phoenix Companies.

We held a few investment meetings with the kids where board member, David Neverson, handed out several research reports on each stock and we discussed the importance of understanding (i) the ticker symbol, (ii) stock price and (iii) earnings per share. We also reviewed how professionals looked at investment fundamentals in order to determine whether an investment made sense financially, as well as from a common sense perspective. The fundamentals we focused on were price-to-earnings ratio ("P/E ratio" or "P/E multiple") and earnings growth rate. The following are excerpts from the Shock Exchange website, chronicling the stock picks.[1]

Fundamentals

Price-to-earnings Ratio

A stock's price to earnings ratio is literally its share price divided by its earnings per share. It is one measurement as to how cheap or expensive a stock is. All things being equal between two stocks (the industry they compete in, expected earnings growth rate, etc.), a higher P/E ratio would reflect that a stock is more expensive than the other, and vice versa. A perfect analogy would be that if two professional basketball players had the same off-court image and same statistics, i.e. points, rebounds, assists, and steals, you would expect them to make the same salary. If not, an industry expert would consider the player with the higher salary to be "overpaid" or to have a "rich" contract.

Earnings Growth Rate

A company's earnings belong to the shareholders. That said, it is only common sense to think that if Company One's earnings are expected to grow faster than Company Two's earnings then Company One (and its earnings stream) would be more valuable than Company Two. This "upside potential" may also explain why two professional basketball players with the same stats today may have two different contracts.

Let's assume that Player One and Player Two both average 18/ppg today. However, Player One's point production by year five of his contract is expected to grow to 30/ppg versus 22/ppg for Player Two. It would make sense that Player One's team (assuming equal talent around both players) would win more games, sell more season tickets, sell more popcorn, sell more apparel, and make more money. That said, a team owner should be willing to offer a higher contract to Player One than to Player Two.

As a rule of thumb, there should be a strong correlation between a stock's P/E multiple and its expected earnings growth. For instance, if a stock's expected earnings growth rate is 25% then it should trade at around 25 times earnings/share at a P/E ratio of 25. In the above example, Apple and GameStop trade at a multiple of 2006 expected earnings ("2006E") of 31.6x and 22.1x, respectively. On the surface, this type of "bottoms up" analysis would imply that Apple is more expensive than GameStop. However, the three year compound annual growth rate ("CAGR") in the earnings of Apple is 316.3% versus 23.2% for GameStop, implying that the differential in the P/E ratios for the two companies may be justified.

Obviously the CAGR in Apple's earnings is an anomaly and may be due to some "noise" in its historical earnings, which may be causing the growth rate to be faulty or unrealistic. However, the 23.2% earnings growth rate for GameStop seems to correlate pretty strongly to its P/E multiple of 22.1x earnings, reinforcing the rule of thumb mentioned earlier. Overall, assuming past is prologue for growth in earnings of Apple and GameStop, common sense tells me that investors have done their homework in awarding Apple a higher P/E multiple versus that of GameStop.

Due Diligence

Apple (Recommended by Ralphie Baker III)

We all know that Apple makes interesting computers but the kids are interested in Apple more for its coolest product, the iPod. Personally, I am overloaded with technology. I have a cell phone, stereo, digital television, camcorder, a VCR and a blackberry that I use at about 70% of their technological capacity. I just do not have time to read each manual thoroughly and the cost (time and efforts) to master the other 30% is just not worth it to me. I do not own an iPod so the kids and Mr. Neverson had to educate me.

What the Kids Say
The iPod digitally stores the music in some type of MP3 file. Apple also has iTunes, which is a music store/music organizer. iTunes stores your music library and you can create playlists and another part connects to the Internet with Apple's internet store where you can download music, music videos, television shows and podcasts. So it involves two different types of medium – music and videos. We understand that the MP3 software is needed in order to convert the music into MP3 format.

Apple decided to leverage the MP3 format to download music and the company continues to add additional services such as video.

The iPod has become a status symbol and you are an "outlier" if you do not own one. Every day on the train you will see a person with an iPod. One player said the iPod was so addictive that his mother takes it into the shower with her, which was a little too much information.

The iPod is so easy to use that it takes about 30 minutes to an hour to figure out everything that you need to know.

Competitors

Dell, Creative Zen, and SanDisk have tried to compete with the iPod to no avail. Nothing has really come close to competing with the iPod. The product's platform has become so user-friendly and is so technologically advanced that it is cool to have one. It also cuts across racial lines and ages where people of all ages use the iPod on a regular basis.

Risks

Microsoft . . . period. The kids and I had an interesting debate about the power of Microsoft. I relayed the story of how Microsoft practically ran competing products such as the Macintosh operating system, lotus, etc. out of business by gaining market share with its own competing products (MS-DOS and Excel). In economics there is a term called "network externalities" which implies that when a user joins a network such as Microsoft's operating system, the power of that next user is not linear but exponential (I'm showing off). Microsoft eventually set the standard and customers eventually decided there was no need to buy competing products. I posed the question as to whether Microsoft could do the same with the iPod.

The kids and the precocious Mr. Neverson acknowledged that Microsoft has committed to entering the market using the product. However, they countered that Microsoft does not have stores to sell the product or educate consumers.

Furthermore, the only downside they saw about the iPod was that you had to send it to the store to change the battery. You cannot buy batteries just anywhere, which I found interesting.

GameStop (Recommended by Alexander Williams)

I had never heard of GameStop until Christmas of 2005. I took my son and my nephew to the Tysons Corner mall in northern Virginia to buy my nephew a Christmas present. We walked around for about 30 minutes when they saw GameStop and immediately started running and screaming. My nephew wanted a video game (seemingly only from GameStop) because according to him, GameStop had the best selection.

When I told them I had never heard of GameStop, the boys looked at me as if I were from planet Mars. What I observed was that it was not enough for my nephew to tell his friends that he got a cool game for Christmas, but he had to say he purchased it from GameStop. This past summer when Alexander Williams suggested we invest in GameStop, trust me, he did not have to tell me twice.

What the Kids Say

GameStop has the potential to grow, so there is more upside with earnings and potentially the stock.

Recently GameStop and EB ("Electronics Boutique") Games merged to become the largest video game store in the country. I was actually surprised that the kids knew this, but one of the kids said that on a recent visit to GameStop a salesperson said they were affiliated with EB Games.

Electronics Boutique made its name selling used games. They created an aftermarket for games by buying and selling used games.

Competitors

Best Buy, Target, and Circuit City sell video games as well. But the best quality and selection is at GameStop. One player even said, "I went to the PC section of one store (no name indicated) and the box to the game was ripped open. I also had to take some games back because they did not work. Only once did I have to take a game back to GameStop because of a malfunction, but the game was used."

Also, GameStop and Electronics Boutique specialize in games. The salespeople are very knowledgeable and actually use the product, while the salespeople at Target and Walmart are not as knowledgeable.

Risks

Comparable store sales decline or the stock gets discovered and becomes overvalued.

Phoenix Companies, Inc. (Recommended by Coach Baker)

Phoenix Companies, Inc. (ticker: PNX) provides life insurance, annuities and asset management products. It distributes its products mainly through financial planners, banks, and broker-dealers. Many think the life insurance sector is attractive and may be a seller's market given (i) the number of acquisitive strategic buyers and (ii) the amount of capital pouring into private equity firms with an appetite for insurance. The private valuation may lend a "floor" to the stock over the long-term.

What the Kids Say
"Whatever you say Coach."

Competitors

A plethora of life insurance companies.

Risks

The favorable changes implemented by management may not be immediately reflected in the stock.

Results of the Fund 12 Months Later

			Apple Computer	GameStop	Phoenix
New York Shock Exchange - Stock Investments					
Ticker			AAPL	GME	PNX
Stock Price at:					
8/18/2006			$67.91	$22.22	$13.68
7/27/2007			$143.85	$40.40	$13.50
% Change			111.8%	81.8%	(1.3%)
Earnings per Share					
2007E			$3.70	$1.45	$1.14
2008E			$4.40	$1.87	$1.16
Price / Earnings Ratio					
2007E			38.9x	27.9x	11.8x
2008E			32.7x	21.6x	11.6x
Three Year EPS CAGR (2004-2006)			151.1%	23.6%	4.9%
2006 Sales ($ in millions)			$19,315.0	$5,318.9	$2,578.0
% Y-O-Y Growth			38.6%	72.0%	(1.2%)
Long-term Growth Rate			23.8%	21.1%	11.0%

The previous table illustrates how the returns achieved by the kids' stock picks (Apple and GameStop) trounced the returns on Phoenix Companies. I was actually afraid people would think I was picking on the kids since I was such an "expert" in investing. I chose Phoenix not because of any investment fundamentals but because I thought it would be put "into play" by an acquirer. The results reiterated what happens when you stick to the fundamentals versus investing on a hunch.

Bond Market According to Joe Baker

I spent the summer after graduating from Darden at home with my family. I saw Grandpa several times a week. Either he would stop by our house or I would go visit him. Those were some of the most awkward conversations. For over two decades we had barely spoken and now I was trying to find something to say. As time went on, the conversations became less forced and we began to speak as men. The running joke amongst me and my cousins was that whenever we had gone out into street and done something we were not supposed to, "it was Joe Baker's fault. We couldn't help it. It was in our blood." Whether it was getting into a fight or returning home in the wee hours of the morning and drawing the ire of significant others, we would always exclaim "Grandpaaaaaa!" He would get the biggest kick out of this whenever we recanted these stories. Grandpa and I shared a lot of light moments that summer. He told me stories about how he grew up and what it was really like working the night shift in the boiler room at Longwood. There was the time he opened his paycheck and realized he had received more money than expected; Longwood had accidentally given him a raise. He felt he deserved it since he had toiled there for so long. His boss tried everything he could to have the pay increase reversed but HR refused. Daily, his boss had to face Grandpa with the knowledge that Joe had bested him. He had me laughing so hard that it brought tears to my eyes. Not to be outdone, I told him the story about the Third Rail – an idiot trying to call me out, not knowing that I had been "playing possum" the entire time. Right out of the Joe Baker playbook. When I decided to get married my family asked me who was going to be the best man and I would say "Grandpa." They would then ask, "Have you asked him yet?" To which I would say "No." If Annie Mae had been alive I would have made the request through her and she would have nagged Joe until he acquiesced. That was the way it was. With her gone, I was hoping Grandpa would find out through osmosis. About a month before the big event I had no choice but to ask him, to which he agreed. On the biggest day of my life I wanted him there, out of respect for the man.

When explaining fixed income products to the Shock Exchange, I started with the basics. Fixed income was simply a loan where you received interest payments annually and your principal back at the end of the term. For zero-coupon bonds, both the principal and accumulated interest were returned at the end of the bond's term. Some loans (bonds) traded on the open market and the price was inversely related to interest rates. If rates rose, then the price of the bond declined, and vice versa. That said, interest rates moved not on inflation or rising costs, but on the expectation of inflation. This was the textbook answer that I had heard in Townsend's economics class and in corporate finance class at Darden. However, before I can truly understand something I have to be able to touch it and feel it. I had never owned a publicly-traded bond so my experience was limited. My grandfather had taught me the fixed-income market in a way that I could understand it. After he retired, Grandpa got his monthly retirement and social security checks. He also cut grass for people in the summertime to stay busy. On my trips home I noticed that he had a constant complaint – the price of goods he bought kept rising and inflation was eating him up. He was living on a fixed income and rising prices were his biggest concern. He complained about it so much that I started to think about it what he saying analytically. Assume he received $3,600 in monthly benefits and he bought a basket of goods (food, utilities, gasoline, car insurance, etc.) each month for $1,200. Now imagine if that basket of goods increased to $1,800/month, Grandpa's fixed income stream would be worth less to him since it could buy less. In that same vein, people would be willing to pay less for that fixed income payment stream – explaining the inverse relationship between the expectation of inflation and the price of fixed income products.

All those years I thought Grandpa had never spoken to us. We stayed with him until I was in the fourth grade – he was not obligated to do that for us. We saw him get up and go to work every day, come rain, sleet, or hail. We saw him on his side hustle (which I am not supposed to tell you about). After Suzie died, I was in business school, my sister was at Howard, Mark was at VCU and Dwayne was in the military. Afraid that we really did not have the means to keep up the mortgage payments, Joe suggested that we sell the house and come back and stay with him. In retrospect, it was he who taught us about hard work, family, responsibility, and commitment.

Suzie and My Daddy out on the town.

Annie Mae in New York with
Aunt Shirley and Aunt Josephine.
She usually stayed with her
daughters for an extended
period of time after they had a
child.

Annie Mae, Grandpa, Aunt Frances, Uncle George, Aunt
Ellen, Thomas and Eva Wilson at one of many family
gatherings.

Thomas, Dwayne and I with that "Who Us?" expression.

By his senior year "Shortcake" had turned into a decent football player.

Lamont Lockett (back row, fourth from left) and I made the All-Area Team our junior year in high school. Even in our finest moment we had to share the spotlight with the Cumberland Dukes. (Photo: Farmville Herald)

"Ralph Baker Night" with Suzie which ended in a rout of Bridgewater College. Rumor has it that the ceremony enraged Bridgewater coach Bill Leatherman.

"Ralph Baker Night" at H-SC. From left, Coach House (football), Coach Baker (football), Coach Finney, Coach Holcolmbe (basketball), Mr. Roach, Me, Coach Scott, Coach Miller (H-SC Athletic Director), Suzie, Uncle Norman Neverson.

I received a ride from my teammates after winning the ODAC. I felt vindicated after all the grief we took my freshman year.

With Coach Shaver after winning the ODAC Championship in 1989.

David Stockman (right) was Reagan's whiz kid budget director in the '80s. A decade later I had a chance to challenge his economic acumen, but thought better of it.

Dave Cooks (to my left) and I relaxed in Vegas with the parents of the Stamford Express. (Circa 1997)

Senator Carter Glass: "One banker in my state attempted to marry a white woman and they lynched him."

Neutron Jack (right) was described as "damned mad" after Joe Jett's (left) $350 million trading loss at Kidder. Welch, Gary Lynch and Judge Carol Fox Foelak set important legal precedence in cases involving incompetent traders.

President George W. Bush, Chelsea Clinton, Hilary Clinton and Bill Clinton attend the opening of the $165 million Clinton presidential library in Arkansas. Clinton has declined to provide a list of donors to the library.

The Triumvirate – John Reed, Sanford Weill, and Robert Rubin ushered in a new era with the merger of Travelers and Citicorp. The new "Citigroup" housed insurance, securities and banking under one umbrella. Unbeknownst to them, they had just set in motion the wheels of the next financial crisis.

Tom and I with the champs of the local recreational league. (Circa 2006)

The Shock Exchange earned it stripes at Hoop Connection in Fort Greene.

The Shock Exchange (12U) awaits it next game at Temple University.

The Shock Exchange surprised everyone with a 2nd place
finish in Hoop Connection.

The team warms up
with Coach Fitz. (Circa
2007)

The Shock Exchange (12U) after a long day at
Brower.

The Shock Exchange (12U) at Wingate Park.

Dave held court at the August 2007 investment meeting. We found out that the kids were actually smarter than the adults.

The Shock Exchange (13U) had an iconic moment at Shock Exchange Comes to Harlem 2008. From left, Nick Smith, Garrett Fox, Ralphie, Me, Marquise Cunningham, Christopher Herman, and Freeman Durden.

The Gauchos and MD Ruffriders locked horns.

Sam Cassell All-Stars took the cake in the 12U bracket. Phil Booth (left, front row) is now one of the nation's top recruits in the class of 2014.

Tom, Mickey and Tyrice saved my hide at our first tournament.

The NJ Playaz brought out the competition. Vaughn Gray (second from left) now plays for George Mason.

Abyssinian and the NY Falcons (15U) battled to 3 OTs at Shock Exchange Comes to Harlem 2009.

The Shock Exchange (13U) after a win at City Wide in Harlem. Nick Smith (second from left) played with us every season, which I was most proud of.

After a Shock Exchange investment meeting. From left: Shumba Smith, Mr. Snagg, Sean Snagg, Drew Cary (fixed income salesman), Me, Ralphie, Dave, Garret Fox, Mr. and Mrs. Fox. (Circa 2008).

Former AIG CEOs Robert Willumstad (left) and Martin Sullivan (right). As an executive at Citigroup and prior to joining AIG, Willumstad had not graduated from college.

Dick Fuld (center) was at the helm of the largest bankruptcy in U.S. history ($691 billion). "I will never heal from this."

Hedge fund manager John Paulson channeled National City when he made "the greatest trade ever," netting $15 billion in profits.

President Obama claims to have gotten the "infrastructure idea" from FDR, but I know otherwise.

Stanford Bank customers in Antigua panic after being denied their deposits.

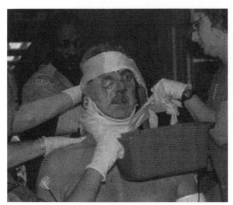

Allen Stanford who bilked depositors out of $7 billion, later panicked after receiving this jailhouse beating.

The progenitors of the financial crisis
were aided and abetted by media types
like Erin Burnett who co-signed their
behavior, while millions tuned in.

Danielle Chiesi, the
"Rasheeda Moore of
Wall Street," seduced
technology executives in
exchange for inside
information.

In 2012 Beyonce performed at Atlantic City's Revel
Casino – a symbol of Wall Street profligacy during the
crisis.

 Joseph Cassano, former head of AIG's Financial Products Unit, nearly bankrupt the earth. Unlike Joe Jett, he was not required to give back his $300 million in bonuses.

When Zhan Qixiong (far right) was detained by the Japanese coast guard in the Diaoyu Islands, China denied rare earth minerals to Japan. Will U.S. treasurys become the next pawn in international relations? (Circa 2009)

Christopher Franklin, CEO Titan Financial, spoke about investment fundamentals and the investing mistakes most professional athletes make. (Circa 2010)

The Shock Exchange (14U) enjoyed D.C. while attending the MD Ruffriders event.

The kids were in a playful mood after providing footage for a docudrama chronicling our travails.

I Caught up with one-half of EPMD at the Puma Clyde event. I told him the Brentwood Ballers would be at Shock Exchange Comes to Harlem so he needed to represent. (Circa 2011)

Sharmane and Mark run Shock Exchange Comes to Harlem from behind the scenes. (Circa 2011)

The team (15U) eventually became a crowd favorite at Brower. Shumba (second from left) was our most sought after player, but he always stayed loyal.

DeSean Fields, Nick and Shumba relax during a due diligence visit to the Apple Store in Manhattan (Circa 2010)

The Motley Crew (16U) poses for a picture after a Hudson Valley Hornets tournament.

NJ Roadrunners took the 17U chip at Shock Exchange Comes to Harlem 2011. Will Tyler Roberson, (back row, fifth from left) become the third McDonald's All-American to attend this event?

Ralphie tried to wreck shop at the Dartmouth Elite camp in 2012.

Mark and I hung out Up the House after church. People don't write books about Ms. Ola, so I wrote it myself.

SHOCK EXCHANGE PREDICTS THE GREAT RECESSION

Shock Exchange Profiled in July Issue of Black Enterprise

During the March 2008 investment meeting with *Black Enterprise* present, I ended it with my take on the impending doom about the economy. I was met with blank stares. In fact nobody was talking about it, anywhere. During previous investment meetings we tracked the declines in housing starts and auto sales – key drivers of the economy. We were also coming out of an extremely low interest rate environment and once rates rose, I figured that (i) there would be a problem with mortgage-backed securities, (ii) like Kidder, at least one investment bank would implode and (iii) a few hedge funds and managers with outsized reputations would be deflated, a la David Askin and Michael Steinhardt. During President George W. Bush's first term in office (long before Hurricane Katrina exposed the U.S.) I had read about the country's crumbling infrastructure and the hundreds of billions of dollars needed for repairs. I thought national infrastructure spending would have been a natural way to jumpstart the economy while modernizing the country. I was so mad that I decided to blog about it.

> The Shock Exchange had its recent investment meeting on March 16, 2008 and it was truly a star-studded event. Jessica Jones and Jerry Jack of *Black Enterprise* were on hand to meet the team and to get a better understanding our investment process. In her article "Round Ball and Round Lots" Ms. Jones documents the various enticements used to teach kids about saving and investing, with sports being one of them. The article goes in depth about the Shock Exchange's basketball program and the performance of the Shock Exchange Fund. I encourage everyone to pick up the July issue of the magazine.

Foreword

There has been a lot of changes to the economy since July 2006 when the Shock Exchange made its first investments. As of March 2008 the U.S. is suffering from declining economic activity, rising unemployment, and record foreclosures caused by real estate speculation. The economy is in the midst of "stagflation" – rising unemployment and rising costs (oil), which is the economic equivalent of the perfect storm. Rising oil prices are caused by external forces such as (i) the war in Iraq which has led to a decline in Iraqi oil production, (ii) reduction in oil production from key producers such as OPEC, Russia, and Venezuela, and (iii) some say oil speculators may be influencing the price (I'm not sure I buy this one).

2008 represents one of the worst U.S. economies since the last time we experienced stagflation – the 1970s when Richard Nixon was in office. Though it is also eerily similar to 1990 which experienced (i) a declining economy and rising unemployment, (ii) the Gulf War which also involved Iraq, (iii) oil price shocks due to a cut in Iraqi oil production, and (iv) the after effects of irrational exuberance from the LBO lending craze and defense spending of the mid to late '80s. What makes the situation even more dire is that there does not seem to be any relief in sight. Our presidential candidates have not acknowledged the situation or devised any concrete steps to address it. If the next president wants to accomplish something concrete then he/she should:

Reign in U.S. Oil Consumption

We cannot control price shocks caused by OPEC or price increases caused by demand from developing countries. However, we can control our own use of oil and gas consumption. With gas prices at $5/gallon in some places, it is almost wasteful to have some Americans driving Hummers and other SUVs through our inner cities. There is a limited supply of oil and such conspicuous consumption costs everybody. Oil/gas is an inelastic good in that demand is not sensitive to its price.

High oil prices hurt lower-income consumers even more because unlike a Mercedes Benz or a pair of Nike Air Force 1's, purchasing oil/gas is a necessity in order to heat homes, drive to work, etc. I am not sure if the solution is a gas guzzler tax or higher emissions standards for automobiles but somehow those who use it inefficiently should pay more for it.

Reign in Healthcare Costs

Healthcare costs are spiraling out of control, with almost no end in sight. Healthcare benefits are some of the largest costs borne by employers and companies are limiting some employees to less than a 40-hour work week in order to avoid paying for healthcare. Healthcare professionals would respond that (i) people are living longer, so they require more complicated healthcare procedures over longer periods as compared to previous generations, and (ii) several procedures, laser eye surgery for instance, have been developed that do not address life-threatening illnesses but help people live better and are billed as "in-network" procedures.

The first issue is sort of a fact of life. The second issue is a case where certain individuals are "taxing" the healthcare system to improve their quality of life, in this case, a procedure to allow them to forgo having to wear glasses. Yet the increase in healthcare costs due to such procedures is borne by everyone, including low-income individuals who can barely afford the cost of basic healthcare. Again, healthcare is another inelastic good where demand is not much affected by the cost. I am not suggesting that certain quality of life procedures be paid for "a la carte" outside of the HMO network, but what I am suggesting is that a plan can be implemented to make basic healthcare more affordable.

Invest in Infrastructure

The U.S. infrastructure, bridges and levees in particular, is in disrepair. Hurricane Katrina, in which the levees protecting New Orleans broke and flooded the city, should have been a wake-up call for America. But everyone was too busy assigning blame to look ahead to attempt to prevent potential future disasters. Repairing our infrastructure should be a high priority for the next president. It is embarrassing that with the U.S. financial might and engineering prowess we are witnessing bridges and levees falter from poor engineering or disrepair. It does present thorny issues as to who will pay the cost for such investment – the federal government or state government(s). Get creative – reallocate some of the federal budget to this initiative in the form of low-interest loans to the states which can be paid back over time.

Reign in Rising Cost of Education

The cost of college is increasing at three times the rate of inflation. This would imply that the inputs (professors' salaries, maintaining buildings & grounds, cafeteria costs, administrative costs, etc.) are also increasing at three times the rate of inflation – this is clearly not the case. What differentiates the U.S. from the rest of the world is our ability to take the best and the brightest and give them access to education and access to capital to allow them to create better and more efficient products and services than are currently available in the marketplace. If the cost of college keeps increasing at its current rate, the only people with access to education will be those from the monied class.

What is really behind the rising cost of education? The administrators I have spoken with say it is the additional costs of amenities that top students demand. Current prospective students look not only at the quality of the education but also demand gourmet meals three times per day, a best in class wellness center, etc. This implies that students who want a basic education, basic amenities and the "option" to eat gourmet meals or join a health spa are being "taxed" by those who not only demand them but whose parents can afford them.

I have another theory on another key driver as well – **the availability of credit**. When I went to college (way back when) there were a couple of student loan marketing agencies. Today there are too many to count. A college education is another one of those inelastic goods – you may not be able to afford college but you cannot afford not to go either. Moreover, a student's ability to pay for college is often directly related to how much he/she can borrow. A student's borrowing capacity has increased dramatically, hence so has the cost of education. A similar phenomenon is LBO lending in the '80's. Oftentimes the amount buyers would offer for a target company was tied to the amount they could borrow – if a bank would lend them $300 million they would offer $375 million . . . if a bank was willing to lend $400 million then they would offer $475 million, and so on.

A solution to these conundrums (and others) will require having to tell the American people that they cannot have their cake and eat it too. This is obviously not what the American public wants to hear and the presidential candidate who suggests such a plan will need backbone and the courage of his/her convictions . . . key attributes of great leaders and of people who have never gotten elected.[1]

Investment Meeting – August 16, 2008

Below are excerpts from our presentation foretelling the stock market decline and corporations' earnings prospects.

The U.S. banking sectors continues to go through its worst crisis in decades

Banks have less liquidity

Eight U.S. banks have failed during 2008

Impact: there is less capital (money) circulating through the economy to stimulate growth

U.S. home prices continue to decline

Home prices are down 15.8% year-over-year and 8.9% YTD

Since our last meeting, home prices have fallen 2.1%

Impact: homeowners feel less wealthy because their primary asset – their home – has depreciated in value

Inflation has soared to a 17-year high from increases in food, energy, transportation and apparel costs

In July, consumer prices increased 5.6% year-over-year

Impact: goods and services cost more, which puts more financial pressure on American households

Job losses have increased

The U.S. has negative job growth since the beginning of 2008

Impact: unemployment is rising and more people are unable to find new jobs

Consumers are spending less

The Consumer Confidence Index (a measure of people's attitudes about the general economy) has declined approximately 40 points since January 2008

Peoples' homes have declined in value, making them feel less wealthy

Households' incomes are strained by higher costs for food, energy and transportation

Less job security causes families to have tighter budgets . . . discretionary purchases (like iPods) are eliminated

Companies see lower sales and profits because people are spending less

This negatively affects companies' growth

When companies begin to earn less they find ways to eliminate costs

Job cuts

Wage reductions

Less spending on growth projects that inject money into the broader economy

Stock prices begin to decline as investors begin to expect lower growth from companies

Economists are worried that the U.S. could slip into a recession with the next six months

Investment Meeting – April 5, 2009

In April 2009 we had Chris Franklin, money manager for professional athletes and high-net-worth individuals for Titan Financial Services, speak to the kids. President Obama had just gotten elected and the group was split on whether he should reign in the Wall Street robber barons or keep them afloat. Coach Baker mentioned how the Joseph Jett fiasco set legal precedence in how regulators should deal with the robber barons. He drew blank stares when he suggested that President Obama was co-signing for the oligarchs and robber barons because he wanted to work for them when he left office, just like every other president and vice president since the H. W. Bush administration. Furthermore, the stock market was in dire need of a "new generation of suckers." One thing not debatable however, was that the U.S. economy was in free fall.

The U.S. banking sector continues to go through its worse crisis in decades

Banks have less liquidity

Impact: there is less capital (money) circulating through the economy to stimulate growth

U.S. home prices continue to decline

Home prices were down 18.2% y-o-y in 4Q 2008

Impact: homeowners feel less wealthy because their primary asset – their home – has depreciated in value

Job losses have increased

The unemployment rate has reached its highest level since 1983 (8.5%)

Impact: unemployment is rising and more people are unable to find new jobs

The federal government has implemented initiatives to prevent economic collapse

Bailout of U.S. banking system

Restructuring of and capital assistance to U.S. automakers

Economic stimulus and housing recovery packages

Impact: limit economic fallout and potentially stabilize the economy

Consumers are spending less

Less job security and less wealth causes families to have tighter budgets

Discretionary purchases (like iPods) are eliminated from families' budgets

Companies see lower sales and profits because people are spending less

This negatively affects companies' growth

When companies begin to earn less they find ways to eliminate costs

Job cuts

Wage reductions

Less spending on growth projects that inject money into the broader economy

Investment Meeting – March 16, 2008

What Happened Since Our Last Meeting [August 2007]

Home prices have fallen significantly across the country

Home prices fell in the 4th quarter of 2007 by 8.9%, the largest year-over-year drop in at least 20 years

Impact: home owners feel less wealthy because their primary asset – their home – has depreciated in value

Banks have less liquidity

Most banks have less money to lend to people and to companies

Impact: there is less capital (money) circulating through the economy to stimulate growth

Job losses have increased

The U.S. has had negative job growth since the beginning of 2008

Impact: unemployment is rising and more people are unable to find jobs

... What Does This All Mean?

Consumers are spending less

The Consumer Confidence Index (a measure of people's attitudes about the general economy) has declined almost 30 points since January 2007

People's homes have declined in value, making them feel less wealthy

Less job security causes families to have tighter budgets

Discretionary purchases (like iPods) are eliminated from families' budgets

Companies see lower sales and profits because people are spending less

This negatively affects companies' growth

When companies begin to earn less they find ways to eliminate costs

Job cuts

Wage reductions

Less spending on growth projects that inject money into the economy

Economists are worried that the U.S. is on the brink of a recession

The Dow Jones Industrial Average is down 7% for the year

Our portfolio's current performance

	Apple	**GameStop**
Stock Price at (8/31/06)	$67.91	$44.43
PE Ratio at (8/31/06)	31.6x	22.1x
Stock Price at (8/31/07)	$138.41	$50.14
Y-O-Y % Change	*103.8%*	*12.9%*
PE Ratio at (8/31/07)	30.7x	37.9x
Stock Price at (3/14/08)	$126.61	$49.05
% Change	*(8.5%)*	*(2.2%)*
PE Ratio at (3/14/08)	24.6x	27.5x

Investment Thesis Review

What was our original investment thesis?

Do we still believe in our thesis given the current economic environment?

What should we do going forward?

Shock Exchange Swagger Jacked by Senator Obama?

Our meetings about the economy's impending doom had seemingly fallen on deaf ears. After the collapse of Fannie Mae and Freddie Mac, guess who was incessantly talking about "this economy" – Senator Barack Obama. By September both presidential front-runners, Senator John McCain and Senator Obama, were engaged in a contest of dueling economic plans. Mr. McCain stayed the party line by promising to preserve existing tax cuts imposed by President George W. Bush. He preached the usual supply-side rhetoric of low capital gains taxes, a reduction in corporate taxes and reduced government spending. Mr. Obama on the other hand, proposed a middle-class tax cut, an investment in alternative energy, and modernization of the country's schools. On September 16, 2008, the day after Lehman Brothers failed, Senator McCain made a fatal flaw. Speaking to a group of supporters in Florida, McCain calmly stated that the "fundamentals of the economy are strong." I thought the guy had completely lost his mind. Senator Obama seized the moment by calling the meltdown of the stock market "the most serious financial crisis since the Great Depression," and Mr. McCain "out of touch." Over a period of mere months, Mr. Obama could see that the economy was near Great Depression status. I surmised that he must have had access to information that McCain, Lehman, MSNBC and the rest of the world did not.

I happened to be home channel surfing one evening when Black Entertainment Television (BET) announced that Senator Obama would be on *106 & Park* to discuss his campaign. Mr. Obama had galvanized the entire country and was on the brink of making history. Here is an excerpt:

Senator Obama: "Thank you for having me . . . This is the last two minutes of the game. I just want to make sure we finish strong . . . We need to change Washington. We are going through some tough economic times. Times could get worse for a while. We need to change Washington and our policy on healthcare, on jobs, on the war in Iraq. Everybody who's watching, I need you to vote."

106 & Park: "Which one [issue] do you think will be the challenge for you to face when you become President?"

Senator Obama: "First item of business is to make sure this financial crisis is stabilized. Even though it starts on Wall Street, if they don't lend money then suddenly people can't get car loans. They can't get loans for their college education. Small businesses can't get a loan which means they have to lay people off. At the same time we have this housing situation with foreclosures and predatory lending and subprime lending crisis. Those are two things we have to work on immediately . . . Education because our school system in too many communities is broken. We have to invest in early childhood education. We gotta give our teachers more money but we also need more accountability from the schools and parents."

106 & Park: "Any issues that weren't discussed enough regarding young people on the campaign trail?"

Senator Obama: "I do think education was something that was neglected a little bit. I am a big proponent of making college more affordable. We didn't talk about it much but I've got a program that says anybody who puts time in community service that we are gonna give a four-thousand-dollar tuition credit to every student every year. That's enough to pay for a community college but it's also enough to pay for two-thirds of the cost of a public college tuition in most states. It will also prevent students from having to take on 60, 70, 80 thousand worth of debt."

106 & Park: "Are there any final words for the young people out there?"

Senator Obama: "Just DREAM BIG DREAMS and know that if you work hard there's nothing you can't achieve, and that includes winning this election."

I sat in front of the television stone-faced. Senator Obama had campaigned hard for the presidency and was considered one of the greatest orators of our time. Of all the speeches and campaigning he had done, Mr. Obama was trying to convince the public that he had actually forgotten something? The only reference he had made to education was modernizing parochial schools and helping educate teachers to improve their competency. Never had he referenced the cost of college. Now in the 11th hour he had a program at the ready to help students pay for an already overpriced product – college education. It was clear why he did not talk about the cost of college that much during the campaign – I had yet to mention it on my website. And the final comment about "DREAM BIG DREAMS" which I had originally thought was so hokey – there was only one place Mr. Obama could have lifted it.

From Senator Obama to President Obama

With the help of Oprah Winfrey's public relations campaign and speeches ringing of "hope and change," Senator Obama gradually became the Democratic frontrunner for the presidential nomination. Due to Senator Obama's obvious brilliant mind and political acumen, every African American I spoke to felt that once he became president the revolution to follow was a forgone conclusion. Yet there were some moments along the campaign trail that raised my antennae. In June 2008 Senator Obama made a Father's Day speech criticizing black fathers and urging them to have the courage to raise their children. The remarks drew national attention and reverberated throughout the black community. His throng of supporters pointed out "how right Obama was" and that "Obama was only telling the truth." I had a different take, however. There were lots of truths he could have mentioned. Why did he pick this one? Secondly, he said it in a venue where he knew the mainstream press would pick up the story and run with it. I saw the speech as nothing more than a veiled attempt to curry favor with white voters. But what struck me was Mr. Obama's willingness, unprompted even, to throw African Americans under the bus in order to do it – just like any other politician. Indeed, he was not in the "truth-telling" business; he was in the business of getting elected. The other incident of note occurred when the Reverend Jesse Jackson criticized Mr. Obama for "talking down to black folks." Mr. Obama's supporters accused Jackson of being a "hater" and urged him to go somewhere and sit down while history was being made. Mr. Jackson and Obama both lived in Chicago and Jackson had heard several of his speeches in local churches prior to Obama reaching the national stage. The nation had only witnessed Mr. Obama during his interview for the presidency. If there was another Obama, those who would have known it could only have hailed from Chicago.

The night President Obama and the rest of the country made history was a surreal moment. African Americans took to the streets around the country, overjoyed at what "we" had accomplished. I walked outside my house in downtown Brooklyn and people were celebrating in the streets. They shut Lafayette Avenue down completely. People were crying, falling out and screaming Obama's name. My first thought was, "Now Obama knows he doesn't have to do anything for you all." The scene struck me as similar to the joy blacks must have felt when Jackie Robinson was admitted into Major League Baseball. Personally I was always a Reggie Jackson fan. Jackson's Yankees played the L.A. Dodgers in the 1981 World Series and surprisingly, the Dodgers were putting up some serious resistance. Late in one of the games Davey Lopes, the Dodgers' second baseman, hit a double that extended their lead. "How does a 'punch and Judy' hitter like Lopes get a double? This entire series is a fluke," I exclaimed. I sat there pouting and Suzie walked in, saw the score and started cheering. I thought she was teasing me for no reason, but she said she was a Dodgers fan. "How could a black woman from Virginia like a team from L.A.?" I asked. "Because they signed Jackie Robinson" she responded. This nearly sent me into a spasm. Jackie Robinson had been signed over 30 years prior – ancient history to a 14-year-old. Then I understood the genius of Branch Rickey, the Dodgers executive who signed Robinson. The moment it happened, black America immediately became Dodgers fans. The history books describe Rickey as a humanitarian. Yet he must have seen the tens of thousands of fans cheering for Robinson at Negro League games, and envisioned their becoming Dodgers fans. If he was such a humanitarian, Rickey would have suggested that some of the Negro League teams be admitted to the majors instead of simply poaching their players. Signing Robinson also meant the death knell of the Negro Leagues and the thousands of black jobs they provided. From an economic standpoint it was probably the worst "trade" in history. African Americans forfeited jobs and baseball revenue every year in perpetuity, for a chance to prove they could compete on the baseball field with their white counterparts. This left me thinking that victories for blacks in America have almost always come at a price.

I listened to President Obama's acceptance speech, awaiting the details of the change about to come. I expected to hear sweeping reforms in the financial services sector, a return to Glass-Steagall and indictments of the Wall Street speculators. What I heard instead was "there can be no strong Wall Street without a strong Main Street." The president sounded more like a consultant from the popular UPS commercial than a revolutionary leader. In the commercial, the consultants tell their client that he needs to "integrate his global supply chain and accelerate inventory velocity." The client pauses and says "Great. Do it," to which the consultants respond: "Sir, we don't actually do what we propose. We just propose it." The world was all topsy-turvy. Obama now had the carte blanche to make bold, sweeping changes without jeopardizing political capital. The American public had no choice but to be open to any proposal that could spur the economy or reform the country, and I anxiously waited for him to put his vision into action.

Infrastructure Investing Key to Economic Recovery

On November 23, 2008 the cover of *The New York Times* caught my eye. There was a digitally altered picture of President Obama dressed up like Franklin D. Roosevelt ("FDR"). The caption read, "Obama Plays FDR In 2.5M Jobs Plan; Pledges Building Blitz to Jump Start Economy." The key plan involved stimulating the economy while overhauling the country's infrastructure:

> In his almost four-minute weekly YouTube-national radio address, Obama outlined his vision to stimulate the economy while overhauling the country's infrastructure by January 2011. 'There are no quick or easy fixes to this crisis,

which has been many years in the making, and it's likely to get worse before it gets better,' Obama said . . . Before outlining his pledge, Obama painted a dire picture of the economy and warned of massive job losses. 'We now risk falling into a deflationary spiral that could increase our massive debt even further,' he said . . . Obama's proposed job jolt has its roots in President Delano Roosevelt's New Deal in the 1930s. FDR created the Public Works Administration and the Works Progress Administration, which hired unemployed Americans to expand the nation's infrastructure . . . Short on specifics, Obama said his economic team would hammer out his plan's finer points by Inauguration Day.[2]

I chuckled at the article. Mr. Obama was trying to convince the world that the infrastructure idea had come to him through a séance with FDR. Did he have a giant weegie board hidden somewhere in the White House? Ironically, FDR was most known for Wall Street reform and breaking up the banks into commercial banks and investment banks. For his efforts, FDR was labeled a traitor to his class – the monied class – by Wall Street sympathizers. Secondly, in giving the credit for his grand plan to FDR, an icon who the country revered, it still struck me as an attempt to curry favor with white voters. "President Obama conveniently failed to mention the true source of his idea to invest in roads and bridges to spur the economy," I surmised. The deterioration in the U.S. economy had materialized when Mr. Obama was still Senator Obama. The article would imply that all along, Mr. Obama had the key to solving the country's economic malaise, yet kept "the infrastructure idea" to himself. As Senator, he had the ability to put the plan into place, but still he kept quiet. Only after he was elected president did he divulge his grand scheme. If that was truly the case then either he was a visionary, or the most unpatriotic person on the planet. Months after President Obama's election victory, I came across an Internet article describing how during the heated presidential campaign, Hillary Clinton accused him of taking credit for ideas that were not his own. Specifically, she accused Obama of plagiarizing an October 2006 speech made by Massachusetts Governor Deval Patrick. The article showed videos of one of Patrick's speeches and Obama's speech from February 2008 as evidence. The public was shocked by the allegations, but I found Mrs. Clinton to be very credible.

Infrastructure Investing "En Vogue"

Atlanta Mayor Shirley Franklin
On the morning of November 17, 2008 CNBC discussed the financial crisis and had Atlanta Mayor Shirley Franklin offer the perspective of someone on the front lines. Ms. Franklin relayed that Atlanta and cities across the country were cash-strapped and in dire need to create jobs before unemployment rose to Great Depression-era levels. She voiced the merits of the federal government offering the city of Atlanta a bailout package for infrastructure investments to create tens of thousands of jobs. Sound familiar?

Joyce Shapiro – Managing Director, Franklin Templeton Real Asset Advisors

By the time Ms. Shapiro spoke to CNBC on August 4, 2011 about infrastructure investing globally the concept, never spoken of prior to the Shock Exchange blog post, had become self-evident.

> This is a great time to be talking about infrastructure investing, actually. This really points to the fact institutional investors are looking for in their portfolios – steady kinds of income, low volatility, the kinds of [investments] taking advantage of the long-term plays related to the shifts in population growth and urbanization. If you look especially in the U.S. where the municipal bond market really was the cornerstone for a lot of infrastructure investing going back several decades, now the opportunity set moves to the private sector because municipalities are somewhat hamstrung financially. The need for capital to move into these markets is very significant whether we look at (i) the developed markets with infrastructure over 50 years old that is aging or (ii) emerging markets needing to meet the needs of population shifts to urban centers. We are looking at over the next several decades 3% - 5% globally of GDP that needs to be spent in this space – $2 trillion a year. That is quite significant. Unfortunately, the municipalities . . . the federal governments around the world are really not in a position to fund all of this. The private sector will have to step in or partner through public-to-private partnerships or look for opportunities from the private-to-private side, clearly a huge growth market. A place like China recently spent $300 billion on rail . . . countries in Europe where the Trans-European network is trying to connect all of its infrastructure systems, or a place like the U.S. looking at waste water systems, that are really aging at this point. The needs are vast and very far fetching.

Infrastructure Investing – China

Global leaders have sought similar stimulus packages to spur their economies and shore up their crumbling infrastructure. In November 2008 China announced a 4 trillion yuan ($630 billion) stimulus package. The lion's share (38%) was earmarked for public infrastructure, which included railway, roads, irrigation, and airport construction. The rest included post-quake reconstruction (25%), social welfare (10%) and technology advancement (9%).[3] China's investment target came directly after President Obama made U.S. infrastructure a priority of his administration.

Infrastructure Investing – India

India meanwhile targeted about $500 billion of infrastructure investments (power plants and roads) around the time of the global financial crisis. The government was hoping to receive about 30% of the necessary capital through private funding. Repairing its crumbling infrastructure is essential if India is to achieve its target of 9% economic growth from 2012 to 2017. India has since increased its five-year infrastructure goal to $1 trillion through 2017.[4] Where space exploration or military buildup occupied developed nations in the past, the two largest global economies (U.S. and China), and the world's second fastest growing major economy (India) are now in a race to shore up its infrastructure to take advantage of future economic expansions.

Infrastructure Investing Politicized?

Nearly 18 months after President Obama took office, hundreds of thousands of unsafe bridges had been passed over for stimulus funds. About 1,300 deficient or obsolete bridges were expected to receive $2.2 billion in stimulus funds for repairs. That compared to over 150,000 U.S. bridges engineers had identified as obsolete or deficient.[5] Instead, the president focused the majority of the $790 billion stimulus package on "shovel-ready" projects. The logic being that shovel-ready projects, such as the repaving of roads, would have stimulated the economy in the short-term, unlike others that needed months of planning and design. My initial reaction was that it was not going to matter anyway. Our crumbling infrastructure was caused by decades of willful neglect. That said, turning around the economy would take years of investment and simply letting nature run its course, if at all. Yet the Obama Administration was under the impression that it could alter the economy's course by the sheer force of the president's will.

Which Companies Will Benefit

Wall Street embraced Obama's stimulus packages and predicted which corporations – from consulting firms to makers of construction material – would most benefit. Corporations' stock prices and takeover prospects rose in lockstep. A review of Sterling Construction by *Seeking Alpha* not only assumed revenue growth from infrastructure construction, but was critical that a long-term bill had not been passed:

> Sterling Construction is a pure-play on transportation and water infrastructure construction . . . Therefore, for investors seeking focused exposure to heavy civil construction, Sterling Construction is the best investment vehicle . . . In addition to the economic slowdown, the absence of a long-term federal funding bill for transportation construction has created constrained infrastructure spending . . . Both transportation and water infrastructure markets have strong long-term growth trends, and Sterling Construction is well positioned to benefit from this. Even with continued uncertainty regarding funding for infrastructure projects, the company should continue to generate steady to higher profitability. However, when a new federal long-term funding bill for transportation infrastructure is passed, or when some other funding mechanism such as an infrastructure bank is established, this could be a catalyst for strong profit growth and stock price gains.[6]

After three years and hundreds of billions of funds allocated to the Treasury Department's "quantitative easing," the U.S. government appears to be cash-strapped. During a January 2011 visit to Washington, the president of China and members of China's business elite met with President Obama. The prospects of China investing in U.S. infrastructure were welcomed by the president. Lou Jiwei, head of China's Investment Corp. (CIC), a $300 billion sovereign wealth fund, thought the idea of the Chinese investing abroad while maintaining jobs in the U.S. could serve symbiotic purposes. In what appeared to be a dramatic policy shift, one White House spokesman was quoted as saying, "'For China to invest in the U.S., in much the same way the Japanese did in the '90s and beyond, to create jobs and manufacture products here, could be quite a constructive contribution to our growth and to better relations between our two countries . . . We see foreign investment as a key part of our effort to create jobs and growth.'"[7] In the past CIC invested $1.6 billion in U.S. infrastructure, taking a 15% stake in AES Corp., a major U.S. power generation distribution company. However, any future investments will have to clear regulatory hurdles and will be fraught with political risks for Mr. Obama. Allowing CIC to invest in a U.S. airport or toll road could cost him a bid for reelection in 2012. How many U.S. workers will CIC employ and what percentage of U.S. building materials will it use? Will CIC "crowd out" companies like Sterling Construction? Nonetheless, at an October 2010 conference in New York, according to Zhou Yuan, head of asset allocation at CIC, implied that infrastructure investing would be more effective than Fed policy: "He said infrastructure projects, such as high-voltage transmission lines, will help create more jobs in the U.S. than the Federal Reserve's quantitative-easing policy."[8]

Buffett To the Rescue

Given the Shock Exchange's prescient call on the Great Recession and recommendations to fix it, one would think we would have been celebrated nationally. President Obama instead sought the counsel of another American icon who could help him curry favor with white voters – Warren Buffett. In July 2010 the president held a secret meeting with Buffett to discuss the economy and get a reaction to Obama's stimulus efforts. America's media darling also made several appearances on CNBC to give his take on the crisis. In a March 2009 interview he explained that "fear is very contagious" and that fear in the markets had been transferred to consumers. Furthermore, the economy had "fallen off a cliff." However, there was one small problem – Buffett, by his own admission, was clueless on the economy. In a June 2010 meeting before Congress, Buffett erroneously admitted that no one, including him, saw the crisis coming. "In the end I don't know who, except for maybe John Paulson or Michael Murray who would have been running Moody's and come up with different ratings. This was the greatest bubble I have ever seen in my life. The entire American public was caught up in a belief that the housing market could not fall dramatically. Freddie Mac, Fannie Mae, Congress believed it, the media believed, I believed. If I had seen what was coming would I have held my Moody's stock?"[9]

Banks Need Bailout Money So They Can Lend

The "grand visionary" also touted the need to supply banks with capital so they could continue to lend; without access to loans, small businesses would not be able to expand, invest in new equipment or hire new workers. The only problem was that banks do not lend out of altruistic motives. They lend because it is a sound business decision. Furthermore, in a contracting economy, banks find it a better business decision to invest in treasury securities – just like they did in the early 1990s. Any funds from the government not specifically earmarked for loans will result in banks investing the funds into treasury securities, and collecting the interest to be paid out in bonuses. That said, banks' penchant for investing in treasury securities during a recession will often lead to an asset bubble in those securities – exactly what Dr. Conroy (Darden finance professor) pointed out in 1992. It did not help Mr. Obama's cause that the Treasury

Department, under President George W. Bush, injected about $700 billion into 21 banks as part of its Troubled Asset Relief Program (TARP) just prior to Obama taking office. The Treasury Department also did not set constraints on how the TARP money could be used. Treasury Secretary Henry Paulson credited himself with saving the U.S. banking industry with his financial ingenuity. However, he struck a deal with the 21 banks that he would never have struck in his capacity at Goldman Sachs. As a Goldman executive, Paulson was known for striking the best deal. "If thirty-two years at Goldman Sachs had taught him anything, it was how to cut the best deal possible. He demanded assurances, in writing, that Treasury would have the same status in the cabinet as Defense and State. In Washington, he knew, proximity to the president mattered, and he had no intention of being a marginalized functionary who could be summoned at Bush's whim but couldn't get the chief executive to return his calls."[10] Yet when representing taxpayers, with Goldman and other members of the Wall Street fraternities negotiating across the table from him, Paulson demanded no assurances in writing – he simply "hoped" they would do the right thing.

Though the TARP investments represented acquisitions of companies on the verge of bankruptcy, the financing arrangements did not reflect that scenario. There should have been covenants, and representations around (i) how the funds were to be spent, (ii) limits on transactions above a certain size (acquisitions, capital outlays, bonuses), and (iii) salary concessions, amongst others. Of the TARP allocated for loans, the Treasury Department should have held that capital back, contingent upon the banks actually making loans. Lastly, investment banks have "elevator assets" – they take the elevator home at night. Prior to distributing the TARP funds, Secretary Paulson and his team should have signed key employees and producers to employment contracts at salaries reflecting their bankrupt status. At that point, the government had TARP recipients "a lil' bit pregnant." In M&A parlance, that is the period that the market knows a company is "in play" or for sale, yet the transaction has yet to be completed. Once the transaction is completed, the leverage in the relationship is reversed. And that is the relationship President Obama inherited from Paulson and President Bush – 21 banks with $700 billion in taxpayer money, with no control over how they could spend it.

Shortly after his election, President Obama spoke about the need for banks to lend. I paced around my house wondering aloud if the man was delusional or simply trying to assuage the public. He and his economic team did not believe banks were going to lend simply because they asked them to, did they? He, Timothy Geithner (Treasury Secretary) and Ben Bernanke (Federal Reserve Chairman) merely had to study the recession of the early 1990s to predict lending patterns. Below are selected quotes by government officials during the credit crunch of the early 1990s. See if they still apply today:

> The Bush Administration is working on ways of encouraging banks to make more loans to ensure that a 'credit crunch' does not hamper the economy's recovery, Treasury Secretary Nichols F. Brady said . . . As a result, the Treasury is rewriting

rules that might discourage lending and is planning other steps to diffuse complaints that high-handed regulators have intimidated bankers out of making loans ... He said bank regulators are only one reason loans are hard to get. 'It is not a single-cause disease like measles or mumps – it is a systemic disease,' the Treasury said, ticking off a list of factors, headed by the massive overbuilding of commercial real estate that has left banks burdened with billions of dollars of mortgages that aren't being paid. Many bankers, Brady said, 'now want to do right because they did wrong before. They made a lot of chancy loans and are now trying to fatten up their balance sheets.' What banks are doing, he added, 'is what always happens at the end of recessions when there is a run to quality. Banks are investing more and more ... in government bonds and less loans to industry.'[11]

Senator Alfonse D'Amato (R-N.Y.), a perennial critic of Federal Reserve Chairman Alan Greenspan, said Greenspan and Brady had failed to tackle one of the biggest impediments to eased bank credit: That banks are finding it more profitable to invest in high-interest Treasury bonds and securities than to make loans to businesses. 'Banks have much more incentive to refrain from lending,' said D'Amato, calling the administration's effort to ease the credit crunch a 'total failure.'[12]

$15 Billion Small Business Loan Funding Program

In March 2009 the Obama Administration announced its intention to buy up to $15 billion in loans made to banks and guaranteed by the Small Business Administration (SBA). The concept was that once the government bought these loans, banks would then have the capital to make new ones. Funding for the program was expected to come from the $700 billion bailout fund enacted during the Bush Administration. It was also an attempt to deflect public criticism that the original outlays from TARP all went to big business. Cynthia Blankenship, head of the Independent Community Bankers of America, trumpeted the program as an incredible tool for community banks to help jumpstart the economy and the credit markets.[13] By March 2011 small business loans outstanding totaled $609 billion, down from 8.6% from the previous year, according to the Federal Deposit Insurance Corporation (FDIC). A similar analysis by the Federal Reserve Bank of Kansas City showed a decline in small business lending by 14% during that period.[14] Of the $609 billion outstanding, the lion's share went to companies with ample collateral and established business histories while smaller companies were left out in the cold. Banks meanwhile blamed regulators' tightening credit standards as a reason many loans were declined. With that backdrop, in December 2010 President Obama released the criteria banks must meet to tap a now $30 billion small lending fund. The new program offered (i) cheap capital (as low as 1%) for banks to lend to small businesses and (ii) an opportunity for banks with TARP funds to substitute them with government funds with fewer strings attached and less stigma.

What Actually Happened

TARP Recipients Reduce Loan Volume

According to a study by the Treasury Department, new loan volume at the TARP recipient banks declined every month from October 2008 to February 2009. New loan volume declined a median of 17.5%, 26.4%, 17.0%, and 2.2% from October - November, November - December, December - January and January - February, respectively. The decline in new loans in February 2009 as compared to October 2008 was a median of 24.2%. The bank with the largest dollar volume decline was JPMorgan Chase, which reduced new loans from $61.2 billion in October 2008, to $39.7 billion in February 2009.[15]

Commercial Banks Invest More Heavily in Treasury Securities

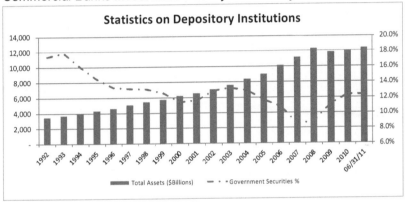

Source: FDIC

As you can see from the above chart, in 1993 commercial banks' holdings of U.S. government securities peaked at 17.9% and declined to 11.4% in 2000. They ramped up their holdings after the economic uncertainty caused by the events of September 11, 2001. Banks reduced their government holdings steadily from 2003 to 2007, and began to hoard cash again when the financial crisis materialized in 2008. Based upon Capital IQ data reviewed by *The Wall Street Journal*, the 382 nonfinancial firms in the S&P 500 that reported results through the fourth quarter of 2009 were holding $932 billion in cash and short-term securities – a record. The cash hoard at those companies was approximately $600 billion in 2005.[16] The cash balance was accumulated via layoffs, inventory reductions and reductions in capital spending – harbingers of economic contraction.

Small Business Lending Fund Recipients Use Funds to Repay TARP

As of October 2011 more than half of the $4 billion in funds disbursed under President Obama's Small Business Lending Fund was used to repay bailout funds received via TARP. The fund was designed to give community banks an incentive to lend to small businesses – banks boosting their small business loans would pay a 1% rate on funds it received under the program. Of the 332 banks that received cash through the fund, 137 used $2.2 billion to pay off their TARP obligations.[17]

Alternative Providers of Capital Stepped in to Fill Void for Small Businesses

Peer-to-Peer Loans

Internet companies like Prosper Marketplace Inc. and Lending Club Corp. have offered small businesses an alternative to bank financing. Peer-to-peer sites cropped up during the beginning of the financial crisis and tend to take on (i) less creditworthy borrowers, (ii) borrowers spurned by banks, and (iii) borrowers with less collateral and a more limited business history. Such sites generated over than $500 million in personal loans in a five-year time span. The business model is to "charge borrowers a fee for connecting them to a network of lenders, who put up anywhere from $25 to $1,000. Lenders are paid back with interest, with the rate set on the basis of a site-assigned credit rating, minus the site's fee . . . Since riskier borrowers offer lenders better returns, the sites often back loans that many banks would reject out of hand or approve with higher interest rates. But by the spreading risk, peer-to-peer loans tend to have lower interest rates than comparable bank loans."[18]

Hedge Fund Lending

Hedge funds flush with cash have stepped in as the lender of last resort for middle market companies unable to tap the corporate bond market. Critics have characterized hedge fund lending as speculative and emblematic of what led to the financial crisis in the first place. Yet, they sound more like opportunists who will extract their pound of flesh as long as the market allows it. With clients who have nowhere else to turn, hedge funds often charge rates that could be characterized as "usury." They also have a penchant for securing nonpublic information on customers during the application process, and either trading on the information or leaking it to others who trade on it. *The Wall Street Journal* recently did a study showing the correlation between (i) a company receiving loans from hedge funds and (ii) the timing of short sales on that company's stock. Don't you just love this country?

Chinese Investment

When peer-to-peer loans and hedge funds are not available, there is always the ubiquitous Chinese, with endless paper to invest. In 2010, Chinese investment in American companies rose to $5 billion; a report commissioned by the Asia Society and the Woodrow Wilson International Center for Scholars, envisions another $1 trillion to $2 trillion of Chinese overseas investment this decade.[19] China not only sees the U.S. as an attractive growth market, but is also looking to obtain American expertise in distribution and marketing. For example, LDK Solar (LDK) of China recently made a $33 million investment in Solar Power, Inc. which installs solar arrays on commercial buildings like the Staples Center and 20th Century Fox. Solar Power had experienced a loss of revenue and income in 2010 when LDK made its investment for 70% of the company. Solar

Power's CEO cited the potential for LDK to "integrate their manufacturing with marketing and distribution on our solar panel projects and then have the know-how to help them in the emerging domestic economy in China."[20] In that same vein, Zhongjixuan Investment Management of Beijing recently acquired a 43% state in Houston's Synthesis Energy Systems for $84 million. Synthesis has the technology to simultaneously upgrade the efficiency of burning low-quality coals and reduce toxic gas emissions. Zhongjixuan hopes it can use the technology to help China produce clean electricity from its low-quality coal reserves. While the U.S. is spending over $2 trillion to help bankers keep their Hermes tie collections and stone mansions in the Hamptons intact, the Chinese are investing in cash-strapped American businesses with marketing, distribution and green energy expertise to make China more competitive in the future. And there is always the risk that once China takes a majority equity stake, it will make the target company its captive supplier.

Banks Need Bailouts in Order to Save Jobs

Mr. Obama also touted the positive impact the government bailouts would have on Corporate America's ability to retain workers. A united America would survive the "Great Recession," he said. However, Wall Street had a different agenda – to fleece the public. In July 2009 New York Attorney General Andrew Cuomo released data that nine banks that received government aid paid out almost $33 billion in bonuses. Almost 5,000 employees received a bonus of at least $1 million. Edolphus Towns, a congressman from Brooklyn, called the payouts "shocking and appalling." Meanwhile, White House Spokesman Robert Gibbs issued a statement that showed Mr. Obama had yet to receive the results of his "pregnancy" test: "'The president continues to believe that the American people don't begrudge people making money for what they do as long as . . . we're not basically incentivizing wild risk-taking that somebody else picks up the tab for.'"[21] The president still had not experienced that Eureka moment. While he was making speeches about spurring the economy, much of the stimulus lay in the $2 trillion in benefits received by the oligarchs and robber barons over the past decade. His failure to claw it back would help keep the economy in a quagmire and define his presidency. And if President Obama did not know who had the leverage in his relationship with Wall Street immediately after his election, he was informed in December 2009. During a scheduled meeting between Obama and CEOs of TARP recipients, several of the CEOs did not even bother to attend. A year earlier they had made the trek down to Washington to collect hundreds of billions in aid. However, after the funds had been distributed, they had little use for the White House.

> President Obama didn't exactly look thrilled as he stared at the Polycom speakerphone in front of him. 'Well, I appreciate you guys calling in,' he began the meeting at the White House with Wall Street's top brass on Monday. He was, of course, referring to the three conspicuously absent attendees who were being piped in by telephone: Lloyd C. Blankfein, the chief executive of Goldman Sachs; John J. Mack, chairman of Morgan Stanley; and Richard D. Parson, chairman of Citicorp. Their excuse? 'Inclement weather,' according to the White House . . . That awkward moment on speakerphone in the White House, for better or worse,

185

spoke volumes about how the balance of power between Wall Street and Washington has shifted again, back in Wall Street's favor . . . Executive compensation, leverage limits and lending standards were all issues that Washington said it planned to change – and when the taxpayers were the shareholders of these firms, it probably could have done so. But now the White House has been left in the position of extending invitations, rather than exercising its clout. And in the figurative and literal sense, it is getting stood up.[22]

Mr. Obama was just beginning to understand what I had learned in my dealings with bankers at Kidder – the government, the public, their employers, et al., only exist for their personal gain. While they owed their very existence to taxpayer bailouts, Wall Street firms then paid themselves billions in bonuses from the public trough. President Obama later reversed course and called the bonuses "shameful" and the "height of irresponsibility." After public outrage over Wall Street pay, Mr. Obama delivered his now-famous plea for investment bankers to "show restraint." Yet the populace was not as patient. The new Tea Party sensed the public's outrage and channeled it to take over 40 seats in the 2010 mid-term elections. The beginning of a protest movement also materialized in January 2010. I went down to the Wall Street area to take a look at what the protests were about. This is what I found:

A coalition led by New York City Councilmember Charles Barron and other activists and organizations will form a protest on Wall Street January 15, 2010 from 3:30 p.m. to 6:00 p.m. at Wall Street and Broad. Coalition members include the Bail Out the People Movement; Rob Robinson of Picture The Homeless; Operation Power; Brenda Stokely of the Million Worker March Movement; Desiree Pilgrim-Hunter of the North Bronx Community Clergy Coalition; Benita Johnson, recording secretary of the Transit Workers Union Local 100; the Harlem Tenants Council; Peoples Organization for Progress; the May 1st Coalition for Immigrant and Worker Rights; labor activists from AFSMCE and the Teamsters; and youth groups like Fight Imperialism Stand Together (FIST). The populous is heated about the government bailing out big business while individuals fight for 'a living wage, affordable healthcare, affordable housing, and ability to use mass transit.' Populist movements are cropping up all over the nation as the 'Tea Party' gains traction down South over government bailouts. The 'Bailout the People' movement seems to be akin to the storming of the Bastille during the French Revolution. Actually, I'm surprised it took this long for mass demonstrations to occur.[23]

After reading the tea leaves, President Obama made another public rebuke of Wall Street in January 2010, claiming "the public wants its money back." He vowed to tax TARP recipients for the $120 billion in TARP that the government expected to lose. And how did Wall Street firms react to the President's threats? They again paid out record bonuses in January 2011. Obama's pleas were in stark contrast to Neutron Jack's reaction after Joe Jett's $350 million trading loss; Neutron Jack was described as "damned mad" about the loss, and reported the incident to the New York Stock Exchange, NASD and the SEC. He subsequently hired Gary Lynch to find someone at Kidder to pay for the wrongdoing. GE's lawyers issued an official statement of Jett's guilt and its corporate communications team delivered it to the media. Lynch then followed up GE's assertions with hard evidence. There were no speeches, no conference calls – just action. In October 2008 Treasury Secretary Paulson touted what a patriot he was for saving the banking system by throwing money at the problem, with no constraints. He and President Bush handed Mr. Obama a fixed deck that would define his presidency. Mr. Obama would have us believe that with no background in economics or in studying economic cycles, he alone had foreseen the Great Recession and come up with infrastructure investing as the elixir – the equivalent of finding a needle in a haystack . . . blindfolded. Yet, he was unable to see the poor political hand dealt by the Bush Administration and placed right in front of him.

President Obama Stares Down Auto Industry . . .

My sophomore year in high school (1983) the Prince Edward County school system invested in about eight K-Cars from Chrysler to be used for Drivers Education (Drivers Ed). We figured they must have gotten them for a steal because they had bought so many, and they were hideous – bright, yellow, box-shaped K-Cars. They were put on display outside the school and the kids would just gawk at them as the bus drove past. If the cars had been sneakers we would labeled them "rejects" or "bobos." I swore I would never get caught dead in one of those cars even if it meant flunking Drivers Ed. "Just give me the 'F'" I exclaimed, as the bus erupted in laughter. Well I almost did get caught dead in one – literally. I was driving 50 miles an hour on route 360 when the car suddenly, inexplicably stalled. Coach Scott, my Drivers Ed teacher and varsity basketball coach, said "Baker restart the car." As he talked I could see a tractor-trailer in my rearview, but it was a pretty safe distance away. There was only one problem, however. I could not get the bright yellow box-shaped K-Car to start! I tried to stay calm but I was literally scared to death. Again, Coach Scott goes, "Baker, start the car." I tried everything, but to no avail. By now you could hear the truck driver blowing the horn behind us. My mind started racing – I figured that by the time he realized the bright yellow K-Car shaped like a box had stalled, it would be too late for him to hit the brakes and he would kill us all. I saw my life flash before my eyes and realized how at age 16, I had actually lived a pretty good life. Coach Scott then yelled, "Baker! Get up!" He made me hop in the passenger side while he took the reins. Embarrassing! There was a girl in the backseat, Brenda, who was literally laughing her rear end off. Like magic, Coach Scott got the bright yellow K-Car with the box shape to start and pulled off just in time to avoid the tractor-trailer. I figured I had just flunked Drivers Ed and gotten cut from the varsity basketball team in one fell swoop – that was how pissed Coach Scott was. I muttered under my breath the entire way home, "If Lee Iacocca gets me cut from varsity there's going to be hell to pay!"

When we arrived back at school I swore Brenda to secrecy. But as always, bad news has a way of reverberating throughout the black community. The kids went wild with talk of "Ralph I heard you can't drive" and "Yo man you still alive? I heard you got Brenda and Coach Scott killed." I retold the story about how the bright yellow K-Car with the box shape stalled in the middle of the road, going 50 miles an hour no less. But everybody found the story too incredible to believe. Who had ever experienced a car doing that? Nonetheless, I was witness to what America was about to find out – the K-Car was a piece of trash. That was my second experience with the Chairman of Chrysler. My first was the $3 billion bailout Iacocca had arranged with the government two years earlier. When news that Chrysler needed a bailout first surfaced I thought the idea was absurd. "There goes Chrysler," I thought. "The government will never go for that." If you started a business and became a billionaire then so be it. If you went bankrupt then that was the risk. That was how America worked. And why should I have cared? My Daddy had never worked for Chrysler. But Iacocca wouldn't give up. He even went to Washington with a plan of how much money Chrysler needed, how it would repay the loan and the salary concessions management would make to get the deal approved – Iacocca personally signed a contract to work for $1. He also negotiated $260 million in wage concessions from the United Auto Workers (UAW), which at the time was a watershed event; prior to the Chrysler bailout, the UAW had always charged the Big Three automakers the same labor rate. In addition, "Chrysler was obliged to submit a yearly operating plan to the Loan Board and had to ask the Board every time it wanted to spend more than $10 million – a fairly small sum in an industry where individual machines can cost that much – and Iacocca and other top executives were required to report monthly. Brian Freeman, head of the Loan Board's staff, had been appalled during the bailout of Conrail that the government had no control over Conrail's spending, however ill-advised. The government had no choice but to guarantee more lending. This time Freeman wanted controls so annoying that Chrysler was motivated to pay loans back as soon as possible."[24] When the loan was announced, it was as if I had seen birds fly north for the winter. Chrysler did not deserve to exist. They were making gas guzzlers with poor quality at a time when gas prices had spiked. Secondly, why should my parents' hard-earned tax dollars go to support those morons who had the world handed to them on a silver platter and screwed it up? Ironically, the Loan Guarantee Act was approved in June 1980, just months before the country was to vote on Carter or Reagan for president. At the time, Lee Iacocca was the biggest "welfare queen" in America, yet Reagan never once referred to him during his war on welfare.

But Iacocca did not stop there; he apologized to the American people and promised to repay every dollar borrowed from taxpayers. He even promised that Chrysler would make cars that Americans would be proud to drive again. I thought Iacocca was smoking something. It seemed as if people had spent more time under the hood of Chrysler-made vehicles than they had actually spent driving them. But guess what? Iacocca pulled it off. He appeared in Chrysler advertising spots touting the company's newest products and quality improvements. Shortly after, Chrysler's cars were built well enough to rival the Germans and Japanese. And you know why? It was because Lee Iacocca looked you in the eye and told you so. The guy had style – pizzazz. Clad in his signature double-breasted suit and striped tie, Iacocca's folksy, down-home public announcements were less commercial and more fireside chat. While we first found these chats annoying, over time we looked forward to them. While we were outside playing someone would yell, "Lee Iacocca's on T.V.!" We would drop everything and come running to see what new product or sales gimmick (five-years or 50,000 mile protection) Iacocca had up his sleeve. Chrysler invented something called the "minivan," capable of seating seven adults. It was a hit with soccer moms because it drove like a car, and with tradespeople who could use it as a delivery van. No other company had a product like it and for the first time in decades, the Japanese were trying to imitate an American manufacturer. And Chrysler's success did wonders for America's bruised psyche. "For five delicious years, Chrysler had the burgeoning minivan market mostly to itself. In the minivan's very first quarter, Chrysler earned $705.8 million, more profit than the automaker had posted the entire previous year and the best results in the company's sixty-year history. By year's end Chrysler racked up nearly $2.4 billion in profit. Rarely had a company so close to bankruptcy sprung back to health with the vigor of Chrysler."[25] Along with Apple Computer, Chrysler has to be considered one of the greatest comebacks in American business history. Chrysler's comeback made Lee Iacocca the face of American business and a national hero.

In the first quarter of 2009 when Chrysler and GM requested $22 billion (in addition to $17 billion already received) in bailout funds from the government, I was not at all surprised. The auto industry is cyclical, experiencing periods of boom and bust; it is their ability to squirrel away earnings for the down cycle, and not get stuck with inventory when consumer tastes change, that separates the quality companies from the pack. I won't spend too much time on the stare down between the Obama Administration and the auto industry. The government could not allow them to fail due to national security issues. If the U.S. were ever attacked or had to go to war, the ability to manufacture jeeps, tanks, and airplanes would be paramount – thus, the need to maintain the Big Three intact. Yet the Obama Administration should be commended for how it handled the situation. Taking a page from the Chrysler bailout, President Obama (i) required the automakers to deliver a realistic operating plan that would ensure their survival, sans taxpayer money; (ii) demanded concessions from the UAW's hourly workers and reductions in contributions for retiree health plans; and (iii) forced the resignation of General Motors chairman, Rick Wagoner, when Wagoner failed to produce a credible operating plan as promised. Mr. Obama even delivered one of the most memorable lines of the entire crisis – "No more kicking the can down the street."

. . . But Blinks at Wall Street

Obama's tone with the auto industry was in stark contrast to the tone he took with Wall Street. The head of the UAW took umbrage with the "kicking the can" comment, and questioned why the president did not take the same hard line with AIG, Morgan Stanley, and Goldman. For while Obama was requiring salary concessions from the Big Three, TARP recipients were paying record bonuses and brazenly thumbing their noses at the rest of the country. In March 2009

AIG, which had received $182 billion in taxpayer bailouts, planned to pay $165 million to the same unit that created the losses. AIG said that since the bonuses were promised before the crisis, the company was obligated to pay them. This came on top of $121 million in previously scheduled bonuses to senior management. In July 2009 Andrew Hall, a Citigroup commodities trader, demanded a $100 million contractual payment based upon his 2008 performance. Citigroup too claimed that the payment to Mr. Hall and a $30 million payment to another trader were negotiated prior to the financial crisis. After hearing that AIG general counsel, Anastasia Kelly, had demanded a $3 million severance package, the Shock Exchange added its two cents:

> AIG's general counsel, Anastasia Kelly, is expected to receive approximately $3 million in severance pay upon her departure from the insurer. In December [2009] Kelly announced she was leaving AIG because of pay cuts imposed by Kenneth Feinberg, President Obama's federal pay czar. Feinberg capped 2009 annual cash salaries for most AIG executives at $500,000 – a significant reduction for Kelly who previously had served as the top lawyer at Fannie Mae, Sears, and MCI/WorldCom. She also drew scrutiny for advising other AIG executives chafing under the pay cuts; at least four other senior AIG executives are expected to join Kelly in departing. According to *The New York Times*, 'her departure comes at a time when the company needs experienced counsel to complete its restructuring, shepherd it through a myriad of legal proceedings and prepare prospectuses for initial public offering of its subsidiaries.' Admittedly the government has less negotiating leverage with AIG (and all TARP recipients for that matter) today than it did in September 2008 before the financial crisis hit. At that juncture, financial services companies like AIG, Lehman, etc. came to the Bush Administration begging for financial assistance, hat in hand, on bended knee. Without TARP funds AIG would be going through bankruptcy proceedings and Kelly would have to stand in line with other AIG creditors for severance or any other kind of pay. That said, today she is no worse off than she would have been had the government not bailed out AIG.[26]

An avid reader of the Shock Exchange blog, Senator Chuck Grassley (R. Iowa), echoed our sentiments, calling the severance a "windfall" and exclaiming, "The taxpayers are fed up with massive payouts to executives at companies that took tax-payer money."[27] Yet, the public was miffed as to why Obama was so draconian with the auto industry, which we needed for national defense purposes, yet pleaded for Wall Street to "show restraint." His administration seemed bipolar when it came to the differing negotiating postures. However, I knew there was a method to his madness. President Obama didn't want to work for the auto industry after leaving office – he wanted to work on Wall Street.

Obama the Investment Banker?

There is something about working in the Oval Office. It must be something in the air. People ascend to the presidency from all sorts of backgrounds – former lawyers, governors, and CIA operatives. But as soon as they leave, they and their family members are suddenly the second coming of Michael Milken – walking, talking redwelds of financial acumen. *Too Big to Fail*, the book detailing events of the financial crisis, described Senator Obama's infatuation with Wall Street –

"[Henry] Paulson finally accepted the position on May 21, but because the White House did not plan to announce the appointment until the following week after running a background check, he was left in the awkward predicament of attending the annual meeting of Goldman partners that weekend in Chicago without being able to tell anyone that he was resigning. (Ironically enough, the guest speaker that day was the junior senator from Illinois, Barack Obama)."[28] The junior senator from Illinois never produced any legislation of note – his day job. However, he found time to be the guest speaker at an annual meeting of Goldman Partners. Presidents have a lot of power but do not make millions of dollars. By championing policies favorable to Wall Street / private equity firms, these firms (i) hire them once they leave office and (ii) reward them with pay packages large enough that they, their children, nor their children's children ever have to work again. These pay packages are not an outright bribe, but a "payment-in-kind" so to speak. For example, after George H. W. Bush left office in 1992 he became a partner at the Carlyle Group, a Washington, D.C. - based private equity firm known for hiring former White House officials. Frank Carlucci (former Secretary of Defense), Jim Baker (former Secretary of State), Richard Darman (former Budget Director) have also worked there. H. W. Bush was not hired for his financial acumen, but to leverage his relationships to secure government contracts for Carlyle's portfolio companies. Carlyle has gained an expertise in, and outsized profits from, investing in U.S. defense contractors where its partners have relationships. During George H. W. Bush's tenure as president, it always struck me as odd that he maintained the country's ballooning military budget, despite Russia's military spending having subsided. My question was always, "If Reagan has indeed broken the Russians, why not reduce the military budget?" After he joined the Carlyle Group, H. W. Bush's stance on military spending made perfect sense.

Even President Clinton was not immune to "the game." I had always recollected that the repeal of Glass-Steagall was the handiwork of Phil Gramm and his fellow Republican revolutionaries, while Clinton was powerless to stop it. When I went back and did the research, I realized that though Clinton had not pushed for its repeal, he was a willing participant in it. When he opened the $165 million Clinton Presidential Library in 2004, the scuttlebutt was the Clintons' decision to make the library's donors a secret. To me, the decision seemed rather arbitrary; I thought it was all much ado about nothing. Besides, what would President Clinton have to hide anyway? After reviewing how rabid financial institutions were about repealing Glass-Steagall, and the hundreds of millions in lobbying dollars they put behind their efforts, the Clintons' "arbitrary" decision appeared more calculated. Below is the list of presidents and their family members who have worked for Wall Street or private equity firms, despite having had no prior experience in those industries.

Presents and Family Members Engaged With Wall Street / Private Equity Firms				
Name	Title	Background	Firm	Industry
George H.W. Bush	President	CIA, Military	Carlyle	Private Equity
Jeb Bush	George H.W. Bush's son, W. Bush's brother	Commercial Banking, Florida Governor	Lehman	Investment Banking
Bill Clinton	President	Governor of Arkansas, Lawyer	Yucaipa	Private Equity
Chelsea Clinton	Clinton's Daughter	McKinsey Consultant	Avenue Capital Group	Private Equity
Dan Quayle	Vice-President	Indiana Senator, Lawyer, National Spelling Bee Champion	Cerberus	Private Equity
Al Gore	Vice-President	Tennesee Senator	Generation Investment Mgmt, Kleiner Perkins	Private Equity
Barack Obama	President	Lawyer, Community Organizer	TBD	TBD

The Great Recession – What Caused It?

After the September 11, 2001 event, Alan Greenspan provided liquidity to the marketplace by lowering interest rates. Investors and businesses were uncertain about the immediate future, so Chairman Greenspan aimed to prevent the economy from going into free fall. That said, the rate on the 10-year government bond declined from 5.01% at the end of 2001 to as low as 4.01% in 2003. Mortgages are priced at a margin above 10-year treasurys. The prevailing theory is that the U.S. government will never default so the rate it pays on borrowings is considered the "risk-free rate." The credit rating for individuals could never be higher than that of the U.S. government, so the rate they pay on mortgages, personal loans and auto loans has to be higher than the risk-free rate. As stated earlier, when interest rates (or prices) decline, fixed-income investments like bonds, commercial real estate, residential homes, and MBS become more valuable. Corporations and individual investors piled into these asset classes during the low interest rate environment of 2002 - 2007, causing an "asset bubble" that burst in 2008.

As an associate at GECC, I thought about the corporate finance and M&A terms we used and wondered how they would apply to basketball. For instance, a mullet was a dumb investor, but on the basketball court it would be a player who constantly made bad decisions. "Big Hat . . . No Cattle" wore an Hermes tie and suit with double vents, yet had never completed a transaction. On the court it would be a player with brand-new Air Jordans, headband and wristbands, but no game. Below is a description of the causes of the financial crisis and their progenitors.

Real Estate Prices to Grow in Perpetuity?
The following chart shows the trend in sales prices of new homes sold from 2000 to 2008. Fixed and adjustable rate mortgages decreased in lockstep with the

decline in 10-year treasury rates, causing an increase in the average sales price of new homes of 51% from 2000 to 2007. Mortgage rates reached a trough in 2003, yet real estate prices kept rising through 2007. Sellers were loath to lower the price expectations for their homes simply because interest rates – which drove home prices higher to begin with – had increased. This asset bubble was a result of (i) real estate brokers who marketed homes based upon what the "last sucker paid" and (ii) banks that pushed low ARMs onto customers to get them initially qualified for higher priced mortgages. These "teaser rates" rose to market rates over time and increased customers' monthly payments. Investment banks and commercial banks flocked to MBS because supposedly, home prices would increase in perpetuity. Thus MBS would have a zero default rate.

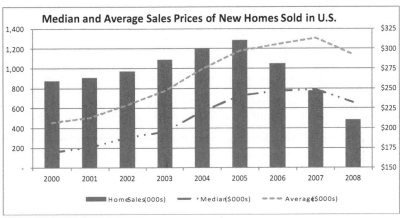

Source: US Census Bureau

Annual Home Sales

Annual home sales grew from 877,000 in 2000 to a peak of 1.3 million in 2005. In 2008 home sales went into free fall as banks reduced credit and increased lending standards after the financial crisis materialized. The average fixed rate mortgage (FRM) reached a trough of 5.85% in 2005 and peaked at 6.24% in 2006. The average ARM reached a trough of 3.76% in 2003 and peaked at 5.54% in 2007. Meanwhile, home sales increased in 2004 and 2005 despite rising rates.

Scapegoating Poor People?

On September 14, 2008 I stumbled upon a *Washington Post* article on the debacles of Fannie Mae and Freddie Mac, which cost taxpayers tens of billions. The article described federal organizations that wanted the below-market financing costs of government-protected entities, yet the carte blanche to take risks and maximize profits like private corporations. Both institutions were set up to provide local banks with federal financing to make housing available for everyone. They helped create a secondary market for these mortgages by (i) packaging them into MBS and (ii) selling them to investors. In doing so, they created liquidity for mortgages, freeing up capital for lenders to make more loans and lowering borrowing costs for prospective homeowners. The article claimed that as Fannie and Freddie became larger they posed a systemic risk to the financial system, yet they spent tens of millions annually to lobby Congress not to rein them in. It alluded that "The Clinton Administration wanted to expand the share of Americans who owned homes, which had stagnated below 65 percent throughout the 1980s. Encouraging the growth of the two companies was a key to that plan."[29] It also showed a picture of Henry Cisneros, Secretary of Housing and Urban Development, looking contrite. Cisneros was quoted as saying, "We began to stress homeownership as an explicit goal for this period of American history . . . Fannie and Freddie became part of that equation."[30] Cisneros' comment hit me like a ton of bricks and suddenly my eyes widened. "They are trying to blame the financial crisis on regular people's pursuit of homeownership," I gathered. It did not take long for me to connect the dots – if they blamed regular people for defaulting on their mortgages, they would eventually scapegoat African Americans. I started to see red.

"Blaming Clinton for pushing home ownership onto the masses was pure folly," I surmised. This economy had the makings of the early 1990s – an extremely low interest rate environment and corporations rushing into fixed income securities, especially MBS. I had known all along that a few corporations were going to blow up when interest rates rose. Just like Kidder, Askin, and Michael Steinhardt, someone's moniker of "Master of the Universe" was going to be exposed for "mistaking success for a bull market." Blaming the "average Joe" was a pure act of cowardice; he was a bit actor in a much bigger script. There were other factors, many of which the article failed to mention.

Wall Street Became Enamored With Anything "Real Estate Related"
When rates dropped, investment banks and commercial banks became enamored with MBS, corporate and government bonds, and commercial real estate. It was like "found money." They borrowed at extremely low interest rates and invested in fixed income, keeping the net interest spread. In some circles these companies "were helping the administration achieve its goal of putting more than 10 million Americans into their first homes," furthering President Bush's "ownership society."[31] However, they were no more altruistic from 2001 to 2008 than they were before Greenspan lowered interest rates.

Biggest Defaulters on Mortgages Are the Rich
The pain of the financial crisis was felt across socio-economic classes. Declining incomes and losses on securities and real estate affected the wealthy as much as middle and lower-income Americans. By late 2009, homes with mortgages greater than $1 million were almost twice as likely to default as compared to other mortgages. According to data compiled by CoreLogic and First American, "Payments on 12 percent of mortgages exceeding $1 million were 90 days or more overdue in September [2009], compared with 6.3% of loans less than $250,000 and 7.4% on all U.S. mortgages."[32] Holding "upside down" mortgages – mortgages greater than the value of the home – the wealthy turned to short sales where the lender agreed to accept less than the value of the mortgage in

order to expedite the sale. The alarming default rates experienced by wealthy individuals were counter to the "spin" coming from Wall Street and the media.

Wall Street Tried to Remove "Cyclicality" From Business Model

Investment banking is a notoriously cyclical business; firms are also notorious for overhiring during good times and firing too many people when the economy contracts. Since the mid-1990s, the trend has been to acquire fee-based businesses that provide a steady stream of revenue during economic downturns. For example, asset management companies were once thought to dovetail nicely with investment banks. The demand to acquire them created a bubble in that industry as well. In the mid-1990s, asset managers were like left tackles in the NFL – everybody wanted one. A 1996 *New York Times* article described the phenomenon: "The money management industry continued its rapid consolidation yesterday as Morgan Stanley confirmed it would pay $745 million to acquire Van Kampen American Capital Inc., a mutual fund company, and Merrill Lynch & Company agreed to pay $200 million to acquire Hotchiss & Wiley, an institutional money manager in Los Angeles . . . Big Wall Street firms, like Morgan Stanley and Merrill Lynch, are aggressively building their money management businesses, believing them to be a good source of fee income."[33] In October 2009, a year after the financial crisis, Morgan Stanley sold Van Kampen to Invesco for $1.5 billion – a semi-acknowledgement that the company was struggling under Morgan's ownership.

Hunger for steady fee-based income also created a big attraction to MBS and commercial real estate. After Greenspan lowered rates, investment banks were making so much income from betting their own capital in the MBS market that they wanted to keep the spigot open. To do so they needed one thing – homeowners. The logic, silly as it may sound, was that real estate prices would rise in perpetuity; and even if a homeowner defaulted they could sell the home and recoup their investment. To keep mortgages flowing, Wall Street firms lowered their underwriting standards and went after riskier borrowers considered "subprime." They became so aggressive that they eventually began to crowd out Fannie and Freddie from the MBS market.

> The subprime mortgages that have failed left and right are the antithesis of the carefully designed, well-supervised loans provided by tightly regulated banks. No law forced a mob of unregulated lenders to make loans in poor neighborhoods. Rather, mortgage companies and Wall Street financiers saw a business opportunity in subprime lending, where the risk of default was high and so were the interest rates . . . When financial firms began buying and bundling mortgages, redividing them into securities, and selling them off, individual brokers had no incentive to make sure any given mortgage would be sustainable if housing prices fell . . . There was enormous pressure in the marketplace. As the *New York Times* reported, Fannie Mae was losing business because of competition from Wall Street and elsewhere, and mortgage lenders and Fannie Mae's own shareholders were pushing the firm to dive into the subprime loan business. The subsequent meltdown of the nation's entire financial system could not have happened without a huge – and entirely voluntary – inflow of money from Wall Street into a sketchy

sector of the mortgage market. Nobody forced investment firms to wager billions of dollars directly on these loans, or to build an elaborate web of complex transactions dependent upon their continued performance. But they did.[34]

Commercial Real Estate Next Shoe to Drop

The other reason the *Washington Post* article stoked my interest was because all the while Wall Street and the mainstream media were scapegoating lower-income Americans, I knew something that they did not. Just like in the year I graduated college – commercial real estate would be the next shoe to drop. And when it did, you would hear no more criticisms from Wall Street or CNBC. All you would be able to hear were "crickets." The following are progenitors of the financial crisis – from the mullets, to the National Cityers, to the co-signers. They would invest trillions in real estate, MBS, and the equity markets years after the real estate market had peaked and macroeconomic forces were working against them. If a bunch of 12-year-olds from the inner city could see it then why couldn't they? They were too dumb.

THE MULLETS

In 1993 John Meriweather, former head of arbitrage trading at Salomon Brothers, set out to construct his new hedge fund, Long-Term Capital Management (Long-Term or LTCM), in the image of Salomon's arbitrage group. He lifted out several of his former colleagues – a mixture of professors and quant jocks with PhDs in math, finance, and economics. Meriweather rounded out his team with Robert Merton and Myron Scholes – two of the most brilliant minds in finance – and on the shortlist for Nobel candidates. The fund raised $1.25 billion, which at the time was the largest start-up ever, and ushered in "the new computer age" on Wall Street. Long-Term's computer-driven trading took investing from art form to a science. The partners exploited price disparities by buying underpriced securities and holding them until prices returned to their long-term averages. The fund bet the farm and initially made millions betting on the "probabilities." Yet, it exposed itself to the "severity" of losing everything, or what Grandma would call "putting all your eggs in one basket." In addition, the fund employed leverage of as much as 28.0x its equity, amplifying returns. At the beginning of 1998, Long-Term had $4.7 billion in capital. In August 1998, Russia defaulted on about $14 billion of its sovereign debt and devalued its currency. World markets crumbled and investors only wanted to hold the safest credits – U.S. treasurys and the German Bund. However, Long-Term had invested in the most esoteric securities with the largest price disparities and profit potential, the very securities investors were suddenly fleeing from. By the time of the Russian sovereign debt default, Long-Term had $3.6 billion in assets. In just five weeks all of it would be wiped out.

As losses mounted, the fund was forced to sell positions in suddenly illiquid markets, sending prices even lower. The lower prices reduced the value of the securities it held as collateral with Bear Stearns, the broker that cleared its trades. When its collateral dropped, Long-Term was forced to sell more securities to avoid a "margin call," creating a circular reference. After the fund's financial woes and trading positions became known all over the Street, rival firms became predatory. Fearing a mass liquidation by Long-Term, investors sold securities held by the fund in advance of such liquidation. For instance, if there was a rally in junk bonds, Long-Term's junk bond holdings remained depressed due to intense selling by others. Long-Term reached out to Goldman Sachs for a capital infusion and divulged its trading positions during Goldman's due diligence of the fund. Instead, Goldman mercilessly pounded Long-Term's trading positions: "According to witnesses, the headstrong Goldfield appeared to be downloading Long-Term's positions, which the fund had so zealously guarded, from Long-Term's own computers directly into an oversized laptop (a detail Goldman later denied). Meanwhile, Goldman's traders in New York sold some of the very same positions. At the end of one day, when the fund's positions were worth a good deal less, some Goldman traders in Long-Term's offices sauntered up to the trading desk and offered to buy them. Brazenly playing both sides of the street, Goldman represented investment banking at its mercenary ugliest. To J.M. and his partners, Goldman was raping Long-Term in front of their very eyes."[1]

Secondly, the fund had to estimate the value of its derivatives and billions of other esoteric holdings which were not publicly quoted. It received its marks from rival traders who added to Long-Term's demise by purposely marking down its holdings. On September 23, 1998 William J. McDonough, President of the New York Federal Reserve, summoned the chiefs of Bear Stearns, Morgan Stanley, Merrill Lynch, Bankers Trust, Lehman, Goldman Sachs, Chase Manhattan, J.P. Morgan and Dean Witter to bail out the fund. Long-Term had over $100 billion in assets, most of it borrowed from the banks summoned to the meeting. Worse yet, it also had over $1 trillion in derivatives exposure that these same banks were counterparties to; saving Long-Term was the equivalent of saving themselves. Together, the Wall Street firms raised $3.65 billion to bail out the hedge fund. A decade later, many of these firms would repeat the same mistakes of Meriweather and his band of geniuses. Moreover, they would employ even more leverage, face larger margin calls and seek bigger bailouts. Dick Fuld of Lehman, James Cayne of Bear Stearns and John Corzine of Goldman and later CEO of MF Global, were all at the table on that September day.

Investment Banks

Below are four investment banks – Bear Stearns, Lehman, Goldman Sachs, and Morgan Stanley – that either imploded, or came close to imploding during the crisis, and the reasons why.

Proprietary Trading

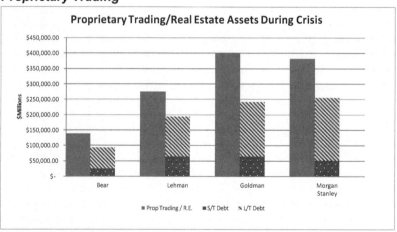

Source: Form 10-K and 10-Q
(1) Bear data at 12/31/07, Lehman at 6/30/08, Goldman and Morgan Stanley at 8/31/08
(2) Lehman financial assets $176.3 billion
(3) Goldman financial instruments $360.7 billion
(4) Morgan Stanley financial instruments $330.9 billion

Bear Stearns

At fiscal year-end (FYE) November 30, 2007 Bear held $138 billion in financial instruments, which contained its proprietary trading portfolio. Included in that amount were $46 billion in mortgage-related securities. Bear funded its prop-trading portfolio with approximately $93 billion in debt, of which $24 billion was short-term. As the company grew its prop-trading portfolio by $48 billion from 2004 to 2007, it funded it not through retained earnings, but via an increase in debt of about $51 billion. Its goal was to earn a spread above the cost to fund its investment securities, which it did until the MBS market collapsed in 2007. In a "run on the bank" scenario where the company's $24 billion in commercial paper and short-term debt were called, Bear would have to liquidate its prop-trading portfolio to repay short-term creditors. In a declining market, much of those securities would have to be redeemed at a discount to its carrying value. As its equity declined from selling securities at a loss to make short-term debtholders whole, the company's clearing broker would potentially demand more capital to support its trades – causing a circular reference.

Lehman

At May 31, 2008 Lehman held real estate-related assets of $96.8 billion while its total trading portfolio, including real estate, was $273.1 billion. Its real estate held for sale of $20.7 billion most likely included the Archstone-Smith Trust portfolio which it acquired in 2007 for $22 billion at the height of the market – one of the largest ever buyouts of a real estate company. As of October 2011, sources thought Lehman could fetch $16 billion - $18 billion for Archstone, an 18% - 27% discount to its original purchase price. The company also made a market in buying and selling credit protection on investment portfolios. I assumed the exposures hedged by its $3.7 billion in credit default swaps were real estate-related. Lehman's financial assets were supported by debt of $192.8 billion, of which $74.6 billion was short-term – a classic case of borrowing short and lending long, or investing in illiquid assets, as the case may be. Lehman also paid out total compensation and benefits of $35.7 billion from 2004 to May 2008, some of which it could have used to fund future growth in lieu of debt. Its leverage ratios from 2006 to May 2008 either approached or exceeded that of LTCM prior to its collapse.

Goldman Sachs

Goldman's proprietary trading business was the envy of Wall Street. It allowed Goldman to earn more than every other firm, and analysts touted its trading prowess as a competitive advantage. Because Goldman had higher earnings, its employees took home the biggest bonuses – how Wall Street keeps score. That said, Bear, Lehman, Morgan Stanley, Merrill Lynch, etc. all tried to replicate it. The prop-trading assets were reflected in its $400.1 billion of "Financial Instruments Owned" at August 2008. These assets were partly financed by $241 billion of debt. The difference between what it earned on its financial instruments and the interest expense on the debt was considered "carried interest." It only made sense that once other firms replicated Goldman's prop-trading model, the margins from the business would eventually decline. Goldman also held real-estate-related assets of $39.4 billion at August 31, 2008.

Morgan Stanley

Morgan Stanley's real estate exposure at August 31, 2008 was $49.7 billion. Of its $6.9 billion in "real estate investments," $3.8 billion represented its ownership of Crescent, which it acquired at the height of the market for $6.5 billion in 2007. Morgan Stanley had expected to place Crescent, owner of office buildings, resorts and housing projects, into a real estate fund it managed for wealthy individuals and institutions. Fund investors were not interested in buying the real estate at peak prices so Morgan Stanley had to keep the assets on its balance sheet. Its total proprietary assets (including real estate) were $380.6 billion, funded partly by debt of $253.3 billion at August 31, 2008.

Leverage

At FYE 2007, the leverage ratios for Bear, Lehman and Morgan Stanley were 32.8x, 30.7x and 32.6x, respectively. They compare negatively to the 28.0x leverage LTCM employed prior to its collapse. Though Goldman's leverage (23.4x) was less than LTCM's, it was still imprudent and a recipe for disaster. After Bear collapsed in the first quarter of 2008 and was taken over by J.P. Morgan, Lehman and Morgan Stanley lowered their leverage ratios while Goldman's increased.

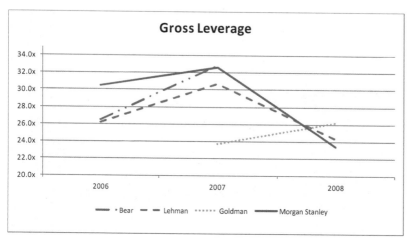

Compensation and Benefits

Cumulative compensation and benefits for the five years leading up to the implosion of these firms, or TARP payouts, was $17.4 billion, $35.3 billion, $69.3 billion and $61.3 billion for Bear, Lehman, Goldman and Morgan Stanley, respectively. Instead of clawing back these compensation payouts to cover losses from real estate and proprietary trading, a la Joseph Jett, these firms lobbied the government for a bailout or filed for bankruptcy.

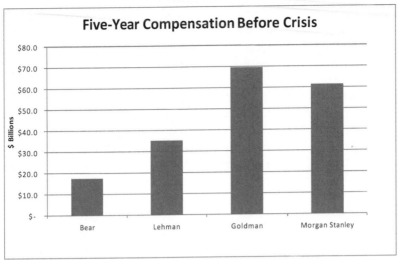

Five-Year Compensation Before Crisis

Source: Form 10-K, 10-Q
(1) Bear from FYE 2004 to FYE 2007
(2) Lehman from FYE 2004 to 6 months ended 5/31/08
(3) Goldman and Morgan Stanley from FYE 2004 to 9 months ended 8/31/08

Run on the Bank

Bear Stearns

Bear had always been a "one-trick" pony, having made the lion's share of its earnings from trading fixed income securities. The fact that a company solely focused on fixed income (so I thought) would collapse coming out of a low interest rate environment was pretty much what I had expected. After doing some additional digging, I learned that Bear's collapse signaled that the Street as a whole was in trouble. The 2007 10-K report highlighted the decline in home sales from 2006 to 2007 and how the subprime industry began to collapse in early 2007, with over 25 subprime lenders declaring bankruptcy, announcing significant losses or announcing their intentions to be sold. The mortgage lenders that retained credit risk were the first to be affected, as borrowers became unable or unwilling to make payments. The significant increase in foreclosure activity and rising interest rates in mid-2007 depressed housing prices further as problems in the subprime markets spread to prime mortgage markets. Prior to its collapse, Bear engaged in investment banking, fixed income trading, global securities clearing, and wealth management. But the lion's share (approximately 45%) of its revenue came from interest and fees on its proprietary trading portfolio that had grown from $90 billion in 2004, to $138 billion by 2007.

Mortgage Write-Downs

Revenues from Bear's prop-trading portfolio declined from $4.2 billion to $685 million from 2006 to 2007. The company recorded inventory markdowns in the second half of fiscal 2007 of approximately $2.6 billion on mortgage-related products and leveraged loans. The third quarter results also included approximately $200 million of losses associated with the failure of its BSAM-management high-grade funds. Despite the revenue and net income declines in

2007, Bear paid cumulative compensation and benefits of $17.4 billion from 2003 to 2007. Instead of squirreling away this money to (i) offset future losses or (ii) invest further in its business, it paid the money out to executives and employees and used debt to fund future operations.

Hedge Fund Collapse "Harbinger of Things to Come"

Bear's MBS investing strategy began to unravel after two of its hedge funds that invested in collateralized debt obligations (CDOs) and derivatives, imploded in early 1997. Their strategy was (i) borrow debt to purchase CDOs and earn a rate above the cost of borrowing and (ii) purchase insurance (credit default swaps) as a hedge against the CDOs falling in value. The end goal was to net out the cost of the debt to purchase "AAA" rated subprime debt, as well as the cost of the credit insurance, and achieve a positive return – referred to as a "positive carry."[2] However, the subprime MBS market declined to levels that could not be perfectly hedged and the funds eventually imploded. The decline in the value of the subprime bonds, some of which Bear had used as collateral for its financing, created a margin call and forced Bear to sell more bonds to increase its collateral. Both funds collapsed and the funds' lenders required Bear to extend $1.6 billion in cash to keep one of the funds afloat.

The Goldman Angle

The Bear hedge funds valued their MBS assets on prices obtained from investment banks like Goldman Sachs, which underwrote them. One of the hedge fund managers implied that of all its counterparties, Goldman offered valuations for securities held by the fund that were starkly lower than competitors, causing the net asset value (NAV) of the funds to decline further. This allegation against Goldman became a prevailing theme during the financial crisis as AIG made similar claims. Some Bear executives implied that Goldman had an incentive to give the securities a lower mark because Goldman had also "sold short" the securities, i.e. made bets that they would decline in value. Goldman shot back that "the value of the mortgage securities underwritten by Goldman and owned by Bear weren't large enough to cause the overall decline in net asset value that sank the hedge funds . . . The steepest markdowns of Bear's holdings were triggered by other securities firms."[3]

Margin Call

In the third quarter of 2007 the mortgage market cratered. In response, the Street slashed its mortgage portfolios, further driving down prices. Internally, Bear was torn about slashing its portfolio because (i) the market for some securities was totally illiquid and almost worthless and (ii) for other securities, Bear would have to incur losses of tens of billions of dollars. It received overtures from KKR and J. Christopher Flowers about providing capital in exchange for equity stakes in the firm, but Bear balked. By early March 2008, rumors circulating the Street were that Bear was strapped for cash, creating a "run on the bank." In a period of one week, clients and short-term lenders pulled out over $18 billion of capital and brokerages and hedge funds refused to trade with the firm. Other short-term lenders followed. Rabobank Group refused to renew a $500 million loan coming due in a week which "meant Rabobank, which was concerned about the overall market, was unlikely to renew an additional $2 billion credit agreement set to expire the next week."[4] The company received emergency funding from the Federal Reserve for a period of 28 days, just enough time to agree to a sale to JPMorgan Chase. The transaction structure included (i) JPMorgan Chase buying the stock for $2/share when it had been as high as $131/share a month earlier, (ii) the Federal Reserve providing a $29 billion loan to a new corporation, Maiden Lane, to acquire $30 billion of mortgages, commercial real estate loans, and securities JPMorgan Chase did not want and (iii) JPMorgan Chase providing $1 billion to finance the new corporation which would be repaid only after the Federal Reserve recovered its investment. At June 2010, the Maiden Lane portfolio had declined about $5 billion due to losses on the residential and commercial real estate assets.

Lehman Brothers

In mid-September 2008 I received a frantic call from my uncle Rufus from Tulsa, Oklahoma wondering "what was going on in New York?" The news hit that Lehman had just filed for bankruptcy. He wanted to know what to do with his 401k assets and I told him "to put it all in cash because the market was about to crash. And whatever you do, don't listen to CNBC or anybody else on television because they do not have a clue as to what is going on." I was pretty calm because the Shock Exchange had been discussing the state of the economy and its fallout for years. Later on that night I received a call from my cousin Donald in Virginia who asked the exact same question, "What are you all doing up there in New York man? How could a big company like Lehman fail?" At that point I started to pay very close attention. "If my relatives who don't follow the market are informing me of what is happening, the financial calamity has just hit Main Street," I thought. In the mid-1990s Lehman was a one-trick pony focused solely on fixed income. Its CEO, Dick Fuld, had brought Lehman back from the brink of bankruptcy several times since then. He diversified its earnings stream with successes in equity underwriting, asset management and mergers and acquisitions – at least I thought. Newspaper articles on Lehman's $691 billion bankruptcy – the country's largest – were pretty high level, citing soured mortgages and credit default swaps. After piecing Lehman's demise together, this is what I found.

After Bear's collapse, 28-day emergency loans by the Federal Reserve became a common occurrence. The repurchase agreement (repo) market froze, and financial institutions grew nervous about lending to Wall Street firms even though the loans were collateralized. At the program's peak, the Federal Reserve loaned $80 billion, with Goldman Sachs taking out the largest loan of $15 billion in late 2008, at rates as low as 1.16%.[5] There were separate reports that Morgan Stanley's crisis loans reached as high as $107 billion in September 2009. Bear's collapse also set other wheels into motion – it put Lehman in the crosshairs of short-sellers betting it too would run out of cash. According to Lehman's May 31, 2008 10-Q, the company's revenue within its Capital Markets division was negative $703 million, driven by $2.7 billion in losses on "principal transactions" which included residential and commercial real estate-related investments.

Pride Before the Fall

In May 2008 Lehman got into a very public spat with Greenlight Capital's David Einhorn, a brash hedge fund manager who had shorted Lehman's stock. Einhorn told anybody who would listen that Lehman's business model was a house of cards, and would crumble just like Bear's. Einhorn held a conference call with Lehman's CFO, Erin Callan, about its first-quarter 2008 financial results. A week later Einhorn delivered a blistering report on the company to a group of high-profile investors, driving the stock price down over 20% the next day.[6] Talks of partnering arrangements with Warren Buffett and the Korea Development Bank, amongst others, fell through as Fuld held out for a better deal. On September 7, 2008 the government placed Freddie Mac and Fannie Mae into receivership, further eroding investor confidence in real estate-related securities and increasing speculation that Lehman was next to fold.

Margin Call

In a written statement before the Financial Crisis Inquiry Commission (FCIC), Fuld described Lehman's final days. Lehman prereleased its third quarter 2008 financial results, reporting a net income loss of $3.9 billion, including $7.8 billion in gross write-downs on residential mortgage and commercial real estate holdings. "The run on the bank then started."[7] Amid souring real estate investments, exiting clients and a frozen commercial paper market, in September 2008 Lehman entered talks to be acquired by Bank of America, but was spurned for Merrill Lynch instead. Citigroup, JPMorgan Chase, Morgan Stanley, and Goldman Sachs, amongst others, entered buyout talks with Lehman, but demanded a Maiden Lane structure used in the Bear transaction. However, the Federal Reserve refused to intervene. Fearing the end was near, J.P. Morgan which acted as Lehman's main "clearing bank" or middleman between Lehman and third-party lenders, demanded more collateral to cover its risk. "Creditors complained soon after Lehman's bankruptcy filing that J.P. Morgan withheld billions in assets from Lehman, contributing to a liquidity crunch that caused the investment bank to collapse . . . As part of a revised guarantee agreement in early September 2008, J.P. Morgan demanded about $8.6 billion from Lehman just days before it filed for bankruptcy."[8]

Goldman Sachs

According to Goldman's August 31, 2008 10-Q, its net revenues for the nine months ending August 2008 experienced significant declines in fixed income trading, principal investments and equities. Fixed income trading was affected by weakness in broader credit markets and broad-based declines in asset values. Credit products included weak results from investments and a $2.1 billion loss related to non-investment-grade credit origination activities. Mortgages included net losses of approximately $1.6 billion on residential loans and $700 million on commercial mortgages. Goldman's leverage of 26.2x at August 2008 was high enough to make it susceptible to a "run on the bank." That scenario was averted when it received approximately $10 billion in TARP and was allowed to convert to a bank holding company, so its debt could be guaranteed by the Term Liquidity Guarantee Program (TLGP) under the FDIC. The FDIC's guarantee of Goldman's debt allowed Goldman to reduce its financing costs by over $205 million per quarter, and helped facilitate a $5 billion preferred stock investment by Warren Buffett. It should be noted that allowing Goldman to convert to a bank holding company was the very thing Glass-Steagall was set up to prevent. It did not want speculators like National City, Goldman or Morgan Stanley to have access to FDIC insurance designed to protect savers.

Relationship With AIG – Back Door Bailout

I was still miffed over the bailout of AIG. I simply was not buying this "too big to fail" story President Bush and Secretary Paulson were pushing. AIG had been one of the largest insurance companies for decades, yet nobody cared. Why was AIG a "company of interest" all of a sudden? Weeks after the AIG bailout was completed, the public became aware as to why bailing out AIG was so imperative – Goldman Sachs was one of AIG's largest counterparties under its credit default swap agreements. The bailout of AIG was nothing more than a "backdoor bailout" of Goldman Sachs; AIG was merely a pass-through vehicle to facilitate that. Below is a list of AIG credit default swap counterparties and how the $62.1 billion payments were allocated.

Total Payments to AIG Credit Default Swap Counterparties			
(in billions)			
AIG Counterparty	Maiden Lane III Payment	Collateral Payments	Total
Societe Generale	6.9	9.6	16.5
Goldman Sachs	5.6	8.4	14.0
Merrill Lynch	3.1	3.1	6.2
Deutsche Bank	2.8	5.7	8.5
UBS	2.5	1.3	3.8
Calyon	1.2	3.1	4.3
Deutsche Zentral-Genossenschaftsbank	1.0	0.8	1.8
Bank of Montreal	0.9	0.5	1.4
Wachovia	0.8	0.2	1.0
Seven Others	2.3	2.3	4.6
Total	27.1	35.0	62.1

Source Office of the Special Inspector General for TARP

Goldman had invested in so many bad mortgages that it literally bankrupted the company insuring them. If you drove down the street blindfolded and caused an accident, I am sure GEICO, Allstate, et al., would deny your insurance claim due to willful neglect. In addition, Goldman paid out nearly $70 billion in compensation and benefits from FYE 2004 through nine months ending August 2008, just before the AIG liquidity problems surfaced. They could have "passed the hat around" to its employees and saved the firm if they wanted. Instead, it made its trading losses, which exacerbated AIG's liquidity problems, an issue for taxpayers. There have been so many Goldman executives appointed to high-level posts within the government over the past few decades that I thought Goldman ran the world. Not only did it control Wall Street, but you couldn't even become a high-level government official without a Goldman pedigree. After the $14 billion in pass-through payments, *The New York Times* dubbed the firm "Government Sachs." The "Goldman Angle" not only explained the $14 billion payment, but it also explained why the government paid the counterparty claims at 100% par. Given the deterioration in AIG's collateral, an "arms-length" transaction would have resulted in the counterparties receiving a steep discount on their claims, if anything at all. And to be clear, the "Washington to Wall Street" conspiracy theory is nothing new. It has been around since the days of John Pierpont Morgan. The list of former Goldman executives with high-ranking positions within the government is too long to count – Steven Friedman (Goldman Chairman, Bush economic advisor, New York Fed Chairman), Josh Bolten (Goldman OMB director, Bush chief of staff), Robert Rubin (Goldman co-chair, Clinton Treasury Secretary) and Hank Paulson (Goldman partner, Nixon White House aide, Bush Treasury Secretary) – are just a few.

Goldman's MBS Valuations Challenged . . . Again

Two years after Goldman's collateral calls sank AIG, Goldman executives submitted documents detailing its pricing methodology for MBS insured by AIG to the FCIC, a panel set up to probe the crisis. AIG had relied on Goldman's pricing methodology in valuing the securities pursuant to Goldman's collateral calls. It was well known throughout the Street that Goldman's prices were much lower than those of other banks in 2007 when the collateral calls began. Rumors swirled that Goldman had an incentive to mark the securities lower than its competitors – the lower the securities were valued, the more collateral AIG was obligated to post under the credit default swap agreements. Bear Stearns' hedge fund managers had made similar claims – the more Goldman lowered the value of the MBS in its hedge fund portfolios, the more Goldman stood to profit from its short sales on the securities. According to documents released by the FCIC, Goldman's valuations were a source of consternation for AIG: "When Goldman began insisting the CDOs had lost value and demanded collateral from AIG, executives at the insurer's derivatives unit repeatedly challenged the demands and questioned the basis for Goldman's prices. In internal discussions, some AIG employees said Goldman's prices were 'ridiculous' and the bank was 'acting irrational.'"[9] Since the CDOs were thinly traded, Goldman claimed to have used actual prices from trades of other CDOs and ABX – a subprime mortgage index – as proxies for valuing the MBS in question. Phil Angelides, former California state treasurer and head of the FCIC, called Goldman's pricing methodology a "stab in the dark."[10] Meanwhile, Joseph Cassano – head of the AIG unit that caused the loss – was still not incarcerated for his role in the debacle. Cassano testified in front of the FCIC that had he still been employed with AIG in 2008, he would have challenged Goldman's lower valuations and saved taxpayers billions of dollars. The fact that Cassano was not testifying from behind bars must have left Joe Jett and Neutron Jack scratching their heads.

Morgan Stanley

Sub-prime related and broad credit markets continued to deteriorate in 2008 and negatively impacted Morgan Stanley's lending business, residential mortgages and commercial real estate products. For the nine months ending August 31, 2008, the company lost $1.7 billion due to valuation adjustments on loans, $2.2 billion of losses on residential and commercial mortgages, and $1.4 billion of losses on bonds insured by monoline insurers and counterparties to derivative contracts. However, it was able to avoid the fates of Bear and Lehman. In September 2008 it received an equity investment of $9 billion from Mitsubishi UFJ Financial Group, Inc. (MUFG) in exchange for a 21% interest in the company, and $10 billion in TARP funds in the wake of the Lehman collapse. Morgan Stanley was also allowed to convert to a bank holding company so its debt could be guaranteed by the TLGP, saving the company $1.1 billion in annual interest expense.

American International Group (AIG)

On September 17, 2008 the government announced it was bailing out AIG for $85 billion in exchange for 80% ownership of the company. According to a speech by President Bush, "We have a big, big problem and we need to act fast." My first reaction was, "So what? There is no threat to national security if AIG fails. There are thousands of other insurance companies that can take its place." My second reaction was, "How do you accidentally lose $85 billion? It seems like you have to try pretty hard to do that." The largest writer of commercial insurance, AIG is one of the truly international financial services companies, rivaled only by Citigroup and J.P. Morgan. It was founded in 1919 when Cornelius Vander Starr established an insurance agency in Shanghai, China. He was the first Westerner to sell insurance to the Chinese. He moved AIG's headquarters to New York in 1949 after the Communist takeover of Mao Ze Dong, but maintained a sizeable presence in Asia. I first learned about the company in the mid-90s after Wall Street analysts found it difficult to understand AIG's accounting for derivatives. Later there were accusations that its mercurial CEO, Maurice Greenberg, was using the company's reserves for insurance losses to manage earnings. Analysts accused Greenberg of over-reserving during good times, i.e. overstating losses, and lowering loss estimates during bad times, which increased earnings. Amid accusations of fraudulent business practices brought on by New York attorney general, Eliot Spitzer, Greenberg stepped down as CEO in 2005. The fact that AIG was again in the news in 2008 for "pushing the envelope" was of no surprise to me.

Liquidity Events of 2008

In the second half of 2008, AIG experienced liquidity pressure from capital calls pursuant to its securities lending business, and credit default swaps underwritten by AIG Financial Products (AIFP) group. The securities lending unit took cash collateral from borrowers in exchange for loans of securities owned by AIG insurance subsidiaries. AIG then invested the collateral primarily in residential mortgage-backed securities (RMBS) and collected a net interest spread. When customers demanded a return of their collateral backing $69 billion of loans outstanding, AIG had to liquidate the RMBS; however, AIG did not want to sell the RMBS securities at steep discounts and reached out to the U.S. government for help. AIG also experienced collateral calls for credit default swaps it had underwritten for everything from credit cards to mortgages. The decline in the CDOs insured by AIG and a downgrade of those securities required AIG to post approximately $20 billion in capital under its swap agreements. Due to AIG's liquidity strain, Standard and Poor's (S&P), Moody's Investors Services (Moody's), and Fitch Ratings Ltd. (Fitch) all downgraded AIG on September 15, 2008. Collateral for the $69 billion in securities loans, and the additional collateral triggered by AIG's debt downgrade required under the swap agreements contributed to the original $85 billion bailout from the government.

Credit Default Swaps

Pursuant to the credit default swaps, AIG received payments from counterparties in return for AIG agreeing to make payments to counterparties if a particular credit action occurred on an underlying security, i.e. if a particular security was downgraded. AIG provided protection for CDOs – a pool of risks – backed by a combination of mortgages, corporate bonds and asset-backed securities. The lion's share of the CDO was backed by mortgages and MBS. I had heard rumors that an executive from AIG, Joseph Cassano, was gallivanting around the world marketing insurance against MBS. He touted to clients and investors the soundness of the product. Since real estate prices would rise in perpetuity there would never be a default and thus, no payouts under the insurance contracts. The beauty was that since there would be no losses and the product was not regulated, AIG was not required to post any reserves for future losses; the business was pure profit, except of course for the huge bonus payments Cassano and his team received to market the swaps. Cassano alone made $300 million in compensation from 2002 until 2008 when he was ousted. The concept of "zero defaults" made no sense to me. Under Hendley's concept of "people are rational," why would clients pay insurance premiums for an event that would never happen? I surmised that either AIG's counterparties were highly "irrational" or Cassano would eventually find himself on the wrong end of a trade.

It's the Model, "Stupid"

AIG's swaps exposed it to three types of events that would trigger a payout or collateral call: (i) if the underlying securities within the CDOs went into default, (ii) if the securities insured by AIG were downgraded or declined in value or (iii) if AIG's own corporate debt was downgraded. AIG relied on financial models built by Gary Gorton, a finance professor at Yale School of Management, in order to underwrite the credit default swaps. There was one caveat though: "Mr. Gorton's models harnessed mounds of historical data to focus on the likelihood of default, and his work may indeed prove accurate on that front. But as AIG was aware, his models didn't attempt to measure the risk of future collateral calls or write-downs, which have devastated AIG's finances. The problem for AIG is that it didn't apply effective models for valuing the swaps and for collateral risk until the second half of 2007, long after the swaps were sold . . . The firm left itself exposed to potentially large collateral calls because it had agreed to insure so much debt without protecting itself adequately through hedging."[11] In effect, AIG covered events under its swaps contracts that it did not include in the financial models it used to actually price the contracts. This little-known fact proved my original point – you have to try really hard to lose $85 billion.

Too Big to Fail?

Officials from the Federal Reserve and U.S. Treasury Department were concerned about the effect an AIG bankruptcy would have on the financial markets, particularly certain retirement accounts held with AIG and credit markets. The Treasury Department realized that AIG's liquidity problems would spark additional debt downgrades and force it to post additional collateral under its credit default swaps. Treasury officials were concerned that a bankrupt AIG would cause systemic risk to the financial system and deemed it "too big to fail." An AIG bankruptcy would have had a negative impact on stable value funds and variable rate annuities within company retirement plans and IRAs. According to a report on TARP, AIG had written approximately $38 billion of stable value fund wrap contracts to more than 200 counterparties, including trustees and investment managers of retirement plans and 401k plans. An AIG failure would have generated losses within those plans.[12] Treasury officials were concerned that an AIG bankruptcy and default on its commercial paper obligations would have caused heavy losses in money market mutual funds holding AIG paper. Such losses would have caused (i) additional money market funds to hoard cash and exacerbate the credit crisis and (ii) retail investors to hoard cash and avoid money market mutual funds.

Maiden Lane III

The Federal Reserve Board of New York created and funded Maiden Lane III as a vehicle to lend up to $30 billion to purchase CDOs from the AIG counterparties. The counterparties agreed to terminate their current credit default swaps (and corresponding collateral calls) in exchange for being allowed to retain the $35 billion in collateral previously posted by AIG.

AIG No Longer a Going Concern?

In February 2010 AIG lobbied the government to exchange $60 billion of its debt for a combination of cash and equity stakes in some of its operating businesses. The plan (i) would have made the government an owner instead of a debtholder and (ii) reduced AIG's burden of paying interest on that debt. The goal was to protect AIG's credit rating, which if cut, would have forced AIG to make additional payments to its trading partners. However, the Shock Exchange found the suggestion pure folly and questioned whether AIG was even a going concern.

> *The Wall Street Journal* is reporting that AIG is seeking to overhaul its $150 billion government bailout package that would substantially reduce the insurer's financial obligations. The crux of the plan is for the government to swap about $60 billion in debt in exchange for certain AIG operating businesses. The first question that arises is, "How do you value the operating companies being sold?" The second question is, "Why should taxpayers make more bets on an AIG turnaround?" AIG does not appear to be a going concern regardless of what the

government does. Do you know of anybody pressing to purchase AIG insurance policies? Me neither.[13]

The government made about $182 billion available to AIG during the crisis. As of September 2011, AIG still owed taxpayers $124 billion in the form of (i) TARP ($49 billion), (ii) preferred interests in AIG overseas life insurance units held by the Federal Reserve of New York ($26 billion), (iii) secured debt owed to the New York Fed ($20 billion) and (iv) debt owed to Maiden Lane II and Maiden Lane III ($29 billion).

Citigroup

Once the government made public its $45 billion in TARP to Citigroup, the size of the bailouts had become mind-numbing. My immediate reaction was "Citigroup again?" The company had been considered too big to fail in the 1980s and now it was back. But how could it possibly lose $45 billion? After looking at Citigroup's crisis-year financials, I saw that it had gone hog wild on real estate , ... again. In 2007 Citigroup's net income from operations was approximately $3 billion, down from $20.5 billion the previous year. In 2008 it recorded a loss of $32.1 billion. The lion's share of its losses was related to subprime mortgages, CDOs, leveraged loans, RMBS, and commercial real estate. Like the other mullets, Citicorp went hog wild over real estate. In 2004 Citigroup's mortgage and real estate-related loan exposure was 42.2% and 3.5% of total consumer and commercial loans, respectively. By 2008 its mortgage and real estate loans had increased to 53.5% of total consumer loans and 7.8% of total commercial loans. Its loan portfolio illustrates the company's bias towards real estate, even as interest rates were increasing and the global real estate market had peaked.

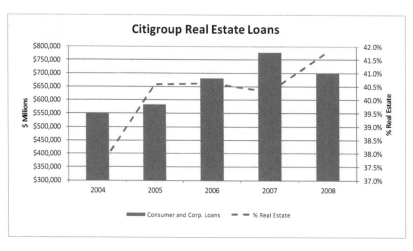

In addition to $45 billion in TARP, the government (i) gave the company $20 billion in exchange for preferred stock and warrants to purchase common stock and (ii) agreed to share in the losses on $301 billion of Citigroup assets in exchange for preferred stock and warrants. The company was a recipient under the FDIC's TLGP which saved Citigroup approximately $2.4 billion in annual interest expense. In February 2009 the government agreed to a third bailout of Citigroup by swapping $27.5 billion of preferred shares in exchange for increasing its common stock ownership from 8% to 36%. The deal reduced Citigroup's dividend payout on the preferred shares and increased its capital ratio. The Shock Exchange questioned whether the deal meant the government was "throwing good money after bad."

> *The Wall Street Journal* reports that the government is considering converting its $45 billion preferred stock investment in Citigroup into common stock. This would move taxpayers' current investment further down the capital structure, i.e., in the case of a bankruptcy (a real risk), taxpayers would be the last to get paid from a sale of Citi's assets. Given Citi's market cap of $12 billion, the government's $45 billion investment represents a de facto takeover already. It is also unclear as to the additional benefits taxpayers would receive by converting the preferreds. It may be more prudent to (i) keep the preferred shares, and (ii) lower the coupon payment (assuming this is "the financial burden" referred to in the article). In exchange for a lower coupon rate, why not request a lower strike price to convert the preferreds? . . . Under a bankruptcy scenario, taxpayers would then have a higher claim on Citi's assets than common shareholders. Moreover, some sources predict that a third bailout of Citi may cost Vikram Pandit his CEO position.[14]

CIT

In July 2009 I learned that CIT was in financial straits; I was surprised because its business should have been insulated from an economic downturn. If customers could not repay their loans, CIT could liquidate the receivables and inventory to cover any exposure. Its commercial paper funding had dried up after the Lehman bankruptcy, its long-term bonds had fallen to junk status and it had billions of debt coming due the following month. Having already received $2.3 billion of TARP, CIT had converted to a bank holding company and returned to the public trough for access to the FDIC's TLGP. With a debt guarantee from the FDIC, the company expected to raise additional capital at the lowest interest rates on the market. CIT argued that its pending bankruptcy would leave its core customer base – millions of middle-market companies, minority-owned firms and entrepreneurs – without a steady source of funds. However, the government looked askance on its TLGP application because (i) unlike the other TLGP recipients, CIT was not considered "too big to fail" and (ii) other banks could serve CIT's customers without causing a dislocation in the middle-market it served.

Loss of Focus

CIT expanded beyond asset-based lending into student loans, subprime mortgages and LBO lending. In 2003 the company hired Jeffrey Peek, an executive from Merrill Lynch, to be its CEO. Peek not only changed CIT's business model, he attempted to change its stodgy, boring culture as well. Subordinates described how he reveled in the pomp and circumstance of being CEO of a publicly traded company. "He installed CIT's top brass in a glitzy office building on Manhattan's Fifth Avenue, eschewing the company's historical base near a big shopping mall in Livingston, N.J., and brought CIT into its high-society orbit as well. CIT became a sponsor of the New York City Opera. Its role as a donor to the Metropolitan Museum of Art may have helped Mr. Peek win a prestigious spot as a museum trustee in 2008 . . . When he arrived, Mr. Peek criticized CIT's culture, which he deemed too cautious, says the former executive. He hired a psychological evaluation firm to 'understand us,' the executive recalled, and used the results to hire hundreds of new sales people who didn't fit the old CIT mold."[15]

In many ways, CIT was a victim of the volatility caused by the lower interest rate environment after the September 11, 2001 Event, and the squeeze investment banks caused when they entered corporate lending after the repeal of Glass-Steagall. Wall Street firms poached CIT's traditional customers by securitizing their loans at rates lower than what CIT could offer. CIT responded by providing riskier, higher margin acquisition loans to buyout shops that were also being courted by commercial banks and investment banks. When CIT attempted to enter the market for corporate loans and LBOs, it faced stiff headwinds. In fact, commercial loan volume for Bear Stearns, Lehman, Goldman and Morgan Stanley at the time of their collapse, or months prior to the crisis, was $15 billion, $37.1 billion, $54.8 billion and $55.8 billion, respectively. These loan commitments would not have been allowed prior to the repeal of Glass-Steagall. Buyout shops played CIT and other LBO lenders against one another to extract the best terms. To make the investment banking model complete, Peek purchased Edgeview Partners, an M&A advisory firm in 2007. One CIT executive I spoke with said CIT wooed Edgeview with guaranteed upfront pay packages, yet its M&A advisory fees were on the come, if at all. Edgeview's guaranteed pay and uncertain value-added may have ruffled the feathers of CIT lifers.

Liquidity Issues

CIT's net income from operations was $925.7 million in 2006 and declined to 664.8 million in 2007. In 2010 it experienced a loss of $633.1 million, driven by write-offs in commercial real estate, asset impairments in its vendor finance unit, and credit losses in both corporate and student loans. After the collapse of Bear Stearns and Lehman, the commercial paper market dried up and caused a liquidity squeeze as CIT had relied heavily on commercial paper to fund itself. CIT's debt ratings were downgraded in 2008 and it had to scramble to raise capital. Its capital raising efforts included (i) raising $1 billion through the sale of common equity, (ii) securing $2.3 billion in TARP funds, (iii) securing $3 billion in long-term financing from Goldman Sachs and $500 million from Wells Fargo, and (iv) selling its home lending and manufactured housing portfolio.

Obama Administration's "Best Deal"

After receiving $2.3 billion in TARP, CIT also pushed to raise $10 billion in debt backed by the FDIC's TLGP. It staked a lot of its survival on additional assistance from the federal government, and spent millions on lobbying efforts. It also hired Evercore Partners, headed by former Deputy Treasury Secretary Roger Altman, to facilitate a government rescue. CIT argued its failure and potential default on over $60 billion in debt would cause a systemic risk to the financial system and leave middle-market lenders without access to capital. In what may have been the Obama Administration's top deal – the deal it did not do – it refused CIT's TLGP application and left it up to the marketplace to rescue the company. In October 2009 the company floated what amounted to a prepackaged bankruptcy that featured (i) the government losing all of its $2.3 billion TARP investment, and (ii) bondholders receiving 70 cents on the dollar for their $30 billion in debt. CIT claimed that had bondholders not accepted the deal, they would have received 6 cents to 37 cents on the dollar. After emerging from bankruptcy, CIT replaced Mr. Peek with John Thain, formerly of Goldman Sachs and Merrill Lynch, reduced its reliance on short-term debt, and shopped its $1 billion portfolio of problem LBO loans. CIT's ability to survive after being denied additional government assistance showed the resilience of the company and its employees, and the flexibility of the U.S. financial markets. If the Bush and Obama administrations had taken this tact with Goldman, Morgan Stanley, AIG, GE, et al., they too would have found creative ways to solve their liquidity problems.

General Electric

After the fall of Lehman and AIG, the news got worse each day. I could not wait to read the newspaper to see which investment bank or hedge fund was about to blow up. But one morning I opened the paper and was thrown for a loop – General Electric had announced that it too was having financial difficulties. Its commercial paper funding had dried up after the collapse of Lehman; not only was its vaunted AAA credit rating in jeopardy, if it could not find an alternative source of capital then filing bankruptcy was an alternative. My first thought was "GE? Not my GE!" My second thought was, "If GE's CEO, Jeffrey Immelt, is crying about his short-term funding drying up then that can only mean one thing – it has been playing the game of borrowing short and lending long . . . just like S&Ls from the 1980s." Commercial paper is super short-term unsecured debt that matures anywhere from overnight to 90 days. It is offered to only the most creditworthy borrowers, like GE or American Express, and designed to meet short-term obligations like payroll and working capital. Given commercial paper's short-term and high quality borrowers, it often fetches the lowest rates. The product really took off in the mid-70s and allowed commercial paper financiers to cherry-pick commercial banks' best customers. Retail money-market mutual funds are currently the main buyers of commercial paper. However, their appetite for the paper contracted after the Lehman debacle and caused liquidity issues for GE, CIT, and American Express whose short-term debt was not renewed.

Borrowing Short and Lending Long

Commercial paper is designed to fund short-term assets. However, GE was using commercial paper to fund long-term assets as well. The following chart illustrates GE's (i) liquid assets, including cash and equivalents, and current receivables, in comparison to (ii) its commercial paper and other short-term debt. In 2006, 2007 and at September 30, 2008, prior to its taxpayer bailout, GE's short-term debt exceeded its short-term liquid assets; at September 30, 2009 GE's short-term debt ($215.4 billion) exceeded its short-term liquid assets ($38.7 billion) by $176.7 billion. Over 95% of the company's short-term debt was borrowed by its finance arm, GECC, to fund its financing receivables. The company's reliance on commercial paper vis-a-vis long-term debt benefited shareholders initially. The interest rate on commercial paper and short-term debt was 4.79% versus 5.25% (per GE 2007 form 10-K for long-term debt) – a 46 basis points (0.46%) differential. However, when its commercial paper dried up and had to be redeemed immediately, the company did not have enough liquid assets to repay it. Therefore, it turned to the government for a bailout in the fourth quarter of 2008. GE lowered its reliance on short-term debt after it received access to government debt guarantees, and raised $3 billion in preferred stock and $12 billion in common equity. After its bailout, GE's short-term liquid assets closely matched or exceeded its commercial paper at year-end 2008 and beyond.

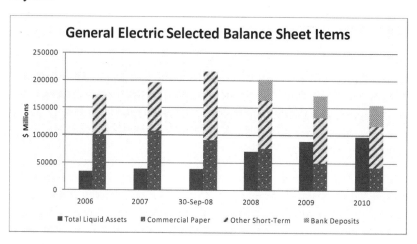

Had the company employed short-term debt to match liquid assets of $38.7 billion instead of the actual $215.4 billion at September 20, 2008, GE would not have needed government assistance. An optimal capital structure best matches its indebtedness to the assets it is designed to fund. Assuming GE borrowed the additional $176.7 billion of long-term debt at its weighted average rate of 5.25% (versus 4.79% for short-term debt), the higher interest rate would have increased GE's run-rate interest expense, and reduced pretax income by approximately $813 million ($176.7 billion * 46 basis points). The following table illustrates

GE's run-rate interest expense given its overreliance on commercial paper, versus its run-rate interest expense had it matched its commercial paper with its liquid assets ($38.7 billion) and increased its long-term debt by the difference ($176.7 billion).

Income Impact From Reliance on Commercial Paper							
	Unaudited		Run-Rate	Pro-Forma			Income
(in millions)	30-Sep-08	Rate	Interest	Debt	Rate	Interest	Impact
Debt:							
Short-Term	$ 215,409	4.79%	$ 10,328	$ 38,740	4.79%	$ 1,857	$ (8,471)
Long-Term	321,019	5.25%	16,868	497,688	5.25%	26,151	9,283
Total	536,428	5.07%	27,196	536,428	5.22%	28,009	813

NOTE: Weighted average interest rates derived from 2007 10-K. Details not provided in 3Q 2008 10-Q.

Government Assistance

In November 2008 the government approved GE's participation in the FDIC's TLGP, under which the FDIC guaranteed GECC's debt up to approximately $139 billion. Instead of issuing overnight loans it raised about $50 billion in guaranteed medium-term debt, more than any other company – a likely savings of about $3.3 billion.[16] In addition, GE turned to famed investor Warren Buffett for a $3 billion preferred stock investment which Buffett only agreed to after GE secured the government debt guarantee. "In reality this is all about protecting GE's credit rating and heading off any funding problems. GE insists it has had no difficulty rolling its paper. The commercial paper market is clearly stressed. Nervous money-market funds, spooked by losses at some funds because of Lehman Brothers Holdings' bankruptcy filing, last week shifted money from commercial paper into Treasurys."[17] The Obama Administration recommended that GE spin-off its GECC financing unit; however, Immelt balked at the idea. GE had been granted the ability to have its cake and eat it too – it had received government debt guarantees and FDIC backing without the capital requirements and regulatory scrutiny reserved for commercial banks.

The Meek Shall Inherit GE?

Gary Wendt built GECC into a juggernaut that eventually grew to represent over 40% of GE's overall earnings. Wendt was the obvious choice to become CEO of the parent company once Neutron Jack stepped down. That said, in 1997 Wendt was party to the most high-profile divorce case of the decade; it was memorable because his wife, Lorna Wendt, was seeking half his assets due to her role as the "corporate wife." Lorna argued that she and Wendt were equal partners in his success at GE. "I was first of all to be his wife, his helpmate, and his partner, his social facilitator, while he carried on the business end of it. I was never hired by GE to know or talk about a deal, but I was there so that when Gary traveled I was an accessory that he liked to have. It made it easier for him."[18] Lorna Wendt's argument was an all too familiar one – the story of the military soldier or corporate executive whose skills in the art of war won him victories on the battlefield and the boardroom. However, it was the military wife or corporate wife who charmed his superiors and their wives, and helped land him the promotion he could not get on his own. The Wendts' divorce case was closely watched by other corporate wives who expected to make a similar legal argument, if need be.

The Wendt divorce garnered a heightened level of media attention for one other reason – it gave the public a rare behind-the-scenes glimpse of the inner workings of GE. Wendt's testimony was so explosive that his attorneys requested that the judge close the proceedings and seal the hearings; they feared his testimony could affect the price of GE's stock, get Wendt fired, or both. In the pretrial deposition, Wendt admitted that being CEO of GECC was not all that it was cracked up to be. He disclosed that he and Neutron Jack had a "rocky relationship." He lamented how at corporate functions Welch all but ignored him. Instead, Neutron Jack stood apart from Wendt, basking in the adulation of younger managers. Wendt was acknowledged to be an uber-talented businessman, but his downfall may have been in not paying proper deference to Welch and having fancied himself the star of his own orbit – he was known for having been the only person to scream at Jack Welch publicly. Any student of history could have predicted the outcome. In 1910 Jack Morgan (Pierpont's son), looked to appoint someone to the role of Chief Operating Officer of the firm; his two choices were Henry Davison and George Perkins. Davison won out over the supremely talented Perkins by default. "Perkins carried several liabilities . . . But the cause of Perkins's downfall would be that he saw himself as a king in his own right, not simply a Morgan vassal. At his Riverdale estate, he had nine servants, a swimming pool, a ballroom, and a bowling alley. In 1906, he bought the world's largest custom-made car – an eleven-foot French monstrosity with ebony woodwork, a writing desk, and a washstand-table. His worst sin may have been not showing due deference to the Morgans. He sneered at Jack and thought he was more highly qualified to run the bank. He sometimes made decisions without consulting the Morgans . . . For those skilled at reading the tea leaves, it grew clear that Henry Pomeroy Davison would become Chief Operating Officer."[19]

Report Card for Immelt

After Welch decided Wendt was not the right man to succeed him, in 1998 he asked Wendt to resign out of fear that Wendt would overshadow his hand-picked successor. At the time I surmised that since Wendt's talent and lack of deference to Welch made him a liability, by definition, the next CEO of GE had to be someone (i) talented, but not talented enough to overshadow Welch and (ii) with a proven ability to pay homage to Neutron Jack. That successor turned out to be Jeffrey Immelt, then head of GE Medical Systems. But unlike my original assumption, Immelt has proven to be anything but "meek." When it comes to exporting jobs abroad and shielding U.S. taxes, Immelt has shown no restraint. Of the multinationals that export jobs overseas, GE has been one of the largest. In 2001 its domestic employees versus those abroad were 158,000 and 152,000, respectively. By 2010 its domestic employees had declined to 133,000 while is multinational employees held steady at 154,000.[20] And this comes from a company whose CEO was appointed as Obama's jobs czar. When analyzing GE's financial statements, I noticed that it paid nearly zero taxes. From 2007 to 2009 its cumulative taxes paid compared to its cumulative pretax income equated to an effective tax rate of about 7.1%. In 2009 it actually received a tax benefit of $1.1 billion on pretax income of $10.3 billion. The bible's reference to "The meek shall inherit the earth" has oft been misinterpreted; some have interpreted "meek" as weak or fragile. However, the word was actually meant to connote a person who was "strong" and "powerful," yet used that strength and power in a controlled way. In that respect, the meek did not inherit GE. After the company's bailout I read an article grading Immelt's performance ten years after taking the helm. Two of the main categories – the ability to pay deference to Welch and the ability to allocate capital efficiently – were not on the list. For the former I would give Immelt an "A+" and for the latter, an "F."

Robert Willumstad

As newly appointed CEO of AIG in June 2008, Robert (Bob) Willumstad found himself at the center of its debacle. Willumstad joined AIG as Chairman in 2006 after Hank Greenberg was ousted. He had the unenviable task of seeking strategic alternatives after its liquidity issues had materialized. His name rang a bell but for the life of me I could not place it. Then it hit me . . . "That's the former executive from Travelers who did not even have a college degree! No wonder AIG was in financial straits. They had people running the company who had barely graduated from high school," I surmised. The name and background were lodged in my mind ever since the groundbreaking merger between Travelers and Citigroup. The unassuming Willumstad started his career on the ground floor at Chemical Bank and joined a consumer finance company that eventually became part of Citigroup. Before you knew it, Willumstad, armed with a high school diploma, was running half of Citigroup and whispered to be the heir apparent to Sandy Weill at the most powerful financial services company in the world – even Spielberg couldn't have made that up.

Quiet, "Predatory" Giant

Mr. Willumstad spent his formative years in a Norwegian enclave in Bay Ridge, Brooklyn. The family moved to Elmont, New York, where he attended Sewanhaka High School. He later attended Nassau Community College, Queens College, and Adelphi University but did not attain a degree. Willumstad eventually "joined Chemical Bank, now part of JPMorgan Chase, as a systems analyst in 1967, and rose through the operations, retail banking and computer systems divisions. In 1987 he joined Commercial Credit, then a consumer finance company that became part of Citigroup. He was running Travelers Group Consumer Finance Services when Travelers and Citibank merged in 1998. He became head of Citigroup's global lending unit, rising in December 2000 to oversee the global consumer business."[21] In 2002 Mr. Willumstad was named president of Citigroup and prompted speculation that he would eventually succeed Weill. His ascendency caught the attention of Wall Street analysts because his demeanor was the polar opposite of Weill's aggressive, hard-driving style. Analysts dispelled talk of Willumstad becoming CEO of Citigroup, citing that he was "too nice" and lacked the ivy-league pedigree of his colleagues. He may have been too nice to colleagues and subordinates, but when it came to borrowers with impaired credit, to use the word "predatory" to describe Willumstad would be too kind – forcing them to take out unnecessary, overpriced insurance before extending them loans. Citigroup was ordered to pay $215 million by the Federal Trade Commission (FTC) to settle charges that it strong-armed lower credit borrowers into taking out single-premium credit insurance. The suit arose at Associates First Capital Corporation (Associates) which Citigroup had acquired. Willumstad knew about Associates' lending practices, yet consumers claimed Citigroup maintained those practices post-acquisition. The FTC also accused Associates of misleading customers into purchasing credit insurance, "for which the premium was folded into the principal of the loan in a lump sum. Borrowers then ended up paying interest on the insurance, which covered payments in case of unemployment, disability or death and often expired long before the loan was due."[22]

In April 2003 Citigroup paid a $400 million fine – the largest ever for a Wall Street firm – to settle charges that its Smith Barney unit issued misleading research reports on companies in exchange for investment banking business. Weill stepped down amid the scandal and named Charles Prince, Citigroup legal counsel, the CEO. Willumstad was promoted from president to chief operating officer (COO), at the time considered a "consolation prize." Resigned to the fact that he would never get the top job at Citigroup, Willumstad left in 2005 to actively seek a CEO position at a public company. I remember wondering aloud, "What would make this man think he could run a Fortune 500 company armed with nothing more than a high school diploma and a personal friendship with Sandy Weill? Sometimes you have to give people what they're asking for." Willumstad moved on to AIG as Chairman in 2006 and was awarded the CEO role he had coveted in June 2008, albeit among dubious circumstances. He led AIG's efforts to address liquidity issues at its securities lending business and the collateral calls at AIGFP which totaled $16.1 billion at July 2008 – the equivalent of closing the barn door after the horse had left the stable. He met with private equity firms, sovereign wealth funds, and various investment banks to assist in raising capital in advance of a ratings debt grade. On September 15, 2008, S&P downgraded AIG's long-term debt ratings by three notches; Moody's and Fitch downgraded it by two notches. In the following two weeks AIG experienced collateral calls of an additional $32 billion from AIGFP counterparties. On September 16th the Federal Reserve agreed to provide AIG the necessary capital to meet counterparty claims; within a week, Willumstad was replaced as CEO by Edward Liddy.

A year after the AIG bailout CNNMoney interviewed Willumstad. He lamented that he was not allowed to stay on and help, and that he felt confident he knew what AIG's problems were and the necessary solutions.[23] The interview begs the question, "If he knew the problems and the solutions, why didn't he implement them in his capacity as Chairman starting in 2006?" The federal government ultimately provided AIG $182 billion in financial assistance. Meanwhile, AIG's Chairman leading up to its liquidity crisis and acting CEO during it, had never even finished college. Yet no one made the connection that AIG's failure was a direct result of Willumstad and AIG executives making decisions that their educational levels, and technical expertise did not warrant.

David Stockman

After working for an investment bank and the private equity firm where I met him, David Stockman fancied himself as a deal guy. In December 2001 I came across a shocking news story that Stockman had raised a $1.4 billion private equity fund called Heartland Partners, L.P. I wondered, "Who in his right mind would give David Stockman $1.4 billion to invest? He could barely balance Reagan's budget so what makes him think he knows M&A." I envisioned Stockman in his Hermes tie and double-vented suit blabbering about the "trickle-down theory," "buy-out multiple" and "IRR." I kept reading and lo and behold, the article filled me in. The Canadian Pension Plan Investment Board agreed to invest $150 million in the fund with the option to co-invest in Heartland acquisitions. Heartland's master plan was to acquire manufacturing companies, specifically in the auto parts space. It had already paid $260 million for 60% of Collins & Aikman (Collins) Corporation, a maker of car interiors.[24] Other investors in the fund were the Michigan state pension plan, J.P. Morgan Chase, AIG, and the pension fund for the steelworkers of America.

My logic asked, "Why would David Stockman invest in the auto industry? I cannot think of anybody buying cars from the Big Three. They are unimaginative. Furthermore, given the wars in Iraq and Afghanistan, the Big Three's aggressive marketing of SUVs is inappropriate. Young men are risking their lives over oil and the Big Three are devising more ways to guzzle it. When gas prices get out of hand again the Big Three are going to have a big problem and auto parts makers are simply a derivation of the auto industry. When Detroit catches cold, the auto parts makers are going to catch pneumonia." Earlier Collins had acquired Textron's TAC-Trim business for $1.3 billion; the unit produced interior components for automobiles such as instrument panels. Textron sold the business because it wanted out of the boom and bust cycles of the auto industry.

Stockman's Investment Fund in Trouble

In September 2003 Stockman took over as CEO of Collins after the company ran into financial difficulties. The company's stock had declined to about $3/share from a high of $28/share in May 2002 and its debt had declined to junk status. Its problems stemmed from the struggles of the Big Three who responded to shrinking operating margins by squeezing their suppliers, including Collins. Exacerbating the problem was the fact that three-fourths of Collins' $4 billion in revenue came from the Big Three, it was embroiled in a dispute with Chrysler – its largest customer – and the Big Three were playing their auto parts suppliers against one another to extract the best terms. Chrysler contended that Collins owed it $16 million as part of a refund based on cost savings. Signaling who had the leverage in the relationship, Chrysler "stopped using Collins as the supplier for its Jeep Liberty, an unusual step in the midst of a production cycle."[25] Stockman responded to the company's declines in business by promising to close unproductive factories and cut the company's workforce by almost 15 percent. Still, one securities analyst, speaking on condition of anonymity, was unimpressed. "'He's got in over his head, and it's not working out,' he said of Stockman. 'He had a great concept which hasn't panned out. The concept was to consolidate subsectors of the parts industry where he could have a dominant position.'"[26] Having made three acquisitions in 2001, Heartland was named "Buyout Firm of the Year" by Thomson Financial's Buyouts Symposium – proving the adage that "some people are better at getting business than doing business."

Smoking That "Kidder Peabody"

In May 2005 I read that Collins was experiencing serious liquidity issues. It had about $15 million in liquid assets and interest payments totaling approximately $54 million due in June and August. To compound matters, David Stockman was missing in action, having resigned abruptly as CEO. An S&P downgrade of GM and Ford had also reduced the amount Collins could borrow under its receivables-based lending agreement, its main source of funding. Stockman's disappearance amid Collins' liquidity problems did not bode well for him or the company's future. I smelled a soap opera brewing. In March 2007 Stockman was indicted for fraud; he was accused of using accounting tricks to mask Collins' deteriorating financial condition and attain additional debt financing, while simultaneously defrauding investors and debtholders. Collins paid Heartland $45 million in management fees from 2001 - 2004, of which $22 million had gone to Stockman.[27] "I took Stockman for an idiot, but not for a crook. David Stockman's going to jail," I thought. The claims sounded like what is known as "fraudulent conveyance" – when equity holders, management, etc. remove funds from a company at the expense of debtholders. "Yeah, David Stockman's smoking that 'Kidder, Peabody'" I surmised. According to David Cole, chairman of the Center for Automotive Research, "Stockman's biggest error was getting into the supplier business too early. 'He really guessed wrong on the restructuring. Once he got into it with the debt load and falling revenue from his traditional customers, it really was a perfect storm."[28]

Collins filed for bankruptcy in 2005 and was eventually sold to vulture investor, Wilbur Ross, in 2007. At the time of the sale it had 4,150 employees and $600 million in revenue, down from 5,400 employees and $4 billion in revenue when Heartland owned it. Collins sued Stockman, amongst others, seeking a return of the $45 million in management fees paid out by the company. In March 2010 Stockman agreed to pay $4.4 million to resolve lawsuits by Collins. Under the settlements, Collins was to receive $24.6 million in total, the lion's share of which was expected to be paid by Heartland. Since his stint as a private equity investor, Stockman has made a comeback as the "go-to person" to explain the financial crisis and the state of the U.S. economy. He has appeared on MSNBC and been quoted on such popular websites as *The Motley Fool*. He has always been introduced as "Reagan's former budget director" with no caveats as to his proclivity in that capacity . . . sort of like the "Paris Hilton of economics" – famous for being famous. In a 2010 interview on MSNBC's The Dylan Ratigan Show, Stockman reacted to a press conference by Fed Chairman Ben Bernanke. Adorned in his Hermes tie and suit with double vents, it looked like David Stockman may have found his true calling – "talking" instead of "doing."

THE BIG HATS . . . NO CATTLE

Charles Ponzi, for whom the "Ponzi scheme" was named, was an Italian immigrant who came to the U.S. in 1903. Ponzi did not look the part of the typical immigrant. "Truly, for an immigrant, I did not look the part . . . From tie to spats, I looked like a million dollars just out of the mint; like a young gentleman of leisure, perhaps like the scion of wealthy parents on a pleasure tour. And that goes to show that appearances don't mean a thing."[1] Yet, Ponzi had only $2.50 to his name, having lost $200 to a card shark on the voyage from Italy. After a short stint in jail, Ponzi spent his life devising "get rich quick" schemes. None ever panned out until he started the Securities Exchange Company to exploit the price differential between an international reply coupon (IRC) representing the cost of stamps in one country, versus the cost of stamps in another. To raise capital quickly, he offered customers exceptionally high returns on their investments – 50% returns over 45 days and double their money over 90 days. The red tape involved in redeeming large amounts of IRCs at the post office stymied the scheme, so he paid returns to initial investors from monies received from later investors – what Grandma would call "Robbing Peter to Pay Paul." The scheme unraveled after several newspaper articles questioned its soundness and claimed Ponzi was insolvent. The negative publicity prompted investors to demand their money back in droves. The Ponzi schemes during the financial crisis – Bernie Madoff, Stanford Financial and Phillip Barry – would too come unraveled after investors demanded their capital amid stock market declines, and questions from regulators about the fantastically high returns promised to investors.

Bernie Madoff – "All a Big Lie"

Bernard L. Madoff, former NASDAQ chairman and head of Madoff Investment Securities LLC (BMIS) was arrested and criminally charged with running a Ponzi scheme in December 2008. According to an SEC criminal complaint, BMIS, which engaged in market-marking services, investment advisory services and proprietary trading had been operating the scheme since at least 2005. The losses amounted to approximately $50 billion. During the first week of December 2008 Madoff told his sons, Andrew and Mark, that clients had requested approximately $7 billion in redemptions, creating a strain on the firm's liquidity. Madoff later met with his family at his Manhattan apartment and admitted that the investment advisory business was a fraud. He also stated that he was finished, had absolutely nothing, and that "it's all a big lie . . . and a Ponzi scheme." Madoff confirmed that the business had been insolvent for years, and that he planned to turn himself into authorities. Moreover, he had $200-$300 million left that he planned to distribute to certain employees, family members and friends. Immediately after his surrender, the SEC requested a temporary restraining order on Madoff and asset seizure of BMIS.

Background

Madoff began as a wholesale dealer specializing in over-the-counter (OTC) stocks for mostly smaller companies shunned by the New York Stock Exchange

(NYSE). Wholesalers bought and sold stocks from/to brokers whose clients were looking to trade OTC stocks. The transactions took place over the phone, making the OTC market highly inefficient. Moreover, the spreads – the difference between the bid/ask for a stock – could vary amongst dealers. In addition to his market-making activities, Madoff managed money for family and friends. He described his earlier trading strategy as "convertible arbitrage." "Madoff invested in high-yield issues that were convertible into common stocks while simultaneously short-selling the common stock . . . Investors then earned 'the spread between the higher dividend paid on the convertible securities and the lower dividend on the common stock, plus interest from investing the proceeds of the stock short sale.'"[2]

Making OTC Trading More Efficient

Describing the specialist system where OTC stocks were traded as 'inefficient" is another way of saying the dealers ripped off investors by inflating the spread between the "bid" and "ask" prices. Bernie wanted to bring down the corrupt system by automating it, making himself millions in the process. OTC dealers' first attempt at automation was a computer system that simply displayed stock quotes – National Association of Securities Dealers Automated Quotations (NASDAQ). Madoff pushed to list buyers and sellers on a computer that anyone could access. "'We came up with a system of developing a screen-based trading mechanism," Bernie explained at a conference. 'That was the start of the NASDAQ.'"[3] The fortune was not in automating OTC trading, but in designing software that allowed trades to occur in seconds, increasing the ease of use for customers. Madoff marketed his firm as able to complete trades "faster" and "cheaper" than anyone else. "Actually 'cheap' understates the matter. Rather than taking a fee for trading stocks, as NYSE specialists did, Madoff paid firms like Charles Schwab and Fidelity a penny or two a share for their orders, a practice known as 'payment for order flow.'"[4] At the time, the spread between the price market makers bought and sold shares was a customary 12.5 cents. Madoff and discount brokers formed a symbiotic relationship – his cheap prices allowed them to slash commissions and attract mainstream investors, while the volume Madoff generated more than offset the payments for order flow. By the 1980s Madoff had attained a sizeable share of this "third market," or electronic trading outside of the NYSE. Madoff executed trades representing 9% of the NYSE's trading volume, creating a cash cow whose profits could theoretically be deployed into other businesses. However, by 1997 the spread market-makers garnered was reduced to 6.25 cents. It evaporated down to one cent by 2001, and with it Madoff's cash cow.

Sunlight the Best Antiseptic?

Over the decades Madoff marketed his investment advisory business via "word of mouth." The secretive, exclusive nature of the business added to its cache and made clients feel privileged to invest with Bernie, an emotion that could be equated to joining a private country club. The marketing scheme was right out of the Pierpont Morgan handbook: "In a culture that worshipped the hard sell, the reticent J.P. Morgan and Company was a puzzling curiosity. As a private New

York bank, it couldn't advertise, solicit deposits from the general public, or pay interest rates on deposits of less than $7,500. Apparently, getting a Morgan account was like being accepted at an exclusive country club."[5] Everything about Bernie's investment advisory business was cloaked in secrecy – from the stocks he invested in, to his trading strategy. For instance, the investment advisory business used Madoff's related-party broker-dealer to hold its assets – a clear conflict of interest. That said, there was no independent custodian who could confirm its actual AUM at any point in time, and now we know why. In 1992 the SEC closed one of Madoff's feeder funds, Avellino & Bienes (A&B), with charges that the partners at the Florida accounting firm had operated A&B as an unregistered investment company and engaged in the unlawful sale of unregistered securities. The $440 million raised by A&B represented one of the largest sales of unregistered securities in history. Everything about the sale reeked of a scam. First there was the marketing pitch – guaranteed returns of 13.5% to 20.0%. Yet the broker, his investment background or his investment strategy was not disclosed. By not registering the investments with the SEC, A&B was able to skirt disclosure of how the money was being invested, who was investing the money and requirements that annual disclosures and investment returns be sent to investors. When regulators performed due diligence on the funds, they discovered that the assets existed and the money manager – Bernie Madoff – was exceeding promised return horizons. The new investment strategy involved a "market-neutral" approach of buying securities in the S&P and hedging the downside with stock options. At the time, *The Wall Street Journal* questioned Madoff's stock-picking prowess – "Perhaps the biggest question is how the investment pools could promise to pay high interest rates on a steady annual basis, even though annual returns on stocks fluctuate drastically. In 1984 and 1991, for example, the stock market delivered a negative return, even after counting dividends. Yet Avellino and Bienes – and Mr. Madoff – maintained their double-digit returns."[6]

In 2001 media stories from trade publication *Mar/Hedge* and *Barron's* questioned Madoff's consistent double-digit returns and wondered aloud whether he was employing "smoke in mirrors." Rumors on the Street were that Madoff was using his brokerage business to subsidize returns at his hedge fund. How else could he achieve consistent returns even in years where the overall market had declined? However, new details emerged that Madoff was instead using the hedge fund to subsidize the brokerage business. In addition to running a Ponzi scheme, he was charged with laundering millions of dollars from the investment advisory business to the brokerage business. In 2006 after a financial fraud investigator, Harry Markopolos, spent nearly a decade trying to persuade it that Madoff was running a Ponzi scheme, the SEC investigated Madoff. However, the former head of the NASDAQ and Wall Street icon bullied and intimidated SEC investigators. In a taped phone conversation between Madoff and representatives of Fairfield Greenwich, one of Madoff's feeder funds, he called the SEC investigation a "fishing expedition" and implied the SEC "might not press too hard because SEC lawyers have ambitions to go into lucrative private practice and don't want to alienate the sorts of firms that might hire them."[7] The

SEC noted Madoff had lied on occasion and attempted to stonewall the investigation, yet closed the inquiry having found no evidence of fraud.

"I Won't Lie Any Longer"

According to the SEC, Madoff assigned George Perez and Jerome O'Hara to work on investment advisory operations in 1992 after the SEC prohibited A&B from feeding money to Madoff. Afterward, clients of A&B and other accounting firms began investing directly with Madoff instead of going through a middleman. This is clear evidence that Madoff had continued to go through machinations to avoid regulatory scrutiny. At a minimum, the clients of A&B were willing to aid and abet Madoff as long as they continued to receive their guaranteed investment returns. O'Hara and Perez, also computer programmers at Madoff's brokerage business, over the next 15 years developed programs to generate records purporting to show Mr. Madoff's new "split-strike conversion" trading strategy, the SEC complaint says. Prosecutors claimed the men created and maintained hundreds of programs that used sophisticated algorithms to generate random, fictitious trading data for thousands of client accounts.[8] Instead of executing the split-strike conversion trades, Madoff kept investor funds in liquid assets (cash, CDs, treasury bills). A large portion was used to pay investor redemptions and line Madoff's pockets, and the pockets of those around him. In 2006 one of the men told Madoff, "I won't lie for you any longer." Madoff then directed his lieutenant, Frank DiPascali, to pay whatever was required to keep O'Hara and Perez quiet. O'Hara and Perez's counter offer was a one-time bonus of $60,000 each and a 25% salary increase. Federal prosecutors eventually brought criminal charges against the pair and set bail at $1 million each. The financial crisis decimated the stock market in the third quarter of 2008, prompting clients to request over $7 billion in redemptions. Knowing there was no way out, Madoff too refused to lie any longer. He called his sons to his Manhattan apartment to tell them the Ponzi scheme had finally come to an end.

Allen Stanford

After Madoff was arrested in December 2008, Ponzi schemes were popping up seemingly everywhere. In February 2009 I listened to a CNBC story about the scheme orchestrated by Stanford Financial Group (SFG) out of Houston, Texas. Included on the telecast was a gentleman who was intimately familiar with SFG, and raved about what a travesty the $8 billion Ponzi scheme was. He also divulged how for years, regulators were warned about SFG and its CEO, Allen Stanford. The part I couldn't ascertain was, "Why now? What fact pattern had suddenly changed to make regulators file a formal complaint against Stanford?" I chalked it up to recent stock market declines having prompted investors to redeem capital, triggering a liquidity strain at the company. The SEC complaint claimed Stanford used marketing glitz, public relations and fantastically attractive returns on investment to attract and defraud investors. I originally thought he had missed his calling – he would have made an excellent AAU basketball coach, recruiting kids with promises of "going to the league." The complaint accused Stanford and three of his companies – Antiguan-based Stanford International Bank (SIB), Houston-based broker/dealer and investment advisor Stanford Group Company (SGC), and investment adviser Stanford Capital Management (SCM).

False Promises and Fabricated Marketing Material

SIB, acting through a network of SGC financial advisors, sold approximately $8 billion of self-styled CDs by promising high returns that exceeded those offered by traditional banks. However, Stanford was not a traditional bank and did not make loans. SIB invested customer funds in instruments ranging from fixed income to equity, highly liquid to illiquid. According to the SEC, as of November 28, 2008 SIB sold CDs representing historical investment returns ranging from 11.5% in 2005 to 16.5% in 1993. SIB purported that it had never failed to achieve returns in excess of 10% since 1994, and had lost only 1.3% in 2008 while the S&P 500 lost 39% during that time. SIB also offered significantly high CD rates as an enticement to customers. In November 2008 it offered rates of 5.375% on a three-year CD, a full 200 basis points higher than those offered by comparable U.S. banks (3.2%). As recently as February 2009 it offered rates greater than 10% on five-year CDs.

"Bank Crack"

SIB also paid higher commission rates to Financial Advisors. It sold CDs to investors in the U.S. through SGC, which received 3% of sales; Financial Advisors received 1% of sales and a 1% commission throughout the term of the CD. The generous commission schedule allowed SGC to recruit established advisors and provide an incentive to promote SIB CDs over those of competitors. Stanford employees referred to the compensation scheme as "bank crack" because it "seemed so addicting." SIB emphasized the liquidity of its investment portfolio as a protective factor for depositors and that the assets were invested in a well-diversified portfolio of highly marketable securities issued by stable governments and strong multinational companies. However, 90% of the investments was in illiquid assets such as real estate and private equity investments. SIB also painted a picture of having a rigorous investment process with a 20-member analyst team monitoring the portfolio. Yet, only Stanford and SFG Chief Financial Officer James Davis were aware of the majority of the firm's assets. Another successful money maker was a proprietary mutual fund wrap program – Stanford Allocation Strategy (SAS) – that SGC generated over $1 billion in sales of. SGC used false and misleading historical performance data to sway investors to buy this product as well. The false representations helped grow sales from $10 million in 2004 to over $1.2 billion, generating fees greater than $25 million. The fraudulent marketing and "bank crack" helped SGC recruit reputable advisors who were also financially motivated to reallocate assets to SIB's CD program. SGC showed pitch books to investment advisors and prospective clients that from 2000 to 2005, SAS outperformed the S&P 500 every year by an average of over 13%. Shortly after placing their clients into SAS, advisors questioned why its actual performance did not achieve the historical results represented in the pitch books. SGC/SCM hired an outside expert to review SAS historical performance. In late 2006 the expert informed SGC/SCM that SAS performance results for years ended September 30, 2006 and

September 30, 2005 were overstated by 3.4 percent and 3.25 percent, respectively. SAS did not ask the expert to audit performance results prior to 2005, yet kept marketing SAS with unverified fund performance data.

SIB was able to fraudulently market its CDs because it failed to register with the SEC. The SEC complaint represented that had SIB complied with the registration requirement, the SEC could have examined its marketing practices and underlying investment portfolio. After public disclosures surfaced that the SEC was investigating SIB, several customers tried to withdraw their assets, to which SIB refused. In one example, SIB tried to charge a "prepayment penalty" for early withdrawal, yet the prepayment penalty feature was contrary to representations made when the CDs were sold. In another, SIB made representations that there was a moratorium on withdrawals because the SEC had frozen customer accounts for two months. While SIB was stonewalling customers looking to redeem, it was liquidating its investment portfolio and attempting to wire hundreds of millions from customer accounts. The SEC subsequently sought a court order to freeze the accounts of SFG, its subsidiaries and senior officers in the midst of a massive fraud and misappropriation of investor funds.

Ponzi Scheme . . . But for Whose Benefit?

In June 2009 the SEC filed a subsequent complaint against Stanford, certain senior officers of SFG and Leroy King, the Administrator and CEO for Antigua's Financial Services Regulatory Commission (FSRC). The complaint described how SIB had internally segregated the assets backing its $8 billion in CDs into (i) cash and equivalents (Tier 1), (ii) investments with outside portfolio managers (Tier II), and (iii) other assets (Tier III). At June 30, 2008 SIB investments in Tier I, Tier II and Tier III represented 9%, 10% and 80%, respectively. These investment choices were starkly different from the highly liquid "securities issued by stable governments" and "strong multinational companies" SIB had represented during the sale of the CDs. Also undisclosed to investors was that of the $6.4 billion in Tier III assets, $3.2 billion represented overvalued real and personal property that SIB had acquired from Stanford-controlled entities, and $1.6 billion in notes on personal loans to Stanford. The "round-trip" real estate represented Island property that Stanford bought for about $65 million and sold back to SIB for $1.6 billion. In addition, Stanford and certain key executives of SFG were aided and abetted by Leroy King; King did not monitor the value of the underlying securities in SIB's investment portfolio and actually deterred a June 2005 SEC inquiry into a possible Ponzi scheme. In fact, King's official response to the inquiry was actually prepared by Stanford and others. The SEC reported that from February 2005 to December 2008 King deposited over $165,000 into U.S. bank accounts – implying "payments-in-kind" from Stanford entities for his complicity in the fraud.

"Man About Antigua"

By all accounts, Allen Stanford looked and acted "the part" of an international financier and cut a towering swath throughout Antigua. The company's offices were described as "posh" and adorned with green marble and mahogany. He hosted sporting events like the Stanford St. Jude Championship golf tournament in Memphis, Tennessee, signed high-priced athletes to endorse his products and hobnobbed with government officials. He was granted citizenship in 1999 and knighted in 2006. "He served as chairman of the government board that oversaw its offshore financial industry, was a major lender to the government, launched an airline and a construction firm, and purchased the island's biggest newspaper. He poured considerable sums into West Indian cricket, hosting a tournament last fall that awarded the winning team $20 million."[9] Stanford then proceeded to betray the trust of Antiguans who welcomed him into their country and communities, and pillaged their life savings for his personal gain. Yet, there were signs that something was amiss with the Stanford entities. The fact that he sold CDs and invested in the stock market was an oddity unto itself. Offering rates much higher than those offered by the competition ("mullet money") was another telltale sign that SIB was either in financial straits, or headed in that direction. Any reputable financial advisor should have recognized that, even if customers were totally unaware. But Stanford's bank crack was highly addictive – 100% pure, never been stepped on. According to Mark Tidwell, who worked as a financial advisor in SFG's Houston office from 2004 to 2007, advisors sometimes accompanied wealthy potential CD buyers on all-expense-paid, three-day trips to Antigua. "If the potential sales reached $5 million, they flew by private jet. When one of Mr. Tidwell's corporate clients asked what the bank invested in, Juan Rodriguez-Tolentino, the bank's president, replied, 'You don't ask what Bank of America is investing in.'"[10]

Shooting the Messenger?

According to a website devoted to aiding the Stanford victims in recovering lost monies, the Stanford Ponzi scheme was uncovered by a supervisor in the SEC's Fort Worth, Texas office, Julie Preuitt, in 1997. In an appearance before the Subcommittee on Oversight and Investigations, Committee on Financial Services, U.S. House of Representatives in May 2011, Ms. Preuitt testified that part of her responsibilities was to review annual filings of registered broker-dealers. The Stanford filings caught her attention because it was highly profitable after only two years of existence and the revenue it generated on its main product – CDs – was higher than normal. According to Ms. Preuitt, they discovered the following on Stanford after performing a more detailed review:

> In August 1997, I assigned an experienced and highly skilled examiner to Houston to analyze Stanford's revenue stream, its methods of product distribution, and its sales practices. In only a week the examiner was able to collect enough evidence to suggest that Stanford was engaged in a fraudulent scheme – most likely a Ponzi scheme. Our conclusion was based on a significant capital infusion of funds into the broker-dealer, the source of which appeared to be investor funds. We also noted apparent misrepresentations regarding the safety and security of the investments. It was highly unlikely that the high returns being paid to investors from the CDs along with the high recurring referral fees being paid by Stanford's broker-dealer could be generated without engaging in significant risk.[11]

From August 1997 to March 2005 SEC examiners made a total of four investigations into Stanford's business model. They concluded the business to be fraudulent, yet the agency decided not to pursue the investigations further. However, a follow-up SEC report found that conflicts of interest led to the botched investigations. "A report by the SEC's inspector general singled out the former head of the SEC's enforcement office in Fort Worth, Texas, accusing him of repeatedly quashing Stanford probes and then trying to represent Stanford as a lawyer in private practice. The former SEC official, Spencer Barasch, is now a partner at law firm Andrews Kurth LLP."[12] In January 2011 prosecutors were in the midst of finalizing a settlement with Mr. Barasch; he was expected to pay a $50,000 fine and receive a six-month ban on appearing before the SEC. When SEC officials asked Mr. Barasch why he was so adamant about representing Mr. Stanford, he replied: "'Every lawyer in Texas and beyond is going to get rich over this case. Okay? And I hated being on the sidelines.'"[13] It was only after the Bernie Madoff Ponzi scheme was discovered that the SEC decided to act on Stanford. And what was Ms. Preuitt's reward for discovering the Stanford fraud and doggedly trying to protect customers of the Stanford entities? In retaliation, her superiors reprimanded her and reassigned her to a new position to prompt her into leaving the SEC.

Madoff of Brooklyn

A New York City fund manager, operating out of a storefront office in the Bay Ridge section of Brooklyn, was accused of bilking investors out of $40 million via a Ponzi scheme. Phillip Barry, of the Leverage Group, promised investors returns of 12.55% - 21.00% from investments in stock options. Over time Barry strayed from his investment guidelines and invested customers' capital in everything from real estate to a mail-order pornography business. His real estate investments ranged from an office building in Brooklyn, to undeveloped tracts of land in upstate New York. Eventually he stopped investing at all and used new investors' cash to pay returns to prior investors. He is also purported to have used some of the funds to pay for personal expenses and fund a side business. Barry hid his Ponzi scheme from investors by sending them phony financial statements detailing hefty profits that did not exist. Barry ran the scam for over 30 years until the economic crisis caused him to go bankrupt. Investigators learned about the Ponzi scheme in August 2008 when Barry turned himself in to prosecutors. In all, over 800 clients were affected. Some earned profits on their investments while many others lost their life savings.

In June 2011, Barry was sentenced to 20 years in prison on one count of securities fraud and 33 counts of mail fraud. A few of his investors testified in court that Barry promised to invest their savings in safe investments. Instead, he became evasive, ducking their phone calls and promising them payments in the mail that never came. Barry's efforts earned him the nickname "Madoff of Brooklyn," yet unlike Madoff, Barry's clients were mostly working-class individuals less likely to recover from the loss of their savings.

THE INSIDER TRADERS

As an associate at GE Capital, I sometimes researched M&A deals just to see the volume of insider trading. It never failed that the trading volume in the stock of a target company, days before a takeover was announced, was three to fourfold of that on a normal trading day. The increased trading volume only meant one thing – somebody knew something. I would sit back and chuckle at how corrupt this country was. There was white-collar crime being committed on a daily basis and nobody cared. The powers that be were too busy policing black people. But whenever the economy turned down all of a sudden white-collar crime became a problem. Ken Lay and Jeffrey Skilling's true crime was not bilking Enron and defrauding investors – it was bilking Enron and defrauding investors after the economy was headed toward a recession, and the Internet bubble of the late 1990s had burst. That said, the following insider traders had the misfortune of committing crimes during the Great Recession when politicians needed a scapegoat for the public. After the economy regains traction – a decade from now – insider trading will return to normal.

Insider Information Not Confined to Public Deals?

If you heard Campanis tell it, the cheating was not relegated to public deals. One day Campanis insisted on joining me for lunch, which I thought was rather odd. After I found out he had been running around the office throwing shade, I let him know in a quiet, detached way that (i) he was only going to succeed by doing excellent work and not by bad-mouthing me, and (ii) if it wasn't work-related, we had nothing to talk about. The guy made some idle conversation and then brought up Project Edsel – a transaction we had completed almost 18 months earlier. He started talking about the intricacies of the transaction structure and the cast of characters from the target company. The entire time I was thinking to myself, "Is there a point to this? Why would this guy want to revisit something from over a year ago?" Then seemingly out of nowhere he blurted out "Leatherman II tweaked Johnson . . . He got Johnson alone in a room and . . . " I cut him off before he could finish and quickly switched topics. He thought it was going to be a "bonding moment," but my changing the subject signaled I wanted no parts of what he was selling. I sensed that Campanis' star was no longer rising within the group and that Leatherman II had turned his gaze on to Miscellaneous, the mentee. Thinking I was his major competition, Campanis had attempted to undermine me at every turn while trying to bond with Leatherman II and Miscellaneous. Now that Miscellaneous was the "chosen one" he was whining to me about Leatherman II. Why he thought I would be an ally was even more perplexing. I knew that he possessed neither the intelligence nor the work ethic to be successful. And to make matters worse, the guy spent his entire time gossiping, trying to fit in and taking credit for other people's work. Once the deals got more complicated, Campanis' lack of "horse power" had become clear even to Leatherman II. He had now given me an opening to engage in a bitchfest, but I didn't take the bait. I assumed it was a ruse of some kind . . . as soon as I had shown any level of disdain he would have run to Leatherman II with, "Guess what the black guy said." Soon after, he would be back in

Leatherman II's good graces. I found it rather comical, however, that the guy was "Jeffin'." Jeffin' is a term used amongst African Americans to describe blacks who co-sign for the boss to his face – "yessuh boss" – and criticize him as soon as he turns his back. It is a survival instinct. Now after all the years he had tried to poison Leatherman II against me . . . make him think I was disloyal and untrustworthy . . . it was Campanis who was the true turncoat. Yet, he knew better than to undermine Miscellaneous – that would have gotten him fired.

The conversation with Campanis prompted me to revisit the fact pattern on Edsel. The transaction was full of surprises; we bid $400 million for a company that, based on prior deals, was worth about $600 million. Our internal projections also supported the $600 million price tag. We had been searching for an acquisition in Edsel's niche market for years; and now that a company of its caliber was for sale, Leatherman II decided to put in a lowball bid that the seller would never accept. It was also symptomatic of our group. Historically we had always talked a good game, but when it came down to actually purchasing a company, senior management often got cold feet. The investment banking community always assumed we were on a fishing expedition – we would get the offering memorandum and gain market intelligence about our competitors, but were never serious bidders. And the Edsel deal team was "damned mad" too. All that hard work we put in was all for not. The investment bankers helping us with the transaction were also pissed. They received their fee only if the transaction closed. They privately wondered if they had backed the wrong horse.

After the second round of bids had been analyzed by Edsel's bankers, they called to tell us what I thought would be bad news; Edsel's advisor was the firm that Johnson worked for, though he was not staffed on this particular deal. The banker on the other end of the phone informed us that our $400 million offer was spot-on with the other highest bidder's. However, the seller favored our all-cash bid because the competitor's was subject to financing. We were ecstatic! I could not believe we won the company. My country behind would have offered $600 million – what I thought Edsel was actually worth. Because of Leatherman II's "market intelligence" and bid strategy, not only did we win the auction, but we saved our parent company $200 million! "That's why he's in charge of the group" I thought. I was extremely humble. No way would I have ever been smart enough to pull off such a coup. The managing director from the investment bank advising us appeared ambivalent though. He was happy he was going to receive a fee for the transaction, yet upset that his value added was nil. He made a quip to the effect that, "Maybe you all are closer to the seller's bankers than we thought." I surmised he was "hating" because Leatherman II was smarter than him.

After the conversation with Campanis, the quip from that managing director seemed less odd. Maybe he too knew that our offer, having matched that of the next highest bidder, was more than a mere coincidence. It also explained why Leatherman II never spent long hours in my office engaging in idle chitchat or gossip, like he had with the others. I had made it known to everyone, in no uncertain terms, that I was not going to be a party to anything untoward – I wasn't going to the pen for anybody. Still, I could not decipher what the word "tweaked" meant. Maybe it was slang for Caucasians. If it meant some type of subterfuge had occurred on Edsel then it made no sense to me. I found it hard to believe that even Leatherman II could be that petty and low-class. There was no way anyone could be so spineless and insecure that he could not acquire a company unless he knew what the other bids were. Secondly, it would be nonsensical for Johnson to risk his career over a $600 million deal. What did he have to gain anyway . . . additional deal mandates in the future? That was the only angle I could think of, but that was too small a reward for the risk implied. A year later, Leatherman II sent an email to the group announcing Johnson's promotion to managing director. Johnson did not work for our company so what was it to me? Leatherman II was acting as if he had a personal stake in the guy's success. My mind raced back to the conversation with Campanis and I thought, "No way!" I surmised what a big liar Campanis was and how he had made up that story to catch me in a trap. I had been too savvy to take the bait, however. From then on I decided to distance myself from him even further. Below are some of the "known" insider traders from the financial crisis:

Raj Rajaratnam

In what was described as one of the largest insider trading cases in decades, in October, 2009 Galleon Group's Raj Rajaratnam and six others were charged with brazen disregard for U.S. securities laws. And of course, the Shock Exchange posted the story, below:

> In what is being described as the largest insider-trading ring in a generation, six people were charged in October of trading inside information to profit on Google and other big-name stocks. At the center of the scandal is Raj Rajaratnam, founder of Galleon Group, a New York-based hedge fund that at the time managed $3.7 billion. A native of Sri Lanka, Raj spent years carving out a reputation as a meticulous investor in technology stocks. He also prided himself on the speed at which he could make decisions on complex issues and on his ability to gather information that competitors were not privy to . . . He was later charged with conspiracy to commit securities fraud, with bail set at $100 million, a fraction of his estimated $1.5 billion fortune. Relying on phone wiretaps, the criminal complaint described a period from 2006 to 2008 when Mr. Rajaratnam, working closely with Danielle Chiesi of New Castle Partners LLC, swapped potential stock-moving information in stocks like IBM and Akamai Technologies. Others charged in the case include: (i) Robert Moffat, 53, an executive at IBM, (ii) Rajiv Goel, 51, an executive in the treasury department at Intel, (iii) Anil Kumar, 51, a director at management consulting firm McKinsey & Co., (iv) Mark Kurland, 60, of New Castle Partners, LLC, and (v) Danielle Chiesi, 43, portfolio manager at New Castle.[1]

Roomy Khan "Sources of Information"

In the now-famous scene from HBO's *The Wire*, kingpin Marlo Stanfield and his cohorts are behind bars and begin to read the police report on how their operation was found out. The report's descriptions about their business dealings and

232

conversations were scarily accurate, and made several references to the "sources of information." It took them five minutes to decipher that "sources of information" meant there was a snitch among them, and about five seconds to decide who would take the fall. Raj Rajaratnam would build an entire career and massive fortune on such "sources of information." Rajaratnam began his career as a loan officer at Chase Manhattan Bank. He joined the investment bank, Needham & Co., in 1985 as a technology and healthcare analyst. He was promoted to oversee all of research and eventually became Needham's president and COO. Rajaratnam started the Galleon Group in 1997 based on his stock-picking prowess at Needham. Yet, there is evidence that even his career at Needham was built on lies, deception and access to nonpublic information. As an analyst, Rajaratnam had a penchant for accurately predicting revenue projections of some of the companies he covered. For instance, the revenue predictions in his research reports on Intel were so prescient that investors complained to Intel that its confidential information was somehow being leaked. Intel began investigating whether anyone was dialing Rajaratnam's number. They learned that Khan dialed it several times and sent faxes to Galleon as well. Afterward, Intel set up a hidden video camera that on March 6, 1998, recorded Ms. Khan faxing confidential financial documents to Mr. Rajaratnam. The documents contained pricing information for key Intel chips as well as the number of units sold in the first quarter of 1998.[2]

Intel fired Ms. Khan and she later worked directly for Galleon. She subsequently entered a plea agreement with the FBI, describing an insider-trading ring that included her, Rajaratnam and others. The FBI and SEC dropped the investigation because they could not demonstrate that Rajaratnam acted on the confidential Intel information from Ms. Khan. As Rajaratnam and Roomy Khan came to the U.S. and brazenly broke every securities law known to man, one out of every three black men was being profiled and arrested for decades. The FBI would lead one to believe that it could arrest D.C. Mayor Marion Barry, the most powerful African American in the country, on trumped-up drug charges but could not bring Rajaratnam to justice. Rajaratnam and Roomy Khan were not the priority. Black men were.

Roomy Khan – "Sources of Information Again"

The SEC caught its big break in early 2007. Rajaratnam turned over documents to the SEC pursuant to a probe of his brother. Within the documents the SEC found a text message to Rajaratnam that "urged him not to buy video-conferencing firm Polycom Inc.'s stock 'till I get guidance; want to make sure guidance is OK.'"[3] The writer was Roomy Khan, who was working as a hedge fund consultant. Regulators confronted Khan with the text message and she again agreed to cooperate by recording phone conversations via a wiretap. Ms. Khan had developed a personal network of young professionals of Indian descent that provided her with nonpublic information on technology companies, hedge funds and private equity funds. She became privy to pre-deal information on the Blackstone Group's pending acquisition of Hilton Hotels in July 2007 and the fact that Google was going to fall short of its second quarter 2007 earnings expectations. Khan passed this information along to Rajaratnam, who prosecutors say made approximately $13 million on suspicious trading in the shares of Google and Hilton. Taped phone conversations of Rajaratnam passing along inside information to Khan in early 2008 were enough evidence for a Manhattan judge to allow prosecutors to tap Rajaratnam's phone. Those wiretaps eventually led to his prosecution, two decades in the making.

Wiretaps Do in Rajaratnam

After Rajaratnam's arrest in October 2009, his lawyer tried to strike at the heart of the prosecution's defense by making the wiretaps inadmissible in court. He argued that the government violated Rajaratnam's constitutional rights by recording the conversations. His defense suffered a devastating blow when Judge Richard Holwell ruled that the prosecution could use the wiretaps (almost 2,500 recorded conversations) in court. In May 2011 Rajaratnam was found guilty on all 14 counts of securities fraud.

> Raj Rajaratnam, the billionaire hedge fund titan who built his fortune on a byzantine level of corporate contacts cultivated over decades, was convicted on all 14 counts of securities fraud and conspiracy in the biggest insider trading case in history. On Wall Street, Rajaratnam is known as the "Tiger Woods" of insider trading. The case involved over 40 wiretaps with conversations between the founder of the Galleon Group and his corporate contacts discussing nonpublic information that Rajaratnam eventually traded on and made millions of dollars off of. The 12-member jury deliberated for nearly two weeks on a case that began in March 2010. This was the first insider trading case that employed the use of wiretaps previously reserved for organized crime and drug cases . . . *The Wall Street Journal* quoted juror Carmen Gomez as saying the wiretaps were the deciding factor in the case: 'It was a very difficult decision, but the recordings showed Mr. Rajaratnam used confidential information and bought stocks based on that.'[4]

The original six conspirators arrested in the Galleon investigation are below:

Name	Age	Description	Sentence (Months)
		Original Six Conspirators in Galleon Insider Trading Case	
Raj Rajaratnam	54	Native of Sri Lanka, co-founded Galleon Group hedge fund in 1997. Fund once had $7 billion in AUM. Known in industry circles as "Tiger Woods of Insider Trading."	132
Robert Moffatt	53	IBM executive in charge of its supply chain, responsible for its hardware, its server, and its semiconductor business. Considered a potential candidate for CEO. Government argued that Moffatt profited not financially, but from the "favors" of Danielle Chiesi.	6
Rajiv Goel	51	Executive in Intel's treasury department. Provided nonpublic information to Rajaratnam concerning Intel's financial results. Was a classmate of Rajaratnam at the Wharton School of Business in early '80s.	Pending
Anil Kumar	51	Director of management-consulting firm, McKinsey & Company, Wharton Business School classmate of Rajaratnam and Goel. Entered into compensation scheme whereby he received share of profits generated from inside information provided to Rajaratnam.	Pending
Mark Kurland	60	Former partner at New Castle Partners, a stock-trading hedge fund started in 1995 at Bear Stearns Asset Management.	27
Danielle Chiesi	43	Portfolio manager at New Castle. Romantically involved with Moffatt and Kurland. Said, "Trading inside information equivalent to having an orgasm."	30

Rajat Gupta

In April 2010 Wall Street's most powerful firm, Goldman Sachs, was drawn into the fray when prosecutors disclosed they were investigating whether one of its board members gave inside information to Galleon. Government prosecutors issued a March 2010 letter stating suspicious trading by Rajaratnam, amongst others, in the shares of Goldman Sachs from the time Bear, Stearns failed and right after Lehman filed for bankruptcy. Those months were perilous, volatile times for investment banking stocks and the volatility created opportunities for huge trading gains. The government disclosed it was investigating whether Rajat Gupta, Goldman board member and former partner at McKinsey & Co., was the source of nonpublic information to Rajaratnam. In October 2011, exactly two years after the U.S. charged the "Galleon Six," federal prosecutors indicted Gupta on six criminal counts of insider trading. According to an SEC complaint, Gupta aided Galleon in the following ways:

Trading in Advance of Berkshire's $5 Billion Investment in Goldman

After the Lehman bankruptcy filing on September 15, 2008, Goldman senior management considered various alternatives to help it avoid Lehman's fate. One alternative was a potential investment from Warren Buffett's Berkshire Hathaway, which Goldman CEO Lloyd Blankfein discussed with the board on September 21. On September 22, Rajaratnam acquired 100,000 shares of Goldman shortly after a four-minute phone call with Gupta. On September 23, Rajaratnam and Gupta spoke by phone again and shortly afterward, Rajaratnam purchased an addition 50,000 Goldman shares on behalf of Galleon. A special telephonic meeting of the Goldman board convened at 3:15 p.m. on September 23 during which the board approved Berkshire's $5 billion investment. The meeting ended at approximately 3:53 p.m. and Gupta called Rajaratnam from the same phone immediately afterward. At 3:56 p.m. Rajaratnam acquired 217,200 shares of Goldman just before the market closed. On September 24 the market reacted favorably to the news of Berkshire's investment, driving Goldman's shares up approximately $8/share (6.4%). Rajaratnam liquidated Galleon's Goldman shares for a profit of over $800,000.

Trading in Advance of Goldman's Fourth Quarter 2008 Financial Results

On October 23, 2008 Gupta called Rajaratnam just seconds after ending a call with the Goldman board to alert him that Goldman's financial results would come in below expectations. The following morning, Rajaratnam sold 150,000 shares of Goldman stock and avoided $3.6 million in losses. In discussing market information with another Galleon co-conspirator, Rajaratnam explained that the Street expected Goldman to earn $2.50 per share but he had heard the prior day from a member of the Goldman Sachs Board that the company was actually going to report a loss.

Trading in Advance of Goldman's Second's Quarter 2008 Financial Results

Goldman CEO Lloyd Blankfein discussed Goldman's positive earnings results with Gupta during a June 10, 2008 phone conversation. At 9:24 p.m. that night, Gupta placed a call to Rajaratnam. The first of a flurry of calls between the two ended with Rajaratnam reaching out to Gupta the following morning. After the market opened Rajaratnam purchased (i) 7,350 Goldman June $170 call option contracts – the right to buy 735,000 shares at $170 per share (Goldman's share price had opened at $167 per share that morning) and (ii) 350,000 additional Goldman shares on June 11 and 12. After a run up in Goldman's stock price, Rajaratnam sold the call options for a $9 million profit on June 16. He sold the shares on June 17 after the positive earnings announcement, netting an additional $9 million in profits. The SEC complaint states that Galleon earned $18.5 million in illicit profits on Goldman shares.

Trading in Advance of Proctor & Gamble's Second Quarter 2008 Financial Results

On June 29, 2009, the day before Proctor & Gamble's second quarter earnings release, Gupta met telephonically to discuss the release with the Proctor & Gamble (P&G) Audit Committee. A draft of the release stated that sales from pre-existing business segments were less than what the company had previously projected. Gupta called Rajaratnam that afternoon and Galleon sold short (made bets that the shares would decline) about 180,000 shares of P&G. After P&G announced earnings the next day, the stock price declined from $58.22 per share to $54.50 per share, generating $570,000 in illicit profits for Galleon.

Double Life for Gupta?

Gupta was born in India shortly after it won its independence from the British. In 1966 he ranked among the top 20 applicants from hundreds of thousands who apply annually to the prestigious Indian Institute of Technology (IIT). After IIT,

Gupta attended Harvard Business School where he was named a Baker Scholar, given to the top five percent of each graduating class. He later joined the New York Office of McKinsey & Co. where he quickly separated himself from his peers. In 1994 he became worldwide Managing Director – the top spot. At age 45 Gupta was the youngest ever to hold that position. He departed McKinsey in 2003 but years prior, Gupta had sown the seeds for his next venture(s). In 2001 he and McKinsey Consultant Anil Kumar set up their own consulting business on the side, Mindspirit LLC, against firm policy. Mindspirit had a penchant for taking stock options in clients in lieu of consulting fees. By some accounts, Gupta envied Wall Street titans who made multiples of his McKinsey salary; Gupta wanted in, leading him into Rajaratnam's orbit.

> In 2006 he co-founded New Silk Route Partners, which eventually raised $1.3 billion to invest in India and other emerging economies . . . Rajaratnam invested $50 million in the firm and withdrew his stake last year . . . After retiring from McKinsey in 2007, Gupta globe-trotted constantly. He traveled to India to look for investments for New Silk Route and to cities throughout the U.S. and overseas for meetings at the five public companies and many non-profit boards on which he was a director. When Gupta was in New York, he spent time with Rajaratnam. According to testimony at Rajaratnam's trial, Gupta and his New Silk Route co-founders initially worked in cubicles at Galleon's headquarters. New Silk Route later leased an office on Madison Avenue that was less than a half block from Galleon's. Gupta, in 2007, joined Rajaratnam and a third partner to form GB Voyager Multi-Strategy Fund, an investment fund, contributing $10 million of his own money. The $50 million fund invested in Galleon hedge funds, including those that traded on Gupta's allegedly illegal tips, the SEC says.[5]

The insider information to Rajaratnam began in 2008; the surprising part is how brazen Gupta and Rajaratnam were about rapidly trading in and out of positions based on that information. Rajaratnam's "prescience" in deciding when to trade Goldman shares or short P&G was similar to his uncanny ability to predict Intel's future revenue. The theory that Gupta did not personally profit from his tips is also a misnomer. His Voyager Multi-Strategy Fund had investments in Galleon hedge funds; if Galleon profited, then so did Voyager, and ultimately Gupta. The media's "surprise" by the so-called culture on Wall Street of casually trading information amongst friends is also misplaced. Information has always been used as a "currency" on the Street, even during the heyday of the insider trading ring involving Siegel, Milken, Dennis Levine (Lehman) and Ivan Boesky (arbitrager). On the witness stand, Levine, Boesky and Milken disclosed how Wall Street worked according to a system of "favors." Levine marveled at how the beauty of "the game" could be played two ways – he could both trade on the insider information, and use it to land clients for Lehman.[6]

Indian Community on Trial?

After first reading of the Galleon co-conspirators it does not take long to realize that most of them are of South Asian descent. The media never mentions it directly, but the nationalities of the perpetrators linger, like the pink elephant in the room. The case drawing the most visceral reaction is that of Gupta, for years one of the most prominent Indians in corporate America. A popular view in India is that Gupta was ensnared in an anti-Indian backlash in the U.S. According to Dilip Cherian, founder of a Delhi-based communications company, Gupta's prosecution is partly a reaction to the dominance of Indian CEOs in America's boardrooms.[7] However, questions remain, "Was there ever any objective measurement of the effectiveness of his consulting advice? Gupta rose through the ranks at McKinsey, but how did clients fare after implementing his advice?" According to *Bloomberg Markets*, "Gupta pushed McKinsey to take on Internet startups as clients, even when they could only pay in stock . . . Client demand for McKinsey services declined following the bursting of the Internet bubble in 2000. Global Crossing Ltd., Kmart Corp., Swiss International Air Lines AG and other companies McKinsey had advised filed for bankruptcy. The biggest embarrassment was Enron Corp.'s collapse . . . The Houston-based energy trader, which had been the seventh largest company by assets in the Standard & Poor's 500 Index, lost almost all of its value when regulators found the company had used accounting gimmicks to create a massive fraud. Enron had McKinsey in its bloodlines. Jeffrey Skilling, the firm's CEO, had once been a McKinsey partner, and the consulting firm had advised the company for 18 years as it transformed itself from an oil pipeline operator to a derivatives trader."[8]

Overheard speaking to Anil Kumar on an August 15, 2008 wiretap, even Rajaratnam painted a view of Gupta counter to what his resume might lead one to believe: "Plus there's the fact that he's really lazy. It's not like he knows what it's like to do an honest day of hard work. You think Rajat has any idea how exhausting it is gathering inside information to trade on? He doesn't know jack."[9] There is also another rationale behind his insider trading – Gupta was incompetent. The only way he could have made money in private or public equities was by cheating. The $10 million he invested in the Voyager fund with Rajaratnam was wiped out in the 2008 financial meltdown. And his New Silk Route private-equity fund has never turned a profit on any of its investments.

Joseph F. "Chip" Skowron III

In April 2011 the SEC filed formal charges against Joseph "Chip" Skowron III, a former hedge fund manager with Frontpoint Partners, with insider trading in a bio-pharmaceutical company. The confidential information centered on the negative outlook for the commercial appeal of one of the biopharmaceutical company's key drugs. A graduate of Yale School of Medicine, Skowron left a burgeoning career as an orthopedic surgeon to pick biotechnology stocks for Frontpoint. The SEC alleged that Skowron sold holdings of Human Genome Sciences Inc. (HGSI) based on inside information he received from a medical researcher, Dr. Yves M. Benhamou, overseeing one of HGSI's drug trials. HGSI's stock plummeted after a press release on the drug trial and Frontpoint was able to avoid $30 million in losses. According to the SEC, Skowron offered Benhamou cash and free hotel stays, and tried to convince him to cover up their dealings. The SEC also attempted to quell the use of "expert networks" as the sources of information for hedge funds and portfolio managers.

The SEC complaint asserts that Benhamou worked for an expert networking firm that consulted with Frontpoint and other hedge funds on healthcare stocks. Benhamou was part of a five-member Steering Committee overseeing a clinical drug trial (Achieve Trial) for Albuferon, used to treat Hepatitis C (liver disease). The Achieve Trial was administered to over 2,000 patients at different doses and compared to Pegasys, the leading hepatitis C drug on the market. The Achieve Trial was expected to confirm that (i) a 900-microgram dose of Albuferon was as effective as a 1,200-microgram dose of Pegasys and (ii) a 1,200-microgram dose of Albuferon was more effective than a 1,200-microgram dose of Pegasys and improved the quality of the patient's life. HGSI was hoping that Albuferon would replace Pegasys in the marketplace as the drug of choice for Hepatitis C. In 2007 Frontpoint purchased 6.2 million shares of HGSI at an average price of $10.32 per share and expected the stock to increase based upon Albuferon's growth potential. The Achieve Trial was scheduled for November 2007; around April 2007, Skowron met separately with Benhamou in Barcelona, Spain and voiced his happiness with Benahou's services and gave him about $6,700 in cash. Skowron also paid for at least one of Benhamou's hotel stays in New York ($5,152).

There was one slight problem, however. Albuferon didn't perform as expected. Two of the patients who received the 1,200 microgram dose developed interstitial lung disease and one died on December 1, 2007. On December 7, 2007 Benhamou tipped Skowron to the trial results and Skowron began liquidating HGSI shares. By mid-December, Frontpoint had sold over 2.8 million shares at an average price of $10.65 per share; about 3.2 million shares remained. On January 18, 2008, the trial's independent data monitoring committee recommended that all patients on the 1,200-microgram dose be reduced to the 900 microgram dose due to safety reasons. Benhamou immediately contacted Skowron and tipped him to the negative nonpublic information, and Skowron sold 700,000 shares on the open market at $10.72 per share. On the morning of January 22, 2008 Benhamou tipped Skowron again that HGSI planned to issue a press release about the negative results of the trial; Frontpoint sold its holdings at the average market price of $10.37 per share. Near the end of the trading day it entered into a block trade with another investment bank at $9.63 per share. According to the complaint, Frontpoint's sale of HGSI shares represented 47% of that day's total trading volume for HGSI. The next day HGSI issued a press release stating its intention to stop the 1,200 microgram dose of Albuferon as part of the Achieve Trial. The stock dropped 44% from $10.02 per share to $5.62 per share, allowing Frontpoint to avoid over $30 million in losses. The investment bank that was counterparty to the previous day's trade requested to break the January 22 trade, but Skowron refused. During the last week of February, the SEC was scheduled to meet with Skowron surrounding the suspicious January 22, 2008 block trade. Skowron called Benhamou to ask him to lie about the inside information he provided Skowron, paid him $10,000 and agreed to pay Benhamou's legal fees for the SEC investigation.

Skowron was eventually sentenced to five years in prison and Frontpoint agreed to repay over $30 million in ill-gotten gains. Frontpoint was subsequently decimated by client redemptions in the wake of the Skowron insider trading investigation. It had about $7.5 billion in assets when the SEC charges were disclosed in November 2010 and was down to $1.5 billion by July 2011. Many of Frontpoint's pension fund investors (Michigan state pension fund, South Carolina pension system, etc.) exited before Frontpoint could halt redemptions in the wake of the charges. Morgan Stanley, which had previously acquired the fund in 2008, spun it off in 2011.

Wharton Classmates Charged With Insider Trading

Not to be outdone by fellow Wharton alumni Raj Rajaratnam, Anil Kumar and Rajiv Goel, Stephen Goldfield and James Self made approximately $14 million from trading on inside information on the acquisition of MedImmune, Inc. Thinking their insider trading success gave them stock-picking superpowers, they later lost it all by trying to pick stocks based on their business acumen alone. Below is a description of their scheme from the Shock Exchange:

> According to a complaint by the SEC, two former Wharton Business School classmates, Stephen R. Goldfield and James W. Self, Jr., engaged in unlawful insider trading in the shares of MedImmune, Inc. (MEDI). MEDI is a pharmaceutical company headquartered in Gaithersburg, Maryland, which was acquired by AstraZeneca on April 23, 2007. In advance of the announcement, Goldfield received material nonpublic information regarding the MEDI sale process from Self, who was at the time, Executive Director of Business Development at a pharmaceutical company located in New Jersey. Self was assigned to the deal team evaluating an acquisition of MEDI and therefore, was privy to nonpublic information. Goldfield at the time was a retired hedge fund manager trading securities on his own behalf.

> Self and Goldfield originally met while attending the Executive MBA Program at the Wharton School from 1994 - 1996. Self tipped off Goldfield about the pending transaction . . . In mid-March 2007, Goldfield began purchasing large volumes of call options on MEDI stock at strike prices ranging from $37.50 - $47.50/share. According to the SEC:

> *As a matter of routine, Self called Goldfield from his cellular telephone on his way to or from work each day, during which he told Goldfield generally the status of the project, including divulging nonpublic information about the progress and the status of the Company's bid to acquire MEDI . . . During one such conversation regarding the MEDI project, in or around early April 2007, Self told Goldfield that the "weather was in the 50s" or words to that effect, conveying to Goldfield that the Company's bid for MEDI was going to be in the 50s. At that time, MEDI stock was trading at approximately $35-$36 per share.*

> On April 23, 2007 Astraneca announced its $58/share acquisition of MEDI. Four days later Goldfield closed out his MEDI position with realized gains of approximately $14 million. By June of that same year, Goldfield lost all of the MEDI profits from losses sustained from more risky options investing. Goldfied originally settled with the SEC to pay a fine of $16.7 million, representing the $14

million gains plus interest. He will actually pay $600,000 because he lost all of the profits. Self paid a $50,000 civil fine. Neither admitted to any wrongdoing.[10]

Danielle Chiesi

After graduating from the University of Colorado in 1988, Danielle Chiesi began her career as an analyst at Mabon Nugent & Co. There she met Mark Kurland, who served as her mentor. They became romantically involved and worked closely together for over 20 years. In 1997 she joined the asset management group of Bear Stearns, where Kurland was the CEO. Kurland later formed a hedge fund within.Bear called New Castle. Chiesi covered technology stocks at New Castle, where she built an enviable network of CEOs, hedge fund managers, and Wall Street analysts within the technology space. Her skill was gaining access to information that others could not and connecting one member of her network with another – a high-powered matchmaker for those seeking capital and those looking to employ it. In August 2007, during a phone conversation with Steven Fortuna, managing director at hedge fund S2 Capital, Chiesi shared the following on IBM: She "told him she had gotten important information from an IBM manager about its upcoming quarter, prosecutors say. Mr. Fortuna posed a pointed question: 'You flat-out asked him?' 'Yeah,' answered Ms. Chiesi."[11] There was one small problem, or big one, depending on your perspective – the Feds were listening. "It was a response the FBI had hoped for, bolstering their belief that Ms. Chiesi had gotten nonpublic information directly from the IBM insider. Prosecutors say New Castle, Chiesi's employer, made $500,000 trading on the information."[12]

Blonde-haired, blue-eyed and petite, the former teenage beauty queen hailed from Binghamton, New York. She dressed seductively – low-cut tops, short skirts, and close-fitting business suits – and used her sex appeal to gain access to information and build relationships with men in the industry. She built a relationship with IBM CFO, John Joyce, who introduced her to Robert Moffat, another IBM executive, in 2002. Moffat was head of IBM's global supply chain and had a close personal relationship with IBM CEO, Sam Palmisano. Due to his stellar performance, Moffat was viewed as a potential future CEO of IBM. Chiesi's persistence, industry knowledge and extensive network of industry contacts got her foot into the door with Moffat; her sex appeal kept her there. Moffat was smitten by having an attractive, aggressive, much younger woman breathing in his face. The words she uttered may have been "joint venture," "product pipeline," or "network solutions," but her body language and the intonation in her voice screamed "sex!" By her own admission she was attracted to the "three S's – stocks, sex and sports."[13] Moffat was a former All-American track star at Union College in upstate New York and the future CEO of IBM. The romantic relationship they entered into the following year was practically inevitable.

Chiesi's Manhattan apartment was the chill spot for technology industry executives and analysts, partly to network, partly to watch Chiesi sashay around.

There she met Hector Ruiz, CEO of Advanced Micro Devices (AMD). In the summer of 2008, AMD was in talks to form a joint venture (JV) with its manufacturing business, Fabco, and a Middle Eastern investment fund. IBM was asked to provide a license for the use of its technology as part of the reorganization. Moffat acted as the IBM liaison during the discussions. Soon Chiesi was being briefed by both Moffat and Ruiz on how the JV would impact AMD's earnings. Kurland directed Chiesi to buy a few hundred shares of AMD stock, and to cover her tracks. In late August 2008, Moffat told Chiesi, "'The Arabs are gonna pay $2.1 billion . . . for a 50% stake in Fabco.' As Moffat talked, Chiesi allowed Kurland to eavesdrop on the conversation . . . She was also feeding the information she gleaned from Moffat and Ruiz to her friend Raj Rajaratnam" and the FBI was listening the entire time.[14] In October 2009, Moffat was the first of the "Galleon Six" to be arrested for insider trading; he was sentenced to six months in prison. Chiesi and Kurland would later be sentenced to 30 months and 27 months, respectively. The irony was that the market reacted negatively to the AMD JV, and New Castle and Galleon lost money on their AMD trades. Secondly, key to an insider trading case is to prove that one sought to profit from the information. The FBI never accused Moffat of profiting financially; instead, it accused him of using nonpublic information on IBM as a currency to obtain the affections of Chiesi.

The "Rasheeda Moore" of Wall Street

I pictured in my mind Chiesi gaining confidential information over pillow talk with technology industry executives – sort of a "quid pro quo." Yet Chiesi was not the first woman to play "this for that" with powerful men. The first name that popped into my head was "Rasheeda Moore" – the woman who set up D.C. mayor, Marion Barry, in an FBI sting in 1990. I came home early one night after work and waited anxiously for the six o'clock news. I heard Barry had been arrested by the FBI for smoking crack cocaine. All of D.C. was tuned in. The news showed a dark, grainy tape of a woman in a hotel room. Barry walked in shortly afterward and there was this awkward silence between them. Barry waited for a few moments and then approached her and tried to "push up." It was barely audible but it sounded like the woman asked Barry to smoke some cocaine, to which Barry showed no interest. The woman asked again and Barry, annoyed this time, said he didn't want any. The third time, Barry reached for the crack pipe and white men in suits bum-rushed the hotel room from seemingly out of nowhere. Barry then uttered those famous words, "The bitch set me up!" I concluded that the tape was much ado about nothing and all I could think was, "That's the smoking gun the FBI was talking about? Barry will beat the rap on this easily. The man said three times 'I don't want that.' That's entrapment!" However, to hear Barry yell, "The bitch set me up!" had me doubled over from laughing so hard. Details surfaced that Moore was a former girlfriend of Barry's. I did not know Barry or have an opinion of him. My mind again raced back to Ralph Ellison. If the powers that be promoted the worst in African Americans, then wouldn't the opposite also be true – they would undermine the best of us?

Shortly after Barry's arrest, an FBI agent held a press conference explaining how they had been telling people for years that Barry had used cocaine, and how they had finally gotten him. I was appalled – here we were in the middle of a recession and the FBI was spending taxpayer dollars trying to set up Marion Barry. "What other politicians is the FBI tracking and why is Barry being singled out?" I thought. Meanwhile, President George H. W. Bush had been gallivanting around the globe chastising China and others about human rights violations and converting to a more open, Democratic society. I envisioned the look on the Americans' faces if during one of those meetings on human rights, the Chinese had played the tape of the FBI entrapping the most powerful black man in America. Still, I performed my own independent research out in the streets. Several teenagers in the city made T-shirts with the slogan "The Bitch Set Me Up." The kids were jovial about it, thinking it was all a big joke. When I queried people around my age, almost to a man they said, "Marion Barry gave me my first job as a teenager. Because of Barry I had money in my pockets growing up." They adored Barry and never forgot the gesture. They felt that Barry could not be controlled so Congress wanted him out. Others felt the arrest was partly his fault, however. Barry knew "The Man" was after him and he never should have given him an opening. There were Barry's political enemies who cited how he was an embarrassment to the city and how he handed lucrative government contracts to unqualified cronies. With Barry gone, they could hand out lucrative government contracts to their cronies, at least they thought. The real estate developers lamented how Barry wouldn't allow them to build apartment buildings, hire their own workers at the expense of D.C. residents, and raise rents high enough to gentrify the place. Then there was the beltway contingency that worked in the District, but lived elsewhere. They had access to city services like the fire department, police department and hospitals, and taxed its roads as they drove to and fro each day – yet they did not pay taxes in D.C. Barry sought to change that. He wanted those who worked for city agencies to live in D.C. He also wanted those Maryland and Virginia residents who worked in the District to pay city taxes for their use of city services – something places like New York or Philadelphia demanded. Maryland and Virginia residents considered Barry "nervy" and "arrogant" and therefore, had to be removed.

Second Act

Barry's trial lasted over two months, preventing him from seeking a fourth consecutive term as mayor. The FBI presented evidence that he had been a heavy drug user for over a decade. The jury convicted Barry on one count of drug possession in an incident separate from the Rasheeda Moore videotape. I was in a state of disbelief, as a lot of D.C. residents were. "Could this be America? The FBI obviously has too much time on its hands," I surmised. Barry's friends implored him to leave the spotlight, get drug counseling and heal his marriage. He was eventually sentenced to six months at a minimum-security prison in Petersburg, Virginia. In his absence a relatively unknown lawyer, Sharon Pratt Dixon, was elected mayor. The mayoral frontrunners beat each other up with character assassinations, all but ignoring Pratt Dixon. She portrayed herself as a political outsider and showed up at rallies with a shovel, promising to clean up D.C. corruption and slash the city's bloated budget. Yet Barry's shadow still loomed large.

After release from jail in 1992, Barry won a City Council seat in the 8th Ward, known for its poverty and allegiance to him. In 1994 Barry vowed to reclaim what was stolen from him – a fourth term as mayor. He defeated Councilmember John Ray and Mayor Sharon Pratt Dixon, just as he had promised. Washingtonians rejoiced. Barry's victory represented "payback" for the unfair treatment by the FBI. It also symbolized that D.C. was not going to let Congress, the FBI, the White House, or the national media dictate whom they should vote for. Nationally there was outrage; the media had a field day, calling the reelection a "travesty," running non-stop articles about Barry's so-called crack addiction, and questioning the intellect of Washingtonians. It also didn't help that Pratt Dixon left Barry a deficit in the hundreds of millions of dollars. The only place Barry could turn to for help was Congress, which positioned the deficit as a symbol of Barry's ineffectiveness. Congress treated D.C. like a foreign government – squeeze the people long enough via trade sanctions and refusal of aid, and they will overthrow the leader for you. The Republican Congress set up a financial control board that gave it final say over the District's purse strings. Economically at least, D.C. home rule was a misnomer and Barry a mere figurehead. It was a bitter comeuppance for a defiant mayor, and an embarrassment to Washingtonians everywhere.

> By early summer 1997, President Clinton's staff had produced a far-reaching reform package for the city. But as the package moved through Congress, Sen. Lauch Faircloth (R-N.C.), chairman of the Senate Appropriations subcommittee on the District and no fan of home rule, seized the moment. Late one night in July, he inserted language into the legislation that stripped nearly all of Barry's remaining power, transferring day-to-day control over nine major operating departments to the control board. Barry angrily denounced Faircloth's 'rape of democracy,' saying it wasn't just about Marion Barry. But for Faircloth – and many other politicians, pundits and residents of the city – it was about Barry and no one else. And there was consensus among them that as long as the Republicans controlled Congress, Marion Barry would never get his power back.[15]

After Barry was rendered powerless, even his most ardent supporters abandoned him. "Barry's an embarrassment to the city" they said. "It's time we elect someone who can work with Congress. All people talk about is how our mayor's a 'crackhead.' It's time for Barry to go." The low point for me came during Chris Rock's *Bring the Pain*, his stand-up routine held at D.C.'s Tacoma Theatre. During one segment, the comedian went in on Barry:

> Marion Barry . . . at the Million Man March . . . how'd he get a ticket? You know what that means? Even in our finest hour, we had a crackhead on stage. How the hell Marion Barry get his job back. Smoke crack got his job back. How the hell did that happen? If you get caught smoking crack at McDonald's you can't get ya job back. They aren't going to trust you around the happy meals. All I wanna know is who was so bad they lost to a crackhead? What was their

campaign like? What was they on . . . heroin? How you 'gon tell little kids don't get high when the mayor's on crack? [Chris Rock voice] 'Don't get high. Don't get high. You won't be nuthin'.' [Little Kid Voice] 'I can be the mayor.'

Rock's routine was met with raucous laughter from the crowd . . . in Washington, D.C. no less. I was livid at the crowd enjoying the FBI's handiwork. "If any of those black faces ever strived to advance beyond their predetermined stations or refused to be co-opted by the establishment, they too would be called a 'witch,' just like Barry," I thought. While African Americans constantly cried for "change," they laughed while the FBI demonized Barry who it considered an "agent of change." I envisioned that somewhere the Republican Congress was doing a rain dance to ensure Chris Rock's crops reached their full potential.

15 Years After Barry . . . Is D.C. Better Off?

I later discovered that before Barry ever ran for mayor, he was a renowned civil rights activist with the Student Nonviolent Coordinating Committee (SNCC). In the mid-60s Barry was a community organizer in D.C. and recognized for helping black men find jobs through his Pride, Inc. organization. Rioting after the Martin Luther King, Jr. assassination demolished sections of the city. Barry helped black business owners recover, and black families find housing in the aftermath. He was elected to the D.C. city council in 1974 and used it as a launching pad for mayoral office in 1978. By the time I arrived in D.C. Barry had been hounded by federal agencies for over a decade. Every alleged incident, whether it involved a city contract, a woman or drugs, rose to the level of national security. As for Rasheeda Moore, in her youth she embarked on a modeling career, having been signed by Wilhelmina Modeling Agency and appeared on the cover of *Essence Magazine*. She walked the catwalk in New York, where she made from $1,000 to $1,500 a day. According to Frances Rothchild, Executive Vice President of Wilhelmina, Moore was one of the top black models in the industry in her day.[16] Prior to Wilhelmina, Moore trained at the Cappa Chell Finishing School and Modeling Agency in Northern Virginia, where they taught social graces, and how to "turn heads." By all accounts, Moore was one of the school's top students – a looker with social graces. By the late '80s Moore had fallen on hard times and was having trouble caring for her three kids. She became a "person of interest" after an FBI informant told the Feds she and Barry were romantically involved. The FBI tracked Moore down and to secure her cooperation, threatened to charge her with lying to a grand jury over Barry's drug use. And this is where the details get murky. The popular belief is that Moore cooperated to avoid perjury charges. But according to urban legend, the Feds had her cousin on a charge and threatened to put him away for a long time unless she cooperated.

Teacher Can't Teach

I have looked askance on mayors who have followed Barry. My impression is that many have measured success based on positive press from the mainstream media or a collegial relationship with Congress. However, are Washingtonians better off today than they were 15 years ago? Developers have built condominiums with sky-high rents, causing a black flight to the suburbs. Once dubbed "Chocolate City," the District is now predominantly white. In November 2006 Adrian Fenty became the youngest mayor in D.C. history at age 35. He staked his career on fixing D.C.'s broken public school system. By "fixing," he meant repairing run-down buildings and providing new supplies. He embarked on a media blitz to show the millions of dollars invested in D.C. schools' property, plant and equipment. What raised my antennae was an article on Michelle Rhee, Fenty's new schools chief. Rhee was an Asian woman from New York who vowed to fix D.C. schools by "removing the school system's underperforming teachers." "The teacher can't teach," was Rhee's veiled message. By cutting the wheat from the chafe and instituting pay for performance, school test results would miraculously rise. "'Fixing the facilities, getting the books, raising salaries, are the right things to do,' said Michelle A. Rhee, the new schools chancellor. 'They're also things we need to do to take away any excuses for underperformance so that then we can start making personnel changes based on evaluations.'"[17] The teachers who did not meet minimum standards would be dismissed. Rhee was practically throwing the teachers of the D.C. public school system under the bus. And the more "tough talk" she spewed, the more national attention she received. I was miffed by Fenty – a politician who didn't understand politics. "This boy [Fenty] wants to get run out of D.C. doesn't he? I'm not sure what game they are playing, but Washingtonians will surely see through Fenty and Rhee's attempts to scapegoat black teachers for the ineptness of politicians (high unemployment, high rates of incarceration, teenage pregnancy)," I figured.

The motif of the tough-talking administrator coming to save inner-city kids has been played out in the media for decades; Rhee was straight out of central casting. What D.C. needed to fix its school system was "the truth." And it appeared as if Rhee and Fenty were taking cues from the national media attention they were receiving. However, the media is not in the "truth telling" business – it's in the business of selling newspapers and magazines. It was Thomas Jefferson who said, "The only things you can believe in the newspaper are the advertisements." I figured that after Rhee replaced throngs of black teachers with ones who referred to her as "sensei" and the schools still did not improve, she would have looked for another scapegoat. When that tact didn't work, having made millions from book deals and the lecture circuit, she would have exited stage left. During the mayoral election of 2010, word on the street was that the mayor's wife was running around the city lobbying for her husband's job. She had this canned speech reminding Washingtonians that the mayor "had actually done a lot for black folks." After hearing this, I knew Fenty's tenure as mayor was over.

It would be too simplistic to say Fenty lost the reelection bid to Vincent Gray because he lost the teacher vote; he also lost support from middle-class African Americans who helped put him in office. Critics pointed out that he catered to the affluent more so than lower-income residents, and that many residents who voted for him were not allowed to share in the city's revitalization. The affluent class and big business had the resources to offer Fenty the national press coverage he enjoyed, a corporate job or the means to fund his library once he left office. Yet those were not the people who voted him into office. Fenty and Rhee wanted to hold public school teachers accountable with an objective evaluation system. The "truth" that I alluded to earlier is that the parent is the first teacher. The difference between St. Albans, Georgetown Prep, St. Stevens, Sidwell Friends and other private schools in the D.C. area is that those schools have "teachers" at home helping students with their schoolwork. High rates of incarceration, unemployment, and teenage pregnancy (to name a few) are reasons why D.C. inner-city kids do not have "teachers" at home – I never heard whether Fenty was "minimally effective" in those areas. Urban revitalization, and donations from private institutions are great headline-grabbing stories, but D.C. residents and the school system would gain more from jobs that could be created by those efforts.

Privatization of D.C. Public Schools?

Vincent Gray's hands may be tied by some of the school reforms already put into place by Rhee. The national media has zeroed in on whether he will "undermine" Rhee's school reforms or turn back the clock to "corruption" and "cronyism" – implying that either Gray continue Rhee's "pay for performance" plan, or risk being branded the next "Marion Barry." "But Mr. Gray needs to do a lot more to reassure the nation's capital that he will not undermine the school reforms started by Michelle Rhee . . . Mr. Gray can start with the private foundations that have provisionally committed nearly $80 million to support those reforms. To do that, he must resist pressure from the teachers' unions that spent heavily on this campaign."[18] That private institutions and corporations are more focused on breaking the teachers union than on job creation is not a happenstance. They have their own agenda – privatization ("AAU-ization") of D.C. public schools. The first step would be to break the teachers union. The second step involves taking over failing public schools. Once the schools are AAU-itized, these private institutions will (i) recruit the best students – kids of senators, congressmen, and the president, (ii) bribe elite students with iPods, backpacks, and sneakers to attend their schools, (iii) discourage underperforming students from attending so they do not skew test scores, and (iv) once students thought to be "elite" do not perform up to expectations, discourage them from attending and recruit more.

The Truth

The truth is that if you solve the incarceration, unemployment, and teenage pregnancy puzzle, and hold teachers and parents accountable for their child's performance, then you solve your school problem. There was a war going on in 1990 when the FBI entrapped Barry. There is a war going on today – politicians' scapegoating of public school teachers for their own ineptness, and private institutions' desire to manage the public school system. And D.C. is right in the middle of it. The right man for the job is not a politician courting the mainstream media or peddling influence. The right man is the Marion Barry of his youth . . .

the Barry of Pride, Inc. before, even by Barry's own admission, he became drunk with power.

During the financial crisis, lenders restructuring debt on commercial properties or developers handing over the keys to properties altogether, was a common occurrence. Here are a few transactions that were symptomatic of the bubble in commercial real estate and will define the past decade.

Donald Trump

In 1990 I visited Atlantic City for the first time and shortly after arriving, I realized one minor detail – I didn't like to lose money. My girlfriend and I visited a few casinos but they all paled in comparison to the Taj Mahal, owned by Donald Trump. It had been open for about two weeks and gotten rave reviews as a "game changer" in terms of the amount of traffic it would generate, and cache on par with the casinos in Vegas. It was also the envy of the boardwalk, as customers frequented the Taj Mahal at the expense of older properties. I was blown away by the opulence of the place – total excess. At the time, I was a big fan of Trump. He was a real visionary. The Trump Shuttle, though eventually shut down, was a brilliant idea and sparked copycat shuttles from the major airlines. I read his autobiography – *The Art of the Deal*. I also knew that he got his start in real estate with his father, managing middle-income properties in New York. However, after reaching a certain level of celebrity, Trump abandoned his motto of "buy low, sell high" and started collecting trophy properties. His yacht, the Trump Princess, cost $32 million and was totally over the top. In 1988 he bought the Plaza Hotel for $390 million and with additional upgrades, planned to make it the most luxurious hotel in the world. Once I saw the Taj Mahal, I wondered how much Trump could have saved had he not used so much gold and crystal inside the place; Trump called the place the "8th Wonder of the World." I thought the Taj Majal's failure would actually teach him a lesson. The fact that Trump built the $1 billion palace with high-yield bonds (14% interest rate) at the height of the recession did not help matters either. By 1991, the Taj Majal was in bankruptcy; however, debtholders restructured the casino's bonds, reduced the interest rate and stretched out the payments. In exchange, Trump gave up 50% ownership of the casino to the bondholders. From my recollection, creditors kept Trump waiting for a while before they agreed to the final deal. It was a sweetheart transaction for Trump in that it did not reflect his weak negotiating position. For all of Trump's supposed business acumen, creditors have bent over backward to help him when his deals went bust – a courtesy not afforded others. Trump properties have sought Chapter 11 protection on four different occasions.

Trump SoHo

The Trump SoHo hotel and condominium was scheduled to open in April 2009. The 46-story building was one of the more anticipated openings in New York City, not only because Trump talked up the project on his reality show, *The Apprentice*, but because it carried the "Trump" name. The condo-hotel business model seemed like an interesting marketing arrangement – a condominium for part of the year and a hotel when units were not used as monthly condos. The developers, the Sapir Organization and Bayrock Group, were expected to sell the units at a starting price of $1.2 million for a studio. The only caveat was that the owners could not stay for more than four months out of the year or for more than 29 consecutive days. On the face of it, the structure seemed like the best of both worlds – up-front cash from condo owners to cover construction costs and recurring cash flow from hotel visitors. However, a zoning ordinance disallowed permanent residences so the developers came up with the mixed-use structure. Initial sales of the 391 units were strong, but by April 2010, only one-third of the units was under contract. The market for mortgage loans contracted after the recession, which required buyers to pay a substantial cash down payment to secure a mortgage. The quirky arrangement where buyers could not stay more than four months in a year also scared away mortgage lenders. The developers offered discounts of up to 25% off the purchase price to spur buyers to close on deals.

As a proxy for Trump SoHo's prospects, Bank of America sold its mezzanine debt on the project at a discount. The project's biggest lender extended $20 million to developers, in addition to its original $250 million loan. Yet, its future still remains uncertain. Learning from his past bailouts, Trump didn't invest any of his own money in the project. He only agreed to manage the hotel and license the "Trump" name in exchange for an equity stake. For customers, the "Trump" name carries a certain cache and an expectation of quality. For lenders, it connotes that project's debt will eventually have to be restructured.

Trump International Hotel & Tower Fort Lauderdale

The Trump International Hotel & Tower Fort Lauderdale and its 300 luxury hotel suites and condominiums are currently in foreclosure. Again, Trump did not invest any equity into the project, merely licensing the "Trump" name. Trump personally marketed the property and generated the kind of hype and media buzz only "The Donald" could. Aided by Trump's stamp of approval, the condos sold from $500,000 to $1 million, which were considered premium prices. The building included a spa, health club, concierge, valet, restaurant and 24-hour security. However, the developers, SB Associates, LLC, defaulted on a $139 million loan to Corus Construction Venture, which also went belly-up due to its exposure to the frothy South Florida real estate market.[1] When the planned building ran into trouble Trump removed his name from the project, but not before receiving royalties under his licensing agreement with the developers. The agreement states that the building must maintain a certain level of quality. Yet, buyers say Trump did not disclose the licensing agreement to them during the sales process, nor did he represent that he was not the developer. The building is unfinished and buyers, who put down the standard 20% down payment, are out of millions. They have sued Trump for misrepresenting his involvement but as usual, litigation will probably take years to resolve and involve some type of debt restructuring.

666 Fifth Avenue

In 2011 Trump's son-in-law, Jared Kushner, also got his "restructuring" on. In 2007 the 30-year-old developer bought 666 Fifth Avenue for $1.8 billion – the highest price ever paid for a single building. Kushner had previously lost out on bids for 1211 Avenue of the Americas ($1.5 billion purchase price) and Stuyvesant Town and Peter Cooper Village ($5.4 billion purchase price), which were acquired by Beacon Capital Partners and Tishman Speyer Properties, respectively. A sign of the times, 1211 Avenue of the Americas was the second-highest price paid for a single building and Stuyvesant Town was the most ever paid for a multifamily complex. Like Trump, Kushner is also the son of a real estate scion. His grandfather left a real estate empire to Kushner's father, Charles. That empire was worth billions in 2004 when Charles was involved in a scandal for which he served a jail time of two years. Since, Jared has taken a higher profile role in the family's real estate operations. By the fall of 2007 when 666 Fifth Avenue was put up for sale by Tishman Speyer, the Kushners were in "deal heat" according to people close to the negotiations. After a week of due diligence, the Kushners put in the attention-grabbing $1.8 billion bid to focus Tishman Speyer solely on them. Shortly afterward, the two sides signed a contract that included a $100 million nonrefundable deposit, pre-empting the bidding process.

The property was reportedly funded with $50 million in equity and $100 million in reserves, which amounted to less than 9% of the total purchase price; describing the transaction as "highly leveraged" would be an understatement. The property was in financial straits after the recession materialized in late 2008. The record purchase price assumed the buyers could exchange certain below-market leases at market rates once they expired, and sell an equity stake in the retail portion of the property. However, several tenants failed to renew leases after the crisis and Kushner began making debt payments from the $100 million reserve fund. As of March 2011, there was a $3.5 million per month shortfall in debt service, "revenues were only one-fourth of the amount forecast in 2007 . . . and only $10 million remained in a reserve fund used to service the property's $1.22 billion mortgage, which is tied to the office portion of the building."[2] In July 2011 the mortgage holder, LNR Property, agreed to rescue the property by modifying the terms of the mortgage. Ironically, CNBC's Rick Santelli was not seen ranting and raving about the folly of restructuring "losers' mortgages."

Morgan Stanley

Largest Private Equity Real Estate Loss in History

Since the early 1990s Morgan Stanley has been one of the biggest buyers of commercial real estate, completing almost $175 billion in deals through private equity funds it manages. Its funds ran into trouble with acquisitions at the height of the real estate bubble, ranging from office buildings in South Korea and Germany, to an Atlantic City casino. What differentiates Morgan Stanley from Lehman or Bear Stearns is that instead of investing its own capital into transactions, it invested money raised from pension funds, college endowments and high-net-worth individuals. When it announced in 2010 that it expected to lose approximately $5.4 billion of its $8.8 billion (nearly two-thirds) Msref VI real estate fund – the largest loss in the history of real estate private equity –

investors took the loss instead. However, the acquisition fees, financial advisory fees, real estate management fees, and fund management fees it generates from investors may be at risk. In 2007 Morgan Stanley reportedly earned almost $200 million in such fees.[3] Its ability to raise new funds may be in jeopardy given its track record. In addition, Congress may prohibit investment banks from entering new real estate deals given their penchant for leaving taxpayers holding the bag when those transactions do not work out. Certain other Morgan Stanley real estate investments that soured after the global property bubble burst are below.

Revel Casino

In 2010 Morgan Stanley took a 98% write-down of its $1.2 billion investment in a proposed $2.6 billion Atlantic City Casino. Because of the downturn in Atlantic City, Morgan Stanley decided it was better to sell its stake in the property than to "throw good money after bad." The project was also a public relations nightmare for the white-shoe investment bank. Morgan Stanley had received tax rebates pursuant to the project, drawing the ire of New Jersey residents who viewed them as another example of corporate cronyism. Labor unions derided the casino, claiming that instead of creating new jobs, it would create a shell game of taking business and jobs from other casinos. Morgan Stanley purchased the land in 2006 and hired an operator to run the casino. It then tried to sell an equity stake in the property, to no avail. A February 2011 SEC filing revealed that Morgan Stanley sold its stake in the half-built casino to an investor group led by the chairman and CEO of Revel Entertainment. Post write-downs, Morgan Stanley did not record a loss or gain on the sale.

Crescent Real Estate Equities

In 2007 Morgan Stanley acquired Crescent Real Estate Equities Co., a collection of office buildings, resorts, and housing projects from Texas financier Richard Rainwater for $6.5 billion, including the assumption of $3.1 billion in debt. Morgan Stanley was so bullish on the transaction that it closed on the properties prior to forming the investment fund expected to ultimately take claim to the property. This allowed Morgan Stanley to move quickly before Crescent was snapped up by another buyer. However, the properties began to deteriorate in value soon afterward and fund investors refused to buy the property at its inflated carrying value. In a departure for the securities firm, it had to keep Crescent on its balance sheet and expose Morgan Stanley shareholders to a dismal commercial real estate market with no bottom in sight. After taking almost $1 billion in losses on Crescent, Morgan Stanley handed the keys to Barclays Capital, which held a $2 billion mortgage on the properties. John Goff, a partner at the firm that sold Crescent to Morgan Stanley, was involved with a Barclays unit that will manage the properties going forward.

CNL Resorts

Morgan Stanley Real Estate Fund V acquired CNL Hotels & Resorts in 2007 for $4 billion and financed it with $3.3 billion of debt. The resorts included such names as the Grand Wailea Resorts Hotel & Spa in Maui and the Arizona

Biltmore. In January 2011 hedge fund, Paulson & Co., and Winthrop Realty Trust exchanged $600 million of mezzanine debt for equity in the company, taking control of CNL from the fund. Realpoint LLC, a debt research company, calculated that "CNL's resorts collectively are worth less than their total debt, meaning junior claims such as those held by the Paulson - Winthrop group are at risk of being wiped out in a restructuring or bankruptcy."[4] CNL had $1.5 billion of debt due on February 1, 2011. The Paulson-led investor group filed for bankruptcy in advance of the debt coming due in order to give it breathing room for a restructuring.

Flagship Fund in Doubt?

In December 2011 Morgan Stanley returned $700 million to investors in its flagship fund, Msref VII, and cut the fund's management fees. The concessions were in exchange for investors giving Morgan Stanley a 12-month extension (through June 2013) to invest. At the time, Morgan Stanley had only invested about $2.5 billion of the $4.7 billion fund. The negotiations came amid some of the worst investment results in the industry – from 2007 through March 2011 the fund generated losses of 72%. If it had not been granted an extension, Morgan Stanley would have been required to return billions in AUM to investors. "The investors in the fund include the Government of Singapore Investment Corp., Canada Pension Plan, and the China Investment Corp., which is the fund's largest investor, with about $800 million . . . CIC also owns a nearly 10% stake in Morgan Stanley as a firm."[5]

Stuyvesant Town / Peter Cooper Village

In November 2006 Metropolitan Life Insurance Company (MetLife) sold Stuyvesant Town and Peter Cooper Village (Stuyvesant Town) to Tishman Speyer Properties for $5.4 billion – the highest price ever paid for a multifamily complex. The two adjoining complexes, tucked away along the East River, were built for the benefit of WWII veterans and awarded public subsidies to help finance them. The property has remained middle-class ever since and served as a haven for generations of city employees like nurses, firefighters, teachers and police officers. The 110 buildings are located between 14th Street and 23rd Street, and have a combined 11,232 apartments on about 80 acres of the most coveted real estate in Manhattan. When MetLife announced it was selling the buildings at an asking price of $5 billion, I thought a buyer would be getting a steal. The sale and its ramifications – irrational exuberance in commercial real estate, the future of rent-stabilized apartments in Manhattan and gentrification of urban America – would end in a soap opera that New Yorkers will be talking about for decades. It is only fitting because Stuyvesant Town was created amid controversy. When Stuyvesant Town was built in the 1940s, New York City invoked its "eminent domain" to force over 10,000 people, including businesses and schools, to move. Residents balked at being forced from their homes, and challenged the constitutionality of their loss of livelihood and living space. In exchange for land and tax breaks, "MetLife agreed to keep the rents below market to serve moderate-and middle-income families, and to limit their profits to 6 percent for 25 years."[6] When the below-market rent requirement expired in the 1970s, new rent regulation laws required that MetLife continue to charge below-market rent until the vacancy rate exceeded 5%. The city reinstated rent regulations again in 1974, but as a compromise, allowed market-based rents for only those buildings constructed after 1974. After intense lobbying, the state legislature allowed all apartments renting for $2,000 or more to be deregulated and subject to rates that the market would bear. At the time MetLife put Stuyvesant Town up for sale, approximately 70% of its apartments was rent stabilized.

Gentrification

The $5.4 billion sale price for Stuyvesant Town allowed MetLife to monetize the differential between (i) market-based rents, and (ii) the below-market rents that 70% of its tenants was enjoying. The transaction was funded with $4 billion in debt (74% of transaction value) provided by Merrill Lynch and Wachovia, and equity from several pension funds. It also passed along to Tishman Speyer the decades of hard work required to repaper rental agreements to reflect the higher rents, and the ire of the public and thousands of tenants. In effect, Tishman Speyer and its investor group, which included BlackRock, CalPERS (California Public Employees' Retirement System), CalSTRS (California State Teachers' Retirement System), a Florida state pension fund, and the Church of England, paid up-front for synergies that were on the come. Once the transaction was announced, Stuyvesant Town's residents knew there was only one way Tishman Speyer could justify a record purchase price – it had to run them out and bring in more affluent tenants. One of the kids from the Shock Exchange lived there and his mother was wondering if, or when, they would have to eventually move. The game of buying up apartment buildings in the inner city and pricing out low- and middle-income residents was triggered as soon as Alan Greenspan drove rates lower. The game also caused a flight of African Americans to the suburbs while affluent whites, who could afford the higher rates, returned in droves. Mayors like Adrian Fenty beat their chests about the shiny new developments being created in their cities, while those who voted them into office were being priced out.

Adding insult to injury, developers and real estate private equity funds used pension funds of CalPERS and CalSTRS to invest in real estate. In turn, they raised the rent on the acquired properties so high that the underlying pensioners could not afford to live there. However, there was only one small problem for the Stuyvesant Town investor group – the tenants being displaced were Caucasian, and they fought back. When the complex was first built, blacks and Hispanics were not allowed to live there; by 2000 over 80% of the complex remained white. In the "court of public opinion" Tishman Speyer could not win. There would be no Rick Santelli ranting and raving about the ill effects "the losers who could not afford to pay $3,000 per month rent" were having on society.

State Court Deals Blow

In January 2007 tenants filed à lawsuit in the State Supreme Court, naming MetLife and Tishman Speyer. The suit contended that (i) the city's J-51 property tax program (J-51) prohibited landlords from removing apartments from rent regulation, (ii) MetLife had received approximately $25 million in tax breaks under J-51 since 1992 and (iii) MetLife violated the law by charging market-based rents for over 3,000 apartments. The lawsuit requested over $300 million in damages, and that Tishman Speyer re-regulate more than 3,000 apartments until 2017 when the J-51 tax breaks were set to expire. In October 2009 the New York Court of Appeals ruled it was illegal for MetLife and Tishman Speyer to charge market-based rents while simultaneously receiving tax benefits. The decision was a death knell for the Tishman Speyer investor group and other real estate investors who had acquired properties with the intent of repapering rent-stabilized apartments. Tenants paying $3,000 per month for a one-bedroom apartment were ecstatic to see their rents reduced by as much as a third. Meanwhile, landlords affected by the ruling were more sanguine: "'It's terrible for the industry,' said Ed Kalikow, whose family owns 2,000 apartments in the city . . . 'A lot of people bought property with the thought that they would get the rents up. People made decisions on that. Banks made loans. This decision is another nail in the coffin.'"[7]

Tishman Speyer Hands Over the Keys

In late 2008, Moody's downgraded the bonds backing the transaction as Tishman Speyer was having trouble raising rents necessary to service the property's debt. It had also blown through the lion's share of $650 million in reserves due to a shortfall in projected cash flow. The court ruling in October 2009 put investors' equity at risk; meanwhile, the recession caused Stuyvesant Town's value to decline to around $1.9 billion – less than half the $4 billion debt used to finance the transaction. In January 2010 Tishman Speyer turned over the keys to the property's creditors, while the equity holders lost everything. CalPERS, which lost $500 million on the Stuyvesant Town debacle, removed BlackRock from its list of investment managers on a go-forward basis. In total, the $220 billion fund lost over $10 billion on busted real estate deals during the crisis. As of November 2011, Stuyvesant Town still had not been sold.

Below are the estimated losses suffered by the Stuyvesant Town investor group.

Estimated Losses - Stuyvesant Town ($ millions)		
Singapore Investment Corp.	[1]	$ 775
CalPERS	[1]	500
Florida Pension Fund	[1]	250
State of Florida	[2]	250
SL/Green	[2]	200
BlackRock	[1]	112
Tishman Speyer	[1]	112
CalSTRS	[1]	100
Church of England	[2]	70
Total		2,369

(1) Fallout Is Wide in Failed Deal for Stuyvesant Town, NY Times, 10/26/10

(2) The Biggest, Baddest Real-Estate Loan, NY Magazine, 12/18/09

Xanadu – Darden Case Study Waiting to Happen?

It has been called an eyesore, "useless," "wasteful" and the "ugliest damn building in New Jersey," yet the "huge monstrosity that could" is still alive after $1 billion in additional funding from the state of New Jersey in April 2011. The name evokes memories of the palatial estate owned by Charles Foster Kane, the media mogul in Orson Welles' *Citizen Kane*. In one of the scenes, Kane dies alone in Xanadu – a ridiculously huge estate that symbolized his opulence. That said, the name "Xanadu" may also befit the most expensive mall ever built in the U.S. at a cost of over $2 billion. The 2.3 million square facility was expected to have an 800 foot indoor ski slope, indoor snowboarding facility, and the largest Ferris wheel in North America. It was also expected to open during the height of the financial crisis when consumers were trying to reduce discretionary spending.

Delays, Cost Overruns

To say that Xanadu is facing stiff headwinds would be an understatement. Not only did it break ground amid the Great Recession, the concept of a suburban mall goes against current trends. Retailers across the country are struggling and malls are dying a slow, painful death – thousands are set to close each year. The most successful malls are being built in the inner cities; they provide amenities and access where previously there were none. They are also following yuppies' flight back into the inner cities, lured by new apartment complexes and assuaged by shorter commutes to work. In contrast, Xanadu is being built in East Rutherford, New Jersey on a sports complex called the Meadowlands, where the New York Giants, New York Jets and New Jersey Nets play. But even the Nets are leaving behind the suburban sprawl. It will move into its new home, Barclays Center, in downtown Brooklyn in late 2012. Yet the executives at Xanadu are staking the entire complex on New Jersey residents' desire for recreation. "'It's not like people aren't looking to recreate,' says Larry Siegel, president of Xanadu. 'They are.'"[8]

Soap Opera

Xanadu has taken a soap operatic journey with no end in sight. In February 2009 the project was delayed due to financial difficulties. It struggled to line up additional lenders and financial backers to help complete the project. New Jersey Governor Chris Christie, even suggested that Xanadu surrender the property back to the state. In 2004, mall developer, Mills Corp., started the Xanadu project. Mills was acquired in 2007 by Simon Property Group and Farallon Capital Management in the wake of an accounting scandal. Before that deal, a Colony Capital-led group which included German fund KanAm and Dune Capital Management, took over Xanadu from Mills for $500 million. Its lenders, Lehman and Capmark Financial Group, Inc., both filed for bankruptcy during the financial crisis; Xanadu's $500 million of financing needed for completion was cut off in the process. Colony was negotiating feverishly with potential partners for new financing, while Governor Christie was breathing down its neck. In August 2010, Xanadu's banks took control of the property and sold it to Triple Five, owner of Mall of America, for an undisclosed sum four months later. In April 2011, Governor Christie agreed to inject $1 billion of fresh capital into Xanadu to spur its completion. Christie's sudden change of heart may have been politically motivated; the ability to say he personally ended the Xanadu soap opera, started under previous Democratic governors, could be converted into votes during the 2013 election. The positive public relations from a Xanadu opening could also help save his job. The new deal arrangements gave Triple Five until the end of 2011 to put the project financing into place, but it was unknown at deal time when construction would resume. After previous tough talk, Christie blinked: "The administration has argued that the project is too big and too far along to let it lie fallow. There is a strong parallel to the Revel casino project in Atlantic City, where construction stalled after billions had been spent."[9] Whether Xanadu will become an international tourist destination and add new jobs, or simply divert public money from more worthy endeavors like green energy projects and schools, remains to be seen.

The "National Cityers"

During the financial crisis, these investment banks "fobbed their bad loans off" onto unsuspecting investors, similar to National City, the depression-era securities firm.

Goldman Sachs

In April 2010 Goldman Sachs was sued by the SEC for purposely misleading investors to the quality of a CDO offering known as ABACUS. And of course, the Shock Exchange was there to give the public the skinny:

> The SEC has sued Goldman Sachs for fraud in connection with a financial instrument the firm developed through discussions with hedge fund Paulson & Co. . . . According to the complaint, Paulson paid Goldman Sachs approximately $15 million for structuring and marketing the security – ABACUS 2007-AC1 – in early 2007. Goldman let Paulson make bets against the residential real estate market, which the hedge fund believed was going to tank. ABACUS 2007-AC1 was a complex investment vehicle known as a "synthetic collateralized debt obligation," or synthetic CDO, which provided income from a pool of corporate bonds without anyone needing to actually purchase the bonds. In layman's terms: (i) Paulson played a significant role in picking which subprime mortgage-backed securities would be used as the basis for ABACUS 2007-AC1, (ii) Paulson had an incentive to pick securities that would have tanked, since it was betting that the value of those securities would fall, and (iii) Goldman failed to disclose to investors Paulson's role in the portfolio selection process or its adverse economic interests.[1]

Paulson shopped his "CDO shorting" plan to other Wall Street firms also. For Scott Eichel, senior trader at Bear Stearns, the scheme "didn't pass the ethics standards . . . We didn't think we could sell deals that someone was shorting on the other side."[2] According to the SEC, Goldman also misled ACA Management LLC, a third-party experienced in analyzing RMBS credit risk, into believing that Paulson had invested approximately $200 million in ABACUS. Based on internal memos from a Goldman vice president, Fabrice Tourre, he knew that marketing ABACUS would be challenging amid the current market conditions. In a January 23, 2007 email, Tourre stated, "More and more leverage in the system, the whole building is about to collapse anytime now . . . Only potential survivor, the fabulous Fab . . . standing in the middle of these complex, highly leveraged exotic trades he created without necessarily understanding all of the implications of those monstrosities!!!" Moreover, Goldman needed ACA's branding and distribution muscle to distribute the CDO. In a February 7, 2007 internal email, Tourre wrote, "One thing that we need to make sure ACA understands is that we want their name on this transaction. This is a transaction for which they are acting as portfolio selection agent, this will be important that we can use ACA's branding to help distribute the bonds."

Tourre was the only Goldman employee listed as part of the SEC complaint. However, knowledge and approval of ABACUS may have gone as high as CEO Lloyd Blankfein. "But according to interviews with eight former Goldman employees, senior bank executives played a pivotal role in overseeing the mortgage unit just as the housing market began to go south. These people spoke on the condition that they not be named so as not to jeopardize business relationships or anger Goldman . . . According to these people, executives up to and including Lloyd Blankfein . . . took an active role in overseeing the mortgage unit as the tremors in the housing market began to reverberate through the nation's economy. It was Goldman's top leadership, these people say, that finally ended the dispute on the mortgage desk by siding with those who, like Mr. Tourre and Mr. [Jonathan] Egol, believed home prices would decline."[3] The ABACUS 2007-AC1 was one of 25 ABACUS transactions executed by Goldman. AIG insured about $6 billion on other ABACUS securities for which it posted $2 billion in losses – losses included in AIG's $182 billion bailout. In July 2010 Goldman settled civil charges with the SEC by paying a $550 million fine. It neither admitted nor denied any wrongdoing in the matter. However, it did concede that it was a mistake to not disclose to investors Paulson's role in picking the underlying securities held by ABACUS.

J.P. Morgan

The ABACUS complaint touched off an SEC criminal probe into whether other investment banks bet against securities they sold to the public, or allowed select clients to do so. J.P. Morgan, Morgan Stanley and Citigroup, amongst others, were caught in the SEC's dragnet. The SEC filed a complaint against J.P. Morgan for securities fraud related to Squared CDO 2007-1 (Squared). The securities underlying Squared's $1.1 billion portfolio consisted largely of credit default swaps whose value was tied to the residential housing market. J.P. Morgan's marketing materials represented that the underlying securities were selected by GSCP (NJ) L.P., an investment advisor experienced in analyzing credit risk in CDOs. Undisclosed in the marketing materials was that hedge fund investor, Magnetar Capital LLC, played a major role in selecting the securities placed into the portfolio. Both J.P. Morgan and GSC were aware that Magnetar sold short about $600 million in securities of its choosing that were placed in the portfolio. That said, Magnetar made a mint at the expense of unknowing Squared investors. Neither GSC nor J.P. Morgan disclosed the short sale to investors or that Magnetar's economic incentives were counter to buyers of the CDO.

In April 2007 J.P. Morgan was having trouble selling a $150 million mezzanine tranche of the CDO, which held the riskiest securities. To facilitate the sale of the mezzanine portion, it looked outside its traditional customer base to investors in Asia and the Middle East. It talked up GSC's reputation and value-added in selecting the securities, never mentioning Magnetar's role in the process. Of the 15 institutional investors who bought the mezzanine securities, seven were domestic. The domestic investors included Thrivent Financial for Lutherans, a not-for-profit life insurance company based in Minneapolis, Minnesota; Security Benefit Corporation, a provider of insurance and retirement products based in Topeka, Kansas; and MoneyGram International, Inc., a global money transfer firm also based in Minneapolis, Minnesota.

By January 2008, almost 85% of the underlying securities in Squared had been downgraded or placed on "watch" to be downgraded. The buyers of the mezzanine tranche lost all or nearly all of their investment. J.P. Morgan agreed to pay about $154 million to settle civil charges that it misled investors. Again, it neither admitted nor denied wrongdoing in the matter and no individuals of the firm were found liable. The SEC filed a separate civil complaint against Edward S. Steffelin, managing director at GSC, who assisted Magnetar in shorting securities his firm was marketing. Steffelin did not disclose that he was also seeking employment from Magnetar at the time he was marketing the securities on GSC's behalf. J.P. Morgan tried to defend itself with the veiled claim that when it came to mimicking National City, at least we were not as bad as Goldman – "A person close to J.P. Morgan tried to draw a distinction between the Squared and ABACUS deals, citing among other things that J.P. Morgan itself took losses on the offering . . . Unlike Goldman, J.P. Morgan also suffered heavy losses on its mortgage bond deal because the bank held onto a 'super-senior tranche' originally valued at $935 million. That stake became nearly worthless."[4]

Citigroup vs. Rakoff and "Ghosts of Thieves Past"

On October 19, 2011 the SEC accused Citigroup of securities fraud. Amid a weakening MBS market in early 2007, Citicorp created a billion-dollar fund – "Class V Funding III" – which it used as a vehicle to fob off its worthless assets onto unsuspecting investors. Not only did Citigroup take a large portion of assets it expected to decline substantially in value and market them as attractive investments selected by an independent investment advisor, but it took a short position in those assets as well. Citigroup made $160 million in profits from its short positions while investors lost over $700 million. The commission filed a separate lawsuit against Citigroup employee, Brian Stoker, and alleged that Citigroup knew it would have been difficult to sell the fund if it had disclosed to investors in advance that the underlying securities were handpicked by Citigroup and expected to perform poorly. Despite the obvious evidence of fraud, the SEC fined Citigroup $285 million and included boilerplate language that Citigroup "neither admit to nor denies" the allegations in the complaint. However, presiding over the case is Judge "Jed S. Rakoff of Federal District Court in Manhattan, a jurist whom many consider the agency's bête noire."[5]

Rakoff rejected the SEC settlement out of hand and questioned the "fact pattern" in the case. He also intimated that in settling quickly with Citigroup, the SEC was more interested in garnering a quick headline. In a legal shot across the bow, Rakoff publicly reminded the SEC of its duty to "see that the truth emerges."[6] In trying to understand Rakoff's approach to fraud settlements, the media delved into his upbringing in Philadelphia and the influence of his mother. However, I believe his rabid search to uncover the truth lies in his experience representing Martin Siegel, member of one of the largest insider trading rings in U.S. history. The first person in the ring to be discovered was Dennis Levine, the 1980s mergers star who claimed to have gleaned takeover targets by watching for unusual trading activity on a company's ticker tape; all the while Levine was receiving inside information on takeovers from Ilan Reich, a lawyer at Wachtell, Lipton, Rosen & Katz and Robert Wilkis, a banker at Lazard Freres. Once the Feds confronted Levine with evidence of his insider trading, he rolled on Ivan Boesky, the arbitrageur, who then rolled on Siegel. Siegel's original choice for legal representation was Wachtell, Lipton who begged off out of conflict of interest. Siegel's second choice was a partner at Mudge Rose Guthrie Alexander & Ferdon, and former head of the securities fraud unit in the U.S. attorney's office – Jed Rakoff. Rakoff advised Siegel to cut a deal with Charles Carberry, the acting chief of the securities fraud unit Rakoff had departed: "Rakoff took the offer back to Siegel, who told him to cut a deal. Rakoff in turn gave Carberry an informal proffer, promising that Siegel could indeed provide incriminating evidence on the head of arbitrage at another major Wall Street firm [Goldman Sachs], though he didn't mention [Robert] Freeman by name. In return, Carberry offered to drop two of the felony counts."[7]

Rakoff advised Siegel to sell his home in New York and uproot his family down to Florida. After giving prosecutors the details on the elaborate insider-trading ring he was part of, the hundreds of millions of dollars they had made and the "big fish" at Goldman, Siegel felt like he was doing something good for society. However, after Freeman got off with only four months' jail time, Siegel was distraught. The Feds admitted to both Siegel and Rakoff that they bungled the case. The prevailing school of thought was that Freeman got a slap on the wrist because he was a member of the Goldman fraternity and protected by its clout. Decades later, after prosecutions for Levine, Milken, Wilkis, Reich, Siegel and Freeman, nothing has changed. If anybody can understand the culture of the Street – entitled, incorrigible – it is Rakoff. To understand his need to restore the public's faith in the government . . . to "make things right," one would had to have witnessed the "Den of Thieves" firsthand.

The "Pay-to-Players"

The financial crisis also revealed what has become known as "pay-to-play" among pension funds and politicians. Pension funds control trillions of American workers' retirement savings; mandates to manage them represent a windfall for investment managers and private equity funds. In comparison, the professionals and politicians who oversee the funds receive a mere stipend. In turn, overseers of the funds have solicited everything from bribes, to gifts, to jobs for friends and relatives, in exchange for investment mandates. In June 2010 the SEC banned investment advisors from donating to politicians whose funds they want to advise. It stopped short of banning investment advisors from hiring placement agents after firms like the Blackstone Group lobbied heavily against it. Below are some of the pay-to-players who made headlines during the crisis.

Steven Rattner

Steven Rattner is a former *New York Times* journalist turned investment banker and private equity investor with the Quadrangle Group. Eric Gleacher, the '80s mergers star at Lehman, described how he took a chance on Rattner: "Lehman Brothers had a history of hiring people who didn't fit conventional molds; the firm was proud of its willingness to take risks. Gleacher hired Steven Rattner, for example, a reporter from *The New York Times* with no investment banking experience whatsoever, and in Gleacher's view, he turned into a star."[1] Also recognizing the former journalist's financial acumen, the Obama Administration appointed him auto czar, overseeing the bailout of the U.S. auto industry in 2008. Rattner was credited with reducing the debt load of the automakers and cutting costs. In July 2009, he stepped down suddenly from his government position amid whispers of a pay-to-play scandal back in New York. At issue was whether (i) Rattner influenced a company affiliated with the Quadrangle Group to give a movie distribution deal to the brother of a pension fund official, in exchange for a mandate to manage the pension fund's assets, and (ii) Quadrangle paid a $1 million "finder's fee" to an advisor to the state comptroller to influence his decision. The Shock Exchange went into the details:

> The wide-ranging "pay-to-play" probe involving former Quadrangle Group head and Obama automobile czar is still at an impasse. At issue is whether the Quadrangle Group paid fees and provided favors in exchange for lucrative business from New York's $125 billion public pension fund. Rattner has reached a tentative settlement with the SEC over his role, which involved a $6 million fine and a two-year ban from certain work in the securities industry. However, he has been unable to reach a similar deal with New York Attorney General Andrew Cuomo . . . The scandal cost Rattner his role as automobile czar and at age 58, he is still trying to put the incident behind him. He is currently promoting a new book about overseeing the U.S. auto bailout. He was recently on CNBC hawking the book but it is uncertain how his current woes have affected, or may affect future book sales.[2]

In December 2009, Rattner agreed to pay $10 million to settle civil charges involving the alleged kickback scheme and received an SEC ban from certain work in the securities industry for two years.

Alfred Villalobos

In August 2010 the state of California filed a civil complaint against ARVCO Capital Research, LLC, Alfred Villalobos, and Federico R. Buenrostro Jr. for fraud involving solicitation of investment management mandates from CalPERS, in exchange for unlawful commissions to ARVCO and Villalobos. A former CalPERS board member, Villalobos formed ARVCO for the purpose of soliciting investments from CalPERS and other pension funds. The suit claims that ARVCO entered into placement agent agreements with various investment firms, including firms managing investments for Aurora Capital Group, a private equity firm based in Los Angeles, California, and various Apollo Funds. CalPERS committed approximately $4.4 billion to Aurora and Apollo who subsequently paid ARVCO about $47 million in commissions for introducing them to CalPERS. The suit claims that at the time of the arrangement with ARVCO, CalPERS already knew about and had invested millions of dollars in funds managed by Apollo and Aurora before Villalobos and ARVCO started their unlicensed broker-dealer activities. In addition, the placement agency agreements required that ARVCO disclose the agreements, and associated commissions to CalPERS; however, ARVCO and Villalobos concealed them.

Undue Influence Over CalPERS Board Members

In addition to Villalobos' unlicensed broker-dealer activities, the state of California accused him of exerting undue influence over CalPERS' board member, Charles Valdes, its CEO, Buenrostro, and Senior Investment Officer Leon Shahinian. Villalobos bestowed gifts and gratuities on these decision-makers, ranging from (i) campaign contributions for reelection to CalPERS' board, (ii) gifts, and (iii) trips to Lake Tahoe, Dubai, Wynn Resorts Macau and New York City, where all the expenses were paid for or highly subsidized. In violation of firm policy, the gifts were not disclosed to CalPERS. At one point during Buenrostro's tenure as CEO, Villalobos extended him an offer of employment, including a condominium, in order to influence his decisions in favor of private equity firms Villalobos represented. After retiring from CalPERS, Buenrostro went to work for ARVCO as a consultant for $25,000 per month.

Pacific Corporate Group

After the Villalobos scandal, CalPERS decided to rid itself of all board members and placement agents associated with him. In October 2010 CalPERS dissolved its relationship with Pacific Corporate Group (PCG), a placement agent with ties to Villalobos:

> The California Public Retirement Systems (CalPERS) has finally decided to sever all ties with the Pacific Corporate Group (PCG), a financial advisor with relations to former CalPERS board member Alfred Villalobos . . . the SEC and pension

funds are cracking down on insider trading and conflicts of interest involving financial advisors. A placement agent for PCG, Villalobos was charged with fraud by CalPERS in May. PCG also settled with New York attorney general, Andrew Cuomo, in a "pay to play" scandal last year. The firm returned more than $2 million in fees to the state's pension fund in order to avoid corruption charges. The incidences of conflicts of interest and fraud involving CalPERS is a sort of comeuppance for the pension fund known for being a strong investor advocate, and frowning upon similar activities at the companies it invests in.[3]

Revolving Door at CalPERS

The disclosure of conflicts of interest by Villalobos and ARVCO is but one example of the "revolving door" at CalPERS. Several of its board members have found it more lucrative to leave CalPERS and act as middlemen for firms seeking investment mandates from the country's largest pension fund. The proliferation of middlemen calls into question whether pension funds choose investment managers based upon their investment prowess, or their willingness to engage in pay-to-play. In January 2010, CalPERS revealed that William Crist, a former CalPERS official, received approximately $900,000 for helping a U.K - based fund manager land a $300 million investment mandate. The disclosure prompted CalPERS to review such placement fees to ensure that it was not overpaying firms to manage its pension money. Below are the top placement agents for CalPERS based on fees received.

CalPERS Top 10 Placement Agents	
Placement Agent	Fees ($Millions)
ARVCO	$ 58.9
Tullig	17.0
DLJ Securities	12.3
Credit Suisse First Boston	10.8
UBS Securities	8.8
DAV/Wetherly Capital Group	5.9
Presidio Partners	3.5
M3 Capital Partners	3.1
Denning & Co.	3.0
Lazard Freres & Co.	1.8

Source: Craig Karmin, At Calpers, A Revolving Door of Fees For Influence, WSJ, 01/15/10

Alan Hevesi

In October 2010, former New York State Comptroller Alan Hevesi pled guilty to providing investment advisors access to New York's Common Retirement Fund in exchange for gifts, all-expense paid trips and political favors. The personal benefits Hevesi received amounted to nearly $1 million. Hevesi subsequently awarded a $250 million investment contract to private equity firm Markstone Capital Partners of California. Hevesi's conviction was brought about by Attorney General Andrew Cuomo, who had been dogged in the past about eradicating pay-to-play practices in New York. Cuomo agreed not to prosecute Hevesi's two sons who were also involved in politics. Executives of Markstone (i) spent $75,000 on trips for Hevesi, pension fund officials and Hevesi's family, including five jaunts to Israel and one to Italy, (ii) paid expenses on political fundraising trips to California and (iii) entered into a $380,000 "sham" contract to lobbyist and political supporter of Hevesi, Henry "Hank" Morris.[4] Hevesi was later sentenced to one to four years in prison. Elliot Broidy, the Markstone executive who executed the payments, pled guilty to one felony charge and Markstone agreed to repay $18 million in management fees to the New York state pension fund. In February 2011, Morris was sentenced to at least 16 months for influence peddling concerning the New York state pension fund.

THE CO-SIGNERS

Many of the corporate crimes and scandals revealed during the financial crisis had been going on for decades. This can only mean one thing – someone in a position of power was complicit or looked the other way. Below is a list of those who reneged in their role to protect the public, or "co-signed" for the perpetrators of the financial crisis.

Michael Bloomberg

Michael Bloomberg built his fortune on Wall Street long before becoming mayor of New York City. The "Bloomberg machine" which provides business information is practically ubiquitous on Wall Street trading floors. The majority of the insider trading, outsized risks, influence peddling, and corporate greed of the past decade emanated in New York City – the city Bloomberg governed. Yet the one person who understood the various ways in which Wall Street fleeced the public and was in a position to stop it, was oddly silent during it all. Behind the scenes he lobbied the Obama Administration for a bailout of several Wall Street firms; given his city's dependence on tax receipts generated by investment banks, a bailout of Wall Street was a de facto bailout of New York City.

Goes in on Burress . . .

However, when New York Giants wide receiver Plaxico Burress accidentally shot himself inside the Latin Quarter, Bloomberg jumped right into action. In November 2008 Burress was carrying an unregistered handgun when the gun discharged, shooting him in the thigh. He later said he was afraid for his safety after one of his teammates had been robbed at gunpoint a week earlier. Bloomberg held a press conference the day after the shooting and guaranteed New Yorkers that he would personally see that Burress received the maximum jail time possible under the law:

> Our children are getting killed with guns in the streets. Our police officers are getting killed with guns in the hands of criminals. Because of that, we got the state legislature to pass a law that if you carry a loaded handgun you get an automatic 3½ years in the slammer and I don't think that anybody should be exempt from that. I think it would be an outrage if we didn't prosecute to the fullest extent of the law, particularly people who live in the public domain, make their living with their visibility. They are the role models for our kids and if we don't prosecute to the full extent of the law them, I don't know who on earth we would. It makes a sham . . . a mockery of the law. And it's pretty hard to argue the guy didn't have a gun and that it wasn't loaded. You've got bullet holes in and out to show that it was there . . . I don't know if there was any special treatment. The police only found out about this because of a story on television. The hospital didn't call and the Giants didn't call. And the Giants should have picked up the phone right away as good corporate citizens . . . They have a responsibility as a team that depends on the public and wants to be role models to the public.

I watched the press conference and figured that Bloomberg had to have been half-joking . . . Right? Of all the crimes committed in the city of New York, it was only when an African-American professional athlete was injured via a self-inflicted gunshot wound that he demanded justice. Besides, we all know that based on the statistics, black men get away with too much in society. Leave it to Michael Bloomberg to personally put an end to the under-policing of black men in America. But there was another angle. In September 2008, two months before the Burress shooting, Bloomberg announced that he would seek a third term as mayor. His second term was set to end in 2009 and Bloomberg was barred from running again by limits restricting the mayor to two four-year terms. Bloomberg's argument was that it was in the best interest of the public to let him guide the city through the financial crisis. The Burress shooting provided a nice little diversion from the term limit debate. It also allowed Bloomberg to show New Yorkers how tough he was on crime and that they were lucky to have him in charge to beat back the threat, real or imagined, of other black men like Burress who were armed and dangerous.

Burress bit his tongue while in prison. After serving two years (a lifetime for a pro football player) of a potential 3½ year sentence, he signed to play again with the New York Jets. In September 2011 Burress finally let off some steam, criticizing his ex-teammate, Eli Manning, and former coach, Tom Coughlin, for their lack of concern for him after the accidental shooting. He also had the following vitriol for Bloomberg: "The way Bloomberg treated me was totally wrong, stacked those charges so high I had to go to jail."[1] And, "I believe with everything that was said by the mayor and the media . . . that it was just over-generalized and I think it went a little further than it needed to go. But at the same time, I was accountable for my actions."[2]

. . . Yet Co-Signs for Steven Rattner

While others, including President Obama, were distancing themselves from Rattner after evidence of pay-to-play, Bloomberg was embracing him. At a 2009 news conference, Bloomberg introduced a new Home Depot store at New York's Bronx Terminal Market. There, he was bombarded with questions about his friend Rattner:

> Reporter: "Do you think Steve Rattner should step down from his federal post while his pension system investigation [is ongoing]?"
>
> Mayor Bloomberg: "I don't know quite how they phrased it but that he and his company did nothing wrong. If that's the case, there'd be no reason to deprive the country of a very smart guy who's willing to devote himself to public service. And as long as that continues to be the case, I think he'd be a great adviser, but that's up to the President and I really shouldn't weigh in. He's a friend of mine. As you know, his company manages some money for me . . . But I can tell you going back a long way with this guy, he is scrupulously honest and a great public servant."

In April 2010 reports surfaced that Bloomberg urged Rattner to take a hands-on approach to investing his personal fortune. Despite Rattner's legal problems and ban from the securities industry, Bloomberg described Rattner as "a friend whose advice he still valued" . . . and that Bloomberg "always remains loyal to his friends." Even after hard evidence that Rattner paid a $1 million bribe to an advisor to the New York State comptroller in addition to other benefits, Bloomberg still co-signed for Rattner, "making a mockery of the law" that had put others in jail for similar behavior.

. . . Then Sues Science Applications in "Kickback" Scheme

Yet when New York City was on the wrong end of a fraudulent kickback scheme, Bloomberg was not so supportive. In June 2011 a federal prosecutor accused Science Applications International Corp. of defrauding the city. In response, Mayor Bloomberg demanded that Science Applications reimburse the city for all sums paid to it under the project – $600 million. Science Applications was the lead contractor in a project to build an automated payroll system. Executives of the company allegedly hired consultants at "inflated rates, to delay the implementation of the project through fraudulent means and to approve work orders for unnecessary staffing increases. At the end of 2005, there were fewer than 150 consultants on the project; by the end of 2007, the number of consultants more than doubled . . . The fraud allegedly involved more than $600 million in city funds, more than $40 million in kickbacks and an international network of shell companies and accountants created for the sole purpose of laundering cash."[3] If only Burress and the executives at Science Applications had been personal friends of the mayor.

CNBC

Over the years I have used the Internet as a major news source at the expense of traditional media outlets. What I noticed was that online basketball sites like probasketballtalk.com, slamonline.com, and dimemag.com wrote at least an article per day about LeBron James. It would have been just as appropriate for them to change their blogs to LeBronJames.com. I noticed how other sites devoted to gossip and the entertainment industry were as focused on Beyoncé, Rihanna and Chris Brown. Once I actually wrote an article about Dan Gilbert's (Cleveland Cavaliers owner) reaction to LeBron's move to Miami for the Shock Exchange website. The next morning the site went completely haywire with thousands of new visitors. A week later I posted an update on the beef between Gilbert and LeBron and the website went haywire again. I had never received that much interest in an article before. That is when I realized that the aforementioned basketball blogs were not enamored with James – the public was. Secondly, they were not in the "truth telling" business; they were in the business of generating website hits and ultimately, advertising dollars. It gave me better insight into the motivations of blogs, newspapers and television shows like CNBC.

When CNBC was first launched it immediately became one of my favorite shows. I watched it religiously and found it very insightful and informative. However, I noticed disturbing cracks in its news coverage over time. One morning CNBC announced something to effect that "IBM's stock hit an all-time high, Microsoft reported record earnings and Darryl Strawberry had been picked up on drug charges again." What in the world did Darryl Strawberry have to do with business news? Other professional athletes had addictions to drugs or alcohol – Steve Howe, Chris Mullin – why did CNBC not make them a part of their business news program. It was starting to sound like any other news organization – "Let me tell ya'll what I have seen and heard about a black guy" in order to increase its viewership. Since the late 1990s I watched CNBC sparingly, if at all. In August 2008, just before Lehman and AIG failed, I tuned in again for any signs of a decline in the market. The first thing I noticed was that the network had a lot of young women who I would describe as "more photogenic than the normal population." While they came off as journalists who could give a good interview, they hardly offered any insight beyond the superficial. And they had a gift for gab, talking nonstop. In the evening Jim Cramer discussed his thoughts on the market and specific stocks he liked. He was very colorful to say the least, ranting and raving and ringing cowbells. And callers loved him, which seemed to be the most important thing. I was impressed with his encyclopedic memory of various stocks, yet curious as to how his stock picks performed against the broader market. I soon found the gimmicks and nonstop gab of CNBC annoying, and began to tune in with the sound turned off.

Leading up to the crisis, there was never any indication from CNBC that something was amiss. After Lehman failed, it was clear the market declines were not normal, yet the commentators appeared stunned. After each down day they appeared sad, at a loss for words. And on that rare occasion that the market either increased or remained flat, they appeared happy, and cheered the market on. The mere thought that the market could and should decline was beyond their grasp. "And why shouldn't the market crash?" I questioned. The smart money had exited the market a long time ago, so a crash was a good thing. There had been too much speculation in real estate and investors had gotten addicted to easy money; a market crash would have put an end to speculative behavior, at least for a few years. When the government doled out TARP funds to the banks I was appalled. Yet there was no outrage at CNBC. They just delivered the news as if bailing out big business was the way things were supposed to work. Consequently, it only made sense that President Obama offered individuals relief on their mortgages since big business had received taxpayer funds. After the government offered individuals loan modifications, CNBC commentator Rick Santelli literally had a conniption on air. Below is a transcript of his February 2009 rant that went viral on YouTube:

CNBC Commentator: "Rick have you been listening to this conversation?"

Santelli: "The government is promoting bad behavior. We certainly don't want to put stimulus for it. It gives people a whopping $8 or $10 dollars in their check and think that they ought to save it . . . in terms of modifications. I tell you what, I have an idea. The new administration is big on computers and technology. How about this President and new administration, why don't you put up a website to have people vote on the Internet as a referendum to see if we want to subsidize the losers' mortgages or if we would like to at least buy cars and buy houses in foreclosure and give them to people that might actually have a chance to prosper down the road and reward people that could carry the water instead of drink the water."

Trading Floor: "Yeah, What? Yeah!"

CNBC Commentator: "They're like putty in your hands."

Santelli: [Addressing the trading floor] "This is America! How many of you people wanna pay for your neighbor's mortgage that has an extra bathroom and can't pay their bills? Raise your hand."

Trading Floor: "Boooo! Boooo!"

Santelli: "President Obama . . . are you listening?"

CNBC Commentator: "Rick how 'bout the notion that you can go down to 2% on the mortgage and still have 40% not be able to do it so why are we trying to keep them in the house?"

Santelli: "You can go down to minus 2% . . . they can't afford the house!"

After Bear Stearns went bankrupt in January 2008, the Federal Reserve loaned banks hundreds of billions at rates as low as 1.16%. While Santelli, CNBC and Wilbur Ross were questioning the benefit of allowing individuals to borrow at 2%, Wall Street was borrowing at 1% and using the savings to pay themselves billions in bonuses.

CNBC Has a Problem With Michael Vick Earning a Living . . .

In September 2010, Darren Rovell, who covers sports for CNBC, discussed Michael Vick's amazing comeback with commentators, Mark Haines and Erin Burnett. Vick had the hottest selling item in the NFL which Burnett took issue with, under the guise that 10 year old boys may become confused if they ever "Google" Vick:

Rovell: "Three years ago Mark, Michael Vick was the first person to have his jersey sales suspended by the league. Reebok, which made the jerseys, honored any retailer who wanted to cancel their orders. And now Vick is back making cash registers ring again. Vick was named the starter earlier this week and he was back to his old self again and maybe even better, throwing for three touchdowns and running for one more in a 28-3 thrashing of the Jacksonville Jaguars. CNBC has learned that retailers in the Philadelphia, Delaware and New Jersey areas have placed big orders for Vick's #7 jersey."

Haines: "Proving I suppose that nothing succeeds like a winner."

Rovell: "Proving that winning is redemptive. Three years ago a mother would never buy their kid a Vick jersey. And you can buy a dog jersey by the way."

Haines: "What is the special magic of Vick? Is it because he's a quarterback? Is it because his story is so lurid?"

270

Rovell: "I think he's so good. The way he throws the ball is unlike any other quarterback . . . it's like he's throwing a nerf . . . Quarterbacks from a marketing standpoint always rule, even more than running backs and wide receivers. I know a lot of people have a problem with this story, but it is reality. It is business."

Haines: "I have a big problem with it but as you say, it's reality."

Rovell: "I doubt you can get many Eagles fans in a poll to say they would rather have Kevin Kolb or even Donovan McNabb as the starter."

Burnett: "When your 10-year-old boy "Googles" Michael Vick and finds all this other stuff how are you gonna . . . I know it's a teaching moment but the kids will look and they will ask and."

Yet Co-Signs for Steven Rattner . . .

Apparently if you "Google Steven Rattner," the fact that he bribed pension officials would not be revealed. On September 20, 2011 CNBC helped him promote his new book, *Overhaul*, about his experience as President Obama's car czar:

CNBC Commentator: "Right now we have Steve Rattner. He was President Obama's car czar, long well known in the private equity world and he has a new book out called *Overhaul*. It's about his time when he was helping to overhaul the automakers in the United States at a very tough time for them. Mr. Rattner thanks for joining us. So you come from Wall Street and there's this perception on Wall Street that President Obama doesn't like them and isn't very friendly to business. What should President Obama say to Wall Street, to the investor class, to the entrepreneurial class when he is on CNBC less than two hours from now?"

Rattner: "I don't believe that the President is anti-business or anti-Wall Street. I believe that he feels that Wall Street made a lot of mistakes and needs to be regulated in a different way as a result of it and that's part of why the regulatory reform bill was passed. I think he will reassure business that he is not anti-business."

CNBC Commentator: "We have had several people on *Power Lunch* saying we are in danger of becoming very much like Japan. Why do you disagree with that?"

Rattner: "I don't believe we are on the verge of becoming Japan. I think we have this enormously productive, flexible economy, with great innovative skills, particularly out of our tech sector . . . a very vibrant and strong still financial services sector, low inflation, a mobile and talented workforce . . . "

CNBC Commentator: "Why do people feel as negatively about the economy?"

Rattner: "It's understandable why people feel the way they do . . . We've had this wrenching recession. We've had this massive unemployment, worse than anybody would have predicted and it's been sticky and not coming down. And we've had a slow recovery . . . It's destabilizing the people."

271

CNBC Commentator: "What do you see as the proper balance between the government involvement in the economy and not?"

Rattner: "I think you have to distinguish the government's involvement in the economy and government's involvement with business. The government's job is to be involved in the economy . . . to do everything it can with monetary policy, with fiscal policy, with regulatory policy to ensure steady, sustained growth . . . But I don't think the government should step back from that responsibility. The government's role with business is different. I know this administration does not want to see government intrude in the private sector any more than is absolutely necessary. I wrote that in my book. I believe that. But there are occasions as there were in early 2009 when markets fail. When there was no alternative for these car companies but for the government to intervene and provide financing and that is a proper role for government. Without government intervention we would today have no financial sector . . . we would have no automobile sector and those are important things."

And Receives Benefits From Lehman and Citigroup

CNBC's lack of vitriol toward the oligarchs and robber barons put me on pause; I surmised that the commentators must have had some friends and family at those firms. Ms. Burnett confirmed it at the September 2011 launch party for her new show on CNN, *Erin Burnett OutFront*. She also used the moment to introduce her fiancé, who works in Citigroup's high-yield department. Prior to that, he was a trader at Lehman Brothers. Apparently Ms. Burnett never "Googled" those firms beforehand. It struck me as a bit duplicitous that while she feigned having a "big problem" with Michael Vick's jersey being a hot seller, she and her fiancé were receiving benefits from two of the biggest robber barons in our country's history.

Co-opted by Morgan Stanley and General Electric?

Another reason CNBC may have lacked vitriol is because the robber barons lobbied CNBC to quell its public criticism of them. Leading up to the crisis John Mack, CEO of Morgan Stanley and affectionately known as "Mack the Knife," called Jeffrey Immelt of GE to complain about the negative publicity CNBC was giving his firm; GE used to own NBC Universal, CNBC's parent. Mack the Knife assumed his relationship with Immelt would guarantee positive coverage for Morgan Stanley. Along those lines, since CNBC executives did not know Darryl Strawberry or Michael Vick personally or go golfing with them, they were fair game. In the book *Bought and Paid For: The Unholy Alliance Between Barack Obama and Wall Street*, author Charlie Gasparino described how GE executives used its media companies to portray President Obama in a positive light in exchange for government subsidies. Gasparino described how Immelt was a registered Republican but saw it as good business to wave the Democratic flag once Obama was elected. He also used his authority to manipulate how CNBC and NBC Universal portrayed Obama to the public:

> Immelt touted his status as a registered Republican when he stated publicly and infamously among his Republican friends his support of the president, saying, 'We are all Democrats now.' His friends tell me that the reasons Immelt supports

272

Obama came down to the fact that he liked the president on a personal level and believed he was the moderate that he sold himself as on the campaign trail. At CNBC, where I worked for several years, Immelt called a meeting of top talent to discuss coverage of Obama's economic agenda and whether the heavy criticism by on-air commentators (like me) was fair to the president.[4]

Undermining the "Public Trust"

Millions of Americans actually depend upon CNBC for news on the market and where they should invest. Not that CNBC commentators can predict the future any better than the next person, but there is clear evidence that the news organization has gone from simply reporting the news and presenting the facts, to picking those stories it thinks will generate high ratings. Based on experience, it knows that openly criticizing Michael Vick, while promoting Steven Rattner, making Warren Buffett sound smarter than he actually is, and co-signing the corruption and undue income of investment banks will generate ratings. In the process, it has become no more than the public relations arm of Wall Street. Yet, it would be a detriment to the public to have a network present itself as experts in food safety, then promote food processing companies that (i) purposely sell contaminated food to supermarkets and (ii) place bets on how many people will get sick from the contamination. The government would not allow it, yet it allows the business practices of CNBC. The food industry, just like the securities industry, is a regulated industry and underpinned by the public trust. There are thousands of subjects – fashion, relationships, sports, etc. that CNBC could manipulate in its quest for ratings and advertising dollars. CNBC has proven that it is not in the "truth-telling" business; it is in the business of generating ratings. That said, CNBC should no longer be allowed to discuss the securities industry, underpinned by the public trust, and should be removed from television.

Warren Buffett

After Goldman Sachs was accused of misleading investors in its ABACUS CDO offering, you would think that legendary investors would have taken Goldman to task for betraying the public trust. Instead, Warren Buffett, whose Berkshire Hathaway had a $5 billion preferred stock investment in Goldman, actually co-signed for the company. Buffett interviewed with CNBC's Becky Quick in May 2010 prior to Berkshire's annual shareholders meeting. During the interview, he discussed the SEC investigation pursuant to the sale of ABACUS. Buffett praised Goldman CEO Lloyd Blankfein, and exclaimed that Goldman had lost the "PR battle" concerning the SEC's accusations, and he did not believe the firm committed fraud:

> From everything I know about the ABACUS transaction, the answer is no, and I'll go through that transaction in detail at the meeting and we'll see what people think when I get through explaining it. It has not been explained well in the media, so it is part of my job today to actually lay out the facts on it . . . I don't think the media – I think it came out Friday, I think the stories were written very quickly. It was a 22-page complaint, as I remember. I read it. But I think people tried to explain it too fast. And the other side of it is Goldman did not have an immediate response because my understanding is they did not know it was coming, so they

273

have to vet something through lawyers and all of that, and so they missed the news cycle.[5]

Leroy King

Leroy King was the administrator and CEO of the FSRC responsible for regulatory oversight of SIB's investment portfolio, the review of SIB's financial reports, and the handling of requests by foreign regulators pursuant to SIB's operations. In marketing its CDs, SIB represented to the safety of the underlying investments and that the FSRC had reviewed its portfolio and approved its business model. Not only had Leroy King not monitored SIB's investment portfolio, but he was a co-conspirator in defrauding his countrymen who invested their life savings with SIB. Stanford made payments to King so that he would not accurately audit SIB's financial statements. In 2005, four years before Stanford's Ponzi scheme was uncovered, the SEC requested King's assistance in determining if SIB was defrauding investors. Instead, King aided and abetted SIB in concealing its true financial condition. And when he finally responded to the SEC in October 2006, King sent a document actually prepared by Stanford and representatives of SIB.

When the SEC was about to expose the Stanford Ponzi scheme to investors, from February 2009 to March 2009 King transferred approximately $560,000 from a New York bank account to his account in Antigua; these payments may give a more true indication of the total bribes King received from Stanford. In August 2009 James Davis, CFO of SFG, admitted in a Houston courtroom that he and others knowingly bilked investors. He also said that Stanford and King performed a "blood oath ceremony" where King agreed to accept bribes in exchange for his not exposing Stanford's fraudulent activities. As of March 2012, King was still fighting extradition to the U.S.

Securities and Exchange Commission

In January 2009 President Obama nominated Mary Shapiro to head the SEC amid corporate corruption, insider trading, and Wall Street debacles missed by Christopher Cox, her predecessor. Ms. Shapiro was formerly the head of the Financial Industry Regulatory Authority (FINRA), a private agency set up by Wall Street regulatory bodies to protect investors. As the crisis unfolded, details emerged that the SEC was more than a bumbling, stumbling regulatory body. It was at times intimidated by and deferential to the firms it was designed to regulate, and complicit with others. Below is a list of missteps by the SEC during the crisis.

Did SEC Drop the Ball on Lehman?

In March 2010, Ms. Shapiro admitted to the House Appropriations Subcommittee on Financial Services that the SEC's oversight of Lehman may have been lax. During the second half of 2008, Lehman hid losses to present a more positive picture of its financial situation. While it was collapsing, Lehman engaged in an accounting mechanic known internally as "Repo 105." Matthew Lee, a 14-year veteran of Lehman, was fired in June 2008 after he raised issues with the firm's auditors that it was dressing up its balance sheet at the end of each quarter: "Mr. Lee first raised concerns on May 16, 2008, when he sent a letter to senior Lehman management about his concerns over the firm's valuations of illiquid investments and the quality of its accounting controls. In June 2008, Lehman's board instructed Ernst & Young to investigate Mr. Lee's allegations."[6] Lehman allegedly removed $50 billion of the illiquid assets off its balance sheet before the financial reporting period. The SEC was unable to catch Lehman's misleading financial statements, which is particularly damning since the investment community began to look askance on Lehman after the failure of Bear Stearns. Ms. Shapiro told lawmakers that the SEC is "focusing on the integrity of its own staff as part of a top-to-bottom review of its operations," implying that the agency itself was a cesspool of corruption and conflicts of interest described by Julie Preuitt during the Stanford Ponzi scheme allegations.[7]

Bernie Madoff

According to a 2009 SEC Inspector General report (IG Report), the SEC botched attempts to uncover Madoff's Ponzi scheme because of inexperienced staff and delays in investigations. The SEC received six warnings over a period of 16 years about Madoff's trading business but never adequately followed up. The IG report shows in detail how Madoff intimidated examiners:

> Despite three examinations and two enforcement investigations into Madoff, 'at no time did the SEC ever verify Madoff's trading through an independent third-party, and in fact, never actually conducted a Ponzi scheme investigation.' The SEC, during two of the examinations, caught Mr. Madoff in inconsistencies or contradictions, the report said, but the staff only questioned him and took his answers, even those that were 'seemingly implausible,' at face value. The IG report found that Mr. Madoff attempted to intimidate SEC staff during an examination in 2005 by dropping names of senior SEC officials . . . During the review of another firm, the SEC discovered internal emails questioning the firm's investment in Mr. Madoff's business. One email provided a 'step-by-step analysis of why Madoff must be misrepresenting his options trading,' according to the report. The email said Mr. Madoff couldn't have been trading over an options exchange since the volume of trades he would need to execute to match his strategy couldn't be supported by the market. The SEC exam staff in New York said the emails indicated 'some suspicion as to whether Madoff was trading at all.' It took eight months before a team was in place to look into the issue. One SEC examiner said of Mr. Madoff during the examination that 'veins were popping out of his neck.' When examiners reported Mr. Madoff's aggressively pushback tactics to higher-ups, they didn't get any support and were 'actively discouraged from forcing the issue.'[8]

SEC "Revolving Door" Signals Conflicts of Interest

During one of his SEC examinations Madoff delivered a grave insight. He suggested that SEC investigators would not push too hard to uncover his Ponzi scheme out of fear of upsetting the firms they would eventually like to work for. Madoff intimidated SEC employees who were more concerned with their own personal gain than with protecting the public. In June 2010, the Senate asked the SEC's inspector general about the revolving door at the agency where SEC staffers leave, and within days, take jobs at companies they once regulated. Senator Charles Grassley, an avid reader of the Shock Exchange blog, particularly looked askance on the practice. In May 2011 the Project on Government Oversight issued a report documenting the SEC's revolving door. From 2006 to 2010, 219 former SEC employees filed 789 post-employment statements indicating their intent to represent an outside client before the Commission. The Inspector General identified cases in which the revolving door "appeared to be a factor in staving off SEC enforcement actions," including cases involving Bear Stearns and the Stanford Ponzi scheme.[9]

Pequot Capital Management . . . Replay of Stanford Ponzi Scheme?

In June 2010 the SEC agreed to pay $755,000 to settle a wrongful termination suit filed by Gary J. Aguirre, a former staff lawyer for the SEC. Aguirre was fired during an insider trading investigation against Pequot Capital Management and its co-founder, Arthur Samberg. Aguirre pushed to interview Morgan Stanley CEO, John Mack, a personal friend of Samberg, about specific trades by Pequot. Aguirre believed his insistence on having a powerful Wall Street figure like Mack testify is what prompted his firing. Mack was issued a subpoena to testify, but it was later withdrawn. The case was closed in 2006 due to lack of evidence but reopened in 2009 when the ex-wife of David Zilkha, a former Microsoft employee who later worked for Pequot, handed the feds incriminating personal emails revealing evidence of insider trading. At a December 2006 hearing before the Senate Judiciary Committee, Aguirre "contended that the SEC closed the investigation of Pequot because of outside influences."[10] A subsequent Senate report in August 2007 berated the SEC for mishandling the investigation. If Mack the Knife was nervy enough to call Jeffrey Immelt in order to put CNBC in check, do you think he would hesitate to stab Aguirre in the back to avoid the witness stand?

SEC Accused of Destroying Evidence of Fraud

In August 2011 Gary J. Aguirre returned to haunt the SEC, this time as the lawyer for Darcy Flynn, who accused the commission of destroying thousands of sensitive documents to cover-up suspected fraud and influence peddling. Here is what the Shock Exchange had to say on the matter:

> A Securities and Exchange Commission (SEC) lawyer recently accused the SEC of illegally destroying thousands of documents related to early stage investigations over the past two decades. The files contained records of nearly 10,000 inquiries involving the likes of Bernie Madoff, Goldman Sachs, Lehman Holdings, and Citigroup. Apparently the SEC whistleblower, Darcy Flynn, told "what had happened" and "what he had seen and heard" on his previous employer as well. In 1993 Flynn received a $2.7 million reward for exposing alleged Medicare fraud as an insurance claims auditor in Michigan. Flynn joined the SEC in 1995 to probe accounting scams and insider trading, but decided to report wrongdoing orchestrated by the SEC instead. Flynn's current whistleblowing may be financially motivated. He left the SEC in 2005 and invested in commercial real estate in the Washington, D.C. area. His company was affected by the recent economic downturn and faced foreclosure and millions in debt. Flynn rejoined the

SEC in 2008 and was recently in charge of recordkeeping related to enforcement cases already closed.[11]

THE CONTRITIONISTS

Weeks after my Darden graduation ceremony, I was in a rush to clear my belongings out of my apartment before my lease expired. Grandpa had also agreed to carry my furniture back to Farmville on the back of his pick-up truck; I knew I had better have my stuff ready when he got there too or there would be complete silence on the 90-minute ride home. On a trip to the dumpster, an older Caucasian man – he had to have been about 85-90 years old – tried to stop me on the sidewalk. I kept it moving though. On my next trip to the dumpster the guy was still walking down the sidewalk. He tried to flag me down again. This time I stopped, thinking he needed some kind of assistance. However, he just wanted to talk. I stared into his eyes and I swear I could see into his soul – he wanted his contrition. He was about to meet his maker and wanted clean hands. Being nice to me would make up for the decades of sins he had committed against a black man, or black woman, as the case may be. I could not help him. "That is between him and his God," I decided.

As I walked off I surmised that that was how the process usually worked. Before we met our maker, we would all seek contrition. Below is a list of "contritionists" from the financial crisis. Former President Bill Clinton is noticeably absent from this list. He signed the bill to repeal Glass-Steagall; he later had his coffers filled by those who stood to benefit most from its repeal, and tried to conceal it. Eventually, when it's time for him to meet his maker, he will get on his hands and knees and beg the public for forgiveness – they always do.

Bernie Madoff

"As the years went by, I realized that my arrest and this day would inevitably come . . . I am painfully aware that I have deeply hurt many, many people, including members of my family, my closest friends, business associates and the thousands of clients who gave me their money. I cannot adequately express how sorry I am for what I have done."[1]

Phillip Barry

I am "profoundly sorry. If granted leniency I would work to repay the money, possibly as a radio host. I never intended for this to happen . . . No one plans to get lost in the woods. It just happens, one step at a time."[2]

Goldman Sachs

In an eight-page letter addressed to shareholders in advance of Goldman's May 7, 2009 annual meeting, CEO Lloyd Blankfein and President Gary Cohn reaffirmed their commitments to clients and addressed their exposure to AIG. Below are excerpts from that letter:

Government Assistance, Relationship With AIG

"In June 2009, the firm repaid the U.S. government's investment of $10 billion in Goldman Sachs as a participant in the U.S. Treasury's TARP Capital Purchase Program . . . Over the last year, there has been a lot of focus on Goldman Sachs' relationship with AIG, particularly our credit exposure to the company and the direct effect the U.S. government's decision to support AIG had or didn't have on our firm. Here are the facts . . . we purchased from them protection on super-senior collateralized debt obligation (CDO) risk. This protection was designed to hedge equivalent transactions executed with clients taking the other side of the same trades. In doing so, we served as an intermediary in assisting our clients to express a defined view on the market . . . This resulted in collateral disputes with AIG."

Activities in the Mortgage Securitization Market

"Another issue that has attracted attention and speculation has been how we managed the risk we assumed as a market maker and underwriter in the mortgage securitization market. Again, we want to provide you with the facts. As a market maker, we execute a variety of transactions each day with clients and other market participants, buying and selling financial instruments, which may result in long or short risk exposures to thousands of different instruments at any given time . . . Although Goldman Sachs held various positions in residential mortgage-related products in 2007, our short positions were not a 'bet against our clients.'"[3]

Interpretation

In explaining its repayment of TARP, Blankfein failed to mention (i) the $14 billion it received from the U.S. government by using AIG as a pass-through entity, or (ii) the billions in zero interest loans provided by the Federal Reserve after the failure of Bear Stearns, that inured to the benefit of Blankfein and other Goldman executives. Secondly, Goldman Sachs bet against its clients – the type of subterfuge that Glass-Steagall was specifically enacted to prevent. Furthermore, Lloyd Blankfein cannot possibly be African American. Otherwise, it would be a 1-in-3 chance that he would have penned this letter from jail.

Robert Moffat, Jr., IBM Executive

"I made terrible mistakes in judgment, which will haunt me for the rest of my life . . . I am alone responsible for my conduct."[4]

"I disclosed this information to Ms. Chiesi intentionally, and I knew that what I was doing was wrong . . . The biggest thing I've lost 'is my reputation.' Everyone wants to make this about sex . . . I know in my heart what this relationship was about: clarity in the business environment."[5]

McKinsey & Company

When hearing of Raj Gupta's SEC allegations, Ian Davis, who succeeded Gupta as McKinsey Managing Director, feigned surprise: "I was shocked, at the news of the allegations." McKinsey has since tightened its rules. It now bars employees and their families from investing in any company McKinsey has served in the past five years or is cultivating.[6]

"It's beyond shocking frankly when you're talking about a guy like Rajat . . . It's a little like finding out the Pope was an abortionist on the other side and had six wives."[7] – Former McKinsey consultant who asked not to be identified

"Chip" Skowron III

"Your Honor, I was not aware of the changes that were happening in me that blurred the line between right and wrong. They came slowly over several years. I allowed myself to slip into the world of relativism where the ends justified the means . . . Quite frankly, it's hard to imagine how I became that kind of person."[8]

"The last year has been devastating but it's also been incredible. These circumstances have been a blessing because I have turned my life over to Christ. I am not what she [Cheryl Skowron] expected when she married a young doctor 15 years ago."[9]

Cheryl Skowron, Chip's wife, went so far as to ask for leniency. In an impassioned letter to Judge Denise Cote, she wrote, "I'm trying to understand how he could risk so much. He says he had no idea prison was a possibility otherwise he never would have done it."[10]

Danielle Chiesi

"Trading inside information was like an orgasm . . . I love the three S's – sex, stocks, and sports."[11]

William Bischoff

Perhaps signaling an avenue for Chiesi's defense, her former fiancé William Bischoff remarked, "She is a victim of a man who was supposed to be her mentor . . . I think Mark [Kurland] was a psychologically abusive person who took advantage of her and pushed her to the limit. She's a fundamentally good person."[12]

"Fox in the Henhouse"

As a former NASDAQ official, Donald Johnson was privy to major announcements of member firms ahead of the general public. He was entrusted with sensitive information such as earnings shortfalls and major acquisitions and then traded on that information, earning $750,000 in profits. One SEC official likened Johnson's betrayal of trust to that of "the fox guarding the henhouse." During sentencing, Johnson wrote a letter to judge Anthony J. Trenga in hopes of swaying his decision. He was eventually sentenced to 42 months in prison. In the letter, Johnson acknowledged his stupidity:

> The shame, embarrassment, and disappointment I've inflicted on my family, friends, and colleagues, have caused me significant guilt and I'll shoulder the remorse for the remainder of my life . . . First I would like to stress that there's no explanation or justification for the unethical behavior I engaged in during the period of August 2006 through July 2009 . . . In retrospect, an appropriate one-word response (along with additional commentary) would've been 'stupidity.'

Alan Hevesi

"I deeply regret my conduct and sincerely and deeply apologize to the people of the state of New York, to the court and to my family."[13]

Henry "Hank" Morris

"Words cannot express the depth of my remorse . . . Throughout my life, I have believed in the potential for government to be a force for good in the lives of people. In fact, I devoted the bulk of my professional life to achieving that goal . . . To recognize that my actions undermined those efforts has been very painful. Simply put, my actions undermined the integrity of New York State's government, and, most importantly, have led ordinary people to question their faith in the political system . . . [To his friends and family] I love you. I love everybody. Thank you."[14]

Tom Ollquist, Former Lehman Bond Salesman

In acknowledging the role he played in the outsized losses that devastated shareholders and the banking system, Ollquist responded: "I have blood on my hands."[15]

Richard McKinney, Former Lehman Mortgage Trader

"From a policy perspective, the regulators have to step in . . . It would be an awful lot to ask the Street to not look for revenue opportunities where their competitors are finding revenue."[16]

Jeff Schaefer, Former Lehman Executive

"I spent a lot of time being angry . . . Angry for working so hard and doing so much. More importantly, for my family and all the time I was away traveling – the time I put in away from them. Now all that money I earned, the money paid in stock, is gone. I can't go back and remake it."[17]

Ken Linton, Former Lehman Mortgage Trader

"Anyone at our level who had a different view from senior management would find themselves going somewhere else quick . . . You are not paid to rock the boat."[18]

James Cayne, Former Bear Stearns CEO

"In hindsight I would say leverage was too high."[19]

Dick Fuld

Fuld had publicly been unapologetic and blamed everyone from the Bush Administration to Henry Paulson to Lehman's CFO for the company's bankruptcy. In April 2009 during a private address to employees of Matrix Advisors LLC, staffed by former Lehman workers, Fuld finally broke down: "I spent too much time out of the office with clients and trusted other people to manage the risk. I'm sorry . . . I take full responsibility for what happened. I will never heal from this."[20]

"He [Dick Fuld] used to have a certain air about him. But he is here less now and has sort of lost his swagger."[21] – Caddy from the Valley Club in Sun Valley, Idaho

John Whitehead

After Goldman's $550 million SEC settlement over its role in the ABACUS CDO, the former co-chairman of Goldman responded: "There is a lot of work ahead for the management to recover its reputation . . . They need to realize that the business goes in cycles and sometimes the trading aspects are important, but sometimes the investment-banking business of raising money for firms and advising private-sector companies becomes important."[22]

John Mack, Chairman and Former CEO of Morgan Stanley

"I'm somewhat disappointed that we've lost a little of the steam about getting financial reform. We do need system-risk management . . . It's not as simple as (Wall Street) having too much risk . . . Credit was free and you were paid to take risk. What we've learned is that firms at 30 and 40 times leverage is a mistake."[23]

Lloyd Blankfein

"We participated in things that were clearly wrong and have reason to regret. We apologize."[24]

Sanford Weill, Former CEO of Citigroup

No longer able to shoulder the burden of the most unpatriotic act of his lifetime, Weill sought his contrition in July 2012. "I am suggesting that they [huge financial conglomerates] be broken up so that the taxpayer will never be at risk, the depositors won't be at risk . . . Mistakes were made."[25]

THE PRISONER'S DILEMMAS

Several of the insider traders, Ponzi schemers, and co-conspirators found it in their best interests to testify against their cohorts in exchange for a reduced sentence. Below are the "prisoner's dilemmas" from the crisis.

James Davis, CFO Stanford Financial Group

Realizing that Stanford's Ponzi scheme had finally been uncovered, SFG CFO James Davis played the role of turncoat to save his own hide. And of course, the Shock Exchange was there to present the facts in layman's terms:

> On August 28th R. Allen Stanford of Stanford Financial, the Texas financier accused of orchestrating a $7 billion international Ponzi scheme, was hospitalized the same day that Stanford Financial's former CFO pleaded guilty to fraud and conspiracy charges. Stanford was taken to Conroe Regional Medical Center, about an hour north of Houston, after complaining of rapid heart palpitations. Conroe is near the penitentiary where Stanford is being held. That same morning James Davis, Stanford Financial's former CFO, admitted in a Houston courthouse that he and several others knowingly bilked investors for decades. Mr. Davis faces a maximum of 30 years in prison but hopes to receive a reduced sentence. In a classic case of "Prisoner's Dilemma," Mr. Davis is cooperating with federal prosecutors in helping them build a case against Allen Stanford. Davis also admitted that an Antigua banking regulator had accepted bribes from Stanford in exchange for his agreement that the Antiqua Financial Services Regulatory Commission would not destroy the company's Ponzi scheme. Leroy King, the regulator in question, is awaiting extradition to the U.S. from Antigua.

> Prisoner's dilemma involves a scenario where Prisoner "A" and Prisoner "B" are both arrested. Prosecutors separate the two prisoners and offer them a reduced sentence in exchange for "snitching" on the other. In the case of Prisoner B, (i) if he snitches and Prisoner A does not snitch, Prisoner B receives a reduced sentence and Prisoner A gets the book thrown at him; (ii) if Prisoner B does not snitch and Prisoner A does snitch, then Prisoner B receives the maximum sentence while Prisoner A receives a reduced sentence; (iii) if both prisoners snitch then they both receive the maximum sentence; (iv) if neither snitches then they both get off or receive something less than getting the book thrown at them. Allen Stanford has denied any wrongdoing whatsoever. However, playing the odds, Stanford Financial's CFO has decided to tell "what had happened" and "what he's seen or heard" in exchange for a reduced sentence.[1]

Anil Kumar – McKinsey Executive, Galleon Co-Conspirator

In December 2009 the government "turned" McKinsey executive Anil Kumar and convinced him to cooperate as a witness against Raj Rajaratnam. In 2006, Kumar and Rajaratnam entered into a compensation scheme whereby Kumar received a share of the profits generated from inside information he delivered to Rajaratnam. Rajaratnam's biggest score from a single trade – $23 million on the merger between ATI Technologies and AMD – came from Kumar. Faced with uncertain jail time, Kumar found it in his best interest to become the "sources of information" at the expense of his former Wharton classmate:

In a move that could add to the government's arsenal in the Galleon Group insider trading case, prosecutors made a federal court filing on December 30, 2009 that suggests they are on the verge of accepting a guilty plea from former McKinsey & Co. partner Anil Kumar. According to *The Wall Street Journal*, the filing signals that Mr. Kumar may waive his right to an indictment by a grand jury, which could be seen by lawyers as a step toward a guilty plea. Of the 21 people the government has brought charges against, four are acting as cooperating witnesses. They are as follows: (i) Roomy Khan, former Intel employee, and (ii) hedge-fund managers Richard CB Lee, Ali Far, and Steven Fortuna. All four have pled guilty to conspiracy and insider trading charges, and are hoping for reduced sentences for their testimony and aid in gathering evidence . . . As you recall from our earlier post on Stanford Financial . . . James Davis, Stanford's former CFO, admitted to running a Ponzi scheme when faced with prisoner's dilemma.

Mr. Kumar, 51 years old, was a star consultant at McKinsey at the time of his arrest. Prosecutors allege that in August 2008 he tipped off Mr. Rajaratnam, head of Galleon Group, about the timing of a reorganization of AMD involving a spinoff of its manufacturing business. Mr. Kumar, who worked on the transaction and was a direct or indirect investor in certain Galleon funds, told Mr. Rajaratnam (i) when the transaction would occur and (ii) to buy AMD stock. *The Journal* went on to report that Mr. Kumar built his career at McKinsey by building relationships in the technology industry and the Indian business world.[2]

THE FRED SANFORDS

When we were still living with my grandparents they had company over one evening. It was during the holidays and everyone was in a festive mood. I was in a good mood too because football was about to come on. To my dismay, My Daddy turned the channel to *Sanford & Son*, a sitcom I had never seen before. It featured a widowed junk man, Fred Sanford, who lived in Los Angeles with his son, Lamont. The show's plot involved scheming by Fred and his friends gone awry; they kept the audience on edge as they tried to plot their way out of trouble. The second source of tension was Esther, Fred's sister-in-law, who was always meddling to ensure Fred was raising Lamont correctly, and living in a way that honored her sister Elizabeth's memory. Whenever Fred would get himself in a serious bind with no escape in sight (which was practically every episode), he would feign sudden illness, grab his heart and look up to the heavens and exclaim "Lisabeth . . . I'm coming to join ya honey . . . I'll be the one with the pocket full of credit default swaps!" The following executives decided to pull a "Fred Sanford" when faced with corporate crimes, or worse yet, decided to end it all.

Charles Barney, Knickerbocker Trust

The panic of 1907 was brought upon by speculation in commodities and railroad stocks. The speculation was mostly attributable to trust companies, which were supposedly "safe" investment vehicles. At the time, trust companies were insulated from competition because banks were prohibited from executing trust business like wills and estates. They found a legal loophole that let them engage in speculative activities beyond traditional trust business. They provided "mullet money" by paying exorbitant interest rates to attract depositors and using the funds to provide margin loans against stocks and bonds. High-risk margin loans and speculation on copper stocks almost led to their undoing, and at least for one, Knickerbocker Trust, it did. Knickerbocker Trust and other speculators tried to corner the stock of United Copper in advance of irrational exuberance for copper. However, the stock of United Copper tanked and with it, the general market. Panicked depositors of the Knickerbocker created a run on the bank; the only person left for its CEO, Charles Barney, to turn to was J.P. Morgan – "Pierpont wrote off the Knickerbocker as hopeless and it failed on Tuesday afternoon, October 22. 'I can't go on being everybody's goat,' he said. 'I've got to stop somewhere.' A few weeks later, refused admission to see Pierpont, Charles Barney of the Knickerbocker shot himself, an act that produced a wave of suicides among the bank's depositors."[1]

Ken Lay, Chairman Enron

The former Chairman of Enron was convicted of conspiracy and fraud by manipulating Enron's stock price to conceal billions of debt and mislead investors in what was at the time, the largest bankruptcy in U.S. history. After his conviction in May 2006, the 64-year-old Lay was expected to spend the rest of his life in prison. In July 2006 Lay was found dead of an apparent heart attack in Colorado. The timing of his death appeared suspicious but the autopsy revealed no evidence of foul play. Prosecutors were seeking a judgment of over $40 million from Lay's estate; however, the legality of seeking monetary remedies from a dead man was thrown into question.

Jeffrey Skilling, CEO Enron

In February 2004 Jeff Skilling, former CEO of Enron, was charged with 35 counts of conspiracy, fraud, and misleading investors about Enron's financial condition. In April 2004 he was taken to New York Presbyterian Hospital by police due to what they described as "erratic behavior." According to news sources: "Several people called police saying he was pulling on their clothes and accusing them of being FBI agents . . . Police took Skilling to the hospital after finding him at 4 a.m. at the corner of Park Avenue and East 73rd Street and determining he might be an emotionally disturbed person . . . Skilling's attorney said that his client and his wife called police after they were assaulted by two men who had followed them. Police denied that account."[2] After reading this story, my friends and I assumed Skilling was trying to act deranged in an attempt to beat the fraud charges on a plea of insanity. In October 2006 the 52-year-old was sentenced to 24 years in prison and ordered to pay $50 million in restitution to his victims.

Hazem Al-Braikan, CEO Al-Raya Investment Co.

In July 2009 the SEC accused Hazem Al-Braikan, a Kuwaiti resident, of drafting a bogus press release claiming that a Saudi Arabian investor group planned to acquire Harman International for $49.50 per share. Al-Braikan was also the CEO of Al-Raya Investment Company, a Kuwaiti financial services firm started in mid-2008 and 10% owned by Citigroup. At the time of the press release, Harman was trading at $25 per share. The stock shot to the mid-$30s on the news and dropped back to $20.86 after Harman exposed the press release as a hoax. The SEC complaint also claims that Al-Braikan temporarily manipulated the stock of Textron, Inc. via a similar fake press release. Al-Braikan and Al-Raya amassed sizeable positions in the stocks of Harman and Textron prior to the press releases and profited from their initial run-ups; Al-Braikan and Al-Raya realized profits of $1.7 million and $1.1 million, respectively. Within days of the SEC complaint Mr. Al-Braikan was found dead in his home with a self-inflicted gunshot wound to the head.

Jeffry Picower

Jeffry Picower, a philanthropist accused of being one of the biggest beneficiaries of the Madoff Ponzi scheme, drowned while swimming in the pool of his Palm Beach, Florida home in October 2009. The autopsy revealed that Picower suffered a heart attack, causing the accidental drowning. Picower had been sued by Irving Picard, the lawyer handling the claims of Madoff victims. Picard claimed that Picower withdrew more than $7.2 billion from Madoff investment funds over 20 years, at least $5 billion of which were phony profits. Picard alleged that Madoff investors received annual returns as high as 950 percent and sophisticated investors should have known such returns were the result of fraud. After learning of the fraud Madoff had perpetuated for decades, the Picowers

[Jeffry and wife Barbara] maintained that the publicity and controversy surrounding their connection to Madoff had been a great source of heartache and taken a toll on their health.[3]

Bernie Madoff

Madoff was having a pretty rough time of it after entering a federal prison in Butler, North Carolina in early 2009. By August he was diagnosed with cancer and considered terminally ill. In December 2009 he suffered multiple wounds from falling out of bed and was experiencing heart palpitations, among other illnesses.

Heart Palpitations

In December 2009 Madoff fell out of a prison bed and suffered facial fractures, a collapsed lung and broken ribs. He was taken to Duke Medical Center where he was cared for. It was originally thought that Madoff had been the victim of a jailhouse beating but reports surfaced that an assault did not take place. According to his lawyer, Ira Sorkin, Madoff also experienced hypertension, heart palpitations and bouts of dizziness. Sorkin also denied previous reports that Bernie was suffering from cancer and was terminally ill. When I first read the article it did seem rather bizarre. "All of those injuries caused from falling out of bed? Maybe Bernie should sleep on the bottom bunk," I thought.

Jailhouse Beating . . . Prison Officials Deny Incident

In March 2010, new reports surfaced that Madoff was indeed beaten by another inmate. After the attack, he was moved to the low-security medical center at the Butler facility. Madoff was treated for a broken nose, cuts to the face and broken ribs. Former inmates confirmed the attack and one thought the incident stemmed from a dispute over money the assailant claimed Madoff owed to him. The assailant, who was serving time on a drug conviction, was described as a former body builder and black belt in judo.[4]

Allen Stanford

In August 2009 after SFG CFO James Davis became the "sources of information" in the Stanford Ponzi scheme case, Allen Stanford immediately began to experience rapid heart palpitations. He was taken to Conroe Regional Medical Center for examination and an upcoming hearing was rescheduled due to his illness. To make matters worse, Stanford's lawyer, Dick DeGuerin, stopped representing him because Stanford was having trouble paying his legal fees after his assets were frozen by the government.

Jailhouse Beating

In September 2009 the 60-year-old Stanford was the victim of a jailhouse beating that left him wearing a neck brace, his head wrapped in bandages and his eye swollen shut. Allegedly, Stanford had been placed in a cell with 14 other inmates, yet the cell was only designed to hold less than 10 people at one time. There was no electricity or air conditioning either. Stanford claimed that the other inmates complained about him being on the telephone and then attacked him for no reason – punching him and kicking him until he lost consciousness. Stanford was shackled and rushed to a nearby hospital where surgery was performed while he was still in chains. He suffered a fractured eye socket as well as broken bones in his facial area. He was beaten so badly that he lost all feeling in the right side of his face. Stanford spent the next few weeks in solitary confinement after which authorities moved him to the Federal Medical Center at the Butler, North Carolina prison complex – the same complex where Bernie Madoff was being housed.

Psychiatric and Psychological Problems

Stanford claimed that the beating at the hands of the two prison inmates resulted in trauma to his brain. His lawyers also claimed he was overmedicated by medical personnel at the Federal Detention Center in Houston, Texas where he was previously held. Stanford showed a limited ability to assist his lawyers in his defense case, so a U.S. district judge ordered that he receive psychiatric and psychological treatment at Butler, and a trial delayal until he was competent enough to defend himself. U.S. Attorney Gregg Costa, challenged Stanford's claims of mental illness as an attempt to pull a "Fred Sanford." He showed "an e-mail Stanford wrote from prison on December 27 that the prosecutor said was 'gibberish.' He asked the doctor if Stanford was 'trying to game the system' by writing jumbled messages during the time the government was examining his mental state, while earlier e-mails were cogent and showed Stanford to be aware of current events."[5]

Amnesia

Determined not to stand trial, in September 2011 Stanford claimed he could not remember events that occurred before his arrest in June 2009. However, doctors not involved with the Stanford case were skeptical of his claim of amnesia: "Roy Lubit, a forensic psychiatrist in New York . . . said medication and withdrawal are unlikely to cause memory loss. 'If it's being cut at a reasonable pace, that shouldn't stop them from being competent,' he said. Dr. Lubit and Colin Koransky, a forensic psychiatrist in California, both said a head injury – Stanford suffered one in the beating – could cause amnesia for recent events but is unlikely to affect older memories."[6]

Raj Rajaratnam

After Rajaratnam was sentenced to 11 years in jail on 14 counts of conspiracy and securities fraud, out of nowhere he began experiencing "health problems." The former hedge fund trader known for his quick temper, berating subordinates and throwing objects in a fit of rage, suddenly was too meek and feeble to go to jail. Apparently, Mr. Rajaratnam had come down with a sudden case of diabetes that could potentially lead to kidney failure. His lawyers argued that he should receive a lesser sentence because of health problems and that he will "likely die in prison if given a lengthy sentence . . . 'Mr. Rajaratnam is not a healthy man, and his death will be hastened by a term of imprisonment.'"[7] In defending its sentence for Rajaratnam, the government noted that Rajaratnam committed his crimes for years after he knew about his medical problems and thus was in no position to seek leniency based on them.

THE PAIN AHEAD

Like President Hoover, FDR, Senator Carter Glass and Representative Henry Steagall before them, today's politicians and lawmakers have a chance to enact laws to further protect the public trust – it will take decades to restore – and shape U.S. capital markets for the rest of the century. Refusing to both rein in the oligarchs and Wall Street robber barons and bring them to justice has been the biggest failings of both the George W. Bush and Obama administrations. That said, the country is currently at an inflection point – we can form laws and regulations to break these corporate fraternities, or have them broken through class warfare and social unrest. Below are recommendations in the aftermath of the financial crisis, and a description of "the pain ahead" for the market and the U.S. economy.

Re-Institute Glass-Steagall

Instead of devising new laws to address financial reform, lawmakers should (i) re-institute Glass-Steagall and (ii) update it to include those products or business lines that may not have existed in the 1930s, but which the "spirit" of Glass-Steagall was designed to address. Such products and business lines include, but are not limited to:

Holding Mortgage-Backed Securities

The secondary market for mortgage loans did not exist during the time of Glass-Steagall. Holding MBS is merely another way of making loans for mortgages. Investment banks should stick to capital raising and advisory services. However, they should be allowed to hold inventory of MBS for market-making activities only.

Proprietary Trading at Banks

Lawmakers should ban investment banks from trading for their own accounts. We know from the "National Cityers" that when those investments turn sour, investment banks will fob them off onto the public. The Volcker Rule attempted to address proprietary trading in detail. However, investment banks are throwing up a myriad of challenges to the Volcker Rule, including the fact that it disallows legitimate market-making and risk-management activities. It would be less cumbersome to use Glass-Steagall as the starting point for financial reform, and modify it. Volcker's legacy as Fed Chairman was that he never "wanted" or "needed," so he could not be co-opted by politicians or Wall Street. The fact that Volcker "needs" to have his name attached to a financial reform bill instead of recommending a return to Glass-Steagall is evidence that he has already been co-opted. That said, commercial banks and investment banks should also be prohibited from making loans to companies – hedge funds for instance – that engage in proprietary trading. If lawmakers prohibit banks from trading for their own accounts and then to allow them to lend to those who do, the banks would still be exposed to the risks of speculative trading.

Does the Risk Ever Go Away?

Goldman shut down its proprietary trading desk in response to the Dodd-Frank Act. KKR then hired a nine-person team from Goldman's former proprietary trading unit, led by Bob Howard; KKR expected to raise money from outside investors for a hedge fund to be run by the new unit. If banks were to lend to such a hedge fund, it would still expose its depositors to the whims of speculators and create the same risk within the financial system that Goldman did. Loans against securities are nothing more than margin loans. When banks make margin loans to individuals, those individuals' personal assets are at stake when the value of the securities falls below the loan value. However, based upon their legal structures, hedge funds have limited liability when it comes to losses. A bank's sole recourse in its loans to hedge funds – officially known as "prime broking" – is from the value of the securities it lends against; this calls into question who the ultimate guarantor is. When those loans turn sour, the hedge fund and its partners will walk away and leave the lender and its depositors holding the bag.

Real Estate Investing

Investment banks should be barred from investing in commercial real estate. We know from the recent crisis that firms like Lehman and Morgan Stanley were not "investing," but rather "paying what the last sucker paid." When their real estate investments went belly-up, they turned to the government for a bailout or received investments from third parties backed by a government guarantee. These firms were the de facto real estate investment arms of the federal government, and their investing activities fueled the bubble in commercial real estate. If bankers want to invest their personal money into real estate, then they should be allowed to. But lawmakers should prohibit firms that enjoy a protected status to be the vehicle for such real estate speculation.

The Conspirators of the Financial Crisis – "Joe Jett" Them

The mullets, Ponzi schemers and insider traders will define the past decade of greed, corruption and profligacy. Unfortunately, it will also be defined by the dearth of people arrested for those misdeeds. The media and regulators have offered up a plethora of excuses why the bankers who orchestrated the crisis have not been placed in handcuffs. They claim that traditional fraud cases where crooks use deceit to steal from their victims do not apply to the bankers. U.S. Attorney for the Southern District of New York, Preet Bharara, has become a media darling for his high-profile indictments of the Galleon insider trading ring, amongst others. However, Bharara, the so-called "Sheriff of Wall Street," has been inept in bringing similar indictments against investment bankers, serving as de facto proof that bankers are too politically connected to bring down. "'The civil charges that should be brought against Wall Street are there screaming out to be brought,' former New York governor and attorney general Eliot Spitzer said on CNN. 'And the fact that it hasn't been done yet is really staggering.'"[1] For clues on where to look for charges, start here:

Sarbanes-Oxley

The Sarbanes-Oxley Act (Sarbanes) of 2002 was enacted after corporate scandals surfaced at Enron, WorldCom, Tyco and Adelphia Cable in the early 2000s. Sarbanes requires corporate officers to attest to the accuracy of their companies' financial statements. However, there is evidence that executives hid their companies' true financial conditions during the crisis. Lehman filed for bankruptcy on September 15, 2008, mere weeks after issuing its quarterly financial statements. Those statements never mentioned that Lehman's inability to operate as a going concern was an imminent risk. In fact, it issued rosy financial statements earlier than expected in order to assuage investors. In early 2007 the National Cityers attested to the accuracy of their financial statements. Yet, behind the scenes, they knew the billions in MBS they held were grossly overvalued, and devised a ruse to fob them off on unsuspecting clients. What these firms knew about the losses embedded in their MBS portfolios has never been ascertained by regulators. Not coincidentally, corporate America has tried to do away with Sarbanes, arguing that its costs far outweigh its benefits.

Fraudulent Conveyance

In lending there is a legal term known as "fraudulent conveyance," which describes a scheme where a company's equityholders pay themselves dividends at the expense of bondholders. If such payouts to management or shareholders are considered excessive enough that it renders a company unable to pay debtholders, the debtholders can file suit. Wall Street firms paid themselves hundreds of billions in compensation over the past decade. Oftentimes employee compensation was greater than profits; the lion's share of those payouts should have squirreled away to cover future losses from proprietary trading or busted real estate investments. When the losses materialized, short-term and long-term debtholders had to stand in line to be repaid, if at all. For example, the creditors of real estate developers, Opus Corp., filed suit in 2010, claiming that the parent company siphoned millions from its operating subsidiary, rendering it unable to repay creditors. "The suit argues that the parent should return nearly $150 million in dividends received from Opus West between 2006 and 2008 because the company was at the time insolvent. As early as 2005, Opus West was struggling to meet its loan requirements . . . Distributing funds to the parent 'created, exacerbated and sustained Opus West's crippled cash position.'"[2]

Undue Enrichment ("Joe Jett Rule")

In a blow to authorities attempting to prosecute white-collar crime, in April 2010 the Supreme Court ruled that prosecutors were too aggressive in arguing that Enron's Jeffrey Skilling deprived others of his "honest services." Skilling's use of accounting mechanics to hide billions of debt off Enron's balance sheet gave rise to the argument that he deprived shareholders, bondholders and employees of his honest services. It also determined that the "honest services" law should be applied only to clear evidence of bribes and kickbacks. The legal community predicted the ruling would remove a key tool to fight white-collar crime. However, the Skilling case was not the best example for the wrongdoing during the crisis – for the most relevant legal precedent, one must revisit the Joseph Jett case. GE charged Jett with fraud, undue enrichment, and breach of duty after the Kidder fiasco. According to Jett, they pretty much had him by the short hairs: "They claimed that they would prove me guilty of fraud; but even if the panelists did not believe me to be guilty of fraud, they should at least find me guilty of undue enrichment. Undue enrichment meant that the money that I had been paid, I had not earned. The General Electric attorneys also claimed that even if the panelist did not find me guilty of undue enrichment; they should at least find me guilty of disloyalty. After all, Kidder Peabody no longer existed and I, in their opinion, was the primary cause of its demise."[3] GE's attorneys argued that Jett was both fraudulent and disloyal and demanded that he repay $82 million in compensation and penalties.

The NASD arbitrators exonerated Jett on the charges of fraud, undue enrichment and disloyalty, and required Kidder to return Jett's $5 million in bonuses. The SEC case was heard by a newly appointed judge, Carol Fox Foelak. She found Jett innocent of securities fraud, yet guilty of "intent" to defraud Kidder. Though Jett had told Kidder up front about his trading strategy, Fox Foelak argued that Jett knew his colleagues did not understand the profit implications of what he was saying. The accounting system that tracked Jett's trades and recorded his profits was inaccurate. His failure to bring it to the attention of his superiors exploited their ignorance and represented his intent to defraud. She ordered him to disgorge $8.2 million in profits and fined him an additional $200,000. Fox Foelak's decision had the same impact as GE's "undue enrichment" argument. Of the four investment banks I studied earlier – Bear, Lehman, Goldman and Morgan Stanley – compensation and benefits over the four and a half to five years leading up to the crisis was approximately $184 billion. Instead of clawing back bonuses to cover future losses, these firms lobbied the government for a taxpayer bailout. Collectively they did not turn a profit leading up to the crisis. The Joe Jett case represents legal precedent for a disgorgement of their compensation.

Neutron Jack, Gary Lynch and Fox Foelak
The government's inability to bring investment bankers to justice may mean the wrong people are assigned to the task. Investment banks have gotten so powerful that they are now countries unto themselves. They are politically entrenched, have a war chest available for lobbying and public relations efforts, and have co-opted regulators and elected officials with offers of future employment. Mary Shapiro and Preet Bharara need to be replaced with those with a passion for prosecuting wrongdoing, and proven a track record of success. After all, if you want to bring charges against individuals for huge trading losses, you don't need a reason. All you need are Neutron Jack, Gary Lynch and Carol Fox Foelak.

Revisit the Joseph Cassano Ruling
Despite having caused losses that contributed to AIG's $182 billion bailout, Joseph Cassano avoided fraud, criminal and civil charges. The SEC investigated whether Mr. Cassano misled investors concerning AIG's mortgage losses; it found that Cassano made key disclosures to investors about the mortgage losses

sufficient enough to end the investigation with no charges. However, what disclosures did Cassano make to AIG? His unit sold credit default swaps with features that put AIG at risk for (i) defaults of the underlying CDO securities, (ii) downgrades of the underlying CDO securities' debt ratings, and (iii) downgrades of AIG's debt rating. Yet, Cassano's unit only included the cost of defaults for the CDOs in the price of the swaps. The $300 million income earned by Cassano represents undue enrichment. If he did not disclose to AIG that the pricing for the credit default swaps did not include features for collateral calls from certain debt downgrades, then that represents intent to defraud his employer, similar to the Jett ruling. It is almost criminal that the SEC and the Justice Department have not pursued this angle.

Banks Too Big to Fail? Then Make Them Smaller

The theory that interstate banking laws put the U.S. at a disadvantage to global competitors has been proven wrong. Regulators allowed banks to enjoy the benefits of additional size and scale; however, they merely led to bigger bets, bigger losses and larger taxpayer bailouts. Except during this crisis, there were no healthy banks to buy up the insolvent ones like there were in the early 1990s. To make the case for bailouts, the government invoked the "too big to fail" argument. It in turn begs the question, "Why not make then smaller and return to interstate banking?" A drawback of interstate banking was that it gave banks in large urban areas like New York, Los Angeles and Chicago so-called "money center banks" – a distinct advantage over banks in less populous areas. This time the government should consider "interregional banking." For instance, if Virginia, Maryland and Washington, D.C. were considered an entire region, banks in that region would not be disadvantaged in comparison to banks located in money centers. That said, global banking has not worked and the bad decision-making of these behemoths has caused them to decline in size anyway. The following chart displays the largest financial institutions based on market capitalization in 1999 and 2009. In 1999, 11 U.S. banks were among the 20 largest banks in the world; three were in the top five. Ten years later, due to billions in losses on commercial real estate, MBS and LBO loans, by 2009 only three U.S. banks were in the top 20 and one in the top five.

Top 20 Financial Institutions Based on Market Capitalization				
	1999	Country	2009	Country
1	Citigroup	U.S.	Indl & Commercial Bank	China
2	Bank of America	U.S.	China Construction	China
3	HSBC	U.K.	Bank of China	China
4	Lloyds TSB	U.K.	HSBC	U.K.
5	Fannie Mae	U.S.	JP MorganChase	U.S.
6	Bank One	U.S.	Mitsubishi UFJ	Japan
7	Wells Fargo	U.S.	Banco Santander	Spain
8	UBS	Switz	Goldman Sachs	U.S.
9	Bank of Tokyo	Japan	Wells Fargo	U.S.
10	Chase	U.S.	Bank of Communications	China
11	Morgan Stanley	U.S.	Royal Bank Canada	Canada
12	Credit Suisse	Switz	China Merchants Bank	China
13	Barclays	U.K.	Westpac Banking	Aus
14	First Union	U.S.	BNP Paribas	France
15	Charles Schwab	U.S.	Itau Unibanko	Brazil
16	Freddie Mac	U.S.	Toronto Dominion	Canada
17	Nat'l Westminster	U.K.	Commonwealth Bank	Australia
18	Banco Santander	Spain	Bradesco	Brazil
19	Sumitomo Bank	Japan	Intesa San Paolo	Italy
20	Goldman Sachs	U.S.	Credit Suisse	Switz

Source: "The Decade of Global Banks," http://www.ft.com, March 22, 2009

U.S. Goes Dating in Northern Africa

In 2011 the world witnessed civil unrest that overthrew the governments of Egypt and Libya, and sparked the beginning of the end to President Bashar al-Assad's reign in Syria. In January 2011, protests actually broke out across parts of Northern Africa – Tunisia, Yemen, Jordan, Algeria and Egypt. The uprisings in Tunisia were so strong that they forced President Zine al-Abdine Ben Ali to flee the country by mid-January. Egyptian activists planned a protest in Cairo to coincide with Police Day, a national holiday held every January 25th to honor police. Just a year earlier Khaled Said, a young man from Alexandria, had been beaten to death by police and portrayed as an outlaw. To activists, Said was a symbol of their frustrations against the establishment. A Facebook page called "We Are All Khaled Said" became a conduit for them to organize and vent their frustrations. The combination of Said's beating, November 2010 elections that the populace viewed as rigged by Hosni Mubarak's ruling Democratic Party, and the success of uprisings in Tunisia caused millions of Egyptians to flock to the streets in protest. The government blamed social media and shut down Twitter, Facebook and eventually, the entire Internet. Yet the country's appearance of being a corrupt police state where a few select insiders thrived, while 80 million residents lived in poverty, proved too much. By February 2011, Mubarak conceded that he was not the agent of change the populace needed and agreed not to run for reelection in September.

The success of Egyptian uprisings spilled over into Libya in the form of peaceful demonstrations. Protestors gained worldwide sympathy after Libya's leader, Muammar Gaddafi, tried to quell the demonstrations through violence. Libyans put together a seemingly makeshift army of rebel forces to seize upon the region's frustration with dictatorial rule. The rebel army turned out to be extremely well organized however. The U.S. military and NATO intervened with targeted air strikes against Gaddafi forces. This was aimed at saving thousands of innocent civilians. Yet the air strikes actually turned the tide in the conflict as rebel forces overtook the capital of Tripoli in August. In October, a Gaddafi on the run was captured and killed in Sirte, the city of his birth, marking an official end to his 42-year regime. But as they say when deciding to switch dating partners, "You know what you've got, but you don't know what you're going to get." After regime changes in Tunisia, Egypt, Libya and potentially Syria, the leadership the world will have to contend with in those areas is totally unknown.

Be the Change You Would Like to See

During the U.S. presidential election campaigns a voter asked Herman Cain, a leading Republican candidate at the time, "What is going on in Libya?" Cain totally flubbed the question, serving as evidence of his lack of foreign relations expertise; his faux pas later went viral on YouTube. The textbook answer was, "The regime change in Libya provided both opportunities and risks. The people-led revolt demonstrated their distaste for dictatorial rule and a desire for a more participatory form of government. But it was up to the U.S. to help Libyans form a government based on democracy and consistent with our moral values. In the short-term the U.S. could help (i) Libya gain access to billions of the country's frozen assets, and (ii) ensure that the country's disparate fighting forces band together post-regime, in order to avoid the mercenary tendencies that befell Afghan forces after the Afghan-Russian conflict of the 1980s." The Obama Administration offered Libya millions in aid to convert to a democratic government but it was refused. Mahatma Gandhi was once quoted as saying "We must be the change that we would like to see." Given that backdrop, the real answer was, "The challenge for the U.S. is less about preaching the ideals of democracy in Libya and other foreign places, but in being an example for other countries to follow. We must first prove that democracy can work in our own country by reigning in the oligarchs, retrieving the hundreds of billions pilfered by the new-age robber barons, and removing the black tax – for starters. The U.S. is currently the laughingstock of the world. The biggest failure of the Bush and Obama administrations was not bringing the Wall Street robber barons to justice; there is clear legal precedence for what occurred. It is not happenstance that bankers have not been placed in handcuffs and their bonuses clawed back. They have co-opted politicians and lawmakers – the rest of the world sees this. If the U.S. were an example of the 'change we'd like to see,' we would spend less time at the bargaining table and less money in bribes to convince others of our way of life."

China – "Arguing With Our Parents?"

My friends and I were driving through the Chinatown section of D.C. one afternoon when I noticed an African-American man crossing the street with beef and broccoli falling out of his mouth. I pointed out to my boys, "You notice how every time you come through Chinatown there are nothing but black people, but you never see a Chinese person walking out of a soul food restaurant? It seems like the flow of capital is always one way." Unbeknownst to me, I had just explained China's ancient philosophy on trade – "If we sell to you, but never buy from you our country can become rich." In 1793 when Britain sent envoy, Lord George McCartney, to engage China in trade negotiations, China was the world's most populous and prosperous country. McCartney plied China's Qianlong ruling party with gifts, and offered it the opportunity to set up a British embassy. However, China's only use for the British was as ready customers for its tea, China's most popular product.

> Less than a half century later, tea had become Britain's beverage of choice with an annual consumption of 12 million pounds per year. By 1785, Britain was importing 15 million pounds per year from China . . . Although China did buy some British manufactured and raw goods, tea was a much bigger seller in Britain than British calico, iron, and tin were in China. Between 1710 and 1759, the imbalance in trade was staggering, draining Britain of silver, the only form of payment China accepted for its coveted tea. During this period Britain paid out £26 million in silver to China, but sold it only £9 million in goods.[4]

The only solution to Britain's trade imbalance was to (i) find an alternative to Chinese tea and (ii) find a product that China would buy from Britain and pay for in silver. To solve its first problem, Britain stole China's tea-making process and used it to build a tea industry in India. For the solution to its second problem, Britain bombarded China with opium. The first shipment arrived in 1782. By the 1830s China was addicted to the drug; in 1839 the British were smuggling in about 39,000 chests of opium each year – representing $25 million.[5] Its opium sales reversed the balance of trade in Britain's favor and created a large outflow of silver from China.

Lord and Vassal

Other historical events that may have shaped China's present-day political and economic policies are the opening up of China for financial interests, and periods of hyperinflation. The British saw China as a region important to expanding its financial enterprise. Despite Britain's inroads from opium sales, China's closed-door policy prevented it from doing more business there. Its solution – start a war with China in order to colonize it. The so-called "Opium War" lasted from 1840 to 1842 and resulted in Chinese defeat and humiliation. In a November 1841 speech, John Quincy Adams blamed China for the dispute: "The cause of war is the kowtow! – the arrogant and insupportable pretension of China that she will hold commercial intercourse with the rest of mankind, not upon terms of equal reciprocity, but upon the insulting and degrading terms of lord and vassal."[6] The Treaty of Nanking signed between China and Britain marked the end of the war. The treaty's provisions required China to, among other things, cede Hong Kong to Britain and open its ports to foreign trade. Britain Russia, Japan, France, Germany and the U.S. subsequently carved up China for their own commercial interests. The foreign capital entering China led to land speculation and hyperinflation, which priced out the local Chinese from owning land.

By the mid-1940s China was marred in a civil war between the Kuomintang (KMT), led by Chiang Kai-shek, and the communist movement led by Mao Zedong. The KMT's decided advantage in terms of weaponry was muted by the communists' use of guerrilla warfare. Another advantage for the communists was one of economics. China had printed money to finance the Sino-Japanese war (1931-1945), which led to hyperinflation. KMT's inability to contain that inflation made it look inept, and led to popular support for Mao. By 1949 the communists controlled almost all of mainland China, and Chiang Kai-shek and his forces fled to Taiwan. Present-day China has the following strengths that will make it a formidable superpower, and vulnerabilities that could upend its global influence.

Strengths

Excellent Negotiators

The Chinese have always been excellent traders, even before the takeover of Mao Zedong; they are particularly adept at playing competing interests against one another. Hence, they drew the ire of the House of Morgan in the 1920s: "China was unpopular on Wall Street and in the City. It was prone to default and adept at playing foreign bankers against each other. Ever since the abortive China consortium under Woodrow Wilson, Lamont had looked upon the Chinese as wily and duplicitous. He perceived them less as victims of foreign intruders than as two-face opportunists."[7] By the 1980s China had graduated to negotiating with multinationals in their quest for access to China's cheap labor. Having learned from the imperialist nature of the British, today government officials require that multinationals enter into JVs with local firms prior to setting up manufacturing facilities in China. Chinese officials then engage in a competitive negotiating process to secure the best JV terms. Years after striking a deal, the multinational oftentimes has to compete with its former JV partner, armed with the multinational's technology and manufacturing know-how – "China is the world's fastest-growing market, and in return for access the country frequently demands technology or other know-how. China then absorbs that technology and uses it to battle global competitors, selling products heavily subsidized by China. That has happened in a range of industries, including autos, electronics and energy. Siemens now competes internationally against Chinese high-speed rail companies that sell products partly based on technology gleaned from an earlier joint venture with the German firm."[8]

Consider the case of global investment banks. The Chinese government requires foreign firms operating in its capital markets industry to do business through a licensed JV, of which it can own no more than 33%. To keep its license, a foreign firm must employ a minimum of four "sponsors" – bankers licensed by China to execute stock and bond offerings. At least two sponsors are required on every offering; the limited number of qualified sponsors allows China to control the flow of public offerings and limit fraud, since sponsors are personally liable. Despite investing millions and sharing their technical know-how, foreign bankers have made limited inroads into the $68 billion Chinese IPO market – the world's largest in 2010. At May 2010, China's top ten book runners were all Chinese firms with a combined market share of 56.7%, leaving other domestic firms and a host of foreigners fighting over the scraps.[9]

Or imagine the looks on the faces of GM executives when Shanghai Automotive Industrial Corp. (SAIC), its Chinese JV partner, contacted the U.S. in September 2010 about acquiring an ownership interest in GM. GM entered a business relationship with SAIC in 1997; however, SAIC would later use GM's technology and manufacturing know-how against it:

> SAIC Motor Corporation (SAIC), China's largest automaker, has reached out to General Motors (GM) to explore the prospect of taking an ownership interest in the "single digits." SAIC has built autos with GM in China for over 13 years. The U.S. government currently owns a 61% stake in GM after making a $50 billion TARP investment. GM's CEO, Dan Akerson, is keen on repaying taxpayers and removing the stigma of being 'Government Motors.' The U.S. Treasury Department is planning to sell an equity stake via an initial public offering this fall, hopefully in the range of $8 - $10 billion.[10]

Having learned from missteps in China, Western firms have taken pains to better protect their technology. Such tactics range from not sharing their most sensitive intellectual property, to partnering with smaller firms less able to become a rival.[11] Consultants advise clients not to include their entire manufacturing process within their Chinese JV – manufacture some parts in China and other parts elsewhere. Companies are also encrypting the most crucial areas of their intellectual property as well.

Playing Countries Against Each Other

Recently, China has been the fastest growing economy in the world. To fuel that growth, it needs access to raw materials like oil, coal and steel. The country's formula has been to acquire natural resources in Africa and marketing know-how in the U.S. In 2005, China's National Offshore Oil Company (CNOOC) sent ripples through the U.S. oil industry when it attempted to acquire Unocal. However, CNOOC was rebuffed due to concerns over national defense. Undaunted, China simply found those countries – Canada, France and Venezuela – willing to bargain away their natural resources. Over time, the U.S. acquiesced in allowing China to invest in its domestic energy sectors. In 2010 China Investment Corporation (CIC) was part of a 20-member consortium that invested approximately $200 million in Chesapeake Energy, an Oklahoma-based power company. Also in 2010 CNOOC invested about $1.5 billion in AES Corporation, a Virginia-based power company, retaining a 15% equity stake.

While China and President Obama have had discussions about Chinese investments in U.S infrastructure, no formal arrangements have been made. In fact, formal discussions may be untenable during an election year. Meanwhile, CIC has made overtures to the U.K. about its infrastructure investment needs. CIC does not merely want to play the role of contractor in such arrangements; it is interested in being a developer, investor and operator of these projects. The outcome of its negotiations with the U.K. could give it leverage in future negotiations with the next U.S. president. In 2010 the U.S. pushed for trade sanctions against Iran in reaction to its nuclear weapons program; it also reached out to China in its efforts to punish Iran financially. Iran is the third largest supplier of oil to China after Saudi Arabia and Angola. Iran also has some of the world's largest oil and gas reserves, yet lacks the capital and know-how to fully develop those reserves. It has threatened to kick out companies unwilling to make capital investment and offer expertise to help it explore its reserves. And therein lays the opportunity for China. If Western countries eliminate themselves from strategic partnerships in the region due to trade sanctions, China could become Iran's preferred partner. China Petrochemical, CNOOC and China National Petroleum Corp. already have a foothold in Iran. In reaction to claims from the International Atomic Energy Agency that Iran has operated secretive research programs to develop nuclear capabilities, in January 2012 the U.S. asked China and other countries to drastically reduce the amount of oil it buys from Iran. Signaling China's divergent interests, Chinese Vice Foreign Minister Zhai Jun rejected the sanctions: "'Iran is an extremely big oil supplier to China, and we hope that China's oil imports won't be affected, because this is needed for our development . . . We oppose applying pressure and sanctions, because these approaches won't solve problems.'"[12]

What China Cannot Acquire . . . It Steals

So-called "piracy" is rampant in China, particularly copyright infringement for software and music. Lawsuits by software companies are expected to increase to combat the practice. The Business Software Association (BSA), a business advocacy group, estimated that 78% of the PC software installed in China in 2010 was pirated, down from 82% in 2006.[13] According to Steve Ballmer, CEO of Microsoft, though PC sales in China and the U.S. are similar, Microsoft's revenue in China is only 5% of what it receives in the U.S. due to piracy. He also noted that Microsoft's revenue in the Netherlands is more than what it generates in China, yet the populations are 1.3 billion and 17 million in China and the Netherlands, respectively. Despite the efforts of U.S. software companies, there does not appear to be an end to piracy in China anytime soon. As evidence of the Chinese government's cavalier attitude toward piracy, government agencies for years have carried pirated software on their own computers. Furthermore, after assurances to end the use of pirated software, these government agencies have consistently pushed back suggested timetables.

Cheap Labor

China has a low-cost labor advantage over the U.S., making it a big draw for multinationals looking to increase profit margins. Multinationals' hiring abroad, while reducing their domestic workforces, has been a point of contention during the financial crisis. "The companies cut their work forces in the U.S. by 2.9 million during the 2000s while increasing employment overseas by 2.4 million, new data from the U.S. Commerce Department show. That's a big switch from the 1990s, when they added jobs everywhere: 4.4 million in the U.S. and 2.7 million abroad . . . The trend highlights the growing importance of other economies, particularly in rapidly growing Asia, to big U.S. businesses such as General Electric Co., Caterpillar Inc., Microsoft Corp. and Wal-Mart Stores Inc."[14] In July 2011 GE was sharply criticized when it announced it was moving its X-ray unit to China. GE claimed it did not expect to lose any U.S. jobs at the unit, which employed about 120 people. However, implicit in the move was that future jobs within the fast-growing Chinese healthcare market would come at the expense of U.S. workers. Though the gap in the cost to manufacture in China versus the U.S. is slowly closing, for the time being, multinationals are still flocking to China. For instance, in 2010 the world's largest makers of CT scanners – GE, Siemens AG, Royal Phillips Electronics – decided to make the Chinese market a priority. Over the next five years China expects to build tens of thousands of hospitals, creating demand for diagnostic imaging machines. GE's healthcare workforce in China measures over 4,000 and it expects to expand that to maintain its number one market share in Chinese medical imaging devices. Meanwhile, Siemens and Royal Phillips expect to grow their operations on pace, if not faster, than expected market growth.

One Billion Consumers

For multinationals to continue to grow revenues, they must expand beyond their domestic markets, which may already be saturated. China's population of 1.3 billion people represents the Holy Grail for those capitalistic intentions. China is still a largely untapped marketplace; the percentage of its population that is actually ready to consume the toaster ovens, refrigerators, and smartphones multinationals are prepared to sell them is uncertain. Experts peg China's "true" consumer market at around 250 million people; not debatable is that in order to tap into China's potential, multinationals must have manufacturing facilities nearby. "For international multinationals, technology transfer has long been the quid pro quo of landing deals in China. Foreign businesses have meekly gone along with this arrangement because they assume that since the biggest markets in everything from wind turbines to mobile phones have moved to China, you have to be in the country if you want to be No. 1, No. 2 or even No. 3 in the world. Without scale, global businesses can't be industry leaders, they can't remain on the frontiers of technology, and they become vulnerable to competition. But scale means that you've got to be in China."[15] But at what cost? On the front-end, multinationals will invest in manufacturing plants and employee training, and give away valuable intellectual property. Whether they can actually reach 1.3 billion consumers and protect their domestic markets from the competition posed by their Chinese JVs partners, remains to be seen.

Willingness to Make Hard Decisions

China, having learned from the hyperinflation and land speculation of its past, has taken several measures to guard against real estate speculation and the "hot money" from foreigners that causes it. While the U.S. ignored the speculation that created its property bubble, China has taken the following measures:

301

Cracking Down on Real Estate Speculation

In 2010 China raised key interest rates to make it more expensive for businesses and borrow, and to cool the bubble in real estate. The rate increases sparked a world-wide sell off in stocks. China was seen as a key engine of growth for the global economy and investors expected rising rates would cause a drag on its growth, capital expenditures and global profits. In addition, China reported "hot money" inflows of about $36 billion in 2010. Fearing that the rapid movements of foreign capital into the country would lead to speculation, and unsustainable real estate prices, China began strictly monitoring the inflows. It took other measures, ranging from disallowing foreign developers to profit from the sale of land and real estate, to prohibiting foreign developers from investing in the property sector at all. It employed local authorities, the Ministry of Commerce, the Ministry of Land and Resources and the State Administration of Foreign Exchange to aid in the crackdown on hot money inflows.

Government officials saw skyrocketing real estate prices and lack of affordable housing as a catalyst for social unrest. To take the air out of its property bubble they (i) raised down payment requirements for purchases of second homes to 50%, (ii) prohibited banks from issuing loans for the purchases of third homes, (iii) introduced property taxes in some cities, (iv) made plans to build affordable housing, and (v) curbed advance sales by developers designed to add to the frothiness of the property market. "The measures come amid increasing concerns that Chinese property prices are in an unsustainable bubble . . . They follow data last week showing property prices in 70 of China's large and medium-size cities rose 11.7% in March from a year earlier, the fastest pace since China began issuing the data in July 2005. The ministry [Ministry of Housing and Urban-Rural Development] said in a notice on its Web site that developers aren't allowed to receive down payments for unfinished properties unless they have obtained government approval to pre-sell properties . . . The ministry said it has discovered that some developers were hoarding property to illegally push up prices, and added it will punish developers that don't follow the rules or that manipulate the pre-sale process to create the illusion of tight supply."[16]

They Know Us Better Than We Know Them

There is a war going on in the global marketplace and China knows us better than we know them. Oft forgotten is the fact that Pol Pot (Vietnam) and Fidel Castro were both educated in the U.S. and well versed in our culture – and look at how our conflicts with them turned out. China is sending its best and brightest to be educated in the U.S. to master our Western-style business practices. Due to China's thriving economy, its students are attending American business schools in droves. "Graduate schools saw a 21% increase in Chinese applicants from the last school year and a 23% increase in admissions offers, for students slated to start this fall, according to a study by the Council of Graduate Schools. It is the sixth year in a row of double-digit percentage increase for Chinese students . . . More middle-class Chinese professionals can afford U.S. tuition these days . . . Meanwhile, American students may have more difficulty finding the funds to cover tuition given the troubled economy."[17]

Vulnerabilities

Hidden Debt

Despite China's measures to rein in inflation and property speculation, the emergence of "shadow loans" poses a serious threat to its economy. Shadow lenders are unregulated and charge exorbitant interest rates – as high as 70% – with onerous terms. Smaller companies lacking access to traditional debt markets are the typical targets of shadow lenders and they oftentimes go out of business, unable to repay the debt. "Since April, nearly 100 factory owners in Wenzhou alone have fled the city after failing to repay high-interest debt, according state media reports. Such distress, economists warn, could spell bigger problems for China's vast banking sector and the economy at large, potentially leading to defaults even on bank loans at normal rates. That could cause banks to cut credit lines to sound businesses and their suppliers."[18] The capital for shadow loans comes from high-net-worth individuals or from the actual banks themselves. Banks also move loans off their books by repackaging them into sovereign wealth funds and selling them to investors. However, the banks are responsible for making investors whole if the actual returns on the funds fall short of stated returns.

Shadow loans are designed to circumvent government curbs on lending; whether officially on the banks' books or not, the loans still exist. The IMF estimated that loans, on and off banks' books, reached an alarming 173% of China's GDP at the end of June 2011. According to UBS, credit extended through banks, but moved off their balance sheets, stood at roughly 12 trillion yuan ($1.9 trillion). Meanwhile, total loans outstanding, both on and off banks' balance sheets, was 55.7 trillion yuan as of August 2011.[19] Exacerbating the problem is that China does not allow locals to invest abroad, forcing billions of capital to create bubbles from chasing domestic opportunities in property and sovereign wealth funds. Runaway speculation could lead to years of deflation when those asset bubbles burst – making China the next Japan. Japan's debt to GDP was around 200% before its economy went into a death spiral. With $3 trillion in currency reserves, China probably has the necessary capital to bail out the banks if need be. However, if bailouts are necessary, China may be unable to avoid an economic "hard landing."

Social Unrest

With progress has come social unrest among those left out of China's industrial revolution, disillusioned by the supposed higher quality of life offered by market reforms, or priced out by inflationary pressures and land grabs by developers. Clashes with police, local authorities and employers seem to be commonplace occurrences.

Worker Anger Over Industrial Reform

The domestic steel industry has been core to China's identity since the days of Mao Zedong; Mao saw it as key to China's ability to thrive as a communist nation. China boasts the world's largest steel industry, yet it is highly fragmented with over 800 producers and no one company controlling more than 5% of output. Government subsidies allow Chinese steelmakers to be the low-cost producer, drawing accusations of "dumping" from U.S. competitors. Consolidation is seen as paramount to the success of the highly subsidized industry. Experts believe that economies of scale gained through consolidation would allow the 10 or so remaining producers to negotiate better prices for raw materials, rationalize headcount, and produce efficiencies that would pay for necessary capital improvements. In 2005 the government sold a 36% interest in Tonghua Iron & Steel Group to privately held Jianlong Group. Jianlong's goal was to turn Tonghua into a "best in class" producer, expand capacity and wring out costs. However, government-appointed managers blocked Jianlong's ambitions.

In July 2009 Jianlong assigned one of its fast-rising managers, Chen Guojun, as general manager of Tonghua. Rumors circulated among Tonghua employees that Jianlong was going to take control of the steel company and lay off workers. On his first day as general manager, Mr. Chen held a meeting with Tonghua executives. However, the meeting still did not assuage employees' fears of losing their jobs and pensions from a Jianlong takeover. That afternoon, employees confronted Mr. Chen and beat him severely. They blocked the streets and prevented police and paramedics from providing assistance to Mr. Chen, as well.[20] With Mr. Chen still missing and Jianlong executives fearing the worst, local government officials made a public announcement that Jianlong's planned takeover had been scrapped. Nonetheless, by the time the rioting had subsided and authorities were able to reach Mr. Chen, the father of two was already dead. The Tonghua incident has since become a symbol of worker resistance to Chinese industrial reform. Previously, only the benefits of government and companies were taken into account amid corporate restructurings. The Tonghua incident has forced the government and corporations to consider the well-being of employees as well.

Civil Unrest

During a four-week period from mid-May to mid-June 2011, China experienced a wave of violent unrest that required riot police to quell. Though the protests were not part of a coordinated effort like those in Egypt or Libya, they all involved citizens who felt denied rights expected in an industrialized nation. Each protest was triggered by a specific flashpoint – a pregnant street vendor assaulted by security or the death of a man in police custody who had challenged a land deal. Each of the protests resulted in violent clashes with police, local authorities or employers – all symbols of repression. Continuing with its tradition of saving its most controversial arrests and verdicts for Christmas, in late December 2011 Chinese officials sentenced long-time dissident Chen Xi, and blogger, Chen Wei, to prison terms of 10 years and nine years, respectively; both were accused of inciting subversion. Chen Xi's arrest surrounds over 30 political essays he published online, criticizing the government. The 57-year-old was jailed for supporting the student riots at Tiananmen Square in 1989 and served a second prison stint from 1996 to 2005. Chen Wei, who also participated in the Tiananmen Square incident, was sentenced to nine years on December 23rd for essays calling for freedom of speech and political reform. The Christmas verdicts represent China's attempt to avoid the spotlight while the Western media is preoccupied with the holidays.

No stranger to civil unrest, China has experienced tens of thousands of demonstrations each year; a Tsinghua University sociologist estimated that over 180,000 large-scale protests took place in China in 2010.[21] Most of the anti-government demonstrations have taken place in rural areas where farmers have had their land taken away by developers or government officials. Yet the wave of unrest described in May and June of 2011 took place in urban areas, and demonstrated the government's inability to control urban populations through "soft" means like Internet censorship, surveillance, and cyber-spying. Such measures are designed to limit the populous' ability to vent, plan or share information about protests. And when "soft measures" do not work, China can always resort to crackdowns and propaganda. "It is no longer controversial in ruling circles to acknowledge that the Chinese Communist Party and 'the masses' have drifted apart . . . But it's probably more accurate to say the Party is paralyzed by fear, with economic and political reform dead in the water. Observers of the Party's remarkable recovery after the 1989 Tiananmen Massacre have attributed it to the leadership's ability to adapt to changing circumstances with creative policies. That ability is no longer in evidence. The current leadership is leaning heavily on two old standbys: crackdowns and propaganda."[22]

Another Shady Land Deal . . . Another String of Protests

In September 2011 China experienced an uprising in the fishing village of Wukan after government officials sold a pig farm to a real estate developer. The officials did not share the proceeds of the sale with residents, even though the farm was owned by locals. The incident is not uncommon; of the tens of thousands of disputes in China's countryside each year, about 65% is related to land.[23] The village of 20,000 rebelled in protest of yet another shady land deal. Police cars were destroyed, over 10 officers were injured and five residents detained during clashes with the police. The standoff reached a boiling point in December when Xue Jinbo, one of the detainees, died in police custody. The police said he died of a sudden heart attack but residents said he was beaten to death. Provincial officials investigating the dispute subsequently froze the land deal, removed two government officials involved in the illegal sale, and agreed to investigate the death of Xue Jinbo.

As China's economy has contracted, municipalities are having difficulties repaying government loans or completing unfinished projects as their tax revenue has declined. The only way they can repay their debts is through land sales. In 2009 China channeled its economic stimulus package through local governments and bank loans. Municipalities' borrowing spree in 2009-10 was underpinned by the promise of land sales to repay debts. According to a National Audit Office report published in June 2011, local governments are on the hook for 10.7 trillion yuan ($1.7 trillion), and 2.5 trillion yuan of that is guaranteed by land sales. Falling real estate prices will require municipalities to increase the amount of land sales to repay its debts, creating the potential for more social unrest.[24]

Rising Elderly Population

China's one-child policy has been much talked about because of the gender imbalance it has created due to its bias toward male offspring. Less talked about is how the policy has heavily skewed the country's demographics toward the elderly. According to a report on the Elderly Protection Act by the vice chairman of China's National People's Congress, (i) China had 178 million people over the age of 60 (13.26% of the population), (ii) China's elderly will surpass 200 million in three years and surpass 300 million by 2025, and (iii) by 2042, more than 30% of China's total population will be over age 60.[25] Even more damning is that nearly half of the elderly live by themselves and over 30 million are disabled or partially disabled, leaving much of their caretaking responsibilities to the state. Though China has a social pension system in place, its nursing home facilities, as measured by the number of old-age beds, is well below those of other developed countries. According to the report, China has old-age beds for only 1.8% of the population, compared with the typical 5% to 7% in a developed country and 2% to 3% in a developing country.[26] For help, it has turned to U.S. private equity investors and nursing home operators. Whether the investment in senior housing will generate an acceptable rate of return, remains to be seen. The regulatory framework in China is uncertain, at best. Secondly, China's culture is one where the elderly are cared for by their children; whether they will adopt the senior housing model is untested. To share in the costs and risks, U.S. investors are looking to form JVs with Chinese developers. Nonetheless, China's senior living facilities and social care services require substantial investment, and pose a serious risk to its future economic growth.

Negotiating Posture

In world affairs, China has demonstrated a philosophy of "might makes right." In future dealings with the U.S., expect China to negotiate in this vein.

The Kowtow

China overtook Germany as the world's largest exporter in 2010; in 2011 its trade surplus was $155 billion, down from its 2008 peak of $300 billion. However, its trade surplus with the U.S. increased from $181 billion in 2010 to $202 billion in 2011. The trade imbalance between the two countries was so egregious that at one point, U.S. shipping companies began accumulating empty shipping containers with no place to store them. China would ship goods to the U.S. and since they did not want to buy U.S. goods, they would simply tell us to keep the containers. The cost of shipping an empty container is not much cheaper than shipping a fully loaded one; however, maintaining empty shipping containers are costly, transferring the burden of having to "reposition" them to U.S. companies.

In 2008, China overtook Japan as the largest foreign holder of U.S. treasury securities. Our debtor/creditor relationship has been a symbiotic one – the U.S. needs someone to help finance its wars and bailouts to oligarchs and Wall Street robber barons, and China needs somewhere to invest its trillions in accumulated trade surpluses. "According to the International Monetary Fund (IMF), in 2009, the United States was the world's largest importer of foreign capital (at 38.2% of global total), while China was the largest exporter of capital (24.2%). From FY2001 to FY2010, the amount of U.S. public debt that is privately held grew from $3.3 trillion to $9.0 trillion . . . Of the U.S. public debt that is privately held, more than half is held by foreigners. Many analysts argue that heavy U.S. reliance on foreign savings is not sustainable and may undermine U.S. economic interests over time."[27] Presently, the U.S. treasury market may be the only one large and liquid enough for China to invest the world's largest foreign exchange holdings. However, China has conveyed to the U.S. the need to get its runaway borrowing under control . . . or else. At the 2009 U.S. - China Strategic and Economic Dialogue, a forum where both countries discussed cooperation on the economy, security, climate change and foreign policy, Chinese officials reiterated its concern – "But like a banker visiting an overextended borrower, Chinese economic leaders repeatedly conveyed to their U.S. hosts the importance of managing the U.S. debt."[28] Putting its money where its mouth is, China reduced its holdings of U.S. treasury securities by over $41 billion from October 2010 to October 2011.

Major Foreign Holders of Treasury Securities (in billions)				
	October 2011		October 2010	
Country	Holdings	% of Total	Holdings	% of Total
China	1,134.1	24.4%	1,175.3	26.9%
Japan	979.0	21.0%	873.6	20.0%
U.K.	408.4	8.8%	209.0	4.8%
Oil Exporters	226.2	4.9%	207.8	4.8%
Brazil	209.1	4.5%	183.0	4.2%
Carib Bnkng Ctrs	175.2	3.8%	146.3	3.3%
Taiwan	150.1	3.2%	154.5	3.5%
Switzerland	131.7	2.8%	107.6	2.5%
Hong Kong	110.7	2.4%	135.2	3.1%
Russia	92.1	2.0%	176.3	4.0%
All Others	1,039.7	22.3%	1,004.5	23.0%
Grand Total	4,656.3	100.0%	4,373.1	100.0%

Source: Department of Treasury/Federal Reserve Board, December 15, 2011

From year-end 2002 to month-end June 2010, China's foreign exchange reserves grew from $291 billion to $2.9 trillion. Its holdings of U.S. securities grew from $181 billion to $1.6 trillion during that same period. Its $1.6 trillion in U.S. investments included treasury securities ($1.1 trillion), long-term agency ($0.4 trillion) and other ($0.1 trillion). The fact that China is the source of the U.S.'s largest trade deficit and the country's largest creditor is a long-winded way of saying "China owns the U.S." And when China has a strong negotiating position it will invoke the kowtow, as John Quincy Adams alluded to almost two centuries ago.

Sino-Japanese Fisherman Spat . . . Harbinger of Things to Come

In September 2010 a Chinese fisherman was captured by the Japanese coast guard in disputed waters in the East China Sea; China and Japan engaged in a stare down over the fisherman's release. The incident stirred centuries of animosity between the two countries, and may have foretold how China will settle future international disputes:

> On September 19th Japan extended the detention of Zhan Qixion, captain of a Chinese trawler whose vessel rammed into a Japanese coast-guard patrol boat off of China's Diaoyu Islands on Sept 7. China claims that Qixion was being held 'illegally.' Japan accused the captain of 'obstructing public officers' when they tried to detain him and the incident has led to tensions between the two countries . . . The Diaoyu Islands are a group of disputed and uninhabited islands controlled by Japan since 1895 but also claimed by the Republic of China (Taiwan) and the People's Republic of China (China). The U.S. controlled the islands as part of its occupation of Okinawa from 1945 - 1972. Japan's decision to detain Qixion was a de facto claim of sovereignty over the Diaoyu Islands. However, since Japan's economy is largely dependent upon China, Japanese officials released the captain on Saturday September 25th . . . Whether the recent dispute will set precedence for how China deals with other countries in the region remains to be seen.[29]

When Japan refused to kowtow, China punished it economically. Chinese customs agents began heavy inspections of exports/imports to and from Japan. In mid-September, it blocked exports of rare earth minerals needed in the manufacture of high-tech equipment like hybrid cars, smart phones, computer screens and military equipment. In mid-October it blocked rare earth minerals to Europe and the U.S. At the time, China controlled about 97% of the global supply of rare earths. Its embargo touched off an international manhunt for rare earth deposits and instantly made Molycorp, a publicly-traded rare earth mining company, paramount to America's national security: "China, with the world's largest supply, has been ramping up production over the past two decades, leading to steep price drops that eventually forced the Mountain Pass mine to shut down operations in 2002 . . . Over the last year, however, the Chinese government, which views rare earth as a key element in its move from low-cost producer of cheap manufactured goods to a high-tech powerhouse, has drastically reduced its export quotas, particularly for the heavy rare earths, like terbium and dysprosium. That sent prices through the roof last summer . . . Wanting to capitalize on the rare-earth shortage, Molycorp, backed by $1 billion in private equity from Resource Capital Funds in Denver, began selling rare earths at its California mine in October."[30]

Revisit Healthcare Costs

In November 2011 the Supreme Court agreed to decide if President Obama's healthcare reform bill was constitutional. Healthcare reform has been approved by Congress but struck down by federal judges in Virginia and Florida, mainly because it forces people to buy healthcare insurance. A favorable Supreme Court ruling would represent a significant accomplishment by the Obama Administration. Yet outside of some headline grabbing news flashes, what would the healthcare overhaul really accomplish? The rub for healthcare is that runaway costs are making it unaffordable to average citizens and they continue to be a drag on the federal budget. Putting the entire country into an overpriced product and calling it "Universal Healthcare" sounds nice, but runaway costs will eventually render the country unable to fund it. In addition to the fact that people are living longer and taxing the healthcare system for cosmetic procedures, experts list healthcare's "third-party payment system" and unnecessary treatments as other burdens on the system.

Reward Doctors Based on Productivity

Since doctors are paid per visit, keeping patients coming back can be profitable for them, despite being unprofitable for healthcare providers. "Driving ever increasing health costs is 'more, more, more.' Doctors are paid per procedure or per visit, giving them great incentive to perform marginally effective treatments that cost a lot but make only a slight difference in the long run; patients don't see most of the costs either."[31] The solution may be to grade doctors based on profitability or their ability to keep costs down. A similar concept is employed within the property & casualty industry; insurance agents are ranked and compensated based on profitability of the business they underwrite. Such a ranking would give doctors a disincentive to charge providers for treatments considered "marginally effective."

Reward People for Healthy Habits and Vice Versa

An overlooked reason for spiraling healthcare costs is that as a nation, we do not take good care of ourselves. According to Humana CEO Michael McCallister, "We're becoming an obese nation, leading to diabetes and other chronic illnesses. A lot of medical spending is tied to five chronic illnesses (diabetes, stroke, heart disease, pulmonary conditions, and hypertension), all of which are preventable."[32] The healthcare system does not penalize people for not taking care of themselves. Instead, one's additional costs are borne by the entire healthcare system, and not the individual engaging in unhealthy behavior. The healthcare system's "third-party payment system" also separates the payer from the seller and the buyer, encouraging some people to splurge on healthcare insurance at everyone else's expense. One solution would be to ring fence the five or so preventable chronic diseases and charge people based on how much they burden the system for them. For example, if a healthcare provider considered obesity as the cause of a preventable illness and a consumer refused to lose weight, then that consumer should pay more for healthcare. If consumers had to pay more for not living healthier, it would (i) force them to become more accountable in managing their health risks and (ii) drive down healthcare costs for everyone else.

College Tuitions Spiraling Out of Control . . . Still

Almost four years after the Shock Exchange post on the spiraling cost of college, nothing has been done to stem the crisis. A college education is an inelastic good – despite spiraling costs, students will still attend, and borrow to do so. The amount of outstanding student loans has practically made U.S. graduates indentured servants. The New York Federal Reserve estimates there are $550 billion in outstanding student loans while Fannie and Freddie put the figures closer to $760 billion. Moreover, the figure could top $1 trillion shortly: "A bank heavily involved in the area says there is at least another $111 billion in purely private loans, and with new lending estimated in excess of $112 billion for this year alone, the total amount outstanding will surpass $1 trillion in the not-so-distant future. Critics allege a viciously wasteful circle: the size of the loan pool expands to enable students to pay ever higher fees to schools whose costs expand because money is coming their way."[33] According to the Department of Education, those student loans had a default rate of 8.8% for fiscal year-end September 2010, as compared to 7.0% the previous year. President Obama has offered to lower interest rates on student loans – the equivalent of lowering financing costs on an already overpriced product.

Arms Race

Apparently there is a method to the madness of college tuitions. Colleges are spending millions in order to bribe the best students to enroll. It is the equivalent of Nike and Reebok-sponsored AAU teams handing out sneakers, backpacks, and iPods, and free trips to Vegas to entice the best players. By turning grassroots basketball into an arms race, they have weeded out the "old ball coach" who preaches discipline and fundamentals. How long will it be before college too deteriorates from a sanctuary where students undergo rigorous training, to a cesspool of bribes? Or has it already? "If colleges were spending most of their money on initiatives that improve the quality of education for students, you might regard price hikes running at two to four times the rate of inflation as a necessary evil. But spending on palatial dorms, state-of-the-art fitness centers and a panoply of gourmet dining options? Maybe not. Yet that's precisely what many schools are doing to attract students – engaging in a luxury arms race, fueled by the wealth of such elite institutions as Harvard and Yale . . . But they're spending even more on building Hogwarts-style dorms with mahogany casement windows of leaded glass (Princeton's newest $136 million student residence); installing 35-foot climbing walls and hot tubs big enough for 15 people (Boston University)"[34] It all begs the question – "Are elite colleges selling a quality education or something else?"

Gaming the System?

Apparently, "the game" is to attract enough students to apply to one's college (with no intention of admitting them) and then deny their applications. The more students a college rejects, the lower its "acceptance rate," and the more "exclusive" it appears. This is the equivalent of Chinese real estate developers hoarding property to push up prices to create the "illusion" of tight supply; the Chinese government has since cracked down on the practice. That said, giving the appearance of exclusivity makes a college more attractive on the *U.S. News & World Report* college survey, thus garnering a higher ranking. Such rankings have become the de facto standard for parents, students and colleges.[35]

Veblen Effect

A real-world effect of rising tuitions is that parents and students are starting to equate quality with higher prices – the higher the price the better the education. Colleges have already realized that in years when they raise tuition, the number of applications also increase. Moreover, the opposite is also true. Colleges that do not increase tuition in lockstep with the competition have difficulties explaining why their college is as good as those who do. The technical term for this phenomenon is the "Veblen Effect," named for American economist Thorstein Veblen. The son of Norwegian immigrants, Veblen traveled throughout the U.S. and studied human behavior; he noticed how some Americans acquired things based solely upon the social status it gave them. For instance, according to Veblen, many people bought a Mercedes Benz not because of how well the car drove, but because few people could afford it. Thus, some products – Mercedes Benzs, Hermes ties, stone mansions in the Hampton – benefit from the "Veblen Effect." The higher the price or more exclusive they are, the more people want them. The one difference is that people can choose whether or not to buy a Maybach. Attending college in today's environment is not an option.

Study Abroad

Some experts are recommending that students travel abroad to attend colleges that are both cheaper, and offer degrees on par with those in the U.S. In the same vein that U.S. residents have to buy medicine in Canada due to soaring medical costs, college may be the next inelastic good only attainable abroad. "During 2010-11 tuition and fees at U.S. private four-year colleges and universities averaged $27,293, with room and board running another $9,700, for a total of $36,993, according to the College Board. Dozens of top private schools posted tuition and fees exceeding $40,000 and total costs of $50,000-plus . . . But St. Andrews, the oldest university in Scotland and the alma mater of Britain's Prince William and wife Kate, will charge tuition of just 13,500 pounds ($21,650) to U.S. students for 2011-12, while the University of Oxford will charge 12,700 to 14,550 pounds . . . Tuition and fees at Canada's McGill University will total $16,689 Canadian ($17,400 U.S.) for U.S. students studying for a B.A. and $25,722 Canadian for those working toward an engineering degree. Other countries have high-quality universities that, thanks to government subsidies, are cheaper or even free."[36] In 2010 about 4,000 Americans studied at U.K. schools for an undergraduate degree. Those figures will likely increase as college is fast becoming a playpen for the wealthy. As a trade-off for President Obama supporting regime changes in Egypt, Libya and Syria, maybe they can let us attain affordable healthcare and college degrees there. It could be their first tests to prove that democracy can indeed work in Northern Africa.

Not-For-Profits Acting in "For-Profit" Manner

The luxury arms race that colleges are engaging in is evidence of traditional not-for-profit entities behaving in a "for profit" manner. The Harvards and the Yales of the world have the largest endowments and therefore, the necessary war chest to compete based on spending; Harvard's endowment of $35 billion is the country's largest. Yet, how much of the endowment money held by so-called "elite" universities came from the oligarchs, robber barons, and hedge fund managers attending those schools? The hundreds of billions of government bailouts were in effect, bailouts of certain elite universities who use those ill-gotten gains to price out taxpayers. More importantly, when you look at countries in terms of the "competitive advantage" of nations, the U.S. is no longer a leader in autos or other manufacturing industries. Our competitive advantage is in technology, and people like Steve Jobs and Bill Gates who innovate in those fields. To stay ahead of the competition, we must find the next entrepreneur to create the next Facebook or the next Google, and create domestic jobs in the process. Is there any wonder why China has banned Facebook and stymied Google's progress over "trumped up censorship" concerns? The one hope we have is to continue to innovate faster than China can pirate those innovations. To do that, we need to find the next Jobs or Gates – whether they come from the monied class or not – educate them and provide them the necessary capital to grow. Institutions that sell luxury suites, saunas and gourmet meals and offer a college degree as an ancillary service, price out the masses and hurt our country's competiveness. The best solution to institutions that act in a "for-profit" manner is to tax them at the same rate as other spas, real estate developers, and fine dining establishments.

Are Hedge Funds the New Arbitragers?

When I first started the Shock Exchange I explained to the kids how Peter Lynch of Fidelity was considered one of the greatest investors of our time. However, by Lynch's own admission, as an institutional investor he had an advantage over individuals – access to information. He had access to both Wall Street research reports and to the management teams of companies he covered. For instance, Lynch understood the business models and growth potential of Apple and Microsoft years before the general public caught on. Lynch headed the Magellan Fund with less than $20 million in assets in 1977 and when he retired in 1990, the fund had over $14 billion in assets. He is best known for beating the market for 10 consecutive years, and he became the benchmark for other investment managers. Bill Miller, manager of the Legg Mason Capital Management Value Trust Fund, would later exceed that feat by outperforming the market for 15 consecutive years through 2005. Because of this "information arbitrage," individuals almost had to invest with professional money managers rather than go it alone. Since the invention of the Internet, that information arbitrage has all but closed. For instance, individuals can now retrieve Wall Street analyst reports and public company filings online. Hundreds of blogs provide real-time information and analysis on the economy and various industries, rendering traditional Wall Street research less effective. I can personally tell you, without having ever read a Wall Street analyst report, that (i) Internet-related stocks like Groupon, LinkedIn, Twitter and Facebook are overvalued, (ii) the revenue and earnings growth needed to justify their P/E ratios are unrealistic and (iii) the next Mary Meeker or Henry Blodget will be the subject of lawsuits for aggressively marketing those stocks to retail investors.

The amount of information available today has empowered individual investors and rendered professional investors almost irrelevant. That is why I could never understand how scores of bankers and consultants, with no prior stock-picking expertise, were so eager to start hedge funds amid the declining "information arbitrage." As the following chart illustrates, hedge fund AUM grew from $237 billion in 2000 to $1.7 trillion by the third quarter of 2011 – a CAGR of around 20.2%. Meanwhile, the information arbitrage declined from 51% to 22% over that period. In this example, the percentage of the U.S. population without access to the Internet in 2011 was 22% – I used this figure as a proxy for the information gap between professional investors and individuals. AUM declined from a peak of $2.1 trillion in 2007 and gradually recovered. Almost 1,400 hedge funds closed in 2008 amid the financial crisis, as the industry suffered its worst year on record, with the average fund losing 19%, according to Hedge Fund Research Inc. "Hedge funds pulled in $55.5 billion in net new money in 2010, the most since 2007 . . . Figures for this year's [2011] first quarter also are expected to be robust. The gains are coming despite performance that has been lackluster of late. The average fund earned 20% in 2009 and 10.3% in 2010 . . . failing to match the 26.5% and 15.1% gains in the Standard & Poor's stock-index in those two years."[37] Despite hedge funds' underperformance in 2008 and since, new money has still poured into the industry, demonstrating investors' addiction to them.

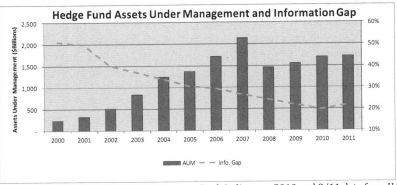

Source: World Bank and World Development Bank Indicators, 2010 and 3/11 data from U.S. Census Bureau and Internet World Stats
Hedge fund data from BarclayHedge, 2011 data at 3Q, rest at year-end

Hedge fund managers have enjoyed a certain level of celebrity over the past decade. The mainstream media sang their praises and gave the public the impression that there were thousands of young, driven managers not named "Peter Lynch" or "Bill Miller" who could best the market year-over-year. Perhaps Lynch's real genius was retiring with his legacy still intact. Yet, like a punch-drunk fighter who did not know when it was time to hang 'em up, Miller never retired from the investing game; instead the game retired him. In 2011 Miller announced he was stepping down from the Legg Mason Capital Management Value Trust Fund with $2.8 billion in AUM – a decline of nearly $18 billion. The fund was down about 36% through year-to-date August 2011 and had trailed the S&P 500 index five of the previous six years.[38] After his running the fund for almost 30 years, Miller's exit was the equivalent of Larry Holmes asking the referee to stop the pummeling he was giving to an aging Muhammad Ali – Holmes could no longer bear to see his mentor take any more punishment.

That mainstream press benefited from the hedge fund hype as the public religiously watched their television shows and read their newspapers. After the near market crash in 2008, the government cracked down on insider trading. As the hedge fund names under investigation poured in – Galleon, Frontpoint, New Castle, SAC Capital, S2 Capital, Citadel, Diamondback, Loch Capital, and Incremental Capital – I wondered if "hedge fund" was synonymous with "insider trading." Even John Paulson's triple-digit returns during the crisis, championed non-stop by CNBC, was a hoax. His ill-gotten gains were achieved by shorting hand-picked MBS he knew would underperform, and convincing Goldman to fob them off on unsuspecting clients. Paulson's investment expertise has nothing to do with mortgages or the real estate industry – he is actually an M&A arbitrager. Ironically, his investment results in arbitrage never came close to his MBS shorting strategy. The media co-signed for hedge fund managers amid clear evidence of insider trading, describing them as "hard-charging," "driven" and generally honest people who may have pushed the envelope. Yet the evidence illustrates that they engaged in insider trading for one reason – incompetence. They have always been incompetent; if you check their backgrounds you would find that they cheated in high school, cheated on their SATs to get into college, cheated to get through college, cheated on their GMATS and LSATs to get into graduate school, etc.

Ivan Boesky, king of the '80s-style arbitragers, once made a speech to the graduation class at Wharton Business School where he advised that "Greed is good." The phrase was made famous by the fictitious Wall Street trader, Gordon Gekko, played by Michael Douglas in the movie *Wall Street*. Yet it was not greed, but Boesky's incompetence that led him to engage in insider trading. In 1982 T. Boone Pickens launched a hostile takeover offer for the oil company, Cities Service. Acting as a white knight to help save Cities Service from Pickens' clutches, Gulf Oil topped his bid. Expecting a bidding war, Boesky plowed $70 million – 90% of it borrowed – into the stock of Cities Service.[39]

Three months later, just before the market closed, Gulf Oil withdrew its bid due to antitrust concerns. In a scenario reminiscent of the movie *Trading Places*, Cities Service's stock plunged in after-hours trading, threatening to destroy Boesky and the firm he launched with capital from his wife's (Seema) family. "Boesky Corporation was in dire straits. It had nowhere near the cash to meet the margin calls, even if it liquidated all its other stock holdings. Worse, Boesky had $20 million in unsecured loans from banks . . . The loans were callable, for any reason, and the banks would almost certainly get wind of Boesky's crisis. Then there was the New York Stock Exchange and the SEC. While much would depend on the price of Gulf stock when trading resumed on Monday, in all likelihood Boesky would be insolvent and in violation of regulatory capital requirements. The firm might be liquidated."[40] Boesky convinced his bankers not to call their loans and worked out a complicated deal with another arbitrager, John Mulheren, which shielded his portfolio from further losses. On the night of the Cities Service stock plunge, Boesky was having dinner with Seema and Mulheren. He made reference to the killing he was taking in the market when Seema abruptly cut him off, "'As far as I'm concerned, this is never going to happen again.' She repeated emphatically, 'Never again.'"[41] Proving his wife a prophet, the next week Boesky set up a meeting at the Harvard Club with Martin Siegel from Kidder's M&A group. There they hatched an arrangement for Siegel to give Boesky inside information on M&A deals involving Kidder, in exchange for a share of Boesky's insider trading profits.

The SEC is "Play-Acting"

The SEC, U.S. Attorney General's Office, et al., have trumpeted their ability to bring insider traders to justice. However, the other piece of the puzzle is to cut off their flow of funds. After Galleon wound down, its investors were allowed to simply take their capital back. It would be naïve to think that sophisticated investors were not aware of Rajaratnam's insider trading. How else could a hedge fund manager generate the lion's share of his returns from stocks he held for less than three months? No one could possibly be that prescient. The harsh reality is that insider trading has become a way of life for hedge fund managers and the investors who fund them. If regulators were serious about stopping insider trading they would have, (i) clawed back ill-gotten trading gains from Galleon investors and (ii) prohibited them from making additional hedge fund investments for a period of time. To stem insider trading they have got to follow the money. After all, the public trust and the country's capital-raising ability are at risk, similar to the aftermath of the 1987 market crash: "Yet the market's plunge left real devastation in its wake. Small investors suffered heavily, and many were so alienated by the experience that they never returned to trading. Already suspicious of the market's integrity, these investors were now convinced that the stock market was a rigged game for professionals. In time, this attitude would seriously impair the country's capital-raising structure – just as the drafters of the original securities laws had feared."[42]

Commercial Real Estate Next Shoe to Drop . . . Further

Prices for commercial real estate peaked in October 2007 and declined gradually through the fourth quarter of 2008. Prices went into free fall thereafter and hit a trough in April 2011. According to Moody's Commercial Property Price Index (CPPI), commercial real estate prices decreased 1.4% in September 2011 as compared to August 2011. The decline followed four months of consecutive price increases and was negatively affected by the number of "distressed" sale transactions. That said, the September 2011 CPPI represented a 42% decrease from the October 2007 peak and a 13.7% increase above the April 2011 trough.

Commercial Real Estate Prices Most Sensitive to Distressed Sales

A key driver of the CPPI is the number of distressed transactions that occur in a given month. Distressed sales often result from banks having to dump properties at fire sale prices in order reduce their problem loans. The market for distressed properties has also fallen more sharply and rebounded slower than the overall market. Moreover, the commercial real estate woes at troubled banks do not seem to be abating anytime soon. Through November 2011, 85 banks had failed, many due to overexposure to problem commercial real estate loans. Of the 11 banks that failed in the month of October, troubled commercial real estate loans accounted for over 65% of problem loans. Of the six banks that failed in September, over 82% of problem loans were commercial real estate related.[43]

In addition, billions of loans are due to be refinanced in 2012 at rates as much as 500 basis points higher than property owners are now paying. At the height of the commercial real estate market in 2007, many property owners took out five-year loans at rates as low as 1%. According to Trepp, a company that tracks mortgages packaged into securities, of the $70 billion in commercial MBS outstanding that are coming due next year, approximately $27.7 billion have been flagged as potentially facing tough hurdles when they try to refinance. In the past few years, low rates have reduced borrowers' expenses and masked problems the properties may be facing.[44] For those properties currently under water, owners will have to inject additional equity. It is uncertain whether lenders will make concessions to borrowers unable to meet obligations at higher rates, or whether borrowers will walk away from the properties altogether. Nonetheless, default rates and distressed sales could rise for the near term.

Demand for Vacant Space

Demand for vacant space is the other lever that drives commercial real estate prices; and that does not bode well for the industry. While landlords face higher interest rates as five-year mortgages are reset, they also face declining rent rolls as five-year leases made at the height of the market expire – property owners' version of the "Malachi Crunch." "Rents in most markets are still well below what they were in 2007, with the drop in some areas as much as 26%, according to data firm Reis Inc. Because of the weak market, landlords with empty space or expiring leases also have to spend large amounts on incentives to attract tenants, like free rent and interior work. Defaults and foreclosures are rising; the delinquency rate securitized office loans hit 9% in December, up from 7.4% in

June. Take the case of BentleyForbes Group LLC, which acquired Atlanta's Bank of America Plaza in 2006 with the help of a $363 million mortgage. At the time, the building was fully leased with Bank of America as its anchor tenant. In 2011 Bank of America reduced its space by over half, which in addition to other departures, caused its vacancy rate to rise to 37% and its income to decline by more than 25% from the time of purchase. In the fall, BentleyForbes defaulted on its mortgage.[45] Then there is 40 Wall Street, the 1.3-million-square-foot-tower owned by Donald Trump. In 2009 40 Wall Street had leases expiring that represented nearly 50% of the building's total space. However, Trump moved aggressively by reaching out to companies beyond the building's traditional Wall Street clientele and offered below-market rents. If this trend continues, the buyer's market for office space may lead to commercial real estate prices revisiting the trough of April 2011.

Farmland – The Next Bubble

At a recent auction for 50 acres of corn and soybean land in Neponset, Illinois, farmer Terry Pratt's winning bid of $7,875 an acre was nearly double the rate he paid for a similar parcel of land nearly four years earlier. Prices for Midwest cropland in other states like Nebraska and Indiana have doubled over the past five years.[46] Driving the land speculation is inflation in prices for corn and soybean which have also doubled in the past five years. The alternative uses of corn to produce ethanol, and China's demand for food to keep pace with its population growth and ascend to the world's second largest economy, are fueling corn prices. That said, farmers and investors are more than willing to buy cropland in anticipation that these dynamics will continue. As China goes, so go commodities; and trying to predict China's future demand for U.S. commodities is the equivalent of trying to navigate a minefield. First, there is the risk of a hard landing in China's domestic economy. If it turns out that China was too draconian in its methods to slow its economy or its ballooning debt sparks deflationary pressures, its demand for commodities will decline. Secondly, there is the risk that China's demand for U.S. corn/soybeans could become a political football pursuant to a trade war with the U.S., or diverging ideologies on Iran, the Koreas, etc. It would be naïve to invest in cropland fueled by demand from China without hedging by (i) locking in crop prices with futures contracts and (ii) buying insurance in case the counterparties on the futures contracts too go belly up. Otherwise, farmers, farm lobbyists, investors and politicians will face a farmland bust not seen since the 1980s.

U.S. – Devoid of Leadership?

In 2007 Iacocca wrote a book that begged the question, "Where have all the leaders gone?" One definition of leadership could be "people who changed the world" – Mother Theresa, John F. Kennedy, Martin Luther King, Jr., Pope John Paul II, and Bobby Kennedy all come to mind. Alec Horniman, my Darden Organizational Behavior professor, pointed out another commonality among them – they have all had assassination attempts on their lives. Leadership could also be defined as "performing small tasks greatly." In that regard, Frank Wills, the security guard who discovered the famous Watergate break-in, and Julie

Preuitt would be exceptional leaders. However, the popular view has morphed into those who are "winning." Our culture extols the CEO simply for being "CEO," or the head coach with multiple championship titles, regardless of the Faustian bargains he made to achieve them.

The mainstream media has sold African Americans on the virtues of Ken Chenault who became the first black CEO of a Fortune 500 company; it cited Chenault's "patience" and "team play" for waiting a decade for a CEO title that Jack Welch, had he been in Chenault's position, would have demanded. Yet, is Chenault any more of a leader than A. Barry Rand, who never became CEO of Xerox? Or take the case of Pat Riley, the former coach of the L.A. Lakers, New York Knicks and Miami Heat. In 1980 Paul Westhead, with Kareem Abdul Jabbar and rookie Magic Johnson, guided the Lakers to the NBA title. In 1981, Johnson suffered a knee injury that caused him to miss over half the regular season, and the Lakers were subsequently bounced in the first round of the playoffs by the Houston Rockets. Eleven games into the 1982 season the Lakers fired Westhead and replaced him with Riley, then the Lakers assistant coach. There were rumors that behind the scenes, Johnson had orchestrated the firing. He and Westhead had not seen eye-to-eye on the team's offense, and instead of "kowtowing" to some punk kid a few years removed from college, Westhead stood his ground. "Two nights before, after the Lakers had beaten the Utah Jazz 113-110 for their fifth straight victory, Westhead had met with Johnson to express his displeasure over what he called a 'lack of concentration on Magic's part.' That reportedly meant that either Johnson hadn't listened to Westhead during a time-out late in that night's game or had failed to run a play to the coach's satisfaction. In the locker room after that meeting, Johnson told the press that he couldn't play under Westhead's system anymore and that he wanted to be traded. After the Lakers arrived back in Los Angeles the next morning, Buss called a press conference, and Westhead was gone."[47] Though there was no logical basketball explanation for his firing, Westhead handled the situation with class and professionalism. Yet even Magic's teammates were taken aback by the news. "But the fact that it happened less than a day after Johnson's outburst in Utah gave some Lakers cause to wonder. [Jamaal] Wilkes, who was 'shocked' by Johnson's statements, had this thought: 'If he got mad at a player, would the player be gone the next day?'"[48] Prior to the 1983-84 season Lakers shooting guard, Norm Nixon, was traded to the L.A. Clippers – the NBA's version of Siberia. Rumors swirled that Johnson had orchestrated that trade too. My cousins and I joked how Johnson had gotten Nixon traded because there was only one ball, and both he and Nixon couldn't dribble it at the same time.

Riley and the Lakers went on to win titles in 1982, 1985, 1987 and 1988 with pretty much the same team Westhead had constructed. With Abdul-Jabbar and Wilkes retired and Magic and James Worthy (first pick in the 1982 NBA draft) aging, the Lakers were knocked out of the second round of the playoffs by the Phoenix Suns in 1990. Riley resigned as Lakers Coach after the 1990 season; he resurfaced in 1991 to coach the New York Knicks and a young Patrick Ewing, the first pick in the 1985 draft. Riley coached them to two NBA finals but never won it. With Ewing and a Knicks team just past its prime, in 1995 Riley left the Knicks to coach the Miami Heat and center Alonzo Mourning, the second player chosen in the 1992 NBA draft. Mourning was diagnosed with kidney disease and missed most of the 2000 season. He did not play at all in the 2002 season, after which Riley resigned due to "fatigue" and took a front office position with the Heat. Prior to the 2004 season the Heat acquired Shaquille O'Neal, the "Wilt Chamberlain" of his era and first pick in the 1992 draft. In 2005 Riley miraculously caught the coaching bug again and replaced Stan Van Gundy. In 2006 Riley coached the Heat to the NBA title – his fifth as head coach. O'Neal battled injuries and off court problems after the 2006 season and was eventually traded in 2008. Riley retired from coaching after the 2008 season when the Heat finished 15-67 – the league's worst record. Riley is widely considered to be one of the greatest coaches in NBA history and a leader of men – his five NBA titles are clear evidence of that. Meanwhile, Riley's former boss, Paul Westhead, has been all but forgotten. However, in my silly mind, Riley did nothing more than win with a championship-ready team inherited from Westhead. And when that Lakers team grew past its prime, he then jumped from situation to situation best in his favor. When he had more talent than everyone else, Riley won. When he didn't, he quit. The true "leader" of the two men was Westhead, who stood up to an impetuous kid questioning his authority, costing Westhead his job and rightful place in history.

Fraternity America

In January 2010 the CEOs of TARP recipients testified before Congress on how they used the funds; I was taken aback at how homogenous they all looked. Vikram Pandit, Lloyd Blankfein, Ken Lewis, Jamie Dimon, John Mack, Ronald Logue, Robert P. Kelly, and John Stumpf, looked like nothing more than members of a social fraternity. If you had queried their employees on how their companies made money from 2000 to 2008, most would have been unable to offer up a cogent explanation. If they got a big bonus at the end of the year then that meant their boss liked them, and vice versa, so they spent the majority of time trying to be "liked." It is these social groups that run the country by filling politicians' coffers with millions in campaign funds and lobbying for policies beneficial to them. They also pay millions to publicists who place favorable articles about them to sway public opinion. Raj Rajaratnam lamented at how the WASP mafia, Irish mafia and Jewish mafia controlled Wall Street and how difficult it was to become a member. Du Bois documented a similar phenomenon in his studies of African Americans. He noted how blacks were all but excluded from industrial jobs in the mid-1800s, in place of European immigrants who possessed neither the skills, nor the formal education to perform the tasks required. However, Midvale Steelworks, located just outside of Philadelphia, was an exception to the rule. It had a quirky manager who actually sought out African-American workers to support his hidden agenda – to counter the clannish behavior of first and second-generation immigrants from Western Europe. That quirky manager, Frederick Winslow Taylor, later became famous for designing methods to improve industrial efficiency, and time and motion studies. The following is an excerpt from interviews at the Steelworks:

In steel manufacture much of the work is done with large tools run by gangs of men; the work was crippled by the different foreman trying to always have men in their gang all of their own nationality. The English foreman of a hammer gang, for instance, would want only Englishmen, and the Irish Catholic only Irishmen. This was not good for the works, nor did it promote friendliness among the workmen. So we began bringing in Negroes and placing them on different gangs, and at the same time we distributed the other nationalities. Now our gangs have, say, one Negro, one or two Americans, one Englishman, etc. . . . Things run smoothly and the output has been noticeably greater.[49]

Taylor's goal was to break a system of ethnic loyalty and inject an atmosphere of competition, where previously workers were resistant to efficiency standards set by Midvale. The group I encountered at GECC's New York office that struck me as rather peculiar because only Italians worked in it, made a lot more sense to me after reading Du Bois' study. If you track the bailout money during the crisis, the lion's share went to such clans bound not by drive or business acumen, but by ethnic loyalties Du Bois documented over a century ago.

The Perfect Leader

We can no longer look to elected officials for leadership. They have for the most part been co-opted by the corporate fraternities they eventually want to join. Leadership will have to come from the people. Recent U.S. presidents have been content with making speeches, "taking care of his base," or writing jingles – (i) "I'd like to teach the world to sing in perfect harmony . . . I'd like to buy the world a Coke and keep it company," (ii) "Two all-beef patties, special sauce, lettuce, cheese, pickles, onions, on a sesame seed bun," or (iii) "Hope and change." To craft the perfect leader I would choose qualities from the leaders of my youth: (i) the "trickiness" of Nixon, (ii) Ford's sense of duty, (iii) Carter's I.Q., (iv) the communication skills of Reagan, (v) the cajones of the Iron Lady, (vi) the patriotism of George H. W. Bush, (vii) the principals of 1980s' Volcker, (viii) the comeback ability of Iacocca, and (ix) the moral compass and social brilliance of Ali. We may need someone with all those qualities to guide us through "the pain ahead."

Market Crash by Year-End 2013?

Shortly after the collapse of Lehman I posted this the following article on the Shock Exchange website advising readers to exit the market. But did they listen?

During mid-September I have received several phone calls from friends and family asking my opinion on the recent financial crisis and what to do with their 401k money and personal investments. This really wasn't news to me because for a while now the Shock Exchange has been screaming about the poor health of the U.S. economy, but our cries seemingly fell on deaf ears. The short answer about the market is . . . GET OUT! There may be short-term upticks in the market due to current or future stimulus packages, but I cannot think of any reason why corporate earnings and ultimately, the market, should rise long-term. Over the past few years the Shock Exchange has discussed the negative trend in the vital signs of the economy . . . and how they will affect the market and our investment portfolio. Nobody has a crystal ball of course, but (i) over the coming weeks I would pay close attention to corporate earnings announcements and Management's outlook for the future and (ii) wait again for 4th quarter earnings announcements in January/February 2009 to determine whether to get back into the market. This 3-4 month period will also give investors a chance to analyze the trend in economic indicators and to wait for any new developments such as more bank failures, hedge fund blow ups, rogue traders, etc., to be priced into the market.[50]

Having missed the market declines after Lehman's bankruptcy filing in September 2009, I bought put options in December, assuming the market would completely implode. Shortly after President Obama was elected, Federal Reserve Chairman, Ben Bernanke, lowered interest rates and signaled he would provide liquidity as necessary to spur economic growth. Meanwhile, the Obama Administration actively propped up the market. The smart money had sat on the sidelines for years, biding its time, waiting for the right moment to pounce. Now the time had come for there to be blood in the streets and here comes the president to save the day . . . but for whom? Rescuing the market salvaged speculative bets made by Wall Street titans; I feared that they and their campaign managers – Paulson, Geithner, Bernanke, CNBC, et al. – were the interests the president was listening to. The market was simply behaving rationally – the outlook for the U.S. economy was dim, corporate earnings were unpredictable and public company financial statements were as clear as mud. How could Lehman report robust financial results one day and less than a month later file for bankruptcy? Investors thought they were buying stock in an investment bank, yet Lehman had been nothing more than a bigger, more complex version of David Askin or Michael Steinhardt.

The Obama Administration's buoying of the market is the equivalent of spending billions to ensure that it does not get cold this winter. You cannot fight nature; at best you can delay the inevitable. The dynamics that brought the market to the brink are still there. The business models of Wall Street firms are still suspect; revenue from capital raising and third-party advisory pale in comparison to the revenue generated from principal trading and real estate speculation. Their earnings will become more cyclical and mirror the U.S. economy. And during the next recession their "going concern" value will also come into question. No longer able to profit from speculative bets while leaving shareholders and taxpayers with future losses, some Wall Street executives will even take their firms private, returning to the partnership structure of the pre-1990s. With partners' personal wealth exposed to their firms' losses, their appetite for risk will all but evaporate. In September 2009, *Seeking Alpha* reiterated our concerns, listing five reasons why the market could crash. It cited the fact that high frequency trading accounted for over 70% of the market's trading volume, to 13 million Americans exhausting unemployment benefits, to a $1 quadrillion derivatives time bomb.[51]

Nature Runs Its Course

I expect nature to run its course by the end of 2013 and what should have taken place in the second half of 2008 will finally come to pass – a market crash.

While the robber barons have been made whole for losses, individuals have returned to the market in droves. Believing news reports of an economic recovery and the safety of the market, individuals will be hit hardest by a market crash. By the end of 2013, the pain ahead will be clear to everyone and expect a crash to be presaged by one of the following events:

Spike in Interest Rates

Whether China dumps large holdings of U.S. debt, S&P issues another downgrade or investors simply demand higher rates to pay them for the country's lack of creditworthiness, a spike in long-term rates will choke off housing starts and auto sales and ultimately, GDP. The dismal outlook for the economy given the country's higher cost of capital would send the market into a tailspin.

Spike in Commodities

A spike in commodities such as oil or food would evoke the dreaded "stagflation." U.S. tensions in Iran and Iraq could cause either of those countries to limit oil supply, increasing its costs. China is rumored to be hoarding oil for its strategic reserves – its crude-oil imports increased to near record levels in March 2012. China's expected increased demand for oil will only push global oil prices higher, and with it, prices from gasoline to transportation to utilities, to consumer goods that use petroleum in their packaging. China's growth could also create a spike in global food costs higher. A spike in energy and food would amplify the pain of rising unemployment in the U.S.

Investment Bank Implosion

Revenue from capital-raising and investment advisory services may not be sustainable long-term given the current economy. By the end of 2013, I expect at least one investment bank to implode or take itself private, a de facto admittance that its pre-crisis earnings levels were predicated on making bets with other people's capital and fleecing the public. Once the public realizes that trillions of taxpayer money went to support an unsustainable business model, expect the market to implode.

The Next Recession and the Pain Ahead

The Federal Reserve embarked on its first quantitative-easing program (QE1) in December 2008 and purchased $1.7 trillion in long-term treasury debt and MBS. It launched its second phase (QE2) in November 2010 and bought $600 billion of long-term treasury securities. Via both programs, the Fed lowered interest rates in order to aid the economy. A historian of the Great Depression and its causes, Fed Chairman Ben Bernanke was determined not to let history repeat itself. There is a common school of thought that the central bank's decision to raise interest rates in the 1930s exacerbated the Great Depression. At a 2002 speech celebrating famed economist Milton Friedman's 90th birthday, Bernanke admitted as such: "'You're right, we did it,' Ben Bernanke told Milton Friedman . . . He was referring to Mr. Friedman's conclusion that central bankers were responsible for much of the suffering in the Depression. 'But thanks to you . . . we won't do it again.' Nine years later Mr. Bernanke's peers are congratulating themselves for delivering on that promise. 'We prevented a Great Depression,' the Bank of England's governor, Mervyn King, told the *Daily Telegraph* in March this year."[52]

Obama Banks His Presidency on "Trickle-down Theory"

In 2011 the lower rates were a boon to corporate America as companies rushed to refinance borrowings and reduce debt service. Highly leveraged companies benefited the most: "Private equity, in particular, has been eager to refinance the massive amounts of debt it accumulated during the leveraged-buyout boom, in addition to raising funds to pay special dividends to private equity sponsors this year. So far this year [through April 2011], $120 billion in leveraged loans have been issued, 62% of which have been used for refinancing. That compares with $158 billion in all of 2010, when 32% were used for refinancing . . . That ability to issue loans and debt should help companies stave off defaults, which have been pushed back down to extremely low levels. Standard & Poor's said last week that its baseline projection for U.S. corporate trailing 12-month speculative-grade defaults is just 1.6%, down from an 11.45% peak in November 2009."[53] The assumption was that in lowering interest rates, Bernanke was hoping to spur the economy through additional business investment and job creation. But that has not occurred; executives whose companies enjoyed lower financing costs repaid Bernanke by hoarding cash. "Lower borrowing costs are a boon to corporate profits, which could in turn benefit the broader economy and hiring . . . But many companies are simply borrowing to refinance old debt. And many are leaving the cash haul on their balance sheets, bracing for the possibility of fresh crises or leaner growth ahead. That suggests the economic benefit of the borrowing boom could be limited."[54] And as if to add insult to injury, from 2008 through March 2009 the Federal Reserve offered banks $7.7 trillion in zero interest loan commitments and tried to hide it from the public. The recipients included, but were not limited to, Morgan Stanley, Citigroup, JPMorgan Chase, Goldman Sachs, Merrill Lynch, Credit Suisse, and Bank of America. *Bloomberg Markets Magazine* estimated the below-market loans equated to an additional $13 billion of income to these banks. [55] The Federal Reserve only divulged the details of the loan commitments after the parent of Bloomberg News won a court case against the Fed and the loan recipients. And what might you ask did those Wall Street firms do with the aid they received from the Fed? They paid themselves record bonuses. In 2009 total compensation and benefits at TARP recipients was a record $128 billion, only to be surpassed by the 2010 record of $135 billion.[56]

Record-low interest rates have been a boon to some homeowners as well. According to Freddie Mac, the average rate for 30-year fixed rate mortgages fell to 3.94% for the week ended October 6, 2011 – the lowest on record. Yet those record low rates have been beyond the reach of many borrowers with substandard credit, behind on their mortgages or with mortgages currently underwater. To give you a sence of the state of the housing market after the crisis, by November 2009 3.4% of U.S. households (1.9 million homeowners) were 120 days or more overdue on their payments, yet not in foreclosure.[57] Secondly, by mid-2011 home prices had fallen about 34% from their peak in 2006, leaving about 10.9 million Americans who borrowed to buy their homes – 22.7% of all homeowners with a mortgage nationwide – underwater on their mortgages.[58] These factors, coupled with lenders' higher credit standards and higher down payment requirements have left millions of individuals sitting on the sidelines during the refinancing boom. And it is among those individuals with lower incomes and higher MPCs that the Obama Administration was hoping to reach by driving down rates. A few hundred dollars per month in savings on mortgage payments for millions of struggling homeowners would have been a boon to the economy. Yet, even in situations where Fannie and Freddie approved loan modifications, they approved them at the highest rates possible. While Fannie and Freddie received record-low financing costs, they did not pass along those full savings to struggling homeowners.

With QE1, QE2, and the Fed's below market loan programs, Obama has attached the success of his presidency to the "trickle-down theory." Those with the lowest MPC – corporations, Wall Street titans, and wealthy individuals – have benefited most from the efforts of Bernanke and the Obama Administration. They have rewarded Bernanke and Obama by hoarding their cash savings. In retrospect, it is somewhat of a misnomer to merely compare the recession of 2008 to the Great Depression. The recent financial crisis is also akin to Japan in the 1980s; it involved both stock and real estate speculation where individuals have become indentured servants to mortgages taken out at the height of the market. Now that the real estate market has collapsed, they are left with mortgages that will take decades to repay, if at all. Moreover, the billions in aid provided by the government have had less of an impact than one would have hoped. President Obama would have been better off simply providing below-market loans to all individuals current on their mortgages. This would have saved the government trillions in stimulus aid and put savings in the hands of individuals who would have spent 90%-95% of it immediately – spurring the economy.

Bubble in Bonds

The Fed's massive bond-buying binge has created a synthetic demand for U.S. treasurys. Even without QE1 and QE2, investors would have bid up U.S. treasury prices and driven down their yields due to a flight to quality. Given the fiscal problems of the EU, U.S. bonds are the safest bets, at least for now. However, a flight to quality does not totally explain record low treasury yields. When the 10-year treasury yield fell to 1.9872% in August 2011, it was the first time it had dipped below 2% since the 1960s. Some bond experts predicted that treasury prices would drop after the Fed's QE2 program ended in June 2011, but that has been anything but the case. Yields declined from 3.158% at June 30, 2011 to 1.871% at December 31, 2011, implying that investors may be acting in a "herd" mentality and prompting questions whether such low yields accurately compensate them for the risk. With housing underwater I expect the U.S. economy to continue to experience deflationary pressures. At some point, I also expect investors to move away from U.S. bonds due to the country's poor creditworthiness. Eventually the EU will get its act together and may become more appealing to global investors vis-à-vis the U.S. Secondly, there is always the risk that China will use its treasury holdings as a political bargaining chip, driving up yields. Moreover, the 50-year average yield on 10-year treasurys is around 6.6% and if yields eventually return to those levels, the potential losses for investors is massive.

U.S. Credit Risk

The debt-to-GDP ratio of 51% during Reagan's last year in office was considered abysmal. From the time George W. Bush took office in 2000, to the end of President Obama's third year, the outstanding debt of the U.S nearly tripled to $14.8 trillion. After wars in two countries, bailouts and zero interest loans to big business with no corresponding increases in hiring, investment in inventory or consumer spending, at year-end 2011 the debt-to-GDP ratio was 99% – figures that would have made even Reagan blush.

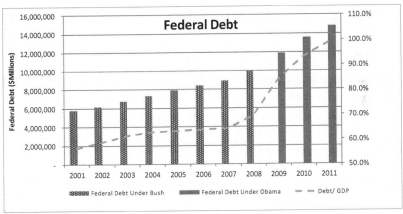

Source: Office of Budget Management

If the U.S. were an individual it would be unable to borrow at the record-low interest rates it has enjoyed. I am not sure whether the U.S. debt rating is "AA+," "BBB" or "CCC." However, I am certain that yields of less than 2% are not high enough to compensate me for the risks of lending to the government. At Sovran Bank I heard wild stories about the double-digit rates of the 1980s – mortgages and CDs as high as 16% - 18%. Paul Volcker raised the fed funds rate during that period to levels he thought would stem inflation. And it would take rates at those levels to entice me to invest in U.S. treasurys.

Treasurys – The New "Rare Earths"?

In the brief fisherman spat with Japan, China tipped its hand as to how it would behave in future global disputes – deny rare earth supplies or extension of credit for political ends. In that vein, China's obvious card would be to dump billions in U.S. debt holdings onto the market. Experts believe this risk is muted by the dearth of alternative investments available to China. Countries in the European Union are in dire straits, but this will not always be the case. President Nicolas Sarkozy of France and other European leaders have made repeated overtures to

China to invest in their debt, and have signaled a willingness to offer concessions. The impact of China dumping billions of U.S. treasury securities onto the market would cause treasury yields to spike. That said, China may not have a choice in the matter. A spike in default rates on its 55.7 trillion yuan (~$8.8 trillion) of public and private debt could force it to sell U.S. treasurys to prop up its fragile banking system; in October 2011, its sovereign wealth fund invested an undisclosed amount to prop up banking stocks deemed vulnerable to an economic collapse. Coupled with the untold billions China will have to allocate to housing and care for its senior population, its holdings of U.S. securities could dwindle overnight.

Nonetheless, there is a credible scenario where China dumps billions of U.S. debt holdings and other investors, knowing the U.S. is in dire straits to borrow, (i) actually trade against treasurys or (ii) become predatory and force the government to raise rates to double digits before they invest. Such a wind-down scenario would dampen housing starts and auto sales, and cause a recession more painful than the last.

Vital Signs
The economy's vital signs have rebounded somewhat since the crisis. However, given record-low interest rates, these statistics are as good as they are going to get.

Housing Starts
Housing starts of 609 thousand in 2011 are less than a third of the 2.1 million starts at the peak of the review period (2005), and about 10% above the 2009 trough of 554,000 – the lowest since WWII. Falling home prices, rising foreclosures, sticky unemployment levels and banks' higher underwriting standards have attributed to some of the most dismal housing starts on record. Contrastly, housing starts during the recession of the early 1990s never fell below 1 million. The "tale of two recessions" reiterates that the crisis of 2008 was driven by real estate speculation – fueled by Wall Street – that will take years to rectify. That said, simply lowering interest rates will not abate the situation if homeowners with the highest MPCs are denied access to those lower rates. Housing starts are driven by both demographics and affordability. For instance, once individuals reach their late 20s or early 30s, they are most likely to marry, start a family and buy a home. The growth in this segment of the population drives housing. The other lever, affordability, may prompt them to buy now or delay their purchase. If mortgage rates reach double digits, housing starts could retest the lows of 2009.

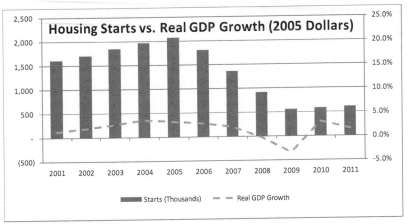

Source: U.S. Census Bureau
Real GDP from World Bank Development Indicators and IMF at 1/26/2012

Auto Sales

2011 auto sales of 13 million are 25.3% below the 17.4 million at the peak of the review period (2005) and about 23% above the 10.6 million trough (2009). Despite less volume in previous years, the auto industry is spilling over with profits. The recession of 2008 forced automakers to become leaner, more disciplined and more fiscally responsible in order to survive. "Auto makers have slashed inventories and emerged from the downturn better able to match output to consumer demand. They also have moved away from relying on margin-eating discounts, and honed their ability to build cars in the colors and configurations that customers want."[59] Another change is that the U.S. auto industry is no longer the Big Three – it is now the "Big Seven." According to motorintelligence.com, through January 2012 industry market share leaders were GM (18.4%), Ford (14.9%), Toyota (13.6%), Chrysler (11.1%), Honda (9.1%), Nissan (8.7%) and Hyundai (4.7%). Again, if interest rates rise, expect auto sales to remain well below levels of four to five years ago.

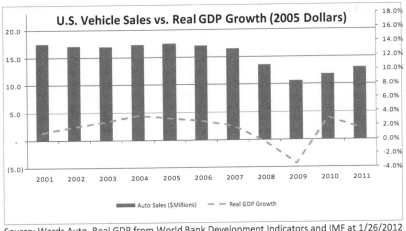

Source: Wards Auto, Real GDP from World Bank Development Indicators and IMF at 1/26/2012

Unemployment

Where housing starts and auto sales are key drivers of GDP growth, unemployment appears to be a derivation of GDP growth. The unemployment rate rose sharply from 5.8% in 2008 to 9.3% in 2009. It peaked at 9.6% in 2010. Meanwhile GDP growth hit a trough at negative 3.5% in 2009, triggering the peak in unemployment the following year. Moreover, as of year-end 2011, about 3.9 million people were out of work for more than a year – the highest total in over 30 years and what Federal Reserve Chairman Ben Bernanke described as a "national crisis."[60] *Fortune Magazine* put the figure closer to 6.2 million (44% of the unemployed), cited them as "dead last on any list of employers seeking to fill positions" and noted, "we risk losing a generation of men and women who won't be able to find meaningful employment ever again."[61] When a double-dip recession materializes, expect unemployment to rise above the 10% level, potentially sparking widespread social unrest.

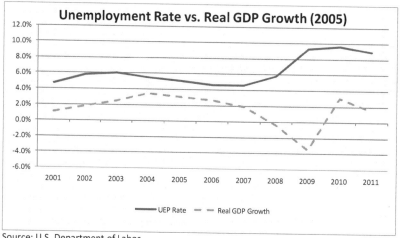

Source: U.S. Department of Labor
Real GDP from World Bank Development Indicators and IMF at 1/26/2012

Real GDP Growth

The correlation between real GDP growth and housing starts and auto sales was more pronounced than it was during the recession of the early 1990s. Both housing starts and auto sales declined from 2005 and hit a trough in 2009. Real GDP growth declined each year beginning in 2005, the sharpest of which occurred in 2009 at negative 3.5%. Real GDP growth appears to be the catalyst to contain the rate of unemployment, and ultimately, social unrest.

Iron Sash Weights

The U.S. has all but escaped the recent violent demonstrations that have occurred in China, Russia and North Africa. Thus far, anger at Wall Street has involved rhetoric and peaceful demonstrations. While some are emboldened by the country's ability to avoid violent conflict, it may simply be the calm before the storm. Fearing a public backlash from record bonuses, in January 2010 Goldman

Sachs placed bomb-sniffing dogs outside its corporate headquarters in advance of its press release on annual earnings. When AIG appeared before the House Oversight Committee in March 2009 to discuss the government's takeover of the company, the hearings reflected the public outrage of the bailout and vitriol at $165 million in retention payments made to AIFP. Former AIG general counsel, Anastasia Kelly, admitted that she was frightened by the public backlash: "Originally they were just supposed to be about the AIG takeover in general. But they became totally consumed by the FP payments, and the whole scene was frightening. By that time some of our employees had received death threats. One person emailing the AIG website said, "'AIG executives and their children should be executed with piano wire.'"[62]

In fact, the U.S. has a history of public outrage against Wall Street. And sometimes it has turned violent. World War I tested America's feigned ambivalence to the goings on in Europe. Though the country sided with the Allies it also wanted to maintain its neutrality. President Woodrow Wilson disallowed Wall Street from providing loans to Allied Powers to help them finance the war. However, Wilson did permit J.P. Morgan to finance Allied purchases of materials, munitions, grain, meat and cotton. The U.S. had previously relied on exports to Europe, and American farmers and businesses did not want those exports curtailed; sales to Allied powers also kept American factories operating at high rates of capacity. In total, J.P. Morgan financed over $3 billion in purchases and its 1% skim of the revenue netted it $30 million in fees – the most important deal in the bank's history.[63] By financing a consistent supply of ammunitions, the U.S. helped turn the tide in favor of Allied forces. However, it nearly cost Jack Morgan his life. In 1915, Jack and his family were assaulted by a lone gunman. They apprehended the intruder, but not before Jack was shot twice in the groin. The gunman was later identified as a former German professor at Harvard. He claimed his intent was to kidnap Jack in order to stop the flow of munitions to the Allies. The assault was one of four such assassination attempts on Jack's life. Immediately after World War I, a global recession materialized and revolution broke out around the world – particularly in Russia and Mexico. Many predicted similar unrest in the U.S., sparked by class warfare. In 1919 Jack was the target of a letter bomb intercepted by the post office. In 1920, Thomas W. Simpkin, an escaped mental patient, wandered into Jack's church and shot his physician whom he mistook for Jack. Again in 1920, a horse-drawn carriage filled with 500 pounds of iron sash weights exploded between J.P. Morgan headquarters and the U.S. Assay Office across the street.[64] The blast killed 38 people (including two Morgan employees) and injured hundreds more.

These are not "captains of industry" who have been bailed out. They are no more than social fraternities. By giving people technical jobs based upon a set of social criteria, the financial crisis was bound to happen. It would be naïve to assume that if the economy goes into a deeper recession the populace won't place the blame at Wall Street's doorstep. Double-digit interest rates, debt-to-GDP ratios approaching 100%, untenable rates of unemployment, and deflation in the housing sector while big business swims in billions of taxpayer funds, will be more powerful than 500 pounds of iron sash weights.

AFTERWORD

"So what is the purpose behind the book," you ask? My ultimate goal with the book was to accomplish the following:

Describe the U.S. Economy in "Black and White"

During my senior year at Hampden-Sydney I had the notion to write a book about the African-American experience – from an economic perspective. I envisioned describing African Americans' trek from the South to northern cities and California in search of jobs, and how the shift from a manufacturing to a service economy was impacting employment trends. Again, letting the facts lead to wherever, I was hoping the conclusion would be that despite unemployment rates of two to three times that of our white counterparts, African Americans were actually doing rather well given the constraints and roadblocks society has presented us with. I used this project to explore that angle.

Describe the Financial Crisis and "The Pain Ahead" in Layman's Terms

While reading newspaper articles and listening to news reports on the failings of Bear, Lehman, AIG, Goldman, et al., even I could not understand exactly what they were doing or how they could collapse seemingly overnight. I wanted to explain the crisis, in addition to the tenets of economics and high finance, in an engaging way. I wanted someone like my mother to be able to read it and understand the wrongdoings of the oligarchs and Wall Street robber barons. I also wanted to describe the role politicians and the mainstream media played in setting the wheels in motion for the crisis to occur, and their culpability afterward. Frankly, I am embarrassed by what has occurred and our refusal to do anything about it. If the reader is not as embarrassed and "damned mad" as Neutron Jack, then I have not done my job. I hope that a century from now someone will read this book and understand what *not* to do prior to the next financial crisis.

Tell "Our Story"

Ironically, the most difficult section of the book to write was the section about my family – and deciding which stories to keep and which ones to discard. People do not write books about Gramma, Grandpa, Grandma, Suzie or My Daddy, the teachers who shaped me, or my Aunt Anna – who died just prior to the book being published. So I wrote it myself. When Grandma recited my family's story over and over and over again, and quizzed me on it, it was unspoken that she had chosen me to retell it. It was Maya Angelou who said, "There is no greater agony than bearing an untold story inside you." I wrote the book partly to put an end to that agony.

NOTES AND SOURCES

Farmville, Virginia – History

1. W.E.B. Du Bois, *The Negroes of Farmville*, Page 5.
2. W.E.B. Du Bois, *The Negroes of Farmville*, Page 17.
3. W.E.B. Du Bois, *The Negroes of Farmville*, Page 38.
4. Taylor Branch, *Parting The Waters*, Pages 19-20.
5. Ronald Heinemann, *Harry Byrd of Virginia*, Page 328.
6. June Kronholz, *Education Gap: In Virginia, School Lockout Still Reverberates*, The Wall Street Journal, May 17, 2004.

Hampden-Sydney College

1. Claudia Perry, *H-SC Coach Ousted After Petition by Players*, Richmond-Times Dispatch, December 18, 1985.
2. http://www.ballineurope.com/national-teams/pau-gasol-prefers-european-style-basketball-fc-barcelona-los-angeles-lakers-9050/
3. Vincent Thomas, *Do You, Jeremy*, http://www.slamonline.com/online/nba/2009/04/do-you-jeremy/, April 29, 2009.
4. John Hollinger, *Stern Foresees 'an NBA China'*, ESPN.com, October 20, 2007.
5. Cindy Boren, *Commissioner David Stern Isn't Ruling Out NBA Contraction*, www.washingtonpost.com, August 15, 2011.
6. Ben Osborne, *#ENDTHELOCKOUT*, SLAM Magazine, February 2012.

Mr. Drysdale

1. Steven Horwitz and G.A. Selgin, *Interstate Banking: The Reform That Won't Go Away, December 15: 1987*, Cato Institute.
2. Steven Horwitz and G.A. Selgin, *Interstate Banking: The Reform That Won't Go Away*, December 15, 1987, Cato Institute.
3. Federal Deposit Insurance Corporation, *Volume I: An Examination of the Banking Crises of the 1980s and Early 1990s*, Pages 208-209.
4. Rudolf A. Pyatt, Jr., *Vast Excess of Retail Space in Area Should Come as No Surprise*, Washington Post, April 18, 1991.
5. *Citibank, and the Rise and Fall of American Financial Supremacy*, www.businessweek.com/chapter/zweigch.htm.
6. Steve Mufson, *Campeau Jitters Send Junk Bonds Down: The Washington Post, Sept. 15, 1989*.
7. *'Welfare Queen' Becomes Issue in Reagan Campaign*, The New York Times, February 15, 1976.
8. Brooks Jackson, *Reagan's "Strategy for Growth" Proposes Spending Restraint to Back Up Tax Cuts*, The Wall Street Journal, September 10, 1980.
9. David Stockman, *The Triumph of Politics*, Page 50.

10. Brooks Jackson, *Reagan's "Strategy for Growth" Proposes Spending Restraint to Back Up Tax Cuts*, The Wall Street Journal, September 10, 1980.

11. David Stockman, *The Triumph of Politics,* Page 268.

12. David Stockman, *The Triumph of Politics,* Page 53.

13. David Stockman, *The Triumph of Politics*, Page 277.

14. Vermont Royster, *Thinking Things Over: The Annual Stockman Show*, The Wall Street Journal, February 8, 1984.

15. Timothy and Lyn Shibut, *The Cost of the Savings & Loan Crisis: Truth and Consequences,* Page 26.

16. David Stockman, *The Triumph of Politics*, Page 275.

17. Saving the Banks: *Done Right, Bank Mergers Can Save Money:* The Wall Street Journal, May 13, 1992.

Top Gun

1. Doron P. Levin, *Behind The Wheel At Chrysler*, Page 62.

2. Doron P. Levin, *Behind The Wheel At Chrysler*, Page 63.

3. Ron Chernow, *The House of Morgan*, Page 304.

GE Capital

1. Robert Shogun, *Affirmative Action May Split GOP*, Los Angeles Times and Las Vegas Review – Journal, August 21, 1995.

2. Steve Daley, *Republicans Seize Senate GOP Ready To Celebrate Biggest Win In 40 Years*, Chicago Tribune, November 9, 1994.

3. Stephen Labaton, *The Debate Over Banking Regulation Reopens*, The New York Times, February 11, 1999.

4. *Clinton Signs Legislation Overhauling Banking Laws,* November 13, 1999, New York Times.

5. *Clinton Signs Legislation Overhauling Banking Laws,* November 13, 1999, New York Times.

6. Joseph Jett, *Black And White On Wall Street*, Pages 8-9.

7. Michael Siconolfi, *Saga of Kidder's Jett: Sudden Downfall of an Aggressive Wall Street Trader,* Wall Street Journal, April 19, 1994.

8. Michael Siconolfi, *Saga of Kidder's Jett: Sudden Downfall of an Aggressive Wall Street Trader*, Wall Street Journal, April 19, 1994.

9. William M. Carley, Michael Siconolfi and Amal Kumar Naj, *Major Challenge: How Will Welch Deal With Kidder Scandal? Problems Keep Coming – GE Chief Stands by His Man; Some Ask How Unit Got So Far Out of Control – A Success Story Frays a Bit*, Wall Street Journal, May 3, 1994.

10. William M. Carley, Michael Siconolfi and Amal Kumar Naj, *Major Challenge: How Will Welch Deal With Kidder Scandal? Problems Keep Coming – GE Chief Sands by His Man; Some Ask How Unit Got So Far Out of Control – A Success Story Frays a Bit*, The Wall Street Journal, May 3, 1994.

11. James B. Stewart, *Den of Thieves*, Page 390.

12. Michael Siconolfi, *To Spin Off Kidder Unit, GE Needs to Inject $2.5 Billion, report says*, Wall Street Journal, September 21, 1994.

13. Alix M. Freedman and Laurie P. Cohen, *Jett's Passage: How a Kidder Trader Stumbled Upward Before Scandal Struck*, Wall Street Journal, June 3, 1994.

14. Stephanie Strom, *Kingpin of the "Big-Time Loan,"* New York Times, August 11, 1995.

15. James B. Stewart, *Den of Thieves*, Page 95.

Key Transactions

1. James B. Stewart, *Den of Thieves*, Page 505.

The Corporate Game

1. Ron Chernow, *The House of Morgan*, Page 88.

New York Shock Exchange

1. Liz Kelly Nelson, http://blog.zap2it.com/pop2it/2011/04/mark-wahlberg-teaming-up-with-justin-bieber-for-movie-for-reals.html, *Mark Walhberg Teaming Up With Justin Bieber for Movie*, April 27, 2011.

2. Kevin Clark, *AAU Helps American Kids Flunk Basketball 101*, The Wall Street Journal, July 13, 2009.

3. Charlie Zegers, *Highest Paid Coaches in Basketball*, http://basketball.about.com/od/coaches/a/coach-salaries.htm, June 27, 2011.

4. Maurice Wingate, *The iHoops Initiative: Friend or Foe*, NYCHoops.net, July 17, 2009.

5. Maurice Wingate, *The iHoops Initiative: Friend or Foe*, NYCHoops.net, July 17, 2009.

6. Maurice Wingate, *Will iHoops Takeover Youth Basketball?*, NYCHoops.net, March 29, 2009.

Shock Exchange Fund

1. *New York Shock Exchange Summer 2006 Investment Meeting*, http://www.newyorkshockexchange.com/content/view/32/59/, July 1, 2006.

Shock Exchange Predicts the Great Recession

1. *New York Shock Exchange March 16, 2008 Investment Meeting*, http://www.newyorkshockexchange.com/content/view/52/59/, July 7, 2008.

2. James Fanelli, *O Plays FDR in 2.5M-Jobs Plan; Pledges Building Blitz To 'Jump-Start' Economy*, The New York Times, November 23, 2008.

3. Sebastian Heilmann and Dirk Schmidt, *China Country Report*. In: Bertelsmann Stiftung (ed.), Managing The Crisis. A Comparative Assessment of Economic Governance in 14 Economies. Gutersloh: Bertelsmann Stiftung, 2010.

4. Mukesh Jagota, *India to Miss Infrastructure Investment Aim*, The Wall Street Journal, September 12, 2011.

5. *Unsafe Bridges Still in Need of Stimulus Funds*, http://www.newyorkshockexchange.com/content/view/99/37/, July 31, 2009.

6. Terry Schumacher, *Sterling Construction: Well Positioned To Benefit From Infrastructure Spending*, http://seekingalpha.com/article/297604-sterling-construction-well-positioned-to-benefit-from-infrastructure-spending, October 5, 2011.

7. Rebecca Blumenstein and Laure Meckler, *Chinese Firms Set Sights on U.S. Investments*, The Wall Street Journal, January 27, 2011.

8. Rebecca Blumenstein and Laure Meckler, *Chinese Firms Set Sights on U.S. Investments*, The Wall Street Journal, January 27, 2011.

9. http://www.newyorkshockexchange.com/content/view/210/37/, Shock *Exchange vs. Warren Buffett? You Decide*, July 13, 2010.

10. Andrew Ross Sorkin., *Too Big To Fail*, Page 42.

11. Jerry Knight, *Administration Seeks Ways to Spur Lending; Regulations a Factor in Squeeze, Brady Says*, The Washington Post, October 3, 1991.

12. Susan Schmidt, *Senate Panel Chides Brady, Greenspan; Administration Ineffective in Easing Credit Crunch, Officials Told*, The Washington Post, February 27, 1992.

13. M. Reynolds, *Financial Crisis: U.S. Easing Credit Crunch for Small Firms*, Los Angeles Times, March 17, 2009.

14. Emily Maltby, Smaller *Businesses Seeking Loans Still Come Up Empty*, The Wall Street Journal, June 30, 2011.

15. *Lending by TARP Recipient Banks*, The Wall Street Journal, April 20, 2009.

16. Jeffrey McCracken and Tom McGinty, *With Fistfuls of Cash, Firms on Hunt*, The Wall Street Journal, March 4, 2010.

17. Emily Maltby and Angus Loten, *Tale of Two Loan Programs*, The Wall Street Journal, October 20, 2011.

18. Angus Loten, *Peer-to-Peer Loans Grow*, The Wall Street Journal, June 17, 2011.

19. James Flanigan, *A Wave of Chinese Money Gives a Lift to Companies Struggling in Tough Times*, New York Times, July 6, 2011.

20. James Flanigan, *A Wave of Chinese Money Gives a Lift to Companies Struggling in Tough Times*, New York Times, July 6, 2011.

21. Susanne Craig and Deborah Solomon, *Bank Bonus Tab: $33 Billion*, The Wall Street Journal, July 31, 2009.

22. *Putting Obama on Hold, In a Hint of Who's Boss*, The New York Times, December 15, 2009.

23. *Storming the Bastille >> Bailout the People Protest*, http://www.newyorkshockexchange.com/content/view/137/37/, January 15, 2010.

24. Doron P. Levin, *Behind The Wheel at Chrysler*, Page 57.

25. Doron P. Levin, *Behind The Wheel at Chrysler*, Page 57.

26. *Does AIG Have the Government "A Lil Bit Pregnant?"*, http://www.newyorkshockexchange.com/content/view/126/37/ , January 4, 2010.

27. *Parroting Shock Exchange, Senator Grassley (R. Iowa), Queries AIG Deal*, www.newyorkshockexchange.com/content/view/140/37/ January 20, 2010.

28. Andrew Ross Sorkin, *Too Big To Fail*, Page 41.

29. *How Washington Failed to Rein In Fannie, Freddie; As Profits Grew, Firms Used Their Power to Mask Peril*, The Washington Post, September 14, 2008.

30. *How Washington Failed to Rein In Fannie, Freddie; As Profits Grew, Firms Used Their Power to Mask Peril*, The Washington Post, September 14, 2008.

31. *How Washington Failed to Rein In Fannie, Freddie; As Profits Grew, Firms Used Their Power to Mask Peril*, The Washington Post, September 14, 2008.

32. Kathleen M. Howley and Dan Levy, *Luxury Homeowners in U.S. Use "Short Sales" as Defaults Rise*, Bloomberg BusinessWeek, December 17, 2009.

33. Peter Truell, *Morgan Stanley And Merrill Set To Add Money Managers*, The New York Times, June 25, 1996.

34. Editorial, *Subprime Scapegoats*, The Boston Globe, October 11, 2008.

The Mullets

1. Roger Lowenstein, *When Genius Failed*, Page 172-173.

2. *Dissecting The Bear Stearns Hedge Fund Collapse*, http://www.investopedia.com/articles/07/bear-stearns-collapse.asp#axzz1szgFGRW2, September 6, 2007.

3. Liz Rappaport, *Goldman: We Didn't Topple Bear Stearns*, The Wall Street Journal, December 14, 2010.

4. Kate Kelly, *Fear, Rumors Touched Off Fatal Fun on Bear Stearns*, The Wall Street Journal, May 28, 2008.

5. Luca Di Leo, *Fed Unveils More Details of Crisis Loans*, The Wall Street Journal, July 7, 2011.

6. Patricia Sellers, *The Fall Of A Wall Street Highflier*, Fortune Magazine, March 22, 2010.

7. *Dick Fuld Testimony: No Apologies Here*, The Wall Street Journal, September 1, 2010.

8. Mike Spector, *Lehman Estate Goes After Banks*, The Wall Street Journal, August 4, 2010.

9. Serena Ng, Carrick Mollencamp, Goldman Defends Valuations With AIG, The Wall Street Journal, August 2, 2010.

10. Serena Ng, Carrick Mollencamp, Goldman Defends Valuations With AIG, The Wall Street Journal, August 2, 2010.

11. *Behind AIG's Fall, Risk Models Failed to Pass Real-World Test*, The Wall Street Journal, November 3, 2008.

12. Office of The Special Inspector General For The Troubled Asset Relief Program, *Factors Affecting Efforts to Limit Payments to AIG Counterparties*, September 17, 2009.

13. *AIG No Longer Going Concern?*, http://www.newyorkshockexchange.com/content/view/79/37/, February 23, 2009.

14. *Throwing Good Money After Bad With Citi?*, http://www.newyorkshockexchange.com/content/view/78/37/, February 23, 2009.

15. Damian Paletta, Serena Ng and Randall Smith, *The CEO Left Off the Lifeboat*, The Wall Street Journal, July 18, 2009.

16. Mark Gongloff, *Banks Profit From U.S. Guarantee*, The Wall Street Journal, August 10, 2010.

17. *Heard on the Street / Financial Analysis Commentary*, The Wall Street Journal, October 2, 2008.

18. *GE at Center of Divorce Case*, Associated Press, January 27, 1997.

19. Ron Chernow, *The House Of Morgan*, Pages 142-143.

20. David Wessel, *Big U.S. Firms Shift Hiring Abroad*, Wall Street Journal, April 19, 2011.

21. Lynnley Browning, *A Quiet Banker in a Big Shadow*, The New York Times, March 10, 2002.

22. Anitha Reddy, *Lending Case To Cost Citigroup $215 Million*, The Washington Post, September 20, 2002.

23. Katie Benner, Bob Willumstad: A 'Bunker Mentality' at AIG, http://money.cnn.com/2009/09/04/news/companies/willumstad_aig_ceo.fortune/ , September 10, 2009.

24. *Firm of Reagan Advisor Raises $1.4 Billion Fund*, The New York Times, December 11, 2001.

25. Danny Hakim, *Selling One (or More) for the Gipper*, New York Times, September 7, 2003.

26. Danny Hakim, *Selling One (or More) for the Gipper*, New York Times, September 7, 2003.

27. Detroit News, *From Budget Whiz to 'Lies, Tricks, Fraud'?*, Detroit News, March 27, 2007.

28. Detroit News, *From Budget Whiz to 'Lies, Tricks, Fraud'?*, Detroit News, March 27, 2007.

The Big Hats . . . No Cattle

1. Charles Ponzi, *The Rise of Mr. Ponzi*, Page 10.

2. James Bandler and Nicholas Varchaver, *How Bernie Did It*, http://money.cnn.com/2009/04/24/news/newsmakers/madoff.fortune/index.htm, April 30, 2009.

3. Steve Fishman, *The Monster Mensch, New York Magazine*, February 22, 2009.

4. James Bandler and Nicholas Varchaver, *How Bernie Did It*, http://money.cnn.com/2009/04/24/news/newsmakers/madoff.fortune/index.htm, April 30, 2009.

5. Ron Chernow, *The House of Morgan*, Page 365.

6. Randall L. Smith, *Wall Street Mystery Features a Big Board Rival*, The Wall Street Journal, December 16, 1992.

7. James Bandler and Nicholas Varchaver, *How Bernie Did It*, http://money.cnn.com/2009/04/24/news/newsmakers/madoff.fortune/index.htm, April 30, 2009.

8. Amir Efrati, Chad Bray contributed, *U.S. Charges Madoff Programmers, Hints at More to Come*, The Wall Street Journal, November 14, 2009.

9. Steve Stecklow, *Hard Sell Drove Stanford's Rise and Fall*, The Wall Street Journal, April 3, 2009.

10. Steve Stecklow, *Hard Sell Drove Stanford's Rise and Fall*, The Wall Street Journal, April 3, 2009.

11. *Stanford's Forgotten Victims: The Stanford Ponzi Scheme: The Whistleblower's View*, http://stanfordsforgottenvictims.blogspot.com/2011/05/stanford-ponzi-scheme-whisleblowers.html, May 16, 2011.

12. Michael R. Crittendon and Kara Scannell, *Report Says Regulators Missed Shots at Stanford*, The Wall Street Journal, April 17, 2010.

13. Jean Eaglesham, *Ex-Official at SEC Nears Deal*, The Wall Street Journal, January 10, 2012.

The Insider Traders

1. *Six Charged in Largest Insider Trading Ring in Decades*, http://www.newyorkshockexchange.com/content/view/119/37/, December 29, 2009.

2. Justin Scheck, Robert A. Guth, and Ben Charny *Rajaratnam Investigated Decade Ago*, The Wall Street Journal, December 3, 2009.

3. Susan Pulliam, *Fund Chief Snared by Taps, Turncoats*, The Wall Street Journal, December 30, 2009.

4. *Wiretaps Do In Hedge Fund Titan, Raj Rajaratnam*, http://www.newyorkshockexchange.com/content/view/342/, May 12, 2011.

5. John Helyar, Carol Hymowitz and Mehul Srivastava, *The Double Life of Rajat Gupta*, Bloomberg Markets, July 2011.

6. James B. Stewart, *Den of Thieves*, Page 92.

7. Vikas Bajaj and Heather Timmons, *Once Revered, Business Icon Is Now Reviled*, NYTimes.com, October 31, 2011.

8. John Helyar, Carol Hymowitz and Mehul Srivastava, *The Double Life of Rajat Gupta*, Bloomberg Markets, July 2011.

9. Bess Levin, *Raj Rajaratnam Did Not Appreciate Gupta's Attempt To Leave The Goldman Board, Join "The Billionaire Circle"*, http://dealbreaker.com/2011/03/raj-rajaratnam-did-not-appreciate-rajat-guptas-attempt-to-leave-the-goldman-board-join-the-billionaire-circle/, March 14, 2011.

10. *Wharton Classmates Charged With Insider-Trading*, http://www.newyorkshockexchange.com/content/view/233/37/, September 9, 2010.

11. Susan Pulliam, *Fund Chief Snared by Taps, Turncoats*, The Wall Street Journal, December 30, 2009.

12. Susan Pulliam *Fund Chief Snared by Taps, Turncoats*, The Wall Street Journal, December 30, 2009.

13. James Bandler with Doris Burke, *Dangerous Liaisons at IBM: Inside the Biggest Hedge Fund Insider-Trading Ring*, FORTUNE, July 6, 2010.

14. James Bandler with Doris Burke, *Dangerous Liaisons at IBM: Inside the Biggest Hedge Fund Insider-Trading Ring*, FORTUNE, July 6, 2010.

15. *Barry's Tenure Was a Roller-Coaster Ride*, http://www.washingtonpost.com/wp-srv/local/longterm/library/dc/barry/barryyears0522b.htm.

16. Elaine Sciolino, *Rasheeda Moore: The Ideal Lure*, N.Y. Times News Service, January 25, 1990.

17. Ian Urbina, *Starting Fast With an Eye on the Long Run*, The New York Times, September 10, 2007.

18. Editorial, *Protecting the Capital's School Reform*, The New York Times, September 16, 2010.

The "Build It And They Will Comers"

1. Candy Evans, *Donald Trump's Foreclosed Condo Hotel in Fort Lauderdale Leaving Buyers in Legal Hell*, http://realestate.aol.com/blog/2010/03/22/trumps-foreclosed-condo-hotel-in-fort-lauderdale-could-leave-buyer-in-legal-hell, March 22, 2010.

2. Eliot Brown, *The Cost of Paying Top Dollar*, The Wall Street Journal, March 30, 2011.

3. Anton Troianovski and Lingling Wei, *Property Loss Pounds Morgan Stanley*, The Wall Street Journal, April 14, 2010.

4. Kris Hudson and Eliot Brown, *Ownership of CNL Resorts at Stake*, The Wall Street Journal, January 11, 2011.

5. Craig Karmin, *Morgan Stanley Faces Fund Troubles, The Wall Street Journal*, December 14, 2011.

6. *A Very High Stakes Deal*, http://nhi.org/online/issues/148/highstakes.html, Winter 2006.

7. Christine Haughney and Charles V. Bagli, *Stuyvesant Town Ruling Worries Tenants and Landlords Alike*, The New York Times, October 22, 2009.

8. Sean Gregory, *The Last Shopping Mall? New Jersey Awaits Xanadu*, Time Magazine, March 9, 2009.

9. Charles V. Gagli and Richard Perez-Pena, *For Xanadu Mall, Stalled and Scorned, Deal May Offer New Life*, The New York Times, April 28, 2011.

The "National Cityers"

1. *SEC Accuses Goldman Sachs of Fraud*, http://www.newyorkshockexchange.com/content/view/168/37/, April 16, 2010.

2. *Bear Stearns Turned Down Goldman Sachs-Type Deal for Failing Ethics Test*, http://www.guardian.co.uk/business/2010/apr/19/bear-stearn-spurned-paulson-deal, April 19, 2010.

3. Louise Story, *Top Leaders at Goldman Had a Role in Mortgages*, The New York Times, April 19, 2010.

4. Jean Eaglesham and Dan Fitzpatrick, *Bank Fine Hints At Feds' Playbook*, The Wall Street Journal, June 22, 2011.

5. Peter Lattman, *Citigroup Deal to Go to Judge Critical of SEC Practices*, The New York Times, October 20, 2011.

6. Chad Bray, *SEC-Citi Pact Rejected by Judge Rakoff*, The Wall Street Journal, November 28, 2011.

7. James B. Stewart, *Den of Thieves*, Page 355.

The "Pay-to-Players"

1. James B. Stewart, *Den of Thieves*, Page 88.

2. *Rattner's "Pay to Play" Probe at Impasse*, http://www.newyorkshockexchange.com/content/view/292/37/, October 28, 2010.

3. *CALPERS Cuts Ties With PCG Over "Pay to Play"*, http://www.newyorkshockexchange.com/content/view/275/37/, October 12, 2010.

4. Michael Rothfield and Chad Bray, *"Pay to Play" Probe Gets Key Guilty Plea; Focus on Rattner*, The Wall Street Journal, October 8, 2010.

The Co-Signers

1. *Plaxico Burress Doesn't Much Care for Bloomberg, Giants, Haters*, http://Gothamist.com, September 10, 2011.

2. Mike Florio, *Plaxico Says His Legal Troubles Were "Totally Blown Out of Proportion"*, http://profootballtalk.nbcsports.com, June 16, 2011.

3. Michael Howard Saul, *Bloomberg Orders $600 Million Payback from CityTime Firm*, Wall Street Journal, June 30, 2011.

4. Jeff Poor, *Fomer CNBC Reporter: GE CEO Immelt Meddled in Network's Editorial Coverage*, http://newsbusters.org, September 14, 2010.

5. Alex Crippen, *Warren Buffett to CNBC: Goldman Sachs Has "Lost the PR Battle At This Point"*, http://www.cnbc.com, May 1, 2010.

6. Michael Corkery, *Lehman's Whistle-Blower's Fate: Fired*, Wall Street Journal, March 16, 2010.

7. Fawn Johnson, *SEC on Lehman Oversight: Not Good Enough*, Wall Street Journal, March 18, 2010.

8. Kara Scannell, *SEC Botched Inquires Into Madoff Scheme*, Wall Street Journal, September 3, 2009.

9. *Revolving Regulators: SEC Faces Ethics Challenges With Revolving Door*, http://www.pogo.org, May 13, 2011.

10. Peter J. Henning, *The Twists and Turns in the Pequot Inquiry,"* http://dealbook.nytimes.com, June 1, 2010.

11. *SEC Whistleblower Tells "What Had Happened" Again*, http://www.newyorkshockexchange.com/content/view/383/37/, September 9, 2011.

The Contritionists

1. Robert Frank, Amir Efrati, Aaron Lucchetti and Chad Bray, *Madoff Jailed After Admitting Epic Scam*, The Wall Street Journal, March 14, 2009.

2. Jessica Dye, *Phillip Barry, "Brooklyn's Madoff," Sentenced For Ponzi Scheme*, Reuters, June 17, 2011.

3. Letter to shareholders in advance of Goldman Sach's May 7, 2009 annual meeting.

4. Chad Bray, *Moffat Sentenced to Six Months in Galleon Case*, The Wall Street Journal, September 14, 2010.

5. James Bandler with Doris Burke, *Dangerous Liaisons at IBM: Inside the Biggest Hedge Fund Insider-Trading Ring*, FORTUNE, July 6, 2010.

6. John Helyar, Carol Hymowitz and Mehul Srivastava, *The Double Life of Rajat Gupta*, Bloomberg Markets, July 2011.

7. Grant McCool and Dena Aubin, *McKinsey Uncomfortable in Rajaratnam Trial Glare*, www.ibtimes.com , May 31, 2011.

8. Chad Bray, *5-Year Sentence of Insider*, The Wall Street Journal, November 19, 2011.

9. *Hedge Fund Manager Is Sentenced to 5 Years*, http://dealbook.nytimes.com/2011/11/18/hedge-fund-manager-is-sentenced-to-5-years/ November 18, 2011.

10. Walter Pavlo, *Insider Trader to Prison, Skowron Gest 5 Years*, http://www.forbes.com/sites/walterpavlo/2011/11/18/insider-trader-to-prison-skowron-gets-5-years/, November 18, 2011.

11. James Bandler with Doris Burke, *Dangerous Liaisons at IBM: Inside the Biggest Hedge Fund Insider-Trading Ring*, FORTUNE, July 6, 2010.

12. James Bandler with Doris Burke, *Dangerous Liaisons at IBM: Inside the Biggest Hedge Fund Insider-Trading Ring*, FORTUNE, July 6, 2010.

13. Michael Rothfield and Chad Bray, *"Pay to Play" Probe Gets Key Guilty Plea; Focus on Rattner*, The Wall Street Journal, October 8, 2010.

14. Jennifer Peltz, *Hank Morris, Political Consultant, Sentenced For Pension Fund Scheme*, The Huffington Post, February 17, 2011.

15. Louise Story and Landon Thomas Jr., *Tales From Lehman's Crypt*, The New York Times, September 13, 2009.

16. Louise Story and Landon Thomas Jr., *Tales From Lehman's Crypt*, The New York Times, September 13, 2009.

17. Louise Story and Landon Thomas Jr., *Tales From Lehman's Crypt*, The New York Times, September 13, 2009.

18. Louise Story and Landon Thomas Jr., *Tales From Lehman's Crypt*, The New York Times, September 13, 2009.

19. *Live Blogging Jimmy Cayne's Testimony*, Wall Street Journal, May 5, 2010.

20. Suzanne Craig and Ianthe Jeanne Dugan, *From Lehman's Wreckage, New Lives*, Wall Street Journal, September 12-13, 2009.

21. Suzanne Craig and Ianthe Jeanne Dugan, *From Lehman's Wreckage, New Lives*, Wall Street Journal, September 12-13, 2009.

22. http://www.efinancialnews.com/story/2010-07-19/goldman-reputation-reclamation, *For Goldman, a Reputation Reclamation Project*, July 19, 2010.

23. *Morgan Stanley's Mack: Reform Of Financial System is Needed*, www.cnbc.com, September 11, 2009.

24. *Goldman Sachs Head Lloyd Blankfein Apologizes for Financial Crisis*, http://articles.economictimes.indiatimes.com, November 18, 2009.

25. E.S. Browning and David Benoit, *Big-Bank Pioneer Now Seeks Breakup*, July 26, 2012.

The Prisoner's Dilemmas

1. *Stanford CFO Admits to Ponzi Scheme . . . Shocker!*, http://www.newyorkshockexchange.com/content/view/105/37/, August 29, 2009.

2. *McKinsey Exec, Galleon Face "Prisoners Dilemma*, http://www.newyorkshockexchange.com/content/view/120/, December 31, 2009.

The Fred Sanfords

1. Ron Chernow, *The House of Morgan*, Page 123.

2. *Ex-Enron CEO Said Taken to N.Y. Hospital*, http://www.usnewslink.com/skillingsplan.htm, April 9, 2004.

3. Mythili Rao, *Madoff Investor Who Drowned in Swimming Pool Had a Heart Attack*, http://articles.cnn.com/2009-10-26/us/madoff.investor.dead, October 26, 2009.

4. Diane Searcey and Amir Efrati, *Madoff Beaten in Prison*, Wall Street Journal, March 18, 2010.

5. Bess Levin, *Did Allen Stanford's Jailhouse Beating Cause Brain Damage? Prosecutors Aren't So Sure*, http://dealbreaker.com, January 6, 2011.

6. Michael Rothfeld, *Stanford Says He Has Loss of Memory*, The Wall Street Journal, September 15, 2011.

7. Chad Bray, *Judge Upholds Galleon Founder's Trial Convictions*, The Wall Street Journal, August 17, 2011.

The Pain Ahead

1. William D. Cohan, *The Enforcer*, Fortune, August 15, 2011.

2. Christina S.N. Lewis, *The Fight With Opus Corp.'s Family*, The Wall Street Journal, April 7, 2010.

3. Joseph Jett, *Black And White On Wall Street*, Page 355.

4. W. Travis Hanes III and Frank Sanello, *The Opium Wars: The Addiction of One Empire and the Corruption of Another*, Page 20.

5. Compilation Group, *The Opium War*, Page 16.

6. Theodore William Overlach, *Foreign Financial Control in China*, Page 8.

7. Ron Chernow, *The House of Morgan*, Page 338.

8. John Bussey, *China Venture Is Good for GE But Is It Good for U.S.?*, The Wall Street Journal, September 30, 2011.

9. Philippe Espinasse, *China's A-Share Market – A Tough Nut To Crack*, The Wall Street Journal, June 2, 2011.

10. *China's SAIC to Acquire GM Stake?*, http://www.newyorkshockexchange.com/content/view/257/37/, September 25, 2010.

11. Dana Mattioli, In China, *Western Firms Keep Secrets Close*, The Wall Street Journal, August 30, 2010.

12. Reuters, *China Defends Iran Oil Trade Despite U.S. Push*, http://www.cnbc.com, January 11, 2012.

13. Owen Fletcher, *Software Group: More Piracy, More Lawsuits Coming in China*, The Wall Street Journal, October 24, 2011.

14. David Wessel, *Big U.S. Firms Shift Hiring Abroad*, The Wall Street Journal, April 19, 2011.

15. Andrew Browne, *Immelt on China: They Won't Let Us Win*, The Wall Street Journal, July 2, 2010.

16. Aaron Back and Joy C. Shaw, *China Tightens Regulations*, The Wall Street Journal, April 21, 2010.

17. James R. Hagerty and Melissa Korn, *China Treads on New Turf . . . While Chinese Students Flood U.S. Grad Schools*, The Wall Street Journal, August 16, 2011.

18. Lingling Wei, *China Puts Light on Shadow Loans*, The Wall Street Journal, October 13, 2011.

19. Lingling Wei, *China Puts Light on Shadow Loans*, The Wall Street Journal, October 13, 2011.

20. Sky Canaves and James Areddy, *Murder Bears Worker Anger Over China Industrial Reform*, The Wall Street Journal, July 31, 2009.

21. Review & Outlook – *Red Ghost Over China*, The Wall Street Journal, June 1, 2011.

22. Review & Outlook – *Red Ghost Over China*, The Wall Street Journal, June 1, 2011.

23. Tom Orlik, *China's Stability Landed in Trouble*, The Wall Street Journal, December 16, 2011.

24. Tom Orlik, *China's Stability Landed in Trouble*, The Wall Street Journal, December 16, 2011.

25. *100 Million Elderly: China's Demographic Time Bomb*, http://www.time.com/time/world/article/0,8599,2091308,00.html, August 21, 2011.

26. *100 Million Elderly: China's Demographic Time Bomb*, http://www.time.com/time/world/article/0,8599,2091308,00.html, August 21, 2011.

27. Congressional Research Service, *China's Holding of U.S. Securities: Implications for the U.S. Economy*, September 26, 2011.

28. Tom Barkley and Deborah Solomon, *Chinese Convey Concern on Growing U.S. Debt*, The Wall Street Journal, July 29, 2009.

29. *China and Japan in Stare Down: Japan Blinks*, http://www.newyorkshockexchange.com/content/view/258/61/, September 26, 2010.

30. Richard Martin, *The $1 Billion Rare-Earth Gamble*, Fortune, December 12, 2011.

31. *Will Health Costs Bankrupt America?*, Forbes, March 14, 2011.

32. Geoff Colvin, *The Business of Obamacare*, Fortune, March 21, 2011.

33. *Student Loans in America . . . Nope, Just Debt*, The Economist, October 29, 2011.

34. Penelope Wang, *Is College Still Worth the Price?*, http://cnnmoney.com, April 13, 2009.

35. Penelope Wang, *Is College Still Worth the Price?*, http://cnnmoney.com, April 13, 2009.

36. Emily Lambert, *Royal College Bargain*, Forbes, August 8, 2011.

37. Jenny Strasburg and Steve Eder, *Hedge Funds Bounce Back*, The Wall Street Journal, April 18, 2011.

38. Joe Light and Tom Lauricella, *A Star Exits After Value Falls*, The Wall Street Journal, November 18, 2011.

39. James B. Stewart, *Den of Thieves*, Page 102.

40. James B. Stewart, *Den of Thieves*, Page 102.

41. James B. Stewart, *Den of Thieves*, Page 106.

42. James B. Stewart, *Den of Thieves*, Page 419.

43. Al Yoon, *Higher Rates in Offing for Commercial Owners*, The Wall Street Journal, December 28, 2011.

44. Craig Karmin and Eliot Brown, *Trouble Is Brewing for Office Market*, The Wall Street Journal, January 11, 2012.

45. Craig Karmin and Eliot Brown, *Trouble Is Brewing for Office Market*, The Wall Street Journal, January 11, 2012.

46. Mark Peters and Schott Kilman, *A Bubble Down on the Farm?*, The Wall Street Journal, December 15, 2011.

47. Anthony Cotton, *Don't Blame Me, I Just Want To Have Fun*, Sports Illustrated, November 30, 1981.

48. Anthony Cotton, *Don't Blame Me, I Just Want To Have Fun*, Sports Illustrated, November 30, 1981.

49. W.E.B. Du Bois, *The Philadelphia Negro*, Page 108.

50. *August 16, 2008: Has President Obama Been on Our Website?*, http://www.newyorkshockexchange.com/content/view/64/59/, November 24, 2008.

51. *Five Reasons Why the Market Could Crash*, http://www.newyorkshockexchange.com/content/view/183/37/, May 7, 2010.

52. *There Could Be Trouble Ahead*, The Economist, December 10, 2011.

53. Emily Chasan, *Before QE2 Ends, Companies Race to Refinance Debt*, The Wall Street Journal, April 27, 2011.

54. Mark Gongloff, Chris Dietrerich and Alex Frangos, *Bonds Soar to Rare Heights*, The Wall Street Journal, July 20, 2010.

55. Bob Ivry, Bradley Keoun and Phil Kuntz, *Secret Fed Loans Gave Banks $13 Billion Undisclosed to Congress*, http://www.bloomberg.com/news/2011-11-28/secret-fed-loans-undisclosed-to-congress-gave-banks-13-billion-in-income.html, November 27, 2011.

56. Aaron Lucchetti and Stephen Grocer, *On Street, Pay Vaults to Record Altitude*, The Wall Street Journal, February 2, 2011.

57. James R. Hagerty and Sara Murray, *Fear of Double Dip in Housing*, The Wall Street Journal, November 19, 2009.

58. Robbie Whelan, *Second-Mortgage Misery*, The Wall Street Journal, June 7, 2011.

59. Neal E. Boudette, *Auto Makers' New Math Drives Net*, The Wall Street Journal, January 27, 2012.

60. Sara Murray and Cameron McWhirter, *Long-Term Unemployment Ripples Through One Town*, The Wall Street Journal, January 18, 2012.

61. Nina Easton, *Politicians Need To Face Harsh Realities About The U.S. Jobs Crisis*, Fortune, September 5, 2011.

62. Carol Loomis, *Inside The Crisis at AIG*, Fortune, March 1, 2010.

63. Ron Chernow, *The House of Morgan*, Page 188.

64. Ron Chernow, *The House of Morgan*, Page 212.